BET 27.50

American Academy of Arts and Sciences
Commission for Racial Equality
Policy Studies Institute

Ethnic Pluralism and Public Policy

Achieving Equality in the United States and Britain

American Academy of Arts and Sciences
Commission for Racial Equality
Policy Studies Institute

Ethnic Pluralism and Public Policy

Achieving Equality in the United States and
Britain

Edited by
Nathan Glazer
and
Ken Young
with the assistance of Corinne S. Schelling

LexingtonBooks
D.C. Heath and Company
Lexington, Massachusetts
Toronto

Heinemann Educational Books
London

Published by Heinemann Educational Books Ltd
22 Bedford Square, London WC1B 3HH

Published in the U.S.A. and Canada by LexingtonBooks,
D.C. Heath and Company, Lexington, Massachusetts/Toronto

© Policy Studies Institute 1983
First published 1983

British Library Cataloguing in Publication Data

Ethnic pluralism and public policy.—(Policy Studies
  Institute series)
  1. Race discrimination—Great Britain—Congresses
  2. Race discrimination—United States—Congresses
  3. Great Britain—Politics and government—Congresses
  4. United States—Politics and government—Congresses
  I. Glazer, Nathan   II. Young, Ken   III. Series
  305 ′.0941   HT1505

  ISBN 0-435-83951-9
  ISBN 0-435-83952-7 (pbk)

Library of Congress Cataloging in Publication Data

Main entry under title:

Ethnic pluralism and public policy.

  At head of title: American Academy of Arts and
Sciences, Commission for Racial Equality, Policy Studies
Institute.
  Bibliography: p.
  Includes index.
  1. Equality—Congresses. 2. Pluralism (Social
sciences)—Congresses. 3. Race discrimination—Law and
legislation—Great Britain—Congresses. 4. Race
discrimination—Law and legislation—United States—Congress.
5. Race relations—Great Britain—Great Britain—Congresses.
6. Race relations—United States—Congresses. I. Glazer,
Nathan. II. Young, Ken. III. Schelling, Corinne
Saposs. IV. American Academy of Arts and Sciences.
V. Great Britain. Commission for Racial Equality.
VI. Policy Studies Institute.
HM146.E83   1983   305.8   83-16283
ISBN 0-669-07345-8

Phototypesetting by Colset Pte Ltd, Singapore.
Printed in Great Britain by Biddles Ltd, Guildford.

Contents

Preface

It is a privilege for me to introduce this book on behalf of the steering committee established by the Commission for Racial Equality, the American Academy of Arts and Sciences and the Policy Studies Institute. It has long been apparent that the United States and the United Kingdom have much to learn from each other in respect of public policy responses to the problems which our societies have encountered in the sphere of race relations. Advanced Western societies today share in the trend towards greater racial and ethnic diversity, with all the attendant problems of securing equality of status and opportunity in housing, employment, education, political rights and many other areas. The United States was the first modern nation to experience large-scale immigration while maintaining a commitment to equal rights, and has much to teach Britain and the other Western democracies.

The specific suggestion that these issues should be pursued by means of a transatlantic conference first arose in informal contacts between the Commission and John Voss of the American Academy of Arts and Sciences, a distinguished institution based in Cambridge, Massachusetts. The idea was originated by Dr Peter Haskell of the Overseas Development Administration, whose wife is a member of the Commission's staff. He put it to John Voss when they met in Kenya. I was asked, with fellow Commissioner Juliet Cheetham, to represent the Commission in the further discussions that were envisaged.

It was agreed that the Commission would seek the help of the Policy Studies Institute in London; PSI had a proven record of research into race relations and the academic expertise and contacts which the Commission needed in support of its own, somewhat different, interests. PSI readily agreed to join with the Commission and the American Academy in sponsoring a joint conference; formal approval for the Commission's participation was obtained in February 1980 and a steering committee was established under my chairmanship. It comprised, for the Commission for Racial Equality: Clifton Robinson (deputy chairman of the Commission and chairman of the steering group); Juliet Cheetham (Commissioner, and senior lecturer in applied social studies and Fellow of Green College, University of Oxford); Peter Tucker (chief executive of the Commission and former head of the Sierra Leone civil service); and Dr. Muhammad Anwar (principal research officer). The American Academy of Arts and Sciences was represented by John Voss (executive officer); Professors Nathan Glazer and Lance Liebman (Harvard) and Donald L. Horowitz (Duke University); and Corinne Schelling (the Academy's associate executive officer). From the Policy Studies Institute we had Ken Young and David Smith (senior fellows) and Colin Brown (research fellow). Professor Nicholas Deakin of Birmingham University was co-opted to the steering committee. Peter Leppard of the Commission's secretariat provided administrative support and was responsible, with a small team of staff, for the organisation of the conference.

The summer of 1981 saw disruptions in many English cities, evoking inevitable parallels with those that had occurred in American cities in the 1960s. The intended comparison between the experiences of our two societies acquired thereby an added urgency: had Britain ignored the US experience to its cost? Was there anything for us to learn from the American responses to that earlier wave of urban violence? The plans for the conference were accelerated by these questions; at the same time, we were determined not to be blinded by the immediacy of the riots to the longer-term questions of discrimination and distribution where, again, the US experience might offer, if not lessons, some relevant questions and welcome illumination.

The Commission accordingly authorised the financial support which enabled the conference to take place at Middle Aston House, Oxfordshire, in May 1982. Further funding was provided by the American Academy of Arts and Sciences, the Sloan Foundation, and the German Marshall Fund of the United States. The support of these foundations enabled the American participants to join us at the conference, and we appreciate their involvement with the Commission.

We were determined that the conference should include as wide a spectrum of people as possible, yet, limited as we were by financial considerations, the numbers attending the seminar at any one moment had to be kept to just over 30. Many who should have been there were not invited for this reason. However, the seminar provided an opportunity for an unusually candid exchange between people whose time for reflection is often limited by the demands of their work. It was always our intention that some of the key papers from the conference would, after discussion, be revised and published in a single volume. It was hoped that this volume would be a major contribution to the debate on public policy responses to a multi-racial society and would be able to influence the thinking and actions of policy makers and administrators. Whether that objective has been attained only time will tell. We, the partners, hope that this is only the beginning, not an ending, of the interchange of ideas and experiences which democratic societies have to share in finding solutions to common problems and needs.

Many people contributed to the work of preparing the conference and it is not possible to thank each of them individually here. However, I should make some specific acknowledgements on behalf of the steering committee. Peter Tucker's long experience of race relations in the United Kingdom was called upon and he gave freely of his wisdom and insight as well as his experience in the public service and the law. Nathan Glazer and Ken Young worked together to map out the conference and to invite and brief the contributors. They also had the more arduous task of selecting from and editing the papers, working closely with authors in several countries to secure the final edited versions which appear in this volume. Nathan Glazer took responsibility for the American contributors with the able assistance of Corinne Schelling; Ken Young worked with the British authors and prepared the eventual manuscript for publication. During the aftermath of the conference, Peter Leppard continued to serve the steering committee and must take credit for his organisational and budgetary skills.

Brian Box and his staff at Middle Aston House did much to ensure the comfort and congeniality of the conference itself. We were delighted to be joined during the seminar by Robert d'Agostino, Deputy Assistant Attorney General of the US Department of Justice and by our guest speaker at the conference dinner, the then Minister of State, Home Office, the Rt. Hon. Timothy Raison MP. That the minister was able to join us for a day and to participate in the discussion sessions was a great pleasure to us and we were grateful to him for his contribution to our debates. Finally, I cannot overlook the many contributors and participants who enabled the conference to take place by attending for at least part of the time and by putting their own experience and expertise at our disposal. The views expressed in the chapters which follow are of course those of the authors alone, and not those of their institutions.

Clifton Robinson OBE, JP
Deputy Chairman
Commission for Racial Equality

LIST OF PARTICIPANTS IN THE US-UK CONFERENCE, MIDDLE ASTON HOUSE, OXFORDSHIRE, 23–27 MAY 1982

USA/CANADA

Robert J. D'Agostino
  Deputy Assistant Attorney-
  General
  US Department of Justice

Professor Richard B. Freeman
  Harvard University

Professor Bernard R. Gifford
  University of Rochester
  New York

Professor Nathan Glazer
  Harvard Graduate School of
  Education

Professor Donald L. Horowitz
  Duke University

Professor Lance Liebman
  Harvard Law School

Corinne S. Schelling
  American Academy of Arts
  and Sciences

Professor Lawrence W.
  Sherman
  The Police Foundation,
  Washington DC

Professor Robert C. Wood
University of Massachusetts at
  Boston

Dr Bhausaheb Ubale
  Commissioner, Ontario
  Human Rights Commission

UNITED KINGDOM

Dr Muhammed Anwar
  Commission for Racial
  Equality

Geoffrey Bindman
  Legal Adviser, Commission
  for Racial Equality

Colin Brown
  Policy Studies Institute

Juliet Cheetham
  Commissioner, Commission
  for Racial Equality

Professor Ivor Crewe
  University of Essex

Dr Malcolm Cross
  University of Aston,
  Birmingham

Professor Nicholas D. Deakin
  University of Birmingham

Dr Valerie Karn
  University of Birmingham

David Lane
  Chairman, Commission for
  Racial Equality

Professor Alan Little
  Goldsmiths' College,
  University of London

Dr Laurence Lustgarten
University of Warwick

Dr Christopher McCrudden
Lincoln College, Oxford

Neville Nagler
Home Office

Susan Ollerearnshaw
Commission for Racial
Equality

Nadine Peppard
Home Office

Clifton E.B. Robinson
Deputy Chairman,
Commission for Racial
Equality
Gurbux Singh
Commission for Racial
Equality

David J. Smith
Policy Studies Institute

Peter Tucker
Chief Executive,
Commission for Racial
Equality

Chief Superintendent R.C.
Marsh
Metropolitan Police

Peter Murphy
Department of the
Environment

Peter A. Newsam
Chairman-designate,
Commission for Racial
Equality

Dr. Bhikhu Parekh
Vice Chancellor, University
of Baroda, India

Professor John Rex
University of Aston,
Birmingham

Dr Peter Sanders
Commission for Racial
Equality

Stephen Small
Policy Studies Institute

Graham Sutton
Home Office

Dr Ken Young
Policy Studies Institute

SECRETARIAT
Peter Lee Leppard, with the assistance of Eatel Houston, Anna
Kingsmill-Stocker and Michael D. Start – Commission for Racial
Equality

1 Introduction
Nathan Glazer

The Western world is becoming increasingly heterogeneous, racially and ethnically. In the countries of Western Europe, the United States, Canada, and Australia, relative economic vigour, higher standards of living, and liberal political traditions have attracted immigration from less favoured countries. In some cases, the heritage of Empire has impelled these nations to make special provision for immigration from those they once governed. As a result, what was once the great distinction of the United States among the developed nations – its formation from streams of immigrants from diverse sources, and the deep racial fissure that has marked its domestic history – is now shared by many other countries.

For nations with liberal and democratic traditions, committed to individual freedom by their history and political constitutions, the first question such heterogeneity brings is ensuring the rights of individuals to equal treatment by the state, by social agencies, employers, and educational institutions. No matter how we try to answer this question, no matter how sweeping the principles we enact into law – and the United States and the United Kingdom have both enacted into law very sweeping principles indeed – difficult and divisive questions emerge immediately. What *are* equal rights in these various spheres? Is it equal for government to provide its services in English to the English-speaking and non-English-speaking alike? For employers to establish requirements that natives or whites can meet more frequently than immigrants or blacks? For schools to provide a common curriculum, regardless of student backgrounds? What are the obligations of societies that view themselves as liberal and democratic to those of different colour or ethnic origin, the long resident and the recent immigrant, the 'legal' and the 'illegal'? It is characteristic of our polities that almost all who enter our countries have *some* rights, even those who enter illegally. Great principles to which commitment seems easy at the outset must thus be defined by concrete law, regulation, practice – and around these there is inevitable conflict. And beyond the immediate questions of equal treatment other more difficult questions arise. What is to be the relation of new groups to the polity they have entered? How do they define their relation to their new society? Will they retain a corporate identity? Of what kind? With what provision by government? And to what degree are the identities and organisations of racial and ethnic groups compatible with the loyalty every state demands?

Inevitably, the distinctive political, cultural, and social characteristics of a nation will determine how it approaches these issues, and it would seem perhaps a vain hope that nations can learn from each other, from failures and successes, in dealing with ethnic and racial diversity. Yet if any two nations can learn from each other in dealing with these problems, it would appear to be the United States and the United Kingdom.

So it seemed a few years ago to the initiators of this volume, who were associated with the American Academy of Arts and Sciences in the United States, and the Commission for Racial Equality and the Policy Studies Institute in the United Kingdom. The American Academy had earlier sponsored a number of conferences and investigations on problems of ethnicity in the modern world.[1] The Commission for Racial Equality is a government agency charged with combating racial and ethnic discrimination. The Policy Studies Institute is engaged in research on policy issues of significance for Britain, notably in the field of race. This volume is the result of our common agreement that it would be worthwhile to bring together, in a conference and in a volume of papers, analyses of where our two nations stand in dealing with issues of ethnic and racial heterogeneity.

It would seem that our very similarities, initially in a century and a half of shared history, in a common language, in closely linked cultures, and in legal and political institutions that because of our common origin are closer together than those of any other two great nations, would add to the value of such an investigation. Any comparison and attempt to learn from difference needs points of similarity to make the exercise worthwhile. Perhaps the greatest point of similarity – stemming from their common political history – is that both nations recognise that those who have come within their political perimeters have rights against the state: even the stranger, the immigrant, the alien. Perhaps a second point of comparison – one in which the United States and the United Kingdom are by no means unique – is that many people in the two countries hold ethnocentric views as to who qualifies as a full member of their country and community, socially and politically. Such views seek to exclude many people of diverse racial and ethnic origins who have entered these societies to work, to bring up families, to educate their children, and eventually to participate in their polities as full members.

The openness of political traditions and the judicial determination of rights thus contrast with what are often narrow and illiberal definitions of who is properly to be considered American or British. This division between principles which stress universal rights and practices which limit them has perhaps been the central fissure in American life. Britain has not suffered such a deep divison. Yet, if Gunnar Myrdal could describe, in the 1940s, an American dilemma in which constitutional commitment to individual equality struggled with the reality of prejudice and discrimination against blacks and in lesser degree those of other non-white races, we can, in the 1980s, in the aftermath of Empire and the emergence of a substantial non-white population in Britain, speak of a similar British dilemma.

Our similarities in this respect grow apace. In 1981 Britain suffered from a series of explosions of inner-city violence which inevitably evoked comparison with the riots of the 1960s in American cities. As sponsors of this volume we were already planning our conference for May 1982; we decided to take as one of our chief concerns the problems of violence and policing in a multiracial society, problems which are addressed here by Horowitz, Sherman, and Lustgarten.

In planning the conference, our aim was not a review of the condition of minorities in the two nations; an enormous literature deals with these issues. Our concern was with policy: how were issues of equal treatment in law, in employment, in housing, in education, dealt with? How should they be dealt with? To what extent were ethnic and racial groups becoming part of the polity – and what policies were being developed to bring them into it? The subject was so huge that only a foray could be hoped for. Our initial plan of parallel articles on a range of topics would have led to a volume twice as long. It was also in some respects naive: similar as are the issues raised by racial and ethnic diversity in the two nations, there are sufficient differences for a simple parallelism of treatment to prove unresponsive to them.

Three differences in particular dictated our approach. First, the United States has dealt with these issues for a much longer time than Britain. Blacks were among the first settlers of what became the United States. American Indians were the first occupants of that territory. Spanish-speaking colonists in the Southwest were established generations before English immigrants landed on the Eastern shores of North America. American attempts to apply the principles explicit in the American Constitution and implicit in the American creed, as Myrdal called it, also long preceded any similar British efforts – inevitably, since racial minorities of any size in Britain were, as Colin Brown's chapter shows, created only as a result of immigration in the 1950s and 1960s. This difference is reflected in the American essays in the volume. Whether we deal with principles of law, with policies in employment or education or housing, or policies affecting police, or with the issue of political representation, American experience has been longer than that of Britain. This is evident in the American essays; they tend to reflect on our long experience, to summarise complexity, rather than deal with specific current issues at the cutting edge of policy. We have no shortage of such issues, but our experience is long enough, our research rich enough, for the American essays to take a longer view. Liebman, Freeman, Kirp, Horowitz, and Sherman draw from this experience and research to see what lessons we have learned. The British contributions, on the other hand, deal with problems that are still comparatively new there and, as Young argues, with policies which are yet to be fully shaped.

A second difference dictates a difference in treatment: our political system, despite its close connections with that of Britain, contains many more separate points at which policy can be and is created and carried out than does the British. We have not only a Congress and Executive engaged in making law, parallel to Parliament and Cabinet, but we also have a powerful judiciary, often acting at odds with Congress and Executive. The individual states are meaningful political entities: in some, equal employment and fair practice agencies long preceded those created at the national level, while in some cases they dispose of budgets, resources, and powers which match those of the Commission for Racial Equality in Britain. Our cities and towns also dispose of independent authority that exceeds that of our national and Federal authorities, particularly in the realms of education and police. Discussion of American policy must thus begin with the assumption of diversity; for the British, on the other hand, diversity is a departure from attempts to establish national norms and standards.

Of course the greatest difference is in scale. The US population is four times the size of Britain, but its minorities (counting blacks, Hispanics, Asian and Pacific islanders, and American Indians alone) are proportionately much greater. Clearly racial and ethnic issues must therefore involve more levels and branches of government, must be taken more seriously by domestic policy-makers than they are in Britain; and they will have a greater impact on domestic policy. Civil rights, and questions of civil rights enforcement, are front-page news in the United States. Civil rights leaders are major figures, as are elected officials from minority groups. Perhaps the most significant effect of size, as noted in Ivor Crewe's paper, is that minorities inevitably have more political weight in the United States. And while this political weight does not as yet fully reflect the numbers of minorities (owing in varying degrees to lesser participation, younger ages, recency of arrival), it inevitably affects policy to a degree one cannot expect in Britain. Nevertheless, while the New Commonwealth population may be less than four per cent of British population all told, we find the same type of residential concentrations in Britain that we find in the United States: concentration in urban areas, in older neighbourhoods, on some housing estates, in some schools.

Of course there are other differences, and some of these are taken up in the papers that follow. I will add two more here. One is the question of obligation. What does one owe to minorities? Lance Liebman raises this question sharply in his paper, and any American would agree that Negro slavery places the obligations of our polity to blacks in a special category. But American Indians are also in a special category. And some of the Spanish-speaking (those from Mexico, now largely resident in states that were once part of Mexico; or those from Puerto Rico, once a colony of the United States, and in the minds of many still a colony) would also argue for a special status. In the United Kingdom, the argument could be made that since the New Commonwealth immigrants and their descendants are there as part of the aftermath of Empire, some obligation is imposed on Britain beyond that owing to immigrants from nations with which Britain had no Imperial relationship. But obligation arises not only because of a previous condition of slavery or colonialism now recognised as wrong. What are the obligations of countries such as the United States and Britain to people who want to migrate to those countries for political or economic reasons? It is no simple matter to define these obligations. In the United States, as a country of free immigration for so long a part of our history, this obligation is taken seriously, and it would be hard to advocate a closing of our doors as abrupt as that which has occurred in Britain; our history (and the political power of ethnic minority groups) argues for a much greater volume of immigration.

A final point of difference emerges sharply in Valerie Karn's paper. While we are both 'welfare states', Britain long preceded the United States in taking on public obligation for the health, housing and welfare of all its people. Much of what Valerie Karn has to say about the action of local housing authorities can be paralleled in the United States, but they control a much smaller, indeed a miniscule, part of the housing stock. Most of our housing stock is in the free market, bought and sold by individuals or rented out by individual landlords. As in Britain the actions of these many actors are affected by major institutions such as banks and by local government authorities: but government in the United States still resists a general responsibility for the fate of minorities because it has taken on fewer responsibilities overall. Immigrants and minorities are always in large measure reliant on their own efforts: perhaps this independence is somewhat greater in the United States than Britain.

But standing above all the differences is what I conceive of as the great similarity: the commitment to universalistic principle rather than to ethnic particularism in determining the nature of the polity and in legitimating the participation of those people of varied ethnic and racial origins who become part of it. I am impressed that Britain passed a Race Relations Act long before immigrant groups had any power to demand it, to exert political pressure to gain it, or to threaten disorder so as to force its enactment. The current legislation expresses the principle that all individuals are in essence of the same worth. Others may be more impressed by the fact that this Act still has – as we see from the contributions of McCrudden, Sanders, and Ollerearnshaw – only a modest impact on British employment practices, compared with the enormous impact of the US Civil Rights Act and federal requirements for affirmative action on American employment practises, documented by Freeman.

The larger implication of this commitment to political principles rather than to race or ethnicity or cultural heritage as the basis for the polity is that both the United States and Britain are willing to contemplate more varied relationships between minority and immigrant communities and the state than are, I believe, France or Germany. These issues of how one envisages the relationship of minority communities to the state come up sharply in education, where one objective is to mould citizens. In both the United States and Britain, as they are described by Kirp and Parekh in this volume, we see a considerable degree of openness to these issues. Political leaders in both societies are able to contemplate with equanimity a situation in which ethnic communities maintain themselves – in part with state assistance – as independent entities, and exert a legitimate political influence in defence of what they see as their interests. There is something in the Anglo-Saxon political tradition – we must call it Anglo-Saxon because we see the same thing in Canada and Australia – that is able to accept a remarkable degree of pluralism, not only in culture and society, but also in politics, and which manages to bind together this pluralism with common principles.[2] Of how many societies can this be said? It offers hope that we may yet manage to contain these difficult problems of ethnic and racial diversity, and to become richer societies as a result.

Notes

1 For two of these see Nathan Glazer and Daniel P. Moynihan (eds) *Ethnicity: Theory and Experience*, (Cambridge, Mass.: Harvard University Press, 1975) and William H. McNeill and Ruth S. Adams (eds) *Human Migration: Patterns and Policies* (Bloomington, Indiana: Indiana University Press, 1978).
2 On these points see, Nathan Glazer, 'Race Relations in Britain – an American

Perspective', *Sociology*, Vol. 6, No. 1, January 1972, pp. 97–100, a review of E.J.B. Rose, *Colour and Citizenship*, (London: Oxford University Press, 1969); and Nathan Glazer, 'Another Democracy's Quest for Racial Equality', *Harvard Civil Rights-Civil Liberties Law Review*, Vol. 9, 1974, pp. 403–411, a review of Anthony Lester and Geoffrey Bindman, *Race and Law in Great Britain*, (Cambridge, Mass.: Harvard University Press, 1972.

Ethnic Pluralism and The Law

2 Anti-Discrimination Law: Groups and the Modern State
Lance Liebman

Law and groups

Legalisation is a worldwide phenomenon of our times. In the United States, but also in both parts of Europe and in the Third World, relations among individuals and between individuals and the state are increasingly subjected to official regulation. Counter-movements asserting claims of liberty, decentralisation, private autonomy, freedom of contract, and the validity of market transactions all urge various sorts of deregulation. Nevertheless, it is inconceivable that government – official social orderings – will withdraw. Individual and collective private action has too many consequences for others. At least some of those consequences (pollution, inflation, depletion, inequality) are regarded as appropriate concerns of the nation. Demands for public intervention will continue to exceed desires for a return to private ordering.

If there is to be official rule, there must be law to discipline authority with a degree of fairness, equality, and process. Thus a central question for modern society will continue to be the effort to make regulatory regimes effective and efficient. We must find better ways to reach agreement on the wider public interests that are insufficiently achieved by private action, more effective devices for pursuing those public goals, and a greater degree of integrity in connecting the grandest of our goals to the resources represented by the limited capability of our intervention mechanisms.

The discongruity between social goals and mechanisms for pursuing those goals is apparent as to legal devices. Law promises process, rationality, respect for the individual, and protection of reasonable expectations. Each is an important goal. But law also means crippling proceduralism, unfair benefits to those who can invest most in legal representation, and power to unelected judges. To give only a single example, the loudest voices in legal scholarship in the past decade have been the group calling for extension of due process rights to aspects of life affected by the welfare state – to jobs and housing benefits and medical care and regulated urban services;[1] and the group calling for an unshackling of competitive enterprise from the burdens and costs of regulation.[2] Each is of course correct to an important degree. What is absent is effective confrontation between what are inevitably competing arguments. We have no methodology for deciding when the benefits of law outweigh the costs; no way to think of law as a costly good that should be allocated to the social tasks where it can be most effective. We have as yet no ideology that asserts both the capacities and the limits of legal ordering.

Happily for readers, this paper does not address all of these issues. Rather, it is about one question of great importance, considered in the context of the larger set of social concerns listed above. The question discussed in this paper is legal protection of the relationship between social groups and the state, especially in a racially diverse society. Individual freedom and individual rights are the central mission of the legal system, and are probably unachievable in a lawless state. That is even more true when a society contains a diverse population. The United States sees itself as made up of racially and ethnically diverse groups. It has historical evidence for the proposition that citizens are not all blind to these distinctions. Its different and identifiable groups of citizens are at different socio-economic levels. That makes the US a society that must consider legal regulation of the impact of important decisions, public and private, on ethnic and racial sub-groups of the population.

Now add two other facts of contemporary society. Many valuable goods (jobs, university places, public housing, and so forth) are allocated by rationalisable norms, yet with important room for discretionary judgments. Also, much of social life is carried on in complex organisations. This is not the frontier or the ocean, where individuals are pitted against nature. Finally, and most difficult to make harmonious with ideas of fairness, much power rests with the complex of procedures and institutions that can be summed up as democratic politics, where outcomes depend greatly on effort, economic and other resources, and institutional arrangements (in what single-member district is my vote cast, for example).

In such social settings, both the United States and Britain have used law to attack discrimination and inequality. One aspect of those efforts is conventional: giving an individual an opportunity to assert that he or she has been the victim of unjustified or forbidden discrimination.[3]

Important questions of implementation result. Is individual enforcement sufficient? What penalties are appropriate, for example when government itself was the violator? How can what statutes sometimes call 'patterns and practices' of discrimination be halted? Contemplation of the US experience suggests, however, that it is immensely difficult to confine the anti-discrimination principle to the individualist legal and political context from which it is proclaimed;

and that the effort to protect individuals against discrimination leads with what seems like inevitability to arguments concerning collective rights of racial and other sub-groups. The social context seems to require that legal institutions, unfamiliar with concepts of group right, at least wrestle with such assertions.

Three stories

As a background to discussion, consider three stories of the 1970s, each located at the intersection of law and politics.

A group of black parents in Atlanta filed suit against the local school board in 1958, seeking desegregation. For various reasons, the suit was still in litigation in 1973, by which time two things had happened: other desegregation cases had made clear that Atlanta parents could achieve a broad busing remedy by which more than a hundred years of racially separate schools would finally be altered; and demographic changes had occurred, especially white migration to the Atlanta suburbs and black migration into the city of Atlanta, with the result that the Atlanta school population was more than 80 per cent black. In that situation the black parent plaintiffs, organised by the local chapter of the National Association for the Advancement of Coloured People (NAACP), decided that an Atlanta busing plan would not serve their interests. This group negotiated a settlement with the school board under which the lawsuit was dropped in return for the board's promise to make a variety of changes in school policies including appointment of black educators to various leadership jobs in the school system. The national NAACP cried foul, saying that the agreement – with its implied denigration of busing – was a bad outcome for blacks nationally, even if correct for the Atlanta circumstances. The national NAACP tried to persuade the federal judge with jurisdiction over the case to reject the settlement. But the judge certified the negotiated agreement, and his decision was affirmed by the US Court of Appeals for the Fifth Circuit.[4]

In a second matter, parents of retarded youths living at Massachusetts institutions sued the state Department of Mental Health in federal court in 1972, alleging that conditions in the institutions deprived their children of their constitutional rights. Facing a long trial, Governor Sargent and his Secretary of Human Services decided that improvement in conditions was a goal they shared and entered negotiations. An agreement was reached, a consent decree signed 'settling' the federal lawsuit, and a court monitor appointed. The result has been divided control over the institutions, with many specific matters of policy and programme referred to the judge by the monitor. The judge held that the state is required to provide the funds that he believes are needed for adequate compliance with the consent decree. Funding has generated controversy in a period of general budget-cutting, and on one occasion the judge threatened the chairmen of the state House and Senate Ways and Means Committees with a contempt of court proceeding if their committees did not approve a budget containing the judge's view of necessary funding. Yet no court has ever decided what are the constitutional rights of retarded children, and indeed recent cases from other states suggest that, had the Massachusetts case been fully litigated, it is unlikely the children would have received the gains the state promised them in the consent agreement.[5]

In a third dispute, present members of the Passamaquoddy Indian Tribe in Maine sued the US Secretary of the Interior, alleging that the US was obliged to assert a claim on their behalf to about two-thirds of the land in the state of Maine, because land sales by the ancestors of the Indians in the nineteenth century had been in violation of the federal Nonintercourse Act of 1791, an enactment that barred white men from purchasing Indian land without US government permission. Current landowners (rather, those who thought they owned land until they learned of this lawsuit — individuals, the state government, local governments, and big timber companies) would have had many possible defences if the Indians' land claims had ever come to trial: that longstanding non-enforcement of the Nonintercourse Act rendered it inapplicable; that in any event too much time had passed for the claim to be asserted now; that any wrong that did occur 150 and more years ago was a violation as to Indians then alive (whose rights were assertedly violated when they were not forbidden to sell' their land for a price they preferred at the time), but not a violation that should give rights to persons alive now whose only connection to those mistreated long ago is to be a member of a continuing tribe. Yet even though the likelihood of current Indians recovering large parts of Maine seemed remote, the existence of the lawsuit, and certain procedural judgments rendered by a federal judge on preliminary issues, cast such a cloud on title as to be a major deterrent to real estate activity. After six years of citizen anxiety and political posturing, a retired Georgia judge appointed as mediator by President Carter achieved a negotiated agreement by which present members of the tribe are to receive money and some undeveloped land – the money for the Indian plaintiffs and the cash compensation to those giving up land coming from the US Treasury. Ahead lie disputes over who is now eligible to share in the tribe's recovery and how decisions about investing the tribe's new capital should be made.[6]

The challenge to individualism

The US legal system is founded on an ideology of individualism. The Constitution speaks of 'persons' and 'citizens'. Even the vast business collectivities – the biggest corporations – take their legal identity as fictional persons. The Constitution recognises states (though not as entities with legal significance predating the Constitution itself), but it and later history refused federal status to municipalities, counties, neighbourhoods, and regions, much less to professional societies, economic interest groups, social movements, unions, or families. Invented in the Enlightenment, reared at the height of British empiricism, positivisim, and utilitarianism, our legal system is not, or at least was not, at all corporativist, fascist, or collectivist. Our image of law is always of an individual plaintiff and an individual defendant, of equality before the law, of individual rights and responsibilities, of freedom from the sins of one's fathers, of no liability without proof, of individual obligation or responsibility. Professor Paul Brest has written:[7]

> If a society can be said to have an underlying political theory, ours has not been a theory of organic groups but of liberalism, focusing on the rights of individuals, including rights of distributive justice. Of course, we recognize the sociological fact that people desire to affiliate and associate with others who share common interests or characteristics . . . We grant rights to associations or treat them as fictitious persons only to protect the rights of their individual members . . . Most societies in which power is formally allocated among racial and national groups are strikingly oppressive, unequal, and unstable.

Yet modern circumstances challenge the reality of that individualist image. Two facts challenge it in particular. First, laws work by creating groups and by assigning consequences to being placed in particular groups. Laws apply to categories of events and to classes of people. They make one rule for optometrists and another for oculists, one subsidy for raspberry growers and another for the artichoke industry, one outcome for those who score seventy-five in a civil service examination and another for those who score seventy-four, one tax rate for the city and another for the suburb, a military draft for those who are aged twenty-five but not for those who are twenty-six, and so on. As perhaps it is the nature of human thought, so it is the nature of law to proceed by presumptions, assumptions, inferences, and generalisations. These group people. And that makes inevitable the question (not the answer) of which groupings are wise/permitted/appropriate and which are not.

Second, groups come to law. Law makes groups, but it also

responds to groups. As legislatures are lobbied by groups of constituents who find it efficient to proceed collectively (whether their
goal is public housing, nuclear power, sex education, or Ukrainian
independence), so opportunities arise to advance common interests by
lawsuit, and every sort of economic, geographic, and social group
sues and is heard. Assessing this phenomenon, Professor Abram
Chayes has written: 'Perhaps the dominating characteristic of modern
federal litigation is that lawsuits do not arise out of disputes between
private parties about private rights. Instead, the object of litigation is
the vindication of constitutional or statutory policies'.[8] Chayes called
this new model 'public law litigation'. Observing it, we may well be
tempted to say that the idea of a legal system oriented to individual
rights and individual disputes is charming but naive, and that the only
prudent intellectual course is to study a legal system now inevitably
altered toward a concern for groups and to concentrate our energies
on understanding and civilising that system.

Because the ideology of this society is so clearly oriented toward
individualism, the cases summarised above seem strange to us. The
courts in each case seem to be acting in an 'unjudicial' manner. The
questions that must be asked are whether there is something new and
important about these instances of legal controversy, whether the
courts are really overstepping their bounds, or whether there is some
substantive aspect of these cases or of contemporary circumstances
that alters the role that the courts must play.

In this light, the interaction between America's legal system and its
ethnic groups has been important. Controversies over immigration
quotas, access to education and jobs, and arrangements for political
representation have required judicial interpretations of the Constitution and of statutes. This much is generally clear and understood. Yet
just as important and far less widely perceived is the significance of
ethnic developments and controversies for our legal system. Civil
rights, desegregation, reapportionment, due process, freedom of
speech, dissent and protest, entitlements to minimum income, death
penalty, and exclusionary zoning are ethnic issues, frequently fought
over in court, that have provided much of the substance for the
legal/procedural transformations of the recent past. But what are the
consequences of treating social groups as litigants? Is the law playing
a role in fragmenting the population and then crystallising that
fragmentation? Is it, by giving legal significance to groups, ethnic or
otherwise, giving them a stability that may ultimately be harmful to
our political system? If we give rights to an Indian tribe or to black
parents or even to retarded children, do we make official groups of
what might otherwise be – and should be – temporary and shifting
alignments? Do we thereby force citizens to classify themselves?

Rights

The individualist, personal anti-discrimination ethic does not capture the most interesting assertions of discrimination and inequality that are made today. One model case is the individual denied a job because he is black. The 1964 Civil Rights Act largely ended that explanation. Now comes the black denied a job as a garbage-man (environmental control officer is the civil service title in some cities) because he did not score high on an IQ test. Has the test an appropriate relationship to qualification for the job? Is it not as likely to correlate negatively as positively with job performance? Is use of the test racial discrimination? What if blacks were for generations denied the opportunities that translate into high test scores? What of the employer who previously discriminated openly against blacks? What of seniority systems when they perpetuate advantages won in an era of straightforward discrimination? The answers are not obvious, and the questions must be faced. But as assertions of legal right, these contentions have a different, a less individualist, nature than the assertion of undisguised racial exclusion.

Legal rights take on a different dimension when they are being asserted by groups rather than by individuals. Is there a right to be educated in an integrated school? No, but there is a right not to be a member of a group victimised by political acts motivated by a segregatory purpose, a right 'remedied' (to a degree) by a rearrangement of school districts. Or there may be a 'right' that one's school district not suffer from state taxing and spending rules that leave some districts with large resources and few students and other districts with many students and a small tax base. The remedy may be a revised tax system, but it will by no means assure a certain level of school spending, much less a certain sort or quantum of education. Is there a 'right' to a pension? Perhaps not, only a right to have a large fund invested carefully, for the benefit of all those retired, and to have rules of distribution meet a judge's standard of fairness and relevance. Education, zoning, taxation, job opportunities, pensions – each, by its nature, is a social good that is significant for an individual in the context of his or her relationships with other people.

When government becomes a major actor concerning land use and job distribution and benefits, its involvement – whether it is regulating or distributing or taking – must meet the standards of due process, and so the rights to these benefits become to a degree 'legalised'. We thus begin to use the language of 'right'. But as to this sort of social claim, the 'right' is collective or relative or contingent or procedural. The claim itself has much of its meaning in status, in relative position. With these claims, therefore, the questions of which group one is in, with whom one is classified, and where different groups stand with regard to one another become absolutely central. Some legal claims always had these characteristics. But there has been a change in degree – an increase in the significance of assertions of these sorts that has by now probably become a change in kind.

Of course the questions about standing and about rights, which are really questions about how attenuated the effect of unlawful action can be on the person who brings a lawsuit, are trickier than those that arise in the traditional litigation. The victim, the person punched or the person trespassed upon or the person who did not receive the hay, could sue. But who is the victim of racial segregation in housing, and who is in the group that has a legal right to sue to stop it? The US Supreme Court recently decided that a legal challenge to housing discrimination can be brought by a 'tester' – a person hired by a private anti-discrimination organisation in Richmond, Virginia, to visit real estate brokers in order to document racial 'steering' to neighbourhoods.[9] If discrimination is an offence only against the black family that genuinely wants an apartment and is falsely told there are no vacancies in a white building or subdivision, then the 'tester' would not have 'standing' to sue because he or she would only be claiming that someone else's legal rights have been invaded rather than asserting that his or her own rights were directly injured. But if non-discrimination is a right of all who care, because integration is a value protected for all, then those concerned about the racial composition of neighbourhoods should be able to sue, even if they are not themselves looking to buy a house. Or perhaps an out-of-neighbourhood tester would not have standing but someone residing in the neighbourhood would. Is preservation of a mountain the right only of the person who hikes on it, or also of one who hopes to hike on it some day, or who looks at photographs of it with extra pleasure because it is still there, or who only knows in general that mountains are being protected? Because we have ordered society in new ways, granting 'rights' much subtler and more diffuse than the traditional assurances against concrete and personal injury; because, it can be said, we have enough to eat and can indulge in more sophisticated claims; and because technology connects us to distant consequences and science lets us see new causal relationships (think of a 'right' that aerosol sprays not destroy the ozone layer in ways tragic for our grandchildren), we confront these questions of standing, which alter the nature of the lawsuit.

Ability to sue

In a group context, the ability to sue raises more questions than the subtle relationship between the right and the harm. Because the 'party' involved, plaintiff or defendant, is not an individual but a group of individuals, there may be disagreement within the single party over how the legal claim should be managed, what the real issue is, and who should be chosen to argue the case. In the school busing example, who picked the Atlanta NAACP, or the national NAACP, to represent the black parents? How do we know that parents prefer an associate superintendent's job to busing? Dean Derrick Bell of the University of Oregon Law School has written incisively of the power that inevitably flows to interest-group lawyers – whether working for the Legal Defense Fund, the Sierra Club, Ralph Nader, or, indeed, the US Department of Justice.[10] Their sense of the possibilities, their knowlege of the system, means that their values play a large role, especially since the members of the client organisations get most of their knowledge from the lawyers and since individuals among the client groups rarely have enough at stake to become sufficiently knowledgeable to play a major role.

But the issue is more complicated than merely a matter of relations between group members and lawyers or the inevitably chaotic arrangements for selection of leaders and internal decision-making in a private organisation. We are now recognising that important matters are being decided by 'political' lawsuits, in which non-governmental groups are litigants: parties plaintiff and parties defendant. Those groups – environmental groups, fair-housing groups, neighbourhood associations, ethnic associations – have neither the regular and governmentally regulated structure of the corporation nor the single focus on profit of the corporation and the partnership. Legislative decision-making long ago made such groupings (known there as lobbies, pressure groups, interest groups) important. But the legislative process contains mechanisms for screening and weighing group representations and is suited to an endless overlap and flux of groups as the agenda of issues changes. By contrast, the traditional lawsuit is a single formal event. It takes place by procedures premised on the model of the search for truth about a single past event, that truth to be determined after adversary participation by two parties whose interests are opposed. Now we have lawsuits vastly more like legislative proceedings: they have many parties, arranged in shifting alliances; they go on for a long time; they look to the future instead of resolving a matter from the past; they often seek 'equity' or 'balance' or 'fairness' instead of determining which of two opposed contentions is correct; the result is sometimes a compromise among values that cannot all be achieved and the creation of procedures for living together in the future.

Lawmaking in elected legislatures, while presenting ancient and serious questions of representation, conflict of interest, resolution of differences, and unfairness to permanent minorities, is a satisfactory means of making official decisions drawing upon the preferences of a diverse and diversely organised citizenry. With the lawsuit as a process for making a sub-set of those decisions (decisions about the distribution of income, about control over public services, about institutional rules for making other ongoing decisions), we must face the problem of the formal legitimation of parties at law, instead of the mere inducement to groups to seek a voice in the legislature.

When the doctrine of standing announces finally who has an adequate 'interest' to sue, it certifies the group's membership and goals and procedures for making decisions. The legal process holds the group together, at least for purposes of sharing in legal winnings and being responsible for legal liabilities.

The problem that this raises is made very clear in the ethnic context. We hear often that 'blacks' or 'Italians' or 'Mormons' or 'Catholics' have a view about legislation: for busing, against abortion, for school prayers, against the MX missile, for stricter enforcement of immigration rules. We know that the statements we read are only more or less accurate, that representatives express what they want as a group's view, that some members of the broad group may be fervently opposed to the supposed group position, and that indeed the position may have the support (much less the attention and enthusiasm) of group members to a wide extent, but may well not. It is altogether different when 'the Passamaquoddy Tribe' or 'a class consisting of all non-white children in Atlanta' or 'parents of all retarded children in Massachusetts' are plaintiffs in a lawsuit and so only one voice is being heard as representative of the group's goals. Yet we should not rush to the conclusion that the courts are the wrong place to resolve group disputes.

Is it inevitable, or even happy, that urban politics is so often an ethnic battleground? Is it not the case that that has been true in our cities since the earliest waves of immigration? Have we not always had ethnic disputes over jobs, turf, and schools? Is it important that the forum for these disputes now is often the courtroom? Is that not just a sign that we have taken steps toward codifying aspects of social life, and that modern explicitness about officially valid claims imports the courts as interpreters and regulators of processes of government allocation?

The real question is whether a larger degree of agreement can be reached about the boundaries of rights. While public sector services and tasks were expanding after 1960, but also more recently as retrenchments have occurred, we have made very little progress toward agreed assumptions about minimal entitlements or citizen responsibilities or appropriate shares. By certain measures, our welfare state arrangements are now comparable with those in Europe.

But we have nothing like the European *theory* – the agreement as to what a citizen can expect. Without theory and explanation, we have to proceed chaotically, with every public service and every public decision being a matter to be fought over. Given the different levels of government that result from federalism and the unrestricted range of claims that can be asserted, it has to be that ambiguity and overlap make courts the agency of reconciliation and minimal coherence. Unless we clarify our promises and understandings, we must continue to battle in court.

The law will muddle through the procedural difficulties that result from group social controversies. All the complexity of standing and representation and remedy only reflects difficulty in defining rights. It is hard for a society to decide what retarded children are entitled to, whether Indians (or Japanese-Americans forced from California during the Second World War) should be compensated today because of what now looks like mistreatment of their ancestors, what rights should result from proven illegal school segregation. But it is not unworthy when a society tries to decide them. Given our traditions, lawsuits will be a significant part of the decision process. If the cases are not traditional – if the judges become managers of ongoing group disputes with very little stable law to guide them – then the courts might do less good work than they do in conventional law-suits. But the question that will remain is whether we can proceed institutionally in ways that would make these imperfect judicial efforts unnecessary.

If the lawsuit is a branch of politics, then our concerns about ethnic explicitness in the courtroom should be similar to the concerns we have when ethnicity is at the centre of legislative and electoral battles. If ethnicity is important to individuals, then they will formulate claims against society in ethnic terms. They will form groups, select leaders, find money, and generally fight to seek or to defend what is important to them. In legislative and administrative processes and in the hurly-burly of electoral contests, this is normal and traditional. Now it is becoming normal and traditional in court as well, because the court is the forum for part of the action. When the court hears the case, it confers legitimacy on the association or organisation or merely on the unorganised collection of people with a similar interest around whom the lawyers have thrown their net. This makes for disorderly lawsuits, for internal disputes among groups of litigants, and for new doctrinal complexities about who is later barred because someone claiming to speak for them has had a day in court. By itself, however, it is only a problem in judicial management, not a threat to society. The asserted threat arises when legal outcomes, whether statutes or court decisions, grant rights according to ethnic or racial classifications. That is the issue now posed at the forefront of equal protection analysis, and it is discussed in the next section.

Equal protection of the laws

The law's relationship to groups of citizens has received its most interesting and important development in the context of judicial inter-pretation of the equal protection clause, an ambiguous section of the Fourteenth Amendment with open-ended wording ('. . . nor shall any state deprive any person of life, liberty, or property without due process of law; nor deny to any person within its jurisdiction the equal protection of the laws') and a history that are surely an invitation to and a sanction for an active judicial role of interpretation and enforcement.

What is 'equal protection of the laws'? The law cannot be equal to the person who steals and the person who does not, the person who scores higher on a civil service test and the person who scores lower, the person whose taxes are levied on an income of $10,000 and the person who reports income of $300,000. Laws classify and distin-guish. Thus the constitutional question must be which classifications, which distinctions, are constitutionally acceptable.

The Fourteenth Amendment does not speak of blacks. It thus seems to establish an ideal of equal treatment that is relevant to the entire population. Yet, as stated above, laws must discriminate; that is their nature. Thus we must ask which discriminations, which inequalities, are forbidden by the Constitution. Considering everything that we know about the circumstances of 1868, it must be the case that dis-criminations against blacks on account of their race were the chief purpose the amendment's draftsmen had in mind. Certainly nothing in the intervening years makes that purpose any less essential to a con-stitutional regime today.

But why do we want our Constitution to bar, and our judges to prohibit, discriminations on account of skin colour? Because the country practised, and the Constitution explicitly sanctioned, slavery; because we believe racial discrimination to be an especially prevalent and dangerous tendency of mankind, needing the most serious insti-tutional barriers that we can construct; because we know that a great deal of racial hostility exists today. We fear that without a constitu-tional barrier to discrimination, government decisions would classify blacks to their detriment, either because of bigotry or because of decisions to treat blacks separately that are efficient but that we have committed ourselves to forbid.

Concentrating on these commitments, it is inevitable that we see the possibility that the same arguments are available regarding other groups in society. Should we not subject to judicial scrutiny legislative and administrative decisions that grant different legal statuses not to whites and blacks but to other groups within the population?

For this paper, it is inappropriate to write at length about sex discrimination and the Fourteenth Amendment. The law classified extensively between males and females at the time the Fourteenth Amendment was adopted. Longstanding interpretations accepted these classifications. The most famous quotation is from Justice Bradley's opinion in *Bradwell v. Illinois*, the 1873 case which upheld the state's refusal to let a woman practice law:[11]

> The natural and proper timidity and delicacy which belongs to the female sex evidently unfits it for many of the occupations of civil life. The constitution of the family organization, which is founded in the divine ordinance, as well as in the nature of things, indicates the domestic sphere as that which properly belongs to the domain and functions of womanhood . . . The paramount destiny and mission of woman are to fulfill the noble and benign offices of wife and mother. This is the law of the Creator.

One approach to that state of the law is a constitutional amendment. And indeed Congress approved the Equal Rights Amendment, but, even after an extended period for ratification, the requisite thirty-eight states failed to approve the amendment.

Nevertheless, Supreme Court interpretations of the Fourteenth Amendment have moved a substantial distance from *Bradwell* and have invalidated a range of government actions classifying by sex. They have, instead, suggested an active judicial role in assuring that government actions not be based on 'old notions' or 'assumptions of dependency' or 'the role typing society has long imposed' or 'the traditional way of thinking about females'.[12] Most recently, however, in the June 1981 opinion upholding males-only draft registration, the Court has turned the other way (though it is easy to imagine a judiciary that struck down much that reflected traditional ideas about sex roles but was not willing to be the institution of government that took even the tiniest step toward sending women into military combat).[13]

It is important to observe the differences from issues concerning racial distinctions. Women are a group not legally barred from political power, not weak because they are oppressed by others, but weak only when women themselves choose not to assert their own claims. Yet history and culture and former legal arrangements play a role in keeping many women from pressing what some women and some men think is their true right and interest. Do judges have the task of 'correcting' for those impacts of culture? If so, their mandate comes only from the words 'equal protection of the laws', a thin support indeed, linguistically and historically. But is it imaginable, in a society in which women's roles are changing, that courts will decline to be one institutional agent of a movement so widely accepted in the circles in which judges travel? Yet does not an active judicial role concerning sexual stereotyping, at a time of judicial hesitation concerning, for example, economic rights, emphasise the charge of elitism and hostility to true democracy so often levelled at judicial review?

For the purposes of this essay, there is a far more important group that has sometimes been accorded status as a sector protected against hostile legislation. The group is aliens. Aliens normally have no voice or vote in politics. Laws, enacted by citizens, often classify aliens unfavourably. In a series of cases concerning eligibility for jobs, the Supreme Court has sometimes required that these laws be supported by a public purpose that is 'substantial' and 'necessary', but in other cases has asked only for 'some rational relationship' between the classification and a public purpose. For example, they allow state government to deny aliens jobs as state policemen (Justice Stevens, dissenting, said the law would deny the New York State Police the services of Hercule Poirot or Sherlock Holmes) and as school teachers, but bar the state from preventing their certification as lawyers.[14] But the issue is immensely important, given the large legal and illegal alien population.

Most of the arguments for judicial protection of blacks apply to aliens. One argument, however, is stronger: aliens have no participation in politics, and so have far less opportunity than blacks to advance their interests without resort to the courts. Like blacks, aliens are a distinguishable group, are often the subject of prejudice, and have difficulty escaping this status to meld into the larger population. Unlike blacks, aliens were not slaves. But a powerful argument can be made that tolerable, not to say decent or defensible, domestic relations in a country with millions of aliens requires active scrutiny of the majority's laws concerning those aliens whom it chooses or permits to enter. Otherwise, the country will contain a substantial population without access to *any* branch of government, a class likely to become entrenched in cycles of inferior position. If the nation is not to repeat its history of tolerating slavery and is not to make all the mistakes of Europe's foreign-worker history, it cannot exclude aliens from all institutional redress.

The Supreme Court took a major step in this area with its 1982 decision that Texas could not deny public schooling to the children of unlawful immigrants.[15] Further cases are inevitable, given the size of the illegal population. Meanwhile, we can speculate briefly about the contexts in which constitutional litigation on behalf of aliens, both legal and illegal, is certain to be brought:

i) Must government (or perhaps a private firm) keep its promises to aliens? For example, what of the promises implicitly made when a worker pays the social security tax?

ii) Are unequal work conditions constitutional? What of a lesser minimum wage for alien workers, for example? Or reduced Occupational Safety and Health Administration (OSHA) protection for aliens?

iii) Is there a minimal set of 'citizenship' rights (speech? due process? freedom from unreasonable search?) that is an attribute of humanity, not deniable to any human being who is within the country?

iv) It is worth noting that aliens are particularly in need of the group access to the courts discussed above. How will they come to have representation? Will we, for example, permit Mexico to represent its citizens who are temporarily in this country?

Focusing on non-citizen residents, lawful or unlawful, as a group at least arguably appropriate for the special judicial protection that the Fourteenth Amendment certainly grants to blacks and may grant to women opens up the even harder question concerning persons of Hispanic origin. Along a continuum, this categorisation is a short distance from aliens. Many, of course, *are* aliens. The group as a whole faces major barriers in participating politically. Prejudice is substantial. Language is a major barrier. How can one imagine a Constitution that protects black Americans and does not speak to the circumstances, similar in so many ways, of Americans who are recently from Puerto Rico or Mexico or, indeed, Cuba or Haiti?

On the other hand, that is the problem: if blacks mean Puerto Ricans which mean Haitians, how can one stop before Latvians or Japanese or Italians or Scots? But there is an answer. Recall that we are considering here judicial scrutiny of laws which themselves classify in certain ways. Laws disadvantaging blacks have almost uniformly been struck down. Laws disadvantaging and advantaging women are now the subject of extensive litigation. Laws about aliens are frequently litigated. Where there are laws classifying citizens of Hispanic origin, surely they should survive only if their necessity and appropriateness and fairness are reviewed and validated by a court.

And there are such laws, in the form of laws which make the English language this country's official tongue. The hard and immediate question is whether the Constitution should protect citizens (also aliens?) whose English is limited or non-existent by intrusive judicial review of legislative arrangements that insist upon the priority of

English. Sixty years ago, pluralists praised Supreme Court decisions that protected the rights of parents to educate their children in German.[16] How far does the Constitution permit the majority to go in insisting that public business be done in English, and in encouraging all persons to adapt to an English-language country, if the effect is frequent inconvenience, and sometimes real hardship, for those who were reared in other tongues? The question is difficult. But it is impossible to deny that it is a *constitutional* question, appropriate in our system for judicial consideration.

When one begins to list the groups on whose behalf courts have reviewed legislation – blacks, women, aliens, Mexican-Americans – one quickly sees that the list is potentially very large. Are we to accord judicial review to the claim of any group whom society has treated badly? Then why not provide judicial protection for bank robbers! Is our standard 'groups that can't win battles for themselves in the legislature'? Then every law about which someone complains creates a candidate, because in every instance the legislative decision has been adverse to a group that is, therefore, now aggrieved. Is our standard 'groups whom the legislature treats worse than it should'? Then who is to say whether the legislature was right? We can mention the physically handicapped, drug addicts, prisoners, homosexuals, the elderly, and even retarded children. The arguments are subtly different in each case. For now it is only important to say that we have created the potential for very wide judicial involvement in basic and controversial domestic politics, and that we do not yet have a limiting principle that tells why any group other than blacks can successfully request intrusive judicial review when the legislature has acted to their detriment, and yet confines the principle so that it stops short of the groups referred to above. That problem remains very serious for this society.

One way the law has recently grappled with the asserted rights of groups has been in deciding which distinctions require strict judicial scrutiny under the equal protection clause – deciding, in effect, the length of the list of suspicious categorisations, a list that begins with categorisations disadvantaging minority races. The second way the issue of groups has arisen under the equal protection clause has been in judicial review of the *impact*, as opposed to the *motivation*, of government action.

Start with the easy case: the constitutional certainty that in 1981 the legislature cannot deny the vote to blacks or the practice of law to women or driver's licences to persons who cannot speak English. Government cannot draw lines it cannot justify, and in each of these cases the courts will look hard at the justification to see if it fits closely with some legitimate public goal. No fit has been found close enough to justify a law disadvantaging blacks.

Now comes a more complex case: just as the legislature cannot say it is making a category of blacks and treating that category worse (and, in many contexts, cannot do so as regards women or aliens or some of the other groups discussed above), so it cannot make a decision that does not explicitly mention blacks but is *in fact* motivated by an attempt to disadvantage blacks. If it can be shown that a zoning change was denied because the zoning board did not want moderate-income housing that would attract blacks or if a school district was altered to prevent racial integration, the government actions are unconstitutional, even though they appear *prima facie* neutral and conventional. It is hard to prove motivation, especially in a chaotic legislative process; and difficult doctrinal questions arise when an official action obviously stems from a number of purposes, some of them valid and one invalid. But the general principle is clear.

Now comes the third type of case: government makes a decision that does not mention blacks. It reduces public housing subsidies or rezones a city's schools or closes a swimming pool. No anti-black motivation is shown; indeed, there is an entirely legitimate explanation for the decision, for instance, budget-balancing. But the result of the decision – its impact, as opposed to its motivation – is harmful to blacks (or, as the case may be, women or Puerto Ricans or Japanese-Americans or homosexuals).

For a time ten years ago, it appeared that the federal courts were about to interpret the equal protection clause to forbid such decisions, or at least to require that government canvass alternative ways to achieve its legitimate purposes before acting in such a way. That direction in constitutional doctrine could be fairly clearly sketched at the very end of the tenure of the Warren Court. It was, however, swiftly rejected after President Nixon's appointees took their seats, and it is now commonplace that no constitutional violation can be established solely with proof of the racially disparate results of government action.[17]

The idea lives, however, both because certain commentators continue to urge it, and more importantly because statutes have been interpreted as creating something quite like it with respect to important areas of social life. In particular, Title VII of the 1964 Civil Rights Act, the provision barring discrimination in employment, has been held to mean that unless an employer can show a close connection between a job criterion and the requirements of a job, it cannot use the criterion (for example, a standardised 'intelligence' test or a requirement of a high school diploma) if it has a differential impact on black applicants, even if the company established the criterion in good faith.[18] Also, the Voting Rights Act of 1965 bars portions of the country from changing their local election systems, for instance the boundaries of city council districts, if the change diminishes black representation, even if the change was not motivated by racism. Thus, we have major and continuing experience with the idea of making sure that satisfactorily motivated decisions (whom to hire, how to structure local government) do not have a result that is bad for blacks as a group, at least not without a compelling justification. We have also had extensive experience with a 'group-disadvantage'principle in what are essentially remedial contexts: as when, after a finding of so-called *de jure* segregation (by a school board or an employer, for instance), a court orders correction of the present consequences of the former misdeeds, and, in a different sort of remedial context, when the court orders payments of cash and land to Indian groups, to Alaskan natives, and, as is now being discussed, to Japanese-Americans who were victimised during the second World War. (Nearly fifteen years ago, Professor Boris Bittker of the Yale Law School explored in depth the issue of cash compensation for slavery and segregation in his book, *The Case for Black Reparations*.[19])

The questions that are put by these developments are difficult and important. Are we prepared to trust the political process, as it reaches outcomes that affect blacks and whites differently? Can blacks do well enough politically so that we regard the outcomes – even if sometimes difficult for them – as compatible with our ideals of a just society? If they can, then the courts should not evaluate 'consequences', should not be concerned with the 'discriminatory impact' of political decisions. If, on the other hand, an obligation still exists because of slavery and legally-mandated segregation, if racism is prevalent and offensive, if politics remains contaminated as it acts differentially upon blacks and whites, if blacks still need and deserve help as they struggle for full membership in this society, if there is a great deal of political action that we believe is motivated by anti-black animus but we have trouble proving that in particular cases, and if (a very big if) fairness for blacks can be achieved through judicial supervision of political outcomes without that process having unacceptable consequences for our ultimate goals of equality and justice, *then* courts should invalidate under the equal protection clause legislative and administrative decisions that have a differential and negative impact on blacks and which cannot be justified by some adequate showing of necessity or appropriateness. Or, even if we do not wish to apply such review as a constitutional matter to all government decisions, we might regard jobs and voting as so important (and perhaps educational access also) that we would insist that decisions on job criteria and on electoral arrangements *either* be fair to blacks in their results *or* be shown to be necessary to achieve some legitimate purpose.

That said, it is suddenly right to see the difference between blacks in America and all other classifications of persons: women, Hispanics, Italians, Vietnamese, handicapped, homosexuals, and so forth. Only with blacks is the social obligation so clear and so strong. And only as regards blacks is there so much reason to fear that the give and take of politics will have consistently bad outcomes. It is possible to argue, as Professor Glazer has done, that we should let politics work for all groups including blacks and give legal place only to individuals and not to blacks and others as groups. But it is important to note at least the possibility of continuing for a time to accord legal protection to the concerns of black Americans while acknowledging that legal scrutiny of political and economic outcomes should not extend beyond blacks, should not categorise and Balkanise the entire population, should not repress fluid and inevitable group political manoeuvring, should not – except as regards blacks – review the justice of political outcomes as they affect officially classified groups of citizens, but only review allegations of discriminatory motivation.

The final issue that requires discussion is affirmative action. If the Constitution tells legislatures they cannot classify blacks to their detriment, can they none the less classify minority racial groups to their advantage? This is certainly the most divisive constitutional issue of our day. Its difficulty is reflected in the lack of coherence of the major Supreme Court decisions on the subject; the Court, like the country, finds the questions hard, close, and troubling. At the moment, however, the Court seems to have said that the Constitution does permit Congress to make special provision for blacks, at least in certain circumstances of past discrimination and present inequality and at least where the consequences for disfavoured whites are tolerable.[20] And indeed, while it has proved difficult for constitutional scholars and moral philosophers to articulate the explanation, there is certainly a large difference between a legislative attempt to perpetuate a race in an inferior position and efforts to pursue eventual equality by correcting for present consequences of past discrimination.

It is also important, however, to see the way in which efforts at affirmative action tend to legitimise formal categorisations of the population, racial and other, and to transform distributional questions into issues of group share. The reason is not only that the arguments for affirmative protection for blacks have aspects that apply to women, Hispanics, the elderly, and homosexuals. Another, equally important, reason is that subjecting distributional outcomes to justification (as, for instance, when private employers were forced to show a job-related justification for educational criteria or public employers for civil service examinations) has stripped away veils which cannot easily be restored, and that intense scrutiny has been generally delegitimising. If there is no defensible basis for picking a school principal or a factory foreman and if the social significance of and the economic return to the position are so high, how justify any method except a lottery on the one hand or quotas of race and sex and ethnicity and age on the other?

We shall have to struggle with these questions for some time. Meanwhile, perhaps we should hope for a Supreme Court wise enough and ingenious enough to uphold legislative decisions that assist blacks but refuse to uphold, because the justifications are weaker and the costs to the social fabric so great, extensions of those arrangements to other groups. Lincoln said we might suffer for slavery 'until every drop of blood drawn with the lash shall be paid'. As to all other social groupings, all those who were never enslaved, majority attitudes and policies can change and even progress, but an attempt to assess and correct guilt is the wrong, and indeed an unconstitutional, endeavour.

Notes

1 For example, Laurence H. Tribe, *American Constitutional Law* (Mineola, N.Y. Foundation Press, 1978); Reich, 'The New Property', *Yale Law Journal* Vol. 73 1964, p. 733.
2 E.g. Stephen G. Breyer, *Regulation and its Reform* (Cambridge, Mass: Harvard University Press, 1982).
3 What discriminations are barred is of course a difficult question. A New York judge recently allowed a landlord to deny housing to a young lawyer, saying it was reasonable for the landlord to be afraid of complaints or litigation. Another New York judge said that a landlord could not evict a tenant who added a boyfriend to the inhabitants of the apartment because state law barred discrimination 'on the basis of marital status'. *Kramarsky v. Stahl Management*, 401 N.Y.S. 2d 943 (N.Y. Sup. Ct. 1977); *Hudson View v. Weiss*, 431 N.Y.S. 2d 632 (N.Y. Civ. Ct. 1980).
4 *Calhoun v. Cook*, 522 F. 2d 717 (5th Cir. 1975); see Trillin, 'U.S. Journal: Atlanta Settlement', *New Yorker*, 17 March 1973, at 101.
5 *Pennhurst State School and Hospital v. Halderman*. 451 U.S. 1 (1981).
6 *Joint Tribal Council of the Passamaquoddy Tribe v. Morton*. 388 F. Supp. 649 (D. Me. 1975).
7 Paul Brest, 'Foreword: In Defense of the Antidiscrimination Principle', *Harvard Law Review*, Vol. 90, 1976 pp. 1, 49–50.
8 Abram Chayes, 'The Role of the Judge in Public Law Litigation', *Harvard Law Review*, Vol. 89, 1976, pp. 1281, 1284.
9 *Havens Realty Corp. v. Coleman*, 102 Sup. Ct. 1114 (1982).
10 Derrick Bell, 'Serving Two Masters: Integration Ideals and Client Interests in School Desegregation Litigation', *Yale Law Journal* Vol. 85, 1976 p. 470.
11 *Bradwell v. Illinois*, 83 U.S. 130 (1873).
12 *Weinberger v. Weisenfeld*, 420 U.S. 636 (1975); *Stanton v. Stanton*, 421 U.S. 7 (1975).
13 *Kostker v. Goldberg*, 453 U.S. 57 (1981).
14 *In re Griffiths*, 413 U.S. 717 (1973); *Foley v. Connelie*, 435 U.S. 291 (1978).
15 *Plyler v. Doe*, 102 Sup. Ct. 2382 (1982).
16 *Meyer v. Nebraska*, 262 U.S. 390 (1923).

17 Compare *Hawkins v. Town of Shaw*, 437 F. 2d 1286 (5th Cir. 1971), aff'd en banc, 461 F. 2d 1171 (1972), with *Jefferson v. Hackney*, 406 U.S. 535 (1972).
18 *Griggs v. Duke Power Co.*, 401 U.S. 424 (1974).
19 Boris I. Bittker, *The Case for Black Reparations*. (New York: Random House Inc., 1973).
20 *Fullilove v. Klutznick*, 448 U.S. 448 (1980).

3 Ethnic Pluralism in Britain: the Demographic and Legal Background
Colin Brown

Introduction

This paper gives a brief account of the demographic and legal background to the issues of British race relations that are discussed in the following papers. It covers the migration, growth and present size of the British black population, the basic characteristics of that population, the legislation that has been adopted to control immigration, and the legislation concerned with racial discrimination and community relations.

The need for brevity puts constraints on content and structure, and therefore in order to avoid any misunderstanding it may be useful to point out several resulting limitations of the paper. First, it omits any specific discussion of the long-term historical context of race relations problems. There is no coverage of the growth or functioning of the British empire, of the origins of the black Caribbean population in the slave trade, or of the economic relationship between Britain and the former colonies. I should emphasise that this is not to deny the importance of a historical perspective in the discussion of contemporary race relations; the presence of the black population of Britain has its origins in migration that has occurred since the second World War, but racism and racial disadvantage have roots that stretch back further in time. Secondly, I have split the description of the legislation into separate accounts of immigration policy and race relations policy, and this may give the impression that the two developed separately. This was certainly not the case, for the approach of the main political parties has been to see immigration control as a positive factor in race relations policy: limitation of the size of the black population has been regarded as a precondition for harmonious community relations and thus the two sets of policies have developed side by side. Thirdly, because information has been condensed from a large subject area into a very short introductory account, some of the generalisations are bound to have ignored important matters of detail. It is hoped that this reduction of a complex and variegated landscape to its broad contours has not been taken so far as to be misleading.

Much of the absent detail is to be found in the specialist papers that follow.

Several points need to be made concerning definitions. The term 'New Commonwealth' is used throughout the paper, and this refers broadly to Britain's ex-colonies that have achieved independence since the second World War, and includes India and countries in the Caribbean and Africa. Pakistan left the Commonwealth in 1973, and a term that has been adopted widely in order to make allowance for this is 'New Commonwealth and Pakistan', often abbreviated to 'NCWP'; this distinction is generally not of importance within the discussion in this paper, and these terms are used interchangeably. What was once the country of Pakistan (geographically two units, known as West and East Pakistan) is now two countries, Pakistan and Bangladesh (Bangladesh is a member of the Commonwealth); as a consequence the term 'Pakistani origin' in British discussion of race relations often refers both to Pakistanis and to Bangladeshis. References in Britain to the skin colour of the main ethnic minority populations have used several terms over the years: 'coloured', 'black and brown', and, after the American practice, 'black'. My preference is for the last of these, and therefore in this paper the term 'black' is used to refer to non-white people of Afro-Caribbean or Asian origin. The term 'Asian' is by convention used to refer to people from the Indian sub-continent and, confusingly, does not usually include people from elsewhere in Asia; moreover, 'Asian' is used generally as a reference to ethnic origin, while 'African' is used as a description of geographical origin, hence the term 'African Asian'. Ethnic Africans are referred to as 'black Africans'. The system of terminology is both technically incorrect and inconsistent, but it has developed this way and we are rather stuck with it.

The overall size of the British black population

The population of Great Britain (England, Wales and Scotland) is about 54 million, and the most recent estimate of the size of its population with origins in the New Commonwealth was just over 2.2 million, or 4.1 per cent, in 1981.[1] Over four-fifths of these people have their origins in the Caribbean, the Indian sub-continent or Africa; the black population is estimated therefore to be about 3.4 per cent of the general population. Although they clearly do not constitute the entire ethnic minority population of the country, people with origins in these areas will be the main focus of attention for this paper, first because the other minority groups are small and varied, and would therefore be difficult to cover adequately in a general description such as this, and secondly because the Caribbean, Asian and African minorities are all subject to the disadvantages arising from differential treatment based on colour. In practice, information is most readily available on the Caribbean and Asian population, the black African group being very much smaller, and as a consequence most of the data given below are confined to those two main groups.

It is frequently pointed out by researchers that numerous groups of immigrants have settled in Britain over the centuries and that as a result the white population has a considerable mix of ethnic origins. Undoubtedly the most important white immigration has been from Ireland. In 1971 over a million of the people in Great Britain had been born in the Irish Republic, or had parents who had been born there. To these first and second generation ethnic Irish can be added an unknown number of people of more distant Irish descent, for Irish migration has long featured as a contributory factor to British demography: in the 1861 census, some 602,000 people born in Ireland were enumerated in England and Wales.

The migration and growth of the black population
Although for a deeper understanding of the migration of people from the New Commonwealth to Britain we would need to look further into history, the period of actual immigration of any scale begins after the second World War. An initially small migration increased during the 1950s to a substantial flow from the West Indies, India and Pakistan. This peaked sharply in the years before the introduction of immigration control in 1962, and since then there has been an overall downward trend in black immigration, although this has been punctuated by several fluctuations: an increase in the mid-1960s, followed by a sharp decrease; a peak in 1972 when people of Asian origin were expelled from Uganda; and an increase between 1974 and 1976 as a result of changes in the procedures regarding the immigration of spouses and dependants.

Within these broad changes in the level of New Commonwealth immigration there have been substantial changes in the composition of that immigration. First, the peak period of West Indian immigration was before the first immigration controls: in the 1950s there were migrants from both major sending areas, but West Indians predominated. Since then, the position has been reversed, and throughout the 1960s and 1970s migrants from the Indian sub-continent have been in the majority. Secondly, the earlier stages of the migration were characterised by a predominance of adult males, and these were later to be outnumbered by women and children. More than 90 per cent of New Commonwealth citizens accepted for settlement on arrival in 1979 were women, children or elderly men.[2] The shift from primary immigration to immigration of dependants has been particularly marked among Asians.

These changes are the result of a combination of factors resulting from the dynamics of the original migration and from the government's introduction of, and changes to, successive immigration controls. The relationship between migrant flow and the controls is not straightforward – for instance, the increase in migration prior to the 1962 Act was the reaction of potential migrants to the coming legislation – but the controls are the major factors leading to the decline of primary immigration. The legislation itself is discussed later in the paper. The statistical sources documenting post-war immigration present very serious technical problems, but to give an approximate visual guide to the general trends and phases of the migration a number of sources are used in combination in Figure 3.1.

So far this description has concerned immigration from the New Commonwealth for settlement in Britain, but it should be noted that for many years total emigration from the United Kingdom has been greater than total immigration, and the net flow became an inward migration only in 1979, this change being the result of a reduction in the number of people moving to Australia and New Zealand. There has also been a small gross return migration to the West Indies and to the Indian sub-continent throughout the period of immigration; this return migration for settlement should not be confused with return journeys to these countries made by British black people – these temporary visits of course have no effect on net immigration.

Levels of future immigration are very difficult to forecast. With the present legislation it is likely that immigration from the New Commonwealth will continue its downward trend, but it is impossible to predict the actual rate of this decline. As a result of the post-war immigration and natural increases, the population with origins in the New Commonwealth has grown steadily as shown in Table 3.1. Projections to 1991 have been made by the Office of Population Censuses and Surveys using varying assumptions of future immigration and fertility levels. Such projections are of course subject to considerable uncertainty, but it seems likely that in 1991 there will be $2\frac{1}{2}$ – 3 million people in this country with origins wholly in the New Commonwealth and Pakistan; it should be remembered that this projection covers all people of wholly NCWP origin, not just those who are black.

Estimates of the ethnic composition of British population with origins in the New Commonwealth are shown in Table 3.2. It can be seen that nearly half have their origins in India, Pakistan or Bangladesh (although some of these came to Britain after living in Africa for a period); nearly a third are of Caribbean descent; only one

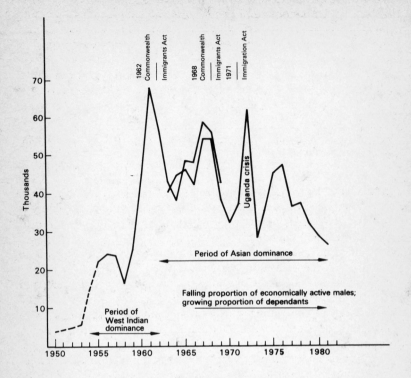

Figure 3.1 General trends in the settlement in Britain of people of West Indian, African and Asian origin, 1950–81

Notes

A = Data from the census. This line represents the numbers of people of NCWP origin born in the West Indies, Africa, India, Pakistan and Bangladesh enumerated in the 1971 census, shown by their year of entry to the UK.

Source: G. Lomas, *Census 1971: The coloured population of Great Britain* (London: Runnymede Trust 1973). Annual totals before 1955 are author's estimates based on five-yearly census figures.

B = Data from immigration control. This line represents the annual number of acceptances of persons subject to control from the West Indies, Africa, India, Pakistan and Bangladesh, and of non-patrial UK passport holders. The totals include those accepted on removal of a time limit.

Sources: (1963–76) Minutes of Evidence to Select Committee on Race Relations and Immigration 1977; (1977–81) Home Office Control of Immigration Statistics.

Table 3.1   Estimates and projections of GB population of New Commonwealth and Pakistan origin, 1966–80

	Numbers	% of GB population
1966	886,000	1.7
1971	1,371,000	2.5
1976	1,771,000	3.3
1980	2,104,000	3.9

Sources: OPCS, *Population Trends*, No. 9, (London: HMSO); *OPCS Monitor PPI 81/6*, December 1981.

in five have their origins in other parts of the New Commonwealth. The dominance of the Asian group is relatively new: the preponderance of West Indians in the early period of the migration meant that they formed the larger group until 1971.

These figures include considerable numbers of people born in Britain; OPCS estimates suggest that in 1976 just under 40 per cent of the population with New Commonwealth origins were born here, and that the proportion will rise to about half by 1991. Because of the differences in the timing of the migration, this process is more advanced for people of West Indian origin than for those of Asian origin.

A fundamental characteristic of the black population is its distinctively young age profile. Table 3.3 shows the OPCS estimates of the age distribution in 1976 and projections to 1991, from which it can be seen that this characteristic will persist for some time.

Table 3.2   Estimates of ethnic origin of population of New Commonwealth and Pakistan origin

Composition in 1980	%
India	22
Pakistan and Bangladesh	17
African Asians	9
Caribbean	31
Africa (other than African Asians)	6
Mediterranean	8
Other	8
	100

Source: *OPCS Monitor PPI 81/6*, December 1981.

Table 3.3   Age profile of population of wholly New Commonwealth and Pakistan origin

Age Group	General population 1976 (%)	Population of New Commonwealth and Pakistan origin 1991 projection		
		1976 (%)	'lower variant' (%)	'higher variant' (%)
0–14	23	37	27	29
15–29	22	28	30	29
30–44	18	22	23	24
45–64	23	11	17	15
65 +	14	2	3	3

Sources: OPCS, *Population Trends* No. 16, Summer 1981 (London: HMSO); Central Statistical Office, *Monthly Digest of Statistics*, February 1978 (London: HMSO).

The geographical distribution of the ethnic minorities in Britain is complex. At both the inter-urban and intra-urban levels, the patterns of settlement and internal migration have been largely shaped by the search for jobs and housing, with the ethnic minorities acting as a 'replacement population' in both cases: black workers generally moved into jobs for which white workers could no longer be found, and into housing that was least desirable to the white population. Thus the ethnic minorities are to be found in large proportion in urban areas, particularly urban areas of previous net outward population movement. The major conurbations of London and the West Midlands, the Midlands towns of Leicester and Nottingham, and the cluster of textile towns in Lancashire and Yorkshire dominate the pattern; other large cities also contain a large proportion of the black population. In 1971 over half the black population lived in London and Birmingham, and 72 per cent lived in cities with over 250,000 inhabitants.[3]

It should be noted that patterns within broad areas of settlement are subject to local variations which become more pronounced as the analysis is focused on smaller geographical units. The result is a bewildering variety of local situations. People of Indian and Pakistani origin are characteristically found in nearly all towns of New Commonwealth immigrant settlement, but the population of West Indian origin is not nearly as widespread, being heavily concentrated in London and the West Midlands. At a small-area level, the patterns of joint settlement by different black groups observable at the inter-urban level often disappear, there being high levels of local residential segregation between Asians and West Indians. This segregation is also apparent between groups from different parts of the Indian sub-continent, and even between people from different islands in the Caribbean. Moreover, the local areas of settlement vary in character from the traditional inner city areas of multiple deprivation to more comfortable suburban and satellite towns and smaller, free-standing industrial towns. The recent disturbances in Britain's inner city areas may have focused attention on grave neglected problems, but their coverage by the media has served to reinforce an unfortunately narrow image of 'the immigrant areas'. The one-to-one association of the problems faced by the ethnic minorities with the problems of urban decay is an incomplete analysis, and is based on a failure to grasp the fact that the geography of black settlement is complex. It is made more unfortunate by one of the features of that geography: simply that the skewed distribution of the minorities has the effect of dividing the white population into two halves – those who live in or near areas settled by blacks, and those who do not. In 1971, 93 per cent of those of Asian or West Indian birth lived in local authority areas containing only 54 per cent of the general population. For a large proportion of British people, black faces are seen on a television screen more frequently than in the street.

Given this highly clustered geographical distribution, it is a question of some importance whether there are any trends towards dispersion or further concentration. What evidence there is suggests that there has been some intra-urban movement towards dispersion, but there is little to suggest that there has been any migration of note into areas not previously settled. In other words, it seems that internal migration from high density ethnic minority areas to lower density areas has occurred, but not any substantial movement into areas of zero density.[4]

The pattern may differ between those of Asian and West Indian origin: evidence from the censuses shows that measures of residential segregation from the general population decreased for West Indians between 1961 and 1971, but increased for Asians.[5] This would make sense in the light of the different positions of the two groups in the housing market, as shown in Table 3.6. Overall, a relatively large proportion of those of Asian origin own their homes, and a relatively large proportion of those of West Indian origin rent from the council or from housing associations. Movement into and between council dwellings is controlled within a local authority by the council's housing department, and although a degree of choice is built into the procedures, housing allocations to any ethnic minority group will inevitably result in some degree of dispersion unless a sustained policy of ethnic concentration is adopted. (The fact that the council's scope for allocation ends at their boundary helps also to explain the lack of inter-urban migration.) In the private sector, there are no such mechanisms acting to disperse any concentrated population; local shortages of supply may act to force people out of an area, but generally there is a greater likelihood within the private sector that the social forces that are working to preserve the concentrated geographical distribution of the Asian community will prevail.

It is quite likely that the factors that produced this differing pattern have continued to have effect, but the absence of an ethnic origin question on the 1981 form will make the Census a rather inadequate data source for further analysis of black internal migration. As a general point it should be noted that the 1981 Census only recorded the individual's birthplace, which for obvious reasons is now a poor proxy indicator of ethnic origin, and the results will therefore be inferior to those of the 1971 Census. The intention of OPCS was to improve on the 1971 proxy (a combination of birthplace and parents' birthplace) by the inclusion of a direct ethnic origin question, but this proposal and the pilot census caused a small political storm, after which both the new question and the parents' birthplace question were scrapped. By classifying people according to the birthplace of their head of household, OPCS estimates that it is possible to identify some 90 per cent of the population of New Commonwealth and Pakistan origin, but these counts will be contaminated by the inclusion of white household heads born in the New Commonwealth; the missing 10 per cent are those in households headed by British-born black people.

What we can already tell from the 1981 Census is that the general population has continued to move out of the principal cities. Table 3.4 shows that this movement, observable between 1961 and 1971, increased considerably in the period to 1981. The most spectacular

Table 3.4   *General population changes, 1961–71, 1971–81*

	1961–1971 % change	1971–1981 % change
Inner London	– 13.2	– 17.7
Outer London	– 1.8	– 5.0
Principal cities	– 8.4	
[Birmingham, Leeds, Liverpool, Manchester, Newcastle, Sheffield]		– 10.0
Other metropolitan districts	+ 5.5	– 2.0
Large non-metropolitan cities	– 1.4	
[over 175,000 in 1971]		– 5.1
Smaller cities	+ 2.2	– 3.2
England and Wales	+ 5.7	+ 0.5

Source: Census 1981, *Preliminary Report*, England and Wales (London: HMSO, 1981).

falls in population have occurred in the inner city areas occupied by the black population, but it is unlikely that this flight from the cities has included a proportionate migration of ethnic minority members.

Diversity among the ethnic minorities

Considering the black population forms only a very small proportion of the general population, the diversity of ethnic and geographical origins, languages and religions to be found among them is dazzling. The largest of the Caribbean groups originates from Jamaica, but the migrants from this area included substantial numbers from Barbados, Trinidad and Tobago, Guyana, the Windward Islands, the Leeward Islands and the Virgin Islands. The Asian migrants can be divided into principal groups by area of origin: those from Gujarat, a western state of India bordering on Pakistan; those from the Punjab area of northern India and Pakistan, and the areas of Pakistan to the north-west of the Punjab; those from Sylhet and the maritime areas of Bangladesh; and those from East Africa, whose family origins were in various parts of India, mainly Gujarat and the Punjab. The majority of Asian families originate from rural areas, although the African Asians generally come from towns and cities.

The first language of most Caribbean immigrants was English. Although there are differences of dialect and patois between the islands, and these have been preserved to an extent within the different communities in Britain, their fundamental closeness to standard English, and the use of English as the official language in the islands, have meant that no language problem can be said to have been encountered by the West Indian immigrants on a scale comparable with that met by the Asians: on arrival most of the Asians had as their first language Punjabi, Urdu, Gujarati, Bengali, Kutchi or Pashto. Most additionally spoke at least one other of these languages, or Hindi, but knowledge of English varied a great deal. Table 3.5 shows the proportions of different Asian groups in the 1974 PEP survey found to speak English poorly.[6] The sample was not confined to recent arrivals, but was a general survey of the ethnic minority population. It can be seen that women were particularly likely to have poor English. The passage of eight years must make these figures out of date, but there is still a substantial proportion of the population of Asian origin who speak little English, and the problem continues to be particularly severe for women. As might be expected, those who cannot speak English are more likely to be found in the more concentrated Asian communities, where it is possible to be insulated from potential language problems, both at work and at other times.

There are several different religions among the Asians in Britain.

Table 3.5   Asians' fluency in English, 1974

	% speaking English 'only slightly' or 'not at all' (interviewer assessment)
African Asian men	19
Indian men	26
African Asian women	41
Pakistani men	43
Indian women	60
Pakistani women	77

Source: D.J. Smith, *The Facts of Racial Disadvantage*, PEP Report 560 (London, PEP, 1976).

Although no strict delineation according to areas of origin can be made, it is possible to generalise: many of those from the Punjab are Sikhs, many from Gujarat are Hindus, and most Pakistanis and Bangladeshis are Muslims. Among West Indians, some of the more enthusiastic Christian sects have a wide following, and the adoption of Rastafarianism by some young West Indian men is very visible. Religious affiliations and observance have very prominent roles in British Asian culture, far more so than among white people or people of West Indian origin.

Housing

The distinctive tenure patterns of the ethnic minorities are shown in Table 3.6. The most notable feature is the different penetration of the owner-occupied and council sectors by the Asian and West Indian groups: whereas a relatively high proportion of Asians have bought or are buying their homes, West Indians have a lower rate of home ownership than the general population; and while the level of council tenancy among West Indians is higher than average, it is very low among Asians. Both groups are more frequently found in non-council rented property than white people, but again there is a difference between the minority groups: Asians tend to be in privately rented accommodation, while West Indians are the group best represented among housing association tenants.

Although these comparisons are striking, there are hidden beneath them even greater differences between white and ethnic minority housing. For the white population, house purchase is associated with good housing quality, and with suburban and rural settlement. For blacks, however, a high level of ownership cannot be equated with

Table 3.6   Tenure patterns, 1977

	West Indian (%)	Indian/Pakistani/ Bangladeshi (%)	White (%)
Owned (outright or with mortgage)	35.9	69.9	54.6
Rented from council	45.2	10.1	30.0
Housing association	4.4	0.4	1.3
Privately rented	14.4	19.6	14.1

Source: Department of the Environment, *National Dwelling and Housing Survey*, (London, 1978).

better housing conditions. Finding it almost impossible to obtain council housing after coming to Britain, and with private rented accommodation becoming too overcrowded as dependants arrived, immigrants were often left with only one option: the purchase of cheap, poor quality housing in the inner urban areas. This process was reinforced by social and cultural factors – the need for larger properties for larger households, the preference for settlement near to other members of the same ethnic and language group, and the emphasis on becoming established in this country by owning property.

Table 3.7   Housing conditions, 1977

	West Indian (%)	Indian/Pakistani/ Bangladeshi (%)	White (%)
In shared dwelling	10.2	14.5	2.8
Without unshared use of all basic amenities (inside WC, fixed bath or shower, piped hot water)	13.2	24.1	8.2
Dwelling built before 1919	46.8	61.7	26.6
Below bedroom standard*	18.3	29.5	4.4

Source: *ibid.*
* The 'bedroom standard' is a calculation of the number of rooms required by a household of given size; if the dwelling is smaller than this, it is classed as 'below bedroom standard'.

Although these factors were particularly strong in the Asian community, house purchase among West Indian immigrants was also more common than among whites, once social class was taken into account: the very much higher proportion of manual workers among

West Indians would have led one to predict a lower rate of owner-occupation. The original tenure pattern has persisted for the Asians, but there has been a general movement by West Indians into council housing and, over the past ten years, a fall in the proportion owning their houses. There is a good deal of research evidence to show that the council dwellings allocated to black families have been those of inferior quality (see Valerie Karn's chapter in this volume). The result of these patterns in terms of housing conditions is shown in Table 3.7, and it gives a depressingly uniform picture: on all four indicators – sharing basic amenities, age of dwelling, and size relative to needs, black people are worse off than whites, and among blacks the Asians are particularly disadvantaged.

The black population at work
Because the ethnic minority population is a very young one, overall economic activity rates are very high, but among some groups the rates are high even after controlling for age. Table 3.8 shows that, among the young and the old, ethnic minority men have higher activity rates than white men, and that in every age group West Indian women have higher rates than white women. The table also shows the enormous differences between the women's activity rates of the various ethnic minority groups. Asian women have far lower rates than West Indian women, and this difference is particularly pronounced when Muslim women are considered. Other Asian women have activity rates which are interesting to compare with those for women in the general population: between the ages of 25 and 44, they are very similar, but for younger women and – more strikingly – for older women, there are fewer of the Asians working.

Just as overall activity rates are high, however, so are unemployment rates. The ethnic minorities are hit particularly hard by unemployment, because not only is the rate always higher than for whites, but also the size of the differential increases when overall levels rise[7]. In 1977 the levels of unemployment were estimated from the National Dwelling and Housing Survey[8] to be 9.6 per cent for the minorities compared with 5.2 per cent for the general population. Among young West Indians the problem is particularly bad, but this is by no means a youth problem alone: the NDHS showed that the proportion of economically active heads of household unemployed was over 10 per cent for West Indians, over 7 per cent for Asians, but under 5 per cent for whites.[9]

Employment patterns among blacks are distinctive. Table 3.9 shows that ethnic minority men are over-represented in manual jobs, and that this is particularly so among those of West Indian, Pakistani

Table 3.8   *Economic activity rates*
           (per cent working full– or part-time)

Age	(i) Asian & West Indian men	(ii) White men	(iii) West Indian women	(iv) Muslim Asian women	(v) Other Asian women	(vi) Women in general population
16–24	80	74	57	21	47	55
25–34	95	96	73	17	47	44
35–44	96	97	83	19	57	58
45–54	96	92	77 ⎱	2 +	28	63
55 +	72	48	65 + ⎰		13 +	20
All ages	91	77	74	17	45	43

Source: Smith, 1976. *op. cit.* (Columns (i) to (v) are based on data from the 1974 PEP survey, Column (vi) on data from the General Household Survey, 1972).

and Bangladeshi origin; the same overall bias towards manual work occurs among women, although there is not the same pattern among the different minority groups. This manual bias is also reflected in the equally distinctive pattern of industries in which black workers are found. The 1974 PEP survey found 47 per cent of ethnic minority men in manufacturing industry, compared with 33 per cent of the general population.[10] Heavy concentrations in vehicle manufacture, textiles and transport can be seen in Table 3.9. Several differences between the ethnic minority groups are noteworthy here: the relatively dense concentration of Pakistanis and Bangladeshis in the textile industry; the relatively low numbers of all groups in the distributive trades, except for African Asians; and the large numbers of West Indians in the 'professional and scientific services', this group probably being composed of health service workers and office staff.

It is not the case that the generally lower job levels occupied by the black population can be explained away by problems caused by recency of arrival, or by differences in educational qualifications, or by regional distribution. Although these factors do serve to reinforce the pattern, there is nevertheless an underlying structure of racial disadvantage in employment, itself the result of a number of historical and contemporary factors which reinforce each other: individual and institutional racism, direct and indirect discrimination, and the legacy of the colonial power relationship. There is research evidence from a number of studies showing the existence of widespread direct racial discrimination in employment recruitment.[11]

Ethnic minority earnings are on average lower than those of the

Table 3.9   *Job levels and industry sectors*

	West Indian (%)	Indian (%)	Pakistani/ Bangladeshi (%)	White (%)
Economically active men:				
(1977) Non-manual	11.6	34.4	14.4	40.7
Manual	88.5	65.6	85.6	59.3
Economically active women:				
(1977) Non-manual	47.4	40.3	53.4	60.2
Manual	52.6	59.7	46.7	39.8

Economically Active Men and Women	West Indian (%)	Indian (%)	Pakistani/ Bangladeshi (%)	African Asian (%)	General Popul'n (%)
(selected industries, 1974)					(1971 Census)
Vehicles & shipbuilding	7	12	12	6	4
Textiles	1	10	26	6	2
Construction	7	4	1	7	7
Transport & communications	10	12	5	11	7
Distributive trades	3	9	7	15	13
Professional & scientific services	19	6	2	3	12

Sources: National Dwelling and Housing Survey, *op. cit.*
Smith, *Facts of Racial Disadvantage, op. cit.*

white population, and this is not entirely the product of their different socio-economic distribution. Within white-collar grades, black men earn less than white men, and it seems that in manual jobs blacks maintain equivalent wages (or, in the case of unskilled manual work, higher average wages) mainly by working longer hours and by working shifts. The prevalence of shiftwork is a major feature of ethnic minority employment. The 1974 PEP survey showed that 19 per cent of male black workers were on shift systems that involved night work, while the corresponding figure for white men was 9 per cent.[12] This is especially a feature of the Asian working population, partly because problems of English language are eased (but inevitably perpetuated) by the insulation of night shifts that are relatively homogeneous in terms of ethnic origin.

Another important characteristic of the black working population is its high level of membership of the trade unions. The overall level for each of the West Indian, Pakistani/Bangladeshi and Indian groups is higher than for whites, and this is not purely a result of the industries and jobs in which they are found: where workplaces are unionised, black workers have been found consistently to have higher levels of membership than white workers. The overall level of membership found by Smith was 47 per cent among white men, and among the ethnic minority men membership ranged from 51 per cent among African Asians to 64 per cent among West Indians.[13]

One of the enduring stereotypes of Asian immigrants held by whites is that of the self-employed small shopkeeper; recently an otherwise well-informed article in *The Economist* referred in passing to 'the industrious and entrepreneurial Patels and Shahs who keep the familiar shops all over England'.[14] The visible presence in the cities and larger towns of Asian shops and restaurants, in contrast to the far less visible industrial workforce, has given rise to something of a myth. The proportion of self-employed shopkeepers in the Asian workforce is, at 5 per cent, indeed larger than the figure of 2 per cent among the general population,[15] but is far smaller than might be inferred from the image so often presented by the media.

The legislation: immigration and nationality

With the labyrinthine nature of today's laws controlling immigration from the Commonwealth and regulating the allocation of British nationality, it is easy to forget that prior to 1948 there were no such laws and no such legal concept as British nationality. The British plundering of the world carried out in the periods of the slave trade and imperialist expansion also served to extend the sovereignty of the British Crown, and the inhabitants of the colonies became subjects of the British monarch. British law recognised no national distinction other than between subjects and aliens, and the status of people in the colonies was identical to that of people living in Britain. Subjects were free to enter and settle in Britain with full rights of citizenship, including the right to vote. This situation persisted even when colonies became self-governing parts of the Commonwealth – the status of subject was not divisible.

The 1948 British Nationality Act made a fundamental change to this state of affairs. The intention of the Act was in no way to restrict immigration (the New Commonwealth immigration had hardly begun) but to attempt to maintain British nationality throughout the Commonwealth while permitting self-governing units within the Commonwealth to develop their own nationality laws. The Act had been pre-empted by the self-governing Dominions that already had their own immigration laws, denying some British subjects the right to settle there. The 1948 Act set up a two-tier system whereby all inhabitants of the Commonwealth remained British subjects, but this status became secondary to their citizenship of their own unit of the Commonwealth. The United Kingdom and its colonies formed one of these units, and the primary status of those within it was Citizen of the UK-and-Colonies (CUKC). It can be argued that the 1948 Act, though itself not part of immigration control, established in British law the essential precondition for control because it broke up the subject-monarch relationship within the Commonwealth; it split the legal atom at the core of the right to free movement from one part to another. In practice the Act left rights of settlement in Britain intact and therefore had no restrictive effect on immigration, and it was after its introduction that the major growth in immigration took place.

Throughout the period of increasing immigration there were discussions at Cabinet level over the possibility of introducing controls on the inflow of black people. In June 1950 the Labour Prime Minister Clement Attlee set up a committee of ministers and civil servants to review 'the means which might be adopted to check the immigration into this country of coloured people from the British colonial territories'.[16] The committee concluded that restrictions were, for the time being, unnecessary, but in accepting this view the Cabinet noted that future immigration might render control essential. Pressure from the right in favour of control increased during the 1950s, and in 1955 the Conservative Cabinet agreed to order the tentative drafting of a Bill to effect this. Prime Minister Harold Macmillan made attempts to check immigration without legal control, and it was not until 1961 that a firm decision was taken to legislate. Fear of an increasingly hostile white response to a tiny but geographically clustered and therefore politically visible black population was a major factor in the government's thinking at this time, although the influence of groups and individuals in Westminster pressing for immigration control from an openly racialist position should not be underestimated. The attempt to avoid internal race relations problems by restricting the numbers of black arrivals has remained at the root of both major political parties' legislative moves in this field. Although the Labour party in opposition fought against the first Commonwealth Immigrants Bill, it later adopted the position that control was essential.

The 'race relations' justification for immigration control has not been publicly presented by the government as an accommodation of white racism, however; rather, it has been explained in terms of problems caused by the presence of black immigrants. It may be that by aiming to appease white opinion by turning first to immigration control, ostensibly as a response to problems caused by black people, rather than by tackling racialism itself, the government has nourished and given legitimacy to anti-immigrant sentiment; thus the outcome of the appeasement policy may have been only a deepening of the racialist currents in British society.[17] It is difficult to analyse the extent to which successive immigration controls have been responses to public opinion, simply because the government's introduction of the controls may itself have been very influential in forming that opinion. It is clear, however, that, at the time of the first Act, most white people were in favour of control, and opposition to further immigration remains a majority response in attitude surveys to this day. Whilst there is academic debate about the actual levels of 'prejudice', 'tolerance' and other measures of white British reaction to black people, it is accepted that opposition to black immigration has become a persistent feature of public opinion, one which has been used as a potent force in electoral politics over the past twenty years.

The 1962 Commonwealth Immigrants Act was the watershed of British policy towards its commitments as the 'mother country' of the Commonwealth. The Act divided British subjects into two groups with different rights of settlement in the UK. Those with passports issued in the UK were permitted free entry, and those with passports issued elsewhere were subject to controls. The controlled group included citizens from the self-governing parts of the Commonwealth and citizens of the UK-and-Colonies with passports issued outside the UK. Control was administered by a system of employment vouchers issued by the Ministry of Labour. The results of this legislation, both in provoking a rush to migrate before the controls became effective, and in the stemming of further primary immigration, were mentioned earlier in this paper.

Within the definition of UK-issued passports were those issued by British High Commissions overseas. Such passports were held by many of the people of Asian origin in the newly independent states of East Africa. When in 1967 Kenya adopted legislation that expelled the African Asians holding these passports, many of them came to Britain. Falling into the UK passport holder category, they were not subject to the regulation controlling the entry of most other black people. The reaction of the Labour Government was quickly to pass the Commonwealth Immigrants Act 1968, denying them the right of entry unless they, or their parents or grandparents, were born or naturalised in the UK or in part of the old Commonwealth. This ensured that most white UK passport holders in East Africa retained the right of entry, while the Asian settlers were brought into the same system of voucher control as other black potential immigrants. A further voucher system was introduced on an annual quota basis for the entry of African Asians. A large proportion of the 28,000 Ugandan Asians who came to Britain in 1972 did not enter under this scheme, as *ad hoc* arrangements were made by the Conservative Government for entry vouchers to be provided following the crisis.

The next major change in the legislation became effective at the beginning of 1973, when the Immigration Act 1971 replaced the 1962 and 1968 Acts. This was an entirely new and very elaborate system which based control on the division of people into *patrials* and *non-patrials*, the former having the right of abode in Britain, the latter being subject to entry regulations. The definition of *patrial* is very complicated, but essentially it consolidated the distinction between those Commonwealth citizens who had a close connection by descent with the UK and those who did not. Outside the UK, this division was effectively between white people in the Commonwealth and all other people. Under the regulations of the 1971 Act, Commonwealth non-patrials were accepted into Britain on a limited work-permit basis or for special categories of employment, but the main category of those permitted to settle was made up of the dependants of non-patrial Commonwealth citizens already settled in Britain, these being mainly wives, children and elderly parents and grandparents. Also entitled to settle were the African Asians holding special vouchers issued under the scheme set up by the 1968 Act. Non-patrials were also accepted on a temporary basis as visitors or students, but some permanent settlement was permitted on expiry of the time limits, mainly for reasons of marriage.

The immigration control system of the 1971 Act remains in operation, but in many respects it has been supplemented by the passing of the 1981 Nationality Act. The effect of this Act is to split the category of 'Citizens of the United Kingdom-and-Colonies' into three new categories: British Citizens, Citizens of the British Dependent Territories, and British Overseas Citizens. The new British Citizen category is similar to the patrial category (the patrial/non-patrial distinction is now abolished) although it includes all New Commonwealth immigrants settled in Britain registered as CUKCs; the Citizen of the British Dependent Territories category covers those closely connected to the dependencies, and so mainly covers people in Hong Kong; British Overseas Citizenship is for the residual category of previously CUKC people. The basis of the new categories of citizenship is the range of immigration statuses with which it is connected; the government White Paper containing the proposals explained that the people to be covered by the residual British Overseas Citizen category could not become British Citizens because it would constitute an unacceptably large immigration commitment. Because it rests on considerations of levels of immigration of people whose movement is already subject to control, the Nationality Act is unlikely to have any effect on actual immigration levels. It has been argued, however, that it represents a major consolidation of immigration policy, because the restrictions which were once based on nationality have, by a remarkable inversion, now come to define that nationality.[18]

Remaining scope for migration from the New Commonwealth is limited mainly to dependants, marriage partners and others with existing connections with the UK, so this immigration is likely to continue to decline.

The legislation: anti-discrimination and race relations

Throughout the 1950s there were individual attempts to introduce legislation to outlaw racial discrimination; most of them were by Fenner Brockway, and all of them were unsuccessful. Eventually the promise of an anti-discrimination law was incorporated into the election manifesto of the Labour party prior to the 1964 general election, and in 1965 the Race Relations Bill was taken through parliament. During its passage the Bill was changed from one prescribing criminal penalties for racial discrimination to one which established a system for conciliation in such cases. Its field of operation was rather narrow, with discrimination in housing and employment falling outside its scope. But the passing of the Act was nevertheless a significant first step into an area previously regarded by many as off-limits to legal intervention.

The 1965 Race Relations Act outlawed discrimination in specified places of public resort, such as hotels, restaurants, cinemas, dance halls and transport facilities, and made it a criminal offence deliberately to stir up racial hatred by publishing or distributing written matter or by speaking in public. The Act set up the Race Relations Board (RRB) which co-ordinated seven regional conciliation committees established to deal with complaints of discrimination. Once a committee was satisfied that a complaint fell within the ambit of the Act and that unlawful discrimination had occurred, its task was to secure a settlement of the difference between the complainant and the discriminator, and an assurance from the latter as to his or her future conduct. In the event of failure to obtain a settlement or a satisfactory assurance, the matter was to be referred to the Race Relations Board, which would, if necessary, refer the matter to the Attorney General, who could seek an injunction restraining the discriminator from further unlawful behaviour. Although the numbers of complaints referred to the committees were small (690 in the year 1967/8), a large majority of them fell outside the scope of the Act, the most frequent of these being complaints about employment, the police and housing. The number of cases referred to the Attorney General was tiny: by 1968 they numbered four.

In 1967 the first PEP research report on the extent of racial discrimination was published, and this confirmed that there were large gaps in the legislation, most notably over employment and housing.[19] The report of the Street Committee was published in the same year; this was an independent examination of the options open to the government to further the legislation on race relations, and its conclusion was that it was both feasible and desirable to extend the law along lines similar to the American model.[20] These and other factors prompted the rapid extension of the anti-discrimination legislation. In 1968 the second Race Relations Act widened the coverage of the law to housing, employment and the provision of goods and services. The Race Relations Board was given power to investigate cases where there was reason to believe that discrimination had taken place but no complaint had been received; the Board was also given the power to bring legal proceedings when attempts to conciliate failed. In addition, the definition of conciliation now included provision for securing redress for the victim of discrimination; the function of conciliation under the 1965 Act had been to right a public wrong, not to settle a private claim.

Part of the 1968 Act was a departure from the straightforward anti-discrimination legislation. This was the setting up of a body in parallel with the Race Relations Board to work to promote good community relations and to act as adviser to the Home Secretary on such matters: the Community Relations Commission (CRC). The CRC replaced the National Committee for Commonwealth Immigrants, a non-statutory body, and took under its wing the Community Relations Councils, the local voluntary bodies through which much of the Commission's efforts were to be channelled.

The second Race Relations Act had a significant effect on the visible extent and nature of discrimination. The more public indications of discriminatory practices, such as advertisements specifying 'no coloureds' and outright statements of racist job recruitment policies, all but disappeared. The PEP research in the early 1970s showed that there had been an actual decrease in direct discrimination in housing and employment since the early 1960s.[21] But there were still high levels of discrimination, on a scale far greater than would have been judged from the still small number of complaints to the RRB. In addition, it had become apparent that direct discrimination was not always at the heart of racial disadvantage: regulations, policies and practices of organisations often discriminated indirectly against ethnic minorities, and the Act lacked any provision for dealing with these cases. Other deficiencies of the Act emerged as time passed, and when the government issued a White Paper in 1974 on equality for women, it was made clear that a model for new legislation concerning both sex and race was under discussion. The option of a joint statute to encompass both fields was rejected in favour of separate but harmonised legislation. The Sex Discrimination Bill was presented to Parliament in 1975, and in the same year a White Paper on racial discrimination was published, containing proposals that closely resembled its sister legislation. This was not merely an extension to the 1968 Act, but was a very different approach to anti-discrimination and race relations policy.

The 1976 Race Relations Act abolished the RRB and the CRC, and replaced them with a single body, the Commission for Racial Equality (CRE). The new Commission had most of the combined duties of its predecessors, but additionally had a wider strategic role to identify and deal with discriminatory practices by employers and other organisations. The legal definition of discrimination was extended to cover individual actions and organisational practices that worked to the disadvantage of the ethnic minorities, regardless of the way they were described or formulated, and regardless of the motive.

The *formal investigation* was established as the main instrument for the exercise of the Commission's strategic role. Organisations or persons suspected of discrimination could be instructed to supply information required for the investigation, and a report would be published by the Commission containing the results of its research and deliberations. Should the report confirm that discrimination had taken place, the offender would be served with a *non-discrimination notice*: an instruction to cease discriminating and to provide information to allow the monitoring of his/her subsequent behaviour in this respect. With regard to discrimination against individuals, the 1976 Act gave victims access to industrial tribunals for employment cases and to county courts for other cases; formerly, all complaints had to be channelled through the RRB.

The 1976 Race Relations Act is still in force. Its provisions and workings are covered in greater detail by other papers in this volume: Christopher McCrudden considers the relationship between the aims of the legislation, the mechanisms of the judicial process, and the enforcement role of the CRE; Peter Sanders deals with the individual complaints procedure and the CRE's formal investigations, and explains the practical difficulties of anti-discrimination law enforcement; and Susan Ollerearnshaw discusses the ways in which racial equality in employment can be promoted by the CRE as a positive policy rather than by relying solely on legal sanctions against discrimination.

Notes

1 Office of Population Censuses and Surveys, *OPCS Monitor PPI 82/1 Sources of statistics on ethnic minorities,* June 1982.
2 The Runnymede Trust and the Radical Statistics Race Group, *Britain's Black Population,* (London: Heinemann, 1980).
3 P.N. Jones, 'The distribution and diffusion of the coloured population in England and Wales, 1961–71', *Transactions,* Institute of British Geographers, New Series Vol. 3, No. 4, 1978.
4 T.R. Lee, 'Immigrants in London: trends in distribution and concentration 1961–71', *New Community,* Vol. V, No. 2, Spring 1973, pp. 145–58; C. Peach and S. Shah, 'The Contribution of Council House Allocation to West Indian Desegregation in London 1961–71', *Urban Studies* 17, 1980, pp. 333–41; V. Robinson, 'Asians and Council Housing', *Urban Studies* 17, 1980, pp. 323–31.
5 C. Peach, S. Winchester and R. Woods, 'The Distribution of Coloured Immigrants in Britain' in G. Gappert and H. Rose (eds), *The Social Economy of Cities,* (Beverly Hills: Sage, 1975).
6 D.J. Smith, *The Facts of Racial Disadvantage,* PEP Report 560 (London: Political and Economic Planning, 1976).
7 D.J. Smith, *Unemployment and Racial Minorities,* PSI Report 594 (London: Policy Studies Institute, 1981).
8 *ibid.*
9 Department of the Environment, *National Dwelling and Housing Survey,* (London, HMSO, 1978).
10 D.J. Smith, *The Facts of Racial Disadvantage, op. cit.*
11 W.W. Daniel, *Racial Discrimination in England* (Harmondsworth: Penguin, 1968); M. Firth, 'Racial Discrimination in the British Labour Market', *Industrial and Labour Relations Review,* Vol. 34, No. 2, January, 1981, pp. 265–72; R. Jowell and P. Prescott-Clarke, 'Racial Discrimination and White-Collar Workers in Britain', *Race,* Vol. XI, No. 4, April 1970, pp. 397–417; N. McIntosh and D.J. Smith, *The Extent of Racial Discrimination,* PEP Report 547, (London: PEP, 1974).
12 D.J. Smith, *The Facts of Racial Disadvantage, op. cit.*
13 *ibid.*
14 'Wool Shrinks, Bradford Crumbles', *The Economist,* 10 April, 1982, p. 34.
15 D.J. Smith, *The Facts of Racial Disadvantage, op. cit.*
16 *The Times,* 2 January 1982.
17 M. Dummett and A. Dummett, 'The Role of Government in Britain's Racial Crisis' in L. Donnelly (ed), *Justice First* (London: Sheed and Ward, 1969).
18 D. Dixon, 'Constitutionalising Racism: The British Nationality Bill 1981', *Critical Social Policy,* Vol. 1, No. 2, Autumn 1981.
19 W.W. Daniel, *Racial Discrimination in England, op. cit.*
20 H. Street, G. Howe and G. Bindman, *Report on Anti-Discrimination Legislation,* (London: PEP, 1967).
21 N. McIntosh and D.J. Smith, *The Extent of Racial Discrimination, op. cit.*

4   Anti-Discrimination Goals and the Legal Process
Christopher McCrudden

British policy-makers in the area of race relations will be increasingly confronted with two major choices. First, should we move further along the road which emphasises legal redress for institutional discrimination? Or should we attempt to use the more traditional political and administrative processes and refrain from putting the legal process in a central role? Secondly, to adopt Leon Mayhew's well-known distinction, should we be concerned to provide 'equal opportunities' or 'fair shares'?[1] The major part of this paper will be concerned with the first issue. I consider the second question more briefly at the end.

Indirect discrimination and institutional discrimination

The earlier Race Relations Act passed in 1968 adopted the principle that, with certain exceptions, colour, race and ethnic or national origin were irrelevant criteria for the distribution of certain resources. The Act provided in part that 'a person discriminates against another . . . if on the ground of colour, race or ethnic or national origin he treats that other . . . less favourably than he treats or would treat other persons'.[2] The use of criteria other than race, colour or ethnic origin, was, however, permissible under this definition.

But this idea of 'direct' discrimination in the 1968 Act came to be regarded as limited for two main reasons. First, it was difficult to establish that discrimination had taken place. Proof was required that a person had a discriminatory *intention*. Secondly, it did not address the use of criteria which had the effect of excluding disproportionate numbers of minority groups *irrespective* of intention. The growing perception that the 1968 Act definition was inadequate coincided with an increasing awareness of 'immigrant disadvantage' and urban deprivation and 'institutional discrimination'.

For example, a number of techniques and methods which are at the centre of the British method of industrial relations were criticised as disproportionately,even if unintentionally, excluding black workers. There is evidence that some work-group and trade union methods of controlling access to employment, such as age restrictions on entry into apprenticeships and what has been called the 'custom of patri-mony'[3] tend to disadvantage black (and women) workers propor-tionately more than white male workers. Similar exclusionary effects have also been found to be a potential side-effect of the use of aptitude testing by management for hiring and promotion, and of reliance on seniority for determining redundancy and promotion and allocation of other benefits.[4]

In the mid-1970s a new policy was adopted, of requiring a consider-ably increased scrutiny of such exclusionary practices in employment and elsewhere. By requiring employers and others to demonstrate the need for such exclusionary practices (educational qualifications, or facility in English, for example) it was hoped to reduce the degree of exclusion. This scrutiny was to be carried out under anti-discrimination legislation, the role of which was to be considerably expanded, particularly through the incorporation of a new meaning of unlawful discrimination.

The Race Relations Act 1976 expanded the meaning of discrimina-tion to include not only the 'direct' discrimination prohibited by the 1968 Act but also 'indirect' discrimination. The concept of 'indirect discrimination' as used in the Act is based on the approach of the US courts to the meaning of discrimination in Title VII of the Civil Rights Act 1964.[5] Each attempts to some extent to circumvent the problems of proof of intentional discrimination, to go beyond its individualised nature, and to provide a basis for intervening against the present effects of past and other types of institutional discrimination. There are, however, several important differences. The new meaning of discrimination serves differing functions in each country. In Britain, exclusionary practices adversely affecting the black immigrant more than the indigenous black are likely to be among those most under attack; in the United States the practices subject to legal attack are largely those which exclude indigenous minority workers. In Britain the purpose is still largely preventative; in the US it is largely remedial.

Some of these differences are reflected in the drafting of the indirect discrimination provisions in the Race Relations Act 1976. There is no requirement in this Act that past discrimination be shown. The indirect discrimination provision applies across the board and is not confined, as it appears to be becoming in the US, to employment situations. Other differences arise from the different institutional origins of the test. The British approach to statutory drafting – spelling out as much as possible in specific language – has led to some issues arising in Britain that do not appear to arise in the US, and vice versa, but these need not detain us here.[6]

The vast majority of racial discrimination cases taken under the 1976 Act involve allegations of discrimination in employment.

Although most allegations are of direct discrimination (in 1979–80 they amounted to 90.2 per cent of race cases, compared with only 7.7 per cent alleging indirect discrimination, and 2.1 per cent alleging victimisation), it is likely that complaints of indirect discrimination will grow. In the equivalent period 1980–81 applications alleging indirect discrimination rose to 20.5 per cent of all racial discrimination cases.[7]

There have been some advances through the existence of the indirect discrimination provision. Some firms have become more aware of the extent of the problem of unintentional discrimination and have adopted equal opportunity programmes to attempt to deal with it. In general, however, the adoption of the indirect discrimination provision in the Race Relations Act 1976 appears, as yet, to have had little effect on institutional discrimination. Serious consideration of the issues raised by it appears to have been minimal, as has any real reduction of exclusionary practices. The changes in the substance of the law have been little reflected in legal or social practices.[8]

There are a variety of possible reasons for this. There are a number of impediments to the effective use of the law which the racial minorities themselves may be able to do something about. There appears to be considerable suspicion among minorities of law and of courts. These are more often viewed from a criminal law perspective than as a potential avenue of redress. There is an absence of training of lawyers in anti-discrimination law. There is little public interest law activity directed against racial discrimination, outside the Commission for Racial Equality. There is as yet no British equivalent of the National Association for the Advancement of Colored People, the Legal Defense Fund or the Lawyers Committee for Civil Rights Under Law.

Turning from the minorities to the majority, there is a lack of understanding of the strategy of using law to attack institutional discrimination among some of those best placed to bring it to public awareness, and a consequent absence of support. The 1981 reports by the House of Commons Home Affairs Committee on racial disadvantage[9] and Lord Scarman's report[10] are key illustrations of either a lack of understanding of the role that the legal process might play in eradicating exclusionary practices or, more likely, of an unwillingness to advocate the effective development of such a role. The potential significance of the new meaning of discrimination has been grossly underestimated. Most observers assume that, in dealing with inequalities between black and white, the legal system should be tied still to the more traditional role of eradicating prejudiced discrimination.

The fault is also partly that of successive governments. There are important respects in which the implications of the change in the meaning of discrimination have not been carried through in the rest of the legislation itself. The enforcement and remedial provisions of the Act specifically distinguish between direct and indirect discrimination in ways which undermine the reasons why the new conceptual meaning was adopted in the first place. Secondly, whereas the equivalent American indirect discrimination test was developed alongside a number of fact-finding and remedial adaptations of the legal process which helped to accommodate this new redistributive role, equivalent adaptations to the British legal process have yet to be made. The tradition of voluntarism in British industrial relations, the absence of a tradition of using law for anti-discrimination purposes, or using regulatory agencies as bodies for law enforcement each contributed to the absence of appropriate institutional adaptation. My argument is that appropriate adaptations should now be made.

Before discussing what these should be, however, it is necessary to confront the preliminary question: why should we place more emphasis on legal redress for racial discrimination and unjustified exclusion? I would argue that there are a number of decisive reasons in favour of taking a legal route. First, there is little in the experience of the past two decades of attempting to bring about a reduction in discriminatory practices which gives confidence that either government, administrators or private businessmen will seek to bring about changes voluntarily.[11] Secondly, the apparent lack of electoral power of minorities in Britain makes one pessimistic about the possibilities for use of the traditional political process.[12]

A possible parallel is to be found in the choice which American blacks made in the 1930s when confronted with a similar lack of political possibilities. A legal strategy was developed in order to counter a lack of political will similar to that which faces the black population in Britain now. Legal rights came to be regarded as political 'trumps' in the hands of those who held them[13], in part because an appeal could be made to the majority on the basis of rights rather than simply political interests or preferences. The issue became 'civil rights' rather than 'race relations'.

Nor is an increased emphasis on legal redress a necessary alternative to the other political pressures, of which involvement of racial minorities in the trade unions is particularly important. Rather, it may well contribute to, rather than retard, the effective use of the political process, by keeping the issue of racial equality on the political agenda where more traditional methods are unable to do so.

It is important, however, not to ignore or discount the problems which will be confronted should the legal process be given more responsibility as a method for bringing about change in this area. First, such a use of the law will emphasise the idea of race. There is a danger that it will encourage racial thinking, perhaps to the detriment of the very groups sought to be protected. Secondly, the approach of sections of the judiciary to the existing legislation has not given grounds for optimism if their role was increased in importance. In Britain it too often appears to be the case that the problem is not one of attempting to stimulate a creative interpretation by the judges of the law (as in the United States) but rather of attempting to prevent its evisceration. An example of the latter is the decision in *Manda v. Lee*[14] in which the Court of Appeal held that Sikhs were not protected by the Act. The definition of 'racial group' in the Act, despite its specifically including 'ethnic group' within it, was held not to apply to them.

Probably even more important is the hesitation over allowing the legal process to be used to counter institutional discrimination on the grounds that such an issue is not 'justiciable' and thus not suitable to be dealt with through court processes. The idea of 'justiciability' involves a number of different issues. In the context of this discussion, however, the question of whether the courts are *competent* to deal with them is the central issue, the core problem, in the courts dealing with institutional discrimination.

In the United Kingdom, two principal methods have been devised to enable the legal process to be used to enforce the anti-discrimination requirements. One method has involved adapting the adjudicatory process so as to enable it to deal with such issues in a more constructive and realistic way, by establishing tribunals outside the ordinary courts and by adapting the traditional courts. Employment discrimination complaints by individuals are heard in industrial tribunals. Appeals are heard by the Employment Appeal Tribunal and thence to the Court of Appeal. Non-employment complaints are heard in modified county courts. Appeals are heard in the Court of Appeal. A second method has been to set up a regulatory agency charged with enforcing the law: the Commission for Racial Equality. My argument is that at the moment the legal process has not been sufficiently adapted to give the courts and these other bodies the powers necessary for them to be competent. This is particularly true in two respects: with regard to remedies and with regard to fact-finding.

Inadequacy of remedies

There is a clear lack of congruence between the substance of the indirect discrimination prohibition and the remedies available once it has been found to exist. Neither the remedies available at industrial tribunals, nor the remedial process in which the tribunals engage, adequately reflect the broadened role which jurisdiction over indirect discrimination complaints seems to require. Remedies in industrial tribunals conform closely to the traditional adjudicatory model.[15] Where an industrial tribunal upholds a complaint by an individual of unlawful discrimination, it is empowered ('as it considers just and equitable') only to make one or more of the following orders: first, an order declaring the rights of the respondent and complainant 'in relation to the act to which the complaint relates'; secondly, an order requiring the respondent to pay damages; thirdly, the tribunal may make a recommendation that the respondent take, within a specified period, 'action appearing to the tribunal to be practicable for the purpose of obviating or reducing the adverse effect on the complainant of any act of discrimination to which the complaint relates'.[16]

The 1976 Act stipulates that such damages may include compensation for injury to feelings whether or not they include compensation under any other head.[17] Damages have another function as well. Recommendations by the industrial tribunal are not specifically enforceable. If not complied with, the tribunal may only make an order of damages or increase an already existing order of damages subject to a maximum.[18]

There is thus in the 1976 Act 'a preference for giving effect to value judgements by providing monetary compensation rather than by granting or withholding reinstatement or re-engagement'.[19] It is important, however, to distinguish the remedy available for an individual proving a breach of the direct discrimination provisions from that of an individual proving indirect discrimination. In the case of the latter no damages may be awarded 'if the respondent proves that the requirement or condition in question was not applied with the intention of treating the claimant unfavourably on racial grounds'.[20] Where a recommendation has not been complied with in an indirect discrimination case the sanction of increasing the damages (or providing them in the first place) as a substitute does not apply therefore.

No injunctive remedy is available from an industrial tribunal under any circumstances in race discrimination cases. Industrial tribunals have no contempt powers. In employment cases, county courts only are empowered to enjoin unlawful acts. Individuals are not permitted to apply for an injunction under the 1976 Act. Injunctions may only be issued by county courts and at the behest of the Commission for Racial Equality in a certain limited range of such cases where persistent discrimination is suspected. Even in such limited circumstances as injunctions are available, negative orders only appear to be permitted. Where the Act permits injunctions to be issued it is in terms of 'restraining the respondent from doing the acts complained of'.[21]

Where a formal investigation by the CRE has disclosed unlawful discrimination (including indirect discrimination), the Commission is empowered to issue a non-discrimination notice requiring the respondent not to commit any such discrimination and, where compliance with that requirement involves changes in any of his practices or other arrangements, to inform the Commission that he has effected those changes and what those changes are, and take such steps as may reasonably be required for the purpose of communicating that information to other persons concerned.[22] A non-discrimination notice may also require the person to provide the Commission with information 'reasonably required' in order to verify that the terms of the notice have been complied with.[23] A period of five years after the notice has become final is the statutory maximum time for which the Commission may impose these requirements. Within this constraint the notice may specify the time at which and the manner and form in which the information is to be furnished to the Commission.[24] The Commission is empowered to make a further investigation at any time within five years to ascertain whether the recipient has complied with its terms.[25]

The remedial powers of the CRE are different from those given to industrial tribunals and county courts. They are more future directed, seeking to alter subsequent behaviour, rather than attempting to compensate for past misconduct. An injunctive-type remedy is relied on to the exclusion of damages. There is a separation of victim and beneficiary; third parties may increasingly be affected by the remedy.

Despite these changes, however, there are considerable limitations to the CRE's powers. Most importantly the extent to which the remedies are more than merely negative prohibitions is uncertain:[26] it is unclear to what extent the statutory provisions permit positive, mandatory requirements to be imposed by the Commission. Secondly, where the Commission has reasonable cause to believe that the person intends not to comply with a requirement in a non-discrimination notice, it may apply to a county court for an order requiring him to comply with it.[27] This is not an injunction, however, and non-compliance with it is not contempt. A small fine is the only remaining sanction.[28] An injunction from the county court is only available where, after a non-discrimination notice (or a finding by a tribunal) has become final, it appears that 'unless restrained he is likely to do one or more' unlawful discriminatory acts in the future.[29]

In both these respects then (lack of wide-ranging mandatory remedial powers and the weakness of sanctions) the CRE appears to be at some considerable disadvantage in putting into effect its remit of removing indirect discrimination. It may well be necessary to amend the Act to permit the CRE to impose considerably more far-reaching affirmative action programmes on respondents found to have discriminated.

It may also be necessary to increase the sanctions available once discrimination has been found in other ways, for example through the use of the government's contracting powers. A precedent may be found in the Fair Employment (Northern Ireland) Act 1976 (FEA). The Act provides that the Fair Employment Agency is to invite such organisations as appear to it to be representative of employers, of organisations of workers and of persons engaged in occupations in Northern Ireland, to subscribe to a declaration of commitment to the principle of equality of opportunity (to be known as the Declaration of Principle and Intent) and to encourage their members to subscribe to it. The Agency is also to use its best endeavours to encourage all employers and all vocational organisations to subscribe to the Declaration. The Agency is to keep a register of those who subscribe to the Declaration and each employer or organisation whose name is on this register is entitled to receive from the Agency and to hold a certificate describing him or it as an equal opportunity employer or organisation.[30] The published list of those who have signed the Declaration is distributed to all public authorities.[31]

The Fair Employment Agency is empowered to require a declarant, as a condition of remaining on the register, to reaffirm at such intervals and in such a manner as the Agency may determine, his intention to adhere to the Declaration. More importantly, the Agency is empowered to remove from the register the name of any person who, among other things, is found by the Agency in consequence of an investigation to have acted in a manner inconsistent with adhering to the Declaration.[32] When an employer's name is removed from the register the Agency is required as soon as reasonably practicable to notify the removal to all the relevant public authorities. In addition, where a public authority forms the opinion that a contractor has acted in the course of performing a contract entered into with the authority in a manner inconsistent with the terms of the Declaration and his name has not already been removed from the register, the authority is required to inform the Agency of this opinion stating the reasons for it.[33] A person aggrieved by the removal of his name from the register may appeal to the Appeals Board against the removal.[34]

At the end of 1981, the government announced a considerable strengthening of the potential effect of these provisions. Tenders for government contracts would not, from April 1982, 'normally' be accepted from firms within the scope of the Act unless they held an equal opportunity certificate issued by the Agency. Any future review of the Race Relations Act 1976 should consider applying a similar requirement with regard to racial discrimination in the rest of the United Kingdom.

Problems of fact-finding

Turning now from the question of remedies to the question of fact-finding, the limitations of the traditional legal process as a vehicle for dealing with issues of social and economic activity and for bringing about social change are well known. As Landis pointed out in 1938, the issues of fact involved in, for example, the disposition of a business problem call not only for legal expertise but also for a 'wisdom in the ways of industrial operation'[35] which the judicial process was unlikely to be able to supply. The breadth of jurisdiction of the ordinary courts tended to make judges 'jacks of all trades and masters of none'.[36]

Moreover, courts are less able than the traditional political process to provide solutions to particular problems requiring consideration of issues other than those raised in individual cases, often involving only isolated aspects of a larger issue. These problems may be thought of as involving 'polycentricity';[37] they have 'many centres of stress and direction of force, only some of which are likely to be the focus of attention when a decision in the area is made'.[38] The consequences of polycentricity are complex. 'Because it has these many different critical areas and because they are all inter-related, a decision's immediate effects are likely to be communicated in many unforeseeable ways and affect many other areas of human concern.[39] The metaphor of a spider's web illustrates the issue – pulling one thread affects each of the other parts of the web.

This is not to say, however, that a judge deciding issues in an ordinary case is divorced from policy problems. In all decisions on a point of law the judge is likely to take into account the consequences as he perceives them of one decision rather than another. Even if the matter is being decided between individuals the question of the general public good is likely to arise in formulating the legal principle which is applied to the specific case. Decision-making in areas with polycentric characteristics is probably not different in kind: the difference lies in the extent to which the judge is unaware of the policy arguments which ought to be brought to bear.

To adjudicate effectively the decision-maker must have information of two broad types: facts concerning the events which have transpired between the parties to the law suit (what Horowitz calls 'historical' facts)[40] and facts which help in the ascertainment of the current patterns of behaviour on which policy should be based (Horowitz's 'social' facts).[41] Consideration of the idea of 'indirect discrimination' in the Race Relations Act 1976 involves issues of public policy, industrial relations, psychology, statistics and sociology of a high degree of importance and potential complexity.

Attempting to use a party-initiated and party-controlled process to provide remedies to polycentric problems may also be seen as giving rise to other associated problems. Here too the primary focus is on the parties rather than the larger issues. In addition, injuries to a group of people may well occur in circumstances in which those involved are in a poor position to seek legal redress individually, either because they do not know enough or because such redress is disproportionately expensive. There are problems relating to the representativeness of the plaintiff. The reactive nature of the courts makes it difficult for them to know the extent to which the situation of litigants illustrates the dimensions of the problem they bring to court. There are problems of timing and problems involving the sequencing of change. There are problems of co-ordination of cases seeking change in a particular area. There are problems concerning review of any policy decided on. The reactive nature of the judicial process makes no provision for automatic examination of the success or even the implementation of the policy decided upon by the court.[42]

The US federal courts have adapted their procedures in a number of ways: reliance on expert witnesses; permitting wide discovery of evidence; widespread use and encouragement of suits which enable large numbers of complainants to seek redress of similar issues together in one action ('class action' suits); relaxation of 'standing' requirements; permitting argument by those interested in the outcome of a case but with no legal standing ('*amicus curiae*' arguments); encouragement of arguments which explain the social facts (so-called 'Brandeis briefs'); acceptance of the expertise of specialist government agencies; and lastly, willingness to examine the legislative history of an Act which they are interpreting.

Comparatively limited changes have been made in the relevant British judicial institutions (the county courts, the industrial tribunals and the appellate courts) the better to adapt these bodies to this role of handling polycentric problems. In view of the minimal number of cases actually brought before county courts, they have had little opportunity to develop desirable features. There is, however, a statutory requirement that race relations assessors sit with the judge hearing cases under the 1976 Act.[43] Industrial tribunals comprise not only a chairman with legal experience, but also two 'wingmen' who are to provide industrial relations experience. Although there is no legal requirement to do so, industrial tribunals normally sit with a wingman who also has experience of racial discrimination issues in appropriate cases.[44] The CRE has power to issue Codes of Practice which industrial tribunals may take into account and may come to regard as authoritative.[45]

More generally, the approach of the courts to the issue of onus of proof[46] and to the availability of discovery[47] has illustrated that the courts may on occasion be sympathetic to the need to construe procedural and substantive law to meet the needs of the legislation. A desire to offset the reluctance and the inability of individuals to litigate prompted the power given to the CRE to grant assistance to individuals who wish to take proceedings under the Act. The Court of Appeal has on occasion allowed the CRE to appear before the court to argue a position in a particular case even though not technically a party to the case (i.e. as an *amicus curiae*).[48]

Despite these changes, however, there are continuing severe problems in the effective use of the courts and the tribunals. Some relate specifically to the use of industrial tribunals. Some arise out of more general problems relating to the use of social science in a legal setting. Turning first to the industrial tribunals, the current attitude of the Employment Appeal Tribunal (EAT) and the superior courts is not consistent on how the tensions should be resolved between, on the one hand, safeguarding the traditional tribunal function of resolving disputes informally, quickly and cheaply, and on the other, providing sufficient 'social fact' information to the tribunal on which to base policy decisions. Different approaches have been taken in different cases. On the one hand, the EAT in the indirect discrimination *Price* case[49] specifically requested that adequate statistical analysis be carried out at a rehearing in an industrial tribunal. On the other hand, some equal pay cases indicate that the answer which the Court of Appeal may eventually give will be that it is not possible to resolve the tension and that informality, speed and lack of expense are more important. Thus in *Fletcher v. Clay Cross (Quarry Services) Ltd*,[50] the Court of Appeal stressed the need to get away from 'legalism' in the interpretation of the Equal Pay Act 1970 and reiterated its desire to return to as uncomplicated a construction of the Act as possible, because the function of industrial tribunals was that of providing speedy and informal resolutions of disputes. In that case the Court deliberately so construed the Act as not to require complicated statistical evidence and contrasted its chosen approach with that of a US case dealing with a similar equal pay issue: 'There will be no need, thankfully, for . . . statistical evidence covering a period of 28 months, supported by four complicated graphs'.[51]

A related issue, and one creating a similar tension, is the issue of representation by lawyers of applicants in industrial tribunals. On the one hand, informality is the preferred method. On the other, the concept of indirect discrimination, and even more its application, is complex and may well involve intricate legal questions. Again, while the form and primary function of industrial tribunals urge a non-legalistic, broad-based approach and a discouragement of further legal participation, the issue of indirect discrimination may require greater involvement of lawyers. Yet legal aid is not provided in cases heard before these tribunals. And in contrast with the United States, additional non-governmental sources of assistance and representation are virtually non-existent, as we have seen. It has been argued that some private organisation is necessary in the employment discrimination law area, not only because it could take advantage of resources which would not be available to the public sector agencies, but also to act as a counterweight to the adverse political climate which might adversely affect the ability of the CRE to assist.[52]

The traditional British judicial process is also itself clearly inadequate in discovering and assessing these social facts itself. The judicial process has no power of independent investigation. The aim of the judicial process is not the fair disposition of the controversy, it is the fair disposition of the controversy upon the record *as made by the parties*. Restricting the judicial role in such cases to that of an umpire presumes that litigants are equally able to put forward facts in support of their claims. In the absence of equal economic power, the umpire theory of administering law is almost certain to fail.

While the appointment of wingmen does go some way towards building an industrial relations expertise into the industrial tribunal, few have so far been appointed with any expertise in the complexities of indirect racial discrimination, and attempts to inform members of tribunals of the social context of the legislation have largely been resisted. In addition, the system of costs in industrial tribunals, whereby each side bears its own costs no matter what the result, will urge greater caution in the use of expensive social science methodology and expert testimony.

Future direct use of social science evidence outside industrial tribunals also seems unlikely. Rather, it will, at best, be only indirectly utilised.[53] There is much less social science research on race discrimination (even apart from specifically socio-legal issues) than is taking place in the USA. Where such work is being done, most of it is unusable directly in a legal setting, often because there is a use of concepts, even, for example, 'discrimination', which may seem similar to legal concepts but which turn out to diverge widely from them.

It would also seem that not only is there little incentive for the complainant to introduce social science evidence, for example by calling expert witnesses, but there is a disincentive for him to do so. In purely financial terms, an individual making an indirect discrimination claim (to take the example which probably most involves the potential for social science evidence) may well be worse off financially by calling expert witnesses, since even if the plaintiff is successful he can get no damages if the discrimination is proved not to have been intentional.

There are further restrictions on significant social science participation. Expert witnesses, for example, face the dual problem that, while their professional standards call for painstaking and possibly lengthy analysis of an issue, the legal process requires relative immediacy. While professionalism calls for the expert not to be more dogmatic than the data will support, the best witness in a legal confrontation may be one who is decisive, and convincing in his certainty. This is in addition to the general unpleasantness of appearing as a witness and the low rates of remuneration. Despite these shortcomings social scientists have been involved in many of the major indirect discrimination cases. It is unlikely, however, that the American empirical approach will be securely transplanted to Britain.

A related reason for this is the restricted extent to which relevant information is likely to be collected in usable form. The opposition of some trade unionists to the collection of work-place statistics on race, and a similar suspicion on the part of some of those in minority groups themselves may well mean that necessary information will not become available in the future.[54] McAuslan's observation in another context is equally relevant here: '. . . our political culture does not believe in or therefore facilitate full disclosure of information, some of which might be inconvenient, and this is an essential pre-condition of a more active judiciary'[55] – and, one might add, of a more active involvement of social scientists.

The extent to which it is believed that legal processes and institutions are malleable and adaptable to any new demands placed on them (largely irrespective of whether their original functions are comparable) will influence the decision whether or not to place greater responsibility for carrying out these new tasks with the already existing adjudicatory bodies of the industrial tribunals, Employment Appeals Tribunal, county and superior courts. If we believe that the undoubted benefits of expertise in historical fact-finding, legitimacy and impartiality can be retained even after adapting these bodies to equip them for their new tasks, then this modification will be preferred to their replacement. If, on the other hand, it is believed that different types of techniques have an 'inner integrity of their own', are not 'all purpose tools of unlimited pliability' and have 'distinctive uses and limits',[56] the opposite conclusion is likely to be arrived at. The extent of the malleability of these social institutions is, in this writer's opinion, largely culturally determined. In the United States courts have been expected to adapt and have adapted to tasks very different from those of traditional adjudication, arguably without the loss of their already existing expertise, legitimacy or impartiality.[57] In Britain the ordinary courts (and the industrial tribunals for that matter) have not been called upon so to adapt in the past and therefore have not done so.

Agency enforcement

It was clearly the intention of the legislators that the CRE would be able, with new increased powers, to deal with indirect discrimination, without major revamping of the established institutions of the county courts and industrial tribunals. This was thought possible, first because of the power given to the CRE to assist individual complainants, and secondly, (and most importantly), by reason of the new formal investigation powers. I want to concentrate on the second of these in this section.

Undoubtedly the powers of formal investigation given to the CRE were a considerable improvement on those granted to the Race Relations Board under the Race Relations Act 1968. In particular, the fact-finding and remedial powers made available appeared adequate to enforce the new indirect discrimination idea. This has not turned out to be the case, however, for a number of reasons, in addition to the absence of adequate remedial powers discussed above. Some constraints are common both to formal investigations and individual complaints. The absence of necessary statistical and other information has already been mentioned. The decentralised nature of much of the decision-making which is being investigated lessens the impact of many findings of discrimination. The interlocking roles of many different persons and institutions often make it difficult to allocate responsibility sufficiently clearly to warrant a legal finding of discrimination by any particular individual or institution.

Other problems arise from the cumbersome nature of the machinery which the CRE has to operate, and the reactions of the ordinary courts to it. Since at least the mid-1960s, judicial intervention to control the exercise of powers by public bodies has developed considerably. In particular in the area of administrative law, the judiciary have 'reasserted their powers', as Wade put it, 'in a succession of invigorating decisions'.[58] De Smith also noted how there had been 'a striking increase both in the frequency with which judicial review has been invoked and in the readiness of the courts to intervene'.[59] What has been invigorating for some has been debilitating for others.

The growth in substantive and procedural review came in time for it to be seen as imposing strict procedural and substantive restrictions on the anti-discrimination agencies. Thus at much the same time as the Race Relations Board was established in the 1960s, judicial review of administrative action took on a new and expanded lease of life. And since that time, and particularly since 1976, judicial review of Commission decisions at every stage of the formal investigation process has increased.

In particular, the relative lack of a tradition of using regulatory agencies as law enforcement bodies has resulted in a somewhat tense evolving relationship between the Commission and the reviewing courts over both the CRE's views of its procedural powers and its interpretation of the legislation. In a number of cases the CRE's interpretation has been upheld. In *Home Office v. CRE*,[60] the Home Office unsuccessfully challenged the power of the CRE to investigate alleged discriminatory acts done in administering immigration control. In *R. v. CRE, ex parte Cottrall and Rothon*,[61] the CRE's procedures relating to the hearing of representations by a respondent prior to the issue of a non-discrimination notice were challenged on the grounds that the respondent should have had an opportunity to cross-examine witnesses. This argument was rejected. So too the CRE was also held to be empowered to delegate to its staff the function of collecting information. Commissioners were therefore entitled to investigate the matter without hearing evidence directly from witnesses and to rely on staff reports. In *London Borough of Hillingdon v. CRE*,[62] however, terms of reference for a formal investigation drawn up by the CRE were held *ultra vires* on the grounds that the terms were too broadly drawn and should have been more limited.

If review on these grounds becomes a source of delay and obstruction, as it well might, then the Act should be amended to ameliorate the problem. One option would be to try to make the Commission's decision to proceed with a formal investigation non-reviewable. Another, preferable, method would be to provide an appeal to the Employment Appeal Tribunal (or the High Court in a non-employment case) within six weeks of a decision to hold such a formal investigation. The grounds of appeal should be restricted to the question of whether the Agency's belief that a person named may have discriminated or may be discriminating is unreasonable, in which case the EAT may amend the terms of reference or require the investigation to cease.

In addition to this inherent power of judicial review there is also a statutory appeal provided against a non-discrimination notice issued by the Commission. Respondents may appeal to an industrial tribunal if it concerns an employment case, to the county courts in other cases. This situation too has resulted in greater judicial involvement in formal investigations than is desirable. The Court of Appeal decision in *CRE v. Amari Plastics Ltd.*[63] is probably the most important of the court's decisions on the role of the Commission to date. The question at issue was the role of the industrial tribunals in appeals against non-discrimination notices. Might the tribunal review only the remedial requirements set out in the notice, or might it also review the finding of facts by the CRE? Should the CRE, in other words, be the body primarily entrusted with fact-finding in formal investigations, or should the investigations be, instead, merely a preliminary to a *de novo* investigation of the facts of the case by the tribunal? A *de novo* hearing would clearly be appropriate after a non-discrimination notice is issued, had the earlier process of investigation been merely a prosecutorial marshalling of evidence. But was this the case?

Griffiths LJ was 'most sympathetic'[64] to the Commission's policy argument. 'If Parliament empowers a body to carry out a formal investigation and hedges the procedures with safeguards to ensure that the person investigated shall have every opportunity to state his case and then requires that body to publish its findings, one might be forgiven for thinking that Parliament intended that this would be the end of the matter'.[65] The Court was unanimous, however, in holding that such was not the case and that 'the language of the statute' provided that appeals might be on both law and fact as well as remedies. Lord Denning, MR, concluded his judgment: 'the machinery is so elaborate and cumbersome that it is in danger of grinding to a halt. I am very sorry for the Commission, but they have been caught up in a spider's web spun by Parliament, from which there is little hope of their escaping'.[66]

Frequently exercised judicial review plus this regular appellate jurisdiction of the industrial tribunals and county courts is likely to have an important effect on the CRE's conduct of its jurisdiction under the Act, because of the desire to avoid successful challenge to its fact-finding and remedial decisions.[67] Intervention to review the CRE's interpretation of both substantive provisions and the procedural requisites of the Act to the extent that is now current, may yet succeed in almost completely eroding the benefits of having an independent, administrative, non-judicial enforcement model, particularly with regard to the fact-finding and remedial process. The Act should be amended to provide that the Commission may effectively carry out its enforcement functions.

One other question has given rise to problems in the context of the equivalent provisions of the Sex Discrimination Act 1975 and its enforcement by the Equal Opportunities Commission. Increasingly there are indications of the unsatisfactoriness of the structure of the legislation which permits an individual complaint to be made and pursued irrespective of whether a formal investigation into the same or a related matter has already begun.[68] The result of individual complaints, over which the Commission may have no control, may be detrimental to the conduct of formal investigations. Lack of full disclosure of relevant facts, and inadequate argument on the relevant law may lead to an adverse decision or a complaint which raises questions of *res judicata* as regards the formal investigations. In order to prevent such problems arising the Act should be amended to allow the Commission to request the EAT (or the High Court in a non-employment complaint), once a formal investigation has begun, to suspend further consideration by an industrial tribunal or county court of any case which relates to, involves, or would be likely to affect a formal investigation in progress. Once the formal investigation had been completed or where it becomes clear that the circumstances leading to the suspension are no longer applicable, the individual complaint would cease to be suspended and would carry on as before.

Reverse discrimination and other approaches

Two caveats are necessary. First, my argument that changes are necessary in the institutional structure and the remedies available in order to make more effective use of the indirect discrimination provision is tempered by a recognition that to place complete reliance on such a strategy would be misguided. The considerable limitations in the procedural and remedial context in which the idea is placed are only one set of restrictions on its usefulness. There are other limitations on the extent to which the eradication of indirect discrimination can or should provide the basis for a complete strategy.

The concept of indirect discrimination, for example, is based on a principle of procedural justice which makes no assumption that a particular pattern of distribution of goods should result. The Race Relations Act 1976 does explicitly permit a limited measure of reverse discrimination in favour of minority groups, in the form of three types of exception to the general prohibition of unlawful discrimination. But they have a number of limiting characteristics: they are permissive but not mandatory; they are detailed; and they are, generally, very specific in their terms. They do not generally make it lawful for the employer to discriminate in favour of minorities at the point of selection for such work or for organisations to discriminate in admitting people to membership or in appointing members to posts in the organisations. Nothing I have written, however, should be taken as necessarily arguing against an expanded role for reverse discrimination in the future.

This caveat is necessary because the adoption of a strategy based on the expanded use of the indirect discrimination approach is sometimes seen as an *alternative* to reverse discrimination. For example, Lustgarten's espousal of an expanded indirect discrimination approach is based at least in part on a desire to prevent the adoption of what he regards as the more extreme policy of 'fair shares' prevalent in the United States.[69]

Such a policy, at least as practised in the US, is unjustifiable, he argues, for a number of reasons. It imposes burdens 'mainly on the young and the relatively less well off'.[70] It creates a 'small group of elite beneficiaries'[71] and sets black and white workers at each other's throats. In so far as Britain is concerned, the different history of the black population here from that of American blacks (voluntary immigration and the absence of legally required discrimination in the past) removes whatever justification there might be for its use in the US. The success of the indirect discrimination approach is, for him, critical, 'if Britain is to avoid having to choose between open acceptance of permanent subordination of minorities and the use of racial preferences as compensation'.[72]

His reasons, however, for rejecting the fair shares approach and 'reverse discrimination' are unconvincing.[73] The interests of white workers are turned, in effect, into rights which can trump egalitarian policies, yet no argument is made for such a move. Nor is such a position consistent with his support for the policy of eradicating indirect discrimination, for he is willing to override white workers' interests in *its* enforcement. Why not, then, in the enforcement of a fair shares approach? Secondly, his implied criticism of the fair shares approach, that it does not break down class barriers but merely creates a similar class structure in the black to that already existing in the white population, not only misses the point that historically that was precisely its purpose, it does not tell us why that is necessarily to be condemned. Thirdly, the choice between the equality of opportunity or the fair shares approach is not quite as clear as he states. At no time, for example, does he distinguish between adopting a fair shares approach as an end in itself and adopting it as a temporary expedient in order to bring about equality of opportunity in the future. Lastly, the complex of American laws, regulations and court judgements which he lumps together under the umbrella term 'reverse discrimination' is much more complex, diverse and sophisticated than he allows for. At a time when British race relations policy is being rethought we should be careful not to dismiss too readily therefore the more difficult alternatives, currently in use in the United States, to which we may have to resort. What is necessary is a greater realisation of the range of different policies available including the effective use of the indirect discrimination provisions of the Act, and the development of a programme which uses these in the best possible mix.

Notes

1 L. Mayhew, *Law and Equal Opportunity* (Cambridge, Mass: Harvard University Press, 1968) pp. 59–74.
2 Race Relations Act 1968, section 1(1).
3 O. Kahn-Freund, *Labour Relations* (London: Oxford University Press, 1977) p. 39.
4 See further McCrudden, 'Institutional Discrimination', *Oxford Journal of Legal Studies*, Vol. 2 (1982).
5 *Griggs v. Duke Power Co.*, 401 U.S. 424 (1971).
6 See McCrudden, *op. cit.*, pp. 347–65.
7 Department of Employment, *Employment Gazette*, October 1978; December 1979; October 1980, pp. 383–6; October 1981, p. 431.
8 See McCrudden, *op. cit.*, p. 366.
9 House of Commons, Home Affairs Committee, Racial Disadvantage, *Report*, London, HMSO 1981, HC4241.
10 Home Office, *The Brixton Disorders: Report of an Inquiry by the Rt. Hon. the Lord Scarman, OBE* (London, HMSO, Cmnd 8427, 1981).
11 See papers in this volume by Peter Sanders and Susan Ollerearnshaw.
12 See paper in this volume by Ivor Crewe.
13 The phrase is Ronald Dworkin's in *Taking Rights Seriously* (London, Duckworth, 1978).
14 [1982] 3 All ER 1108 (CA).
15 See further McCrudden, 'Legal Remedies for Discrimination in Employment', *Current Legal Problems* 1981, from which the following is adapted.
16 Race Relations Act 1976, s. 56(1).
17 s. 57(4).
18 s. 56(4).
19 P. Davies and M. Freedland, *Labour Law: Text and Materials*, (London, Weidenfeld and Nicolson, 1978), p. 379.
20 Race Relations Act 1976, s. 57(3).
21 s. 62(1).
22 s. 58(2).
23 s. 58(3).
24 s. 58(4).
25 s. 60.
26 s. 58.
27 s. 58(7).
28 s. 50(5).
29 s. 62.
30 Fair Employment (Northern Ireland) Act 1976, s. 7.
31 s. 9.
32 s. 7.
33 s. 9(4).
34 s. 8.
35 J.M. Landis, *The Administrative Process* (New Haven and London, Yale University Press, 1938), p. 30.
36 *ibid.*, p. 31.
37 Weiler, 'Two Models of Judicial Decision-Making', *Canadian Bar Review*, Vol. 45, (1968), p. 420.
38 *ibid.* p. 423.
39 *ibid.*
40 D. Horowitz, *The Courts and Social Policy* (Washington DC: The Brookings Institution, 1977) p. 45.
41 *ibid.*
42 See *ibid.* generally.
43 Race Relations Act 1976, s. 67.

44 See L. Lustgarten, *Legal Control of Racial Discrimination*, (London, Macmillan, 1980), pp. 195–6.

45 Race Relations Act 1976, s. 47.

46 See *Oxford v. Department of Health and Social Services* [1977] IRLR 225 (EAT), *Wallace v. South East Education and Library Board* [1980] IRLR 193 (NICA), *Fair Employment Agency v. Craigavon Borough Council* [1980] IRLR 316 (NICA) and *Khanna v. Ministry of Defence* [1981] ICR 653 (EAT).

47 *Nasse v. Science Research Council* [1979] IRLR 465 (HL).

48 As in *Nasse, op. cit.* Often, however, it is unnecessary because the CRE is backing the legislation in any event.

49 [1977] IRLR 291 (EAT).

50 [1978] IRLR 361 (CA).

51 *ibid.* p. 365.

52 CRE, *Commission for Racial Equality Annual Report*, (London, HMSO 1980), p. 5.

53 See further McCrudden, 'Antidiscrimination legislation and the role of the Social Sciences' in S. Lloyd-Bostock (ed.), *Law and Psychology* (Oxford: SSRC Centre for Socio-legal Studies, 1981) from which the following is abridged.

54 Cf. also the opposition to monitoring evidenced in House of Commons Employment Committee questioning of CRE recommendations in Draft Code of Practice – Minutes of Evidence, 17 and 24 March 1982, HC 273(i) and (ii), London, HMSO.

55 P. McAuslan, 'The challenge of the environment' in *English Law and Social Policy*, (London, Centre for Studies in Social Policy, 1975), p. 23.

56 R.S. Summers, 'Pragmatic instrumentalism in twentieth century American thought – a synthesis and critique of our dominant general theory about law and its use', *Cornell Law Review*, Vol. 69, 1981, pp. 861, 923.

57 Although much of the current debate concerning the role of US courts centres around just this question. Contrast, say, L. Fuller, 'The Forms and Limits of Adjudication', *Harvard Law Review* Vol. 92, 1978, with Abram Chayes, 'The Role of the Judge in Public Law Litigation', *Harvard Law Review*, Vol. 89, 1976.

58 H.W.R. Wade, *Administrative Law*, 3rd ed., (Oxford and London: Oxford University Press, 1971) p. 27.

59 S.A. de Smith, *Judicial Review of Administrative Action*, 3rd ed., (London: Stevens, 1973) p. 27.

60 [1981] 1 All ER 1042 (DC).

61 [1980] 1 WLR 1580 (DC).

62 [1982] 3 WLR 159 (HL).

63 [1982] 2 All ER 499 (CA).

64 p. 504.

65 p. 504.

66 p. 503.

67 '. . . if an agency fears challenge to its powers, this may lead to "capture" by vested interests in terms of "safe" decision-making.' (R. Baldwin, 'Regulation by Agency: the Fall and Rise of Government at Arms-Length' (unpublished), citing R. Noll, 'The Economics and Politics of Regulation', *Virginia Law Review*, Vol. 57, 1971.

68 Cf. the circumstances surrounding the Electrolux formal investigations by the Equal Opportunities Commission.

69 Lustgarten, *op. cit.*

70 *ibid.* p. 20.

71 *ibid.*

72 *ibid.* p. 107.

73 See further McCrudden, Book Review, *Ethnic and Racial Studies*, Vol. 5, 1982, pp. 124, 125–6.

5 Anti-Discrimination Law Enforcement in Britain
Peter Sanders

It is now five years since the Race Relations Act 1976 came into force, but there is firm evidence, as Susan Ollerearnshaw demonstrates in her paper, that the patterns of discriminatory behaviour are still deeply entrenched. This may not be surprising in view of the history and nature of our society, but even so it is clear that much more can be done to eliminate racial discrimination. In particular, there are those who argue that the Race Relations Act is too weak, and there are others who argue that, while the Act is strong enough, it has not been properly enforced. It is the aim of this paper to describe the Commission for Racial Equality's experience of the Act so far, and to consider what changes, if any, are needed.

The government's overall strategy

Law enforcement was never intended to be the sole means of eliminating racial discrimination. Rather it was seen as part of a wider strategy, and that strategy was spelt out by the Labour Government in its 1975 White Paper on Racial Discrimination.[1] The other elements of the strategy are discussed in detail in Susan Ollerearnshaw's paper: they are considered here only in so far as is necessary to place law enforcement in context.

First, the then government acknowledged its own special responsibility as an employer to implement an effective equal opportunities policy and accepted that 'a vital ingredient' of such a policy was 'a regular system of monitoring'.[2] In practice, partly because of union opposition, there has been no effective system of monitoring, and it is only recently that the government has agreed to try out monitoring on an experimental basis in one centre alone, the city of Leeds. If that is successful then consideration will be given to extending it to other parts of the country.

Second, the government announced its intention of using government contracts as a lever for achieving equal opportunity. Since 1969 government contracts had contained a standard clause requiring contractors to conform to the provisions of the law against racial discrimination and to take all reasonable steps to ensure that their employees and sub-contractors did the same. In fact that clause had been a dead letter, and the government acknowledged that it could not 'passively assume that a formal condition in a contract is all that is required'. It therefore declared that it would include another standard condition that the contractor should provide on request to the Department of Employment such information about its employment policies and practices as the Department might reasonably require.[3] The Labour Government, however, was extremely cautious in translating this statement of intention into action. In the opinion of the Commission for Racial Equality the arrangements which it proposed fell far short of what was needed to make any significant impact, and its consultations with interested parties dragged on so slowly that they were still continuing when it fell from power in 1979. The present government has simply announced that it does not intend to continue the consultations.

Third, there was the role of voluntary action. The Labour Government expressed the hope that 'most institutions and individuals will respond to the government's positive lead in promoting equality of opportunity and will change their practices voluntarily'[4] and under Section 43 of the Race Relations Act the Commission for Racial Equality was given the duty of promoting equality of opportunity between persons of different racial groups. The promotional work in employment carried out by the Commission is described in Susan Ollerearnshaw's paper, and, although there have been some successes, it is clear that most institutions are still very far from adopting, implementing and monitoring fully effective equal opportunity policies.

Fourth, under Section 47 of the Race Relations Act the Commission was given the power to issue codes of practice containing practical guidance for the purpose of eliminating discrimination and promoting equal opportunity in the field of employment. Any such code, however, could come into force only if it received the approval of the Secretary of State for Employment, and while industrial tribunals would be bound to take its provisions into account where relevant it would not be legally binding. The Commission, after the lengthy consultative processes laid down by the Act, and after detailed discussions at official level, submitted a draft Code to the Secretary of State at the end of 1981, but at the time of writing (August 1982) there has been no definite response.

Enforcing the Race Relations Act 1976

In spite of the intentions expressed in the White Paper, the enforcement of the Race Relations Act has in practice had to stand very much on its own. The provisions of the Act are set out clearly in Christopher McCrudden's paper, and there is no need to repeat them here. Essentially, though, there are two methods by which the law may be enforced. The first is through complaints by individuals; the second is through formal investigations conducted by the Commission.

Individual complaints

Under the 1968 Race Relations Act all individual complaints were investigated by the Race Relations Board and its Conciliation Committee and they were taken to court only if the Board found discrimination and was unable to effect conciliation. It was the Board that instituted proceedings, and not the complainant. Under the 1976 Act complainants themselves have the right to take their cases to litigation, to industrial tribunals in employment cases and to county courts (or sheriff courts in Scotland) in other cases. The main reason for the changes (apart from bringing the law on racial discrimination into line with the law on sex discrimination, which was probably the determining factor) was that the old system was seen as paternalistic: blacks who believed that they had suffered discrimination should have the right of direct access to a judicial hearing. The main worry about the new system was that in practice it might place complainants at a disadvantage, since discrimination had always been difficult to prove, even by the old Race Relations Board, and now complainants would have to do battle with major institutions with no prior investigation by the Board. For this reason they were given the right to apply to the Commission for assistance.

When the Act was first drafted it was envisaged that most complainants would take their own cases to litigation, and that the Commission would concentrate on cases which raised issues of principle. In fact this has not occurred, and in the absence of any powerful outside organisations to assist complainants the Commission has normally given legal representation in any case where the complainant appeared to have a reasonable *prima facie* case or there appeared to be a matter of principle involved. Even those applicants who are refused representation are usually given assistance in other ways, such as advice on marshalling their allegations or putting their questions to respondents. The Commission received 1033 applications for assistance in 1978, the first full year of its operation; 986 in 1979; 779 in 1980; and 846 in 1981. It provided representation in 170 cases in 1978; 141 cases in 1979; 73 cases in 1980; and 135 in 1981.

About two-thirds of the applications that the Commission receives each year are concerned with complaints about discrimination in employment. By comparison the old Race Relations Board used to receive about 1,000 complaints each year of which about half concerned discrimination in employment. This shift towards employment may be because non-employment cases have to go to county courts, where the procedures are dauntingly slow and formal, whereas employment cases go to industrial tribunals, where the procedures are much quicker and less forbidding.

In general there have been about 400 industrial tribunal cases each year, of which just over a half have been settled without a hearing. A considerable number of these have been settled with substantial payments being made to the applicants. Of the applications on which decisions have been reached, however, only about 10 per cent have been upheld. Most of the successful applications have been aided by the Commission, usually with legal representation. Up to the end of 1981 there had been 76 successful cases. In 61 of these the Commission provided representation, and in six assistance in other forms.

As indicated above, about one-third of the applications that the Commission receives each year are concerned with complaints about discrimination in areas other than employment. Yet by the end of 1981 only 39 cases had reached county courts, of which 24, all assisted by the Commission, had been successful, which is a much higher proportion than in industrial tribunals. This success rate is no doubt because, for reasons which need not be examined here, it is generally less difficult to prove discrimination in non-employment cases than in employment cases.

The figures quoted above are insignificant when considered against the amount of discrimination that is occurring. No doubt the publicity given to tribunal and court hearings has had more of a deterrent effect than the conciliation effected privately by the old Race Relations Board, but apart from this the new procedures have not resulted in any significant advance. Indeed in non-employment cases it can be argued that they are less effective. Whereas the old Board towards the end of its existence was forming opinions of discrimination in about 100 cases each year, so far the number of complaints upheld by county courts is less than ten each year.

There are many reasons why victims of discrimination do not complain. Many of them do not realise that they have suffered discrimination. When they are looking for a job, for example, and are told that there are no vacancies whereas in fact there are, or they are told that they do not have the required qualifications whereas a white man with their qualifications would be accepted, they simply believe what they are told. And many who suspect that they have suffered discrimination will not complain because they feel insecure and are afraid of being branded as troublemakers; or they want to forget the humiliation; or they despair of proving their case in court; or they simply do not want all the trouble and bother. Another reason for the low figures is the absence of a powerful civil rights movement. Whereas in America civil rights legislation was the outcome of pressure by the civil rights movement, in the United Kingdom this has not been the case. Apart from the Commission, therefore, there has been no strong organisation which has assisted victims of discrimination to make use of their rights under the Act. The Commission gives training to outside individuals and organisations in aiding complainants, but so far this has had little effect.

Formal investigations

It must be said, however, that the change in the procedures for dealing with complainants, while intended to be an improvement, was never seen by the government as a major springboard for advance. Indeed it was because the government was so well aware of the limitations of the complaints process in general that it gave the Commission the new power of conducting formal investigations and issuing non-discrimination notices.

So far the Commission has started 47 investigations – 24 in employment, 11 in housing, two in education, nine in the provisions of goods, facilities and services, and one into immigration control. Of these one was discontinued, and reports have been published on 14. In 11 of these 14 discrimination was found and non-discrimination notices were issued. In several others the Commission's enquiries are complete and the reports will be published later this year. In eight of them non-discrimination notices have been issued, and in six of these the respondents have appealed against the notices to the tribunals or courts.

Most of the published investigations have been small, and the Commission has recently been criticised by the Home Affairs Select Committee of the House of Commons for its delays in completing some of its larger investigations. The Commission, while accepting that there is room for improvement, argues that large investigations are bound to take a long time, since they are in effect major research exercises conducted within the context of law enforcement; and that there is considerable scope for respondents to slow down enquiries. Whatever the reasons, however, so far the Commission's formal investigations have obviously made little impact on levels of discrimination. It may well be that when the reports on some of the larger investigations are published in the next year or two the effect will be considerable, although a great deal will depend on the attitude taken by the courts and tribunals on the appeals that are still pending and on the sort of publicity given by the media. There are no financial penalties which can be imposed following a formal investigation, and it is difficult to judge to what extent there will be a 'ripple effect', that is, how far companies which have not been investigated will feel under pressure to alter their practices in the light of the reports that are published. Clearly this will be one of the main aims of the Commission's promotional work.

The Commission is at present reviewing its procedures to see whether or not any improvements can be made. Regardless of the outcome of this review, however, it is clear that there are at least three major constraints on the effectiveness of formal investigations.

First, the law is too cumbersome. If, for example, the Commission decides to investigate a respondent who it believes may have discriminated, it must issue terms of reference to the respondent; offer him the right to make oral and written representations about the proposal to conduct an investigation; consider any representations that are made; go through the whole procedure again if, as a result of the representations, it decides to revise the terms of reference; resolve to embark on the investigation (assuming that it still believes that the respondent may have discriminated); conduct its enquiries; issue a *subpoena* notice if the respondent refuses to provide information, and get that notice enforced through the courts if necessary; if it finds discrimination, inform the respondent of its grounds and offer him the right to make oral and written representations again; consider the representations; if it so decides, issue a non-discrimination notice; if there is no appeal against the notice, draft a public report, offer the respondent and other interested parties the opportunity to comment on the report, revise it if necessary, and then publish it. Moreover, while the Commission acts throughout the investigation as an administrative body, with a duty to be fair and to follow the statute, at every stage the respondent may apply for a judicial review and may also appeal against the non-discrimination notice. The implications of these procedures are discussed in detail in Christopher McCrudden's chapter.

Second, the Commission's resources are wholly inadequate. It is expected to tackle unlawful discrimination throughout England, Scotland and Wales in employment, housing, education, and the provision to the public of goods, facilities and services. It has been given substantial powers to this end. Yet to tackle this task and exercise these powers it has been given 34 investigative officers and, since these have a few other functions as well, one can say in effect that it has about 30 officers.

Third, at present there are very few employers who keep records of the ethnic origins of their employees or of the persons who apply to them for work. Moreover, few keep any form of records of unsuccessful applicants after a certain period of perhaps a month or two. When therefore the Commission is trying to find out if there has been any discrimination in recruitment, it can establish what criteria and procedures are used, but it cannot find out whether these criteria and procedures have been applied consistently to all applicants; it therefore has to resort to such expedients as relying on the employer's memory, asking employees if they know of other persons who have applied unsuccessfully for work, consulting local Community Relations Councils and ethnic minority groups, and advertising in the local newspapers. It is not surprising that none of these methods has proved entirely satisfactory. In fact, the difficulties have been so forbidding that in future the Commission, when embarking on an investigation, may in some cases be examining recruitment as it takes place in the future as much as the recruitment that has already taken place. For decisions about promotion evidence is more accessible; but as the Race Relations Board discovered, and as industrial tribunals are discovering now, it is much harder in general to prove discrimination in promotion, at least direct discrimination, than in recruitment.

These are the three main constraints that have become evident so far. Other constraints may become evident later, particularly when the courts and tribunals start to consider the appeals against nondiscrimination notices and the application of the concept of indirect discrimination.

Conclusions

The Commission has not yet decided what changes it would like to recommend in the Act, and it is not the purpose of this paper to anticipate the Commission's recommendations. Clearly, however, when the Commission does address itself to these issues it should consider the following questions:

(1) Are industrial tribunals and county courts the most appropriate forum for the adjudication of complaints about racial discrimination? In industrial tribunals the number of successful cases is very small. Very few cases reach the county courts at all. (Christopher McCrudden, in his chapter, points to other difficulties, and these too raise serious questions.) Should the Commission now be pressing for any changes in these arrangements, for example, the establishment of special Civil Rights Tribunals?

(2) Should the Race Relations Act be amended so that the administrative and judicial procedures relating to formal investigations are simplified and investigations can be speeded up? The Home Affairs Select Committee of the House of Commons has recommended that Section 49(4) should be repealed, i.e.

the Section that gives respondents the right to make representations at the beginning of an investigation if the terms of
reference indicate that the Commission believes that they may
have been discriminating. This seems the very least that should
be done.

(3) Should it be made legally compulsory for large employers in
multi-racial labour markets to keep records of the ethnic
origins of their employees and of all job applicants, whether
successful or unsuccessful, and to submit those records to the
Commission? The Commission could then consider whether
any approach to the company would be appropriate, whether
through promotional work, further enquiries or a formal
investigation. The Commission, of course, already argues that
unless employers monitor equal opportunities policies, using
ethnic records as their base for this, there is no real possibility
of eliminating discrimination. The new proposal would make
this legally obligatory and the Commission, as it were, would
monitor the monitors. Obviously, if the proposal was
accepted, it need not be confined to employment, but could be
extended to other areas, such as local authority housing, and in
any event the Commission's resources would have to be substantially increased.

Apart from strengthening the law, there is other action that the
government should be taking: the effective implementation of its own
equal opportunities policy, monitoring the equal opportunities clause
in government contracts, giving swift approval to the Commission's
draft Code of Practice, and increasing the Commission's resources.
There is action that the ethnic minority groups themselves might be
taking, in particular the development of an organisation or organisations to assist individual complainants. And there is the action that
employers and others should be taking voluntarily.

The Commission has always argued that a national effort is
required if discrimination is to be eliminated. The Commission must
obviously play its part, but the lead must be given by the government
itself. In the 1975 White Paper this was fully recognised, but so far the
actions of successive governments have failed to live up to their words.

Notes

1 *Racial Discrimination*, presented to Parliament by the Secretary of State for the
Home Department, Cmnd. 6234, September 1975 (HMSO).
2 *ibid*. pp. 4–5.
3 *ibid*. p. 5.
4 *ibid*. p. 20.

The Pursuit Of Equality

6 Elusive Equality: Race, Ethnicity, and Education in the American Experience
David Kirp

From the very beginnings of the republic, education has been regarded as an 'American religion',[1] commanding extraordinary public attention and allegiance. In the American vision, schooling is seen as promoting social melioration through self-improvement. The nineteenth-century supporters of the common school proclaimed the institution as at once the 'great equalizer' of individual circumstance and the 'balance wheel of the social machinery'.[2] If education in America can be likened to a religion, blacks and other ethnic minorities have long been among the most faithful worshippers. Their insistence on receiving *some* education in the nineteenth century as well as the push for *equal* education since the middle of this century bespeak the desire of these groups for inclusion into the larger society.

Education has long been a primary focus in the legal and political campaign to eradicate the lingering impress of slavery and, subsequently, to equalise life chances among black and white, old and new Americans. It has been the vehicle through which ethnic groups sought to enter the American mainstream even while preserving their own linguistic and cultural identities.

Legal basis for equal educational opportunity
The Supreme Court's decision, *Brown v. Board of Education*,[3] (1954) on which language minorities as well as blacks rely to sustain their position, recorded a consensus, at least among those who might be termed the enlightened, concerning the meaning of racial justice with respect to schooling. Official segregation of the races constituted bad law and bad social policy; and segregation could be undone by an authoritative judicial decision.

Segregation was legally wrong because it denied blacks the respect that the Constitution bestows equally on all individuals. Segregation embodied a persisting badge of slavery, a symbol of caste, and was for that reason 'inherently unequal'. As a matter of constitutional law, the *Brown* decree seemingly resolved the American dilemma identified by Gunnar Myrdal – the disparity between the nation's formal commitment to equal treatment and its palpably unequal treatment of blacks.[4]

Segregation was equally misguided as social policy, for it kept blacks from achieving equality of educational opportunity. This denial mattered in its own right, since segregation wounded the 'hearts and minds' of black youngsters. It also had important instrumental consequences. Because education was widely viewed as a vehicle of social and economic mobility, unequal education was held to doom blacks to life in the underclass.

Thus were education, race, and equality linked in the prevailing consensus. The remedy for the sins *Brown* identified followed directly from the recital of wrong: abolish state-imposed racial separation. Once racial barriers were lifted, it was supposed, there would exist neither white schools nor black schools but 'just schools'.[5] By dismantling the dual school system, the constitutional rights of blacks would be secured; so too would their opportunity for social and economic equality. Blacks, like whites, would then be free to succeed or fail on the basis of merit, not caste.

The *Brown* decision changed the terms of the policy debate over race and schooling. In pronouncing segregation unconstitutional, the opinion placed supporters of the policy on the defensive, obliged to revise what had been revealed as part of the republic's organic law. Here, as so often in its history, the Supreme Court functioned as 'teacher in a vital national seminar'.[6]

While squarely grounded in positive law, *Brown* also touched profound normative aspirations whose sources lay deeper than the constitution. The case at once confirmed and gave rise to a social movement committed to the moral rightness of civil rights. It is not by accident that the language of the movement was visionary, that Martin Luther King spoke in terms of his 'dream' for the nation, that the leading chronicle of the movement is entitled *My Soul is Rested*.[7] It exaggerates, but only slightly, to equate the ideal of uniform and authoritative justice evoked by the Supreme Court with the image of the Heavenly City. To its most devoted adherents, the *Brown* decree promised a kind of secular salvation.

The campaign for equality waged on behalf of language minorities was pitched in a lower key. The Supreme Court decision, the *Lau* decision, which affirmed the entitlement of the non-English-speaking to some special assistance was designedly of lesser legal moment than *Brown*: the Court chose to rely upon an administrative interpretation of the Civil Rights Act, rather than reaching the constitutional ramifications of the claim.[8] In a broader sense, though, the *Brown* history *is* the salient history, for it was to *Brown* that advocates turned, in search of both a definition of the wrong and an understanding of justice on behalf of those whose first language was not English. Supporters of bilingual-bicultural education echoed the language of *Brown*, seeking to draw moral force for their position from that decision.[9]

Development of race and schooling policy

What once seemed right and inevitable – a great declaration of law, morality, and politics – has been remade and in some sense diminished by subsequent history. Details which were thought a trivial business now dominate discussion. What is the meaning of 'intentional discrimination' in desegregation cases? How should the benefits of desegregation, changes in student attitude and achievement, for example, be measured?[10] What happens when the intended beneficiaries of racial equality resist the practical consequences of desegregation? In contrast to the lofty themes of *Brown*, these seem mere cavils, but they have come to occupy a central place in working out the meaning of equality.

The contemporary reality of race and schooling policy makes a shambles of the hoped-for uniformity. What prevails is not a single national standard, authoritatively set and effectively implemented, but rather a bewildering diversity of arrangements, *ad hoc* in nature, varying enormously both in content and in implementation. Some communities have undertaken to balance their schools racially, others have retained neighbourhood schools while improving the quality of instruction in predominantly black schools, still others have done nothing at all. Similarly, the processes by which these policies come into being vary from place to place. Court orders, federal, state, and local initiatives, and bargaining among political and bureaucratic forces have all played a part. Race and schooling policy is thus predominantly localist, significantly political, and widely varying in its key dimensions.

The publicised stories at the onset of the 1980s illustrate this variability. These tales are less dramatic than they were some years ago, when apparently effortless racial mixing in Berkeley, California, seemed the very embodiment of the Heavenly City, while the bus-burning in Pontiac and the riots in Boston resembled scenes from the *Inferno*. Yet they are no less distinctive. The football team at a predominantly white St. Louis high school welcomes incoming black students; in Los Angeles, whites quietly withdraw from the public schools in sizeable numbers in the face of badly managed desegregation; and parents in a Louisiana community, supported by a state judge, defy a federal judge's order to send their daughters to a newly desegregated school.

The ways in which policy takes shape are equally miscellaneous. Chicago's school board negotiates an agreement with the Justice Department to accomplish both some desegregation and substantial programmatic improvement in the remaining all-black schools (subsequently undone by school board changes of heart and a reversal of policy by the Reagan administration). Seattle, which had voluntarily adopted a modest busing plan, enlarges that plan on its own initiative. By contrast, the federal district court in Cleveland, pronouncing that district's efforts to comply with court-ordered desegregation a failure, in effect takes over the management of the system.

At the national level, Court and Congress seem intent on undoing each other's work. The Supreme Court has continued to expand school district liability for segregation – broadening the meaning of 'intentional' segregation – even as Congress has limited the authority of the Executive to enforce racial remedies.[11]

Similarly, with issues of ethnicity and education variability is a dominant theme. A Congress that with little debate turned the holding of the *Lau* decision into statutory law in 1974 became markedly less sure about the benefits of bilingual education a mere four years later. Lower federal courts, lacking authoritative Supreme Court guidance, are split.[12] The ethnic groups themselves have different agendas: the Chinese, who offer after-school instruction in their own culture, want help in English; Hispanics claim that concern with their culture will foster self-confidence, and hence bolster achievement, among Hispanic students. The Department of Education under President Carter issued detailed rules concerning bilingual education instruction which portended a powerful federal presence; these were subsequently withdrawn by the Reagan administration.

Debate ranges broadly over educational and ethnic policy. Is bilingualism an effective educational strategy or merely a job programme for minority professionals, as some claim? What sort of education should the limited-English-speaking receive: a transitional course, intended to return them to the English-speaking classroom as quickly as possible, or a programme extending the duration of their school careers, which nurtures an appreciation for two languages, two cultures? Underlying discussions over programme specifics are basic disagreements concerning the nature of the society that these students are entering, and the place of 'alien' cultures in that society. A nominally educational concern has been shown to have deeper political roots.

Some of the variability, notably the tension between legislature and judiciary, is troubling because it appears to jeopardize the national commitment to equality. Yet variability itself is not necessarily a concession to parochialism, an irritating problem to be overcome with will and imagination. Rather, I would argue, justice with respect to race and schooling – and ethnicity and schooling – must be in good measure idiosyncratic.

But policy in these areas cannot be *merely* idiosyncratic, a matter of adding up the votes or market preferences. For one thing, the political process may systematically shut out minority voices. Blacks and the non-English-speaking may thus suffer from decisions that they had no hand in shaping. When that happens, the process itself needs to be recalibrated, often by the constitutionally-based decision of a court, to ensure their inclusion.[13] A less frequently discussed problem entails abandoning the field of decision-making to the historic victims, with a concomitant loss of policy sensibility: acceptance of black or ethnic separatism, with its anti-white overtones and emphasis on indoctrination, is the best illustration. It is easy enough to understand how sentiment can dissolve into sentimentality, to the long-range detriment of all concerned. As Daniel Bell writes: 'When a nation has publicly admitted moral guilt, it is difficult to say no to those it has offended'.[14] Too little responsiveness to the schools' constituencies imposes majoritarian policy, while too much responsiveness to black or ethnic extremism sets the schools at odds with social norms.

There are also substantive limits on policies concerning race and schooling which would be thought just. Even if citizens in a community vote unanimously to maintain racially separate schools, we would think that decision unjust and wrong, for this issue is not just a political question. Had the voters rejected the proposed construction of a municipal subway system, that would be the end of the matter. Questions touching on race or ethnicity are different. Education is not a public works project but rather a public good; decisions affect those who are not party to them, and that licenses outsiders to have some say. Moreover, because the policies concern the fair treatment of persons they have a constitutional dimension – a supra-political dimension, if you will – as well as a political one. The idea of equality is indeed ambiguous, but it does retain a core and controlling meaning.[15]

The quest for equality: decision-making processes

The story of race and schooling policy was once a tale of high drama, culminating in *Brown v. Board of Education*, the triumph of a powerful national vision. The hope for racial equality in schools remains as luminous and as elusive as ever, but its dimensions have changed; we are no longer so sure that it is official policy which frustrates achievement of equality or that any particular remedy convincingly relates to the wrong. At the outset, the quest for racial equality centred on a substantive entitlement; yet it was also procedural in nature. The call for equality included a demand that attention be paid, respect accorded. Both aspects of the quest have been complex, the results mixed.

There are some unambiguous successes. Surveys conducted over the past two decades report that Americans increasingly declare colourblindness the appropriate policy in education, as in housing and employment.[16] The shift has been marked – some 20–40 per cent of the white population, depending upon the issue, has abandoned its old prejudices and come to accept the rights of blacks as persons. Compared with a quarter-century ago, blacks and whites are more likely to attend racially mixed schools; resources are more equitably shared by black and white students; blacks are far more likely to stay in school beyond the school leaving age (indeed, black and white college attendance rates are essentially the same),[17] and the gap between the educational achievements of blacks and whites has narrowed considerably, although the pattern varies by region. Similarly, expressions of official antagonism to non-English speakers have become rarities. No school district would dream of suspending a child who spoke Spanish in the playground, as routinely occurred in southwestern schools during the 1960s.

These successes have not been much celebrated. On the contrary: as a society, we are rated as being either too much or too little committed to bringing together white and non-white schoolchildren, over-judicialised or excessively politicised in the way we formulate policy. The critics are various, but they can be loosely grouped into conservative and liberal camps.

Conservatives, who regard self-governing local governments as the norm, decry federal intervention as a heavy-handed and ill-advised attempt to undo healthy differences.[18] They have spearheaded the successful effort in Congress to draw the teeth of the Office of Civil Rights and the Justice Department, and have attempted to curb the courts' authority with respect to race, and sought to get Washington out of the bilingual education business altogether.

The judiciary's role in race questions arouses the deepest conservative ire. Conservatives do not argue with the core proposition of the *Brown* decision, that state-imposed segregation is unconstitutional, but read *Brown* narrowly with respect both to the definition of the wrong and the specification of the remedy. They attack judicial efforts to expand the idea of intentional segregation to embrace almost all racial separation, including segregation that seems to have occurred naturally. Court-ordered busing is the conservatives' *bête noire,* for it is regarded as both inconsistent with the ideal of a colour-blind constitution and a violation of popular preference. Judicial decisions affecting the administration and educational programme of school districts also offend conservatives, for these undermine the capacity of local authority to turn local wants into policy.

Liberal critics, on the other hand, regard present policy as insufficiently constitutionalised, and deeply distrust the decentralisation and politicisation that now exist.[19] When we treated race as a regional and political concern, the liberals remind us, we had Jim Crow laws in the South and their informal (sometimes their official) equivalent in the North. Only an authoritative decision of the Supreme Court occasioned even the semblance of fairness. Determinations of racial policy, liberals believe, cannot as a practical matter be confined to a given setting. The actions of one community will be widely felt, since '[b]lack children in San Francisco do not escape the stigma when the state calls blacks in Los Angeles inferior'.[20]

When conservatives look at communities they see Arcadia, while liberals envisage Sinclair Lewis's *Main Street,* with all its attendant Babbitry. Central government is the liberals' preferred setting for policy, the courts their instrument of choice. Because the issue of racial equality is defined in normative terms, it is thought best handled by the judiciary, the chief norm-setting institution of the society.

A parallel split is evident concerning ethnicity, although it does not necessarily follow liberal-conservative lines. Supporters of bilingual programmes of wide scope, running parallel to English language classes and emphasising cultural separateness, have looked to the national government to specify the particulars and impose them on localities. Those who care less about cultural identity than about bringing non-English speakers into the educational mainstream have been more confident of the willingness of school districts to take the needed steps, less trusting of the Washington educational bureaucracy.[21]

The weakness in both the liberal and conservative viewpoints on race is that each forces a choice between interest politics and constitutionalism. What is needed instead is an amalgam of political and constitutional processes of decision-making, the acceptance of significant but bounded substantive diversity. The variability of the present fully reflects our inability to specify a single vision of the Good Society, either politically or constitutionally driven. 'A judicial model would serve well', Grant McConnell observed, 'if standards existed on which men agreed and which could be readily applied', but these circumstances are not at hand.[22] A political resolution would similarly be acceptable if the full gamut of possible political action commanded broad assent, but that is not the situation. A wholly politicised world might rob minorities of rights to dignity, whose source lies deeper than the momentary action of the electorate, even as a wholly judicialised world could overwhelm the reality of circumstance with the force of principle.

Policy concerning race and schooling has been extraordinarily dynamic in the years since *Brown*, and the deliberate maintenance of tension among the decision-making bodies has fueled that dynamism. The judiciary has historically exercised varying degrees of influence; it has not been the single-mindedly imperialist institution that conservative critics decry. The courts' role has shifted from one of social control in the context of Southern desegregation during the 1960s to managing a reinvigorated polity within a constitutionally-fixed framework in the 1970s. The relationship between central and local government has similarly varied over time. Concerning ethnicity, the involvement of each branch of government – sometimes working in tandem with the others, as in administrative elaboration of remedies, initially set forward in the Supreme Court's decision concerning bilingual instruction, other times in distressing disharmony – has produced a fluid, if stormy, policy.

The present process of decision-making often does not work badly, and its variability contributes importantly to its success, but we could do better. In substantive terms, what is wanted with respect to race and schooling is a policy combining uniform minimum guarantees of equal treatment – including the chance to obtain an integrated education – with idiosyncratically developed school programmes based on the preferences of particular communities. In procedural terms, enhancing the opportunities for black participation in shaping those idiosyncratic decisions and in monitoring uniform minima is the desired end. A similar substantive mix is desirable with respect to ethnicity: guarantees of the effective inclusion of non-English speakers in the life of the school, with wide latitude for school districts to decide for themselves on the forms of instruction. In procedural terms, although fuller participation is certainly to be desired, differences in the histories of blacks and other minorities argue for a lesser level of policy concern with respect to ethnic groups.

Achieving these goals demands some change in the ways both the courts and the political system do business. Constitutional doctrine, as developed by the Supreme Court in the context of Northern segregation, is excessively devoted to fault-finding, insufficiently attentive to the underlying issues of equitable treatment. Lower courts' efforts may jeopardise the distinction between political and judicial action. The negativism of politics at the national level since the mid-1970s has hindered efforts to develop sane policy. At the local level, policy seems increasingly driven by self-interest, less attentive to the claims of the larger community. These are each remediable defects if the will to remedy them can be mustered.

The role of the courts

For nearly two decades following the *Brown* decision, the Supreme Court decided only Southern school desegregation cases.[23] The cause of racial separation in those cases seemed, plainly enough, the officially maintained dual school system, whose impact lingered after its formal abolition. The justices did not belabour this point, but instead stipulated what remedies were constitutionally necessary to undo the continuing impact of segregation.

By 1971, however, when *Swann v. Charlotte-Mecklenburg County School District*[24] was decided, the nexus between pre-1954 segregation and the current racial composition of the schools had become attenuated. The Charlotte-Mecklenburg, North Carolina, school district had some years earlier abandoned such practices as case-by-case review of black student requests to be transferred to all-white schools, which predictably produced dual schools. But new considerations contributed to racial identifiability in the schools, notably an increase in residential segregation coupled with the maintenance of neighbourhood attendance patterns. In this respect, Charlotte-Mecklenburg did not seem so very different from Northern districts which, although untainted by a history of mandated dual schools, none the less operated substantially segregated school systems in which school attendance was largely determined by place of residence. *Swann* emphasised the persisting consequences of the pre-1954 regime – the first time since *Brown* that the Court had spoken of this causal chain – but that portion of the opinion is factually unconvincing. Its very unpersuasiveness prompted speculation that the Supreme Court might abandon the constitutional predicate of fault, treating desegregation as an affirmative constitutional right regardless of the source of racial separation.[25]

In *Keyes v. School District Number 1, Denver*[26] the Court refused to adopt such an approach. In a community with no history of Jim Crow laws, the majority maintained, deliberate intent to segregate had to be shown before relief could be ordered; the mere fact of racial isolation was constitutionally irrelevant. Proof of intentional segregation affecting a substantial portion of a district presumptively demonstrated that deliberate segregation had a district-wide impact, and for that reason district-wide desegregation, including busing if necessary, was the appropriate remedy. Since *Keyes*, the Court has been preoccupied with elaborating the meaning of intent and refining the connection between wrong and remedy. Both are confusing enterprises.[27]

Because Northern school districts had not been formally authorised in modern times to separate students on racial grounds, intentional segregation had to be inferred from the actions of the school board – decisions concerning school boundaries, construction of new schools, teacher assignment, and the like. But how was this inference to be drawn: Was it sufficient to prove that school policy had the predictable effect of segregating students, or did intent carry a stronger meaning, implying some additional element of culpable conduct? Opinions after *Keyes* first contracted and later expanded the possibility of proving intentional segregation. The Court's determinations similarly fluctuated with respect to the fit between wrong and remedy, alternatively increasing and diminishing plaintiffs' legal burdens.

The Supreme Court's vagueness and vacillation have caused considerable trouble. Lower courts, unsure of what standard to apply, have reached varying decisions without being able clearly to explain those differences: why should Pontiac and Kalamazoo, but not Grand Rapids, have to bus their students? Policy-makers have been baffled and infuriated by these inconsistencies. *Brown v. Board of Education* was premised on values understandable and persuasive to the intelligent lay person. *Keyes* and its progeny, by contrast, float in a sea of murky technicality, barely comprehensible to anyone, not obviously anchored to principles of fairness.

The constitutional standard propounded in *Keyes* is the chief culprit. Requiring proof of intentional segregation before calling for any remedy is a defensible reading of the Fourteenth Amendment – the language of equal protection is sufficiently capacious to tolerate a range of understandings – but hardly the most sensible interpretation. The injury that children suffer from racial separation is not attributable to its cause: do black fourth graders realise that their school is 95 per cent black only because officials gerrymandered the attendance zone? Does it matter? Most important, because intentional segregation as the judges have defined the concept is neither a consistent nor a readily understandable basis for judicial intervention, the very legitimacy of the Court's effort is jeopardised. Why should people obey a decision whose rationale they cannot grasp and whose authoritativeness they doubt?

A preferable constitutional approach, well within the Supreme Court's discretion in interpreting the Equal Protection Clause, would recognize the irrelevance of fault-finding with respect to most aspects of segregation. Justice Powell's opinion in the Denver case follows this course, proposing 'a right, derived from the Equal Protection Clause, to expect that once the state has assumed responsibility for education, local school boards will operate integrated school systems':[28]

> A system would be integrated in accord with constitutional standards if the responsible authorities had taken appropriate steps to (i) integrate faculties and administration; (ii) scrupulously assure equality of facilities, instruction, and curricular opportunities throughout the district; (iii) utilize their authority to draw attendance zones to promote integration; and (iv) locate new schools, close old ones, and determine the size and grade categories with this same objective in mind.

This approach, *uniform minimum integration*, attempts to distinguish between the principle-based and policy-based components of the idea of racial justice, assigning only the former element exclusively to the courts. It locates a core substantive right, not appropriately subject to testing against the competing concerns of the larger community, and distinguishes that right from more obviously policy-based claims. Beyond the uniform minimum obligation, racial concerns are, as Justice Powell observes, properly weighed against 'other, equally important education interests which a community may assert'.

Uniform minimum integration is attentive to the need for consistency. Although the scope of the constitutional obligation remains disputable in the marginal instance, the range of differences from place to place is substantially narrowed. Since every school district would have a constitutional responsibility to bring black and white students together, the distinction between North and South, now almost wholly lacking any factual basis, would be abandoned.

Uniform minimum integration, while specifying the most important judicial task, needs to be augmented in several respects. Because the entitlement to an education free from racial stigma is an individual constitutional right – it is, after all, the rights of 'persons' that the Fourteenth Amendment secures – any child, black or white, should be able to attend a school other than the one to which he or she is assigned if that choice reduces racial isolation.[29] The rights of minority children would of course also encompass freedom from intentionally imposed segregation which causes existing racial isolation. Intent is used here in the strong sense, referring to official design as distinguished from inferences made from the effect of a particular practice.

Uniform minimum integration, the right to choose a less segregated school, a broader race-conscious remedy where there is proof of deliberate and effective efforts to separate black and white students within school districts or metropolitan areas: these are the elements of a

Supreme Court standard concerning race and schooling that at once respects the civil rights of individuals and the policy interests of communities.

The challenge confronting the lower federal courts that hear race and schooling suits is different, for they are less the inventors of doctrine than the overseers of institutional reform in the schools. The courts have done reasonably well in setting in motion a new mode of decision with noteworthy social policy effects. Nathan Glazer, speaking generally of institutional reform litigation, notes that courts:[30]

> are beginning to shape the entire structure of social policy. They are determining which of the factions disputing policies and their implementation are to be strengthened, and which weakened. . . . They are significantly determining how resources within any given branch of social policy are to be distributed, and how they are to be distributed among the several branches of social policy.

What licenses judges to act in this fashion? Certainly not the traditional conception of adjudication, which sharply distinguishes judging from politics.[31] Lower courts themselves have sought to maintain the traditional conception. Even as they act in a political setting, they emphasise unbroken links to past legal behaviour. Even as the courts goad a political process, they issue orders; even as they seek to balance interests, they refer to rights.

Yet in the context of contemporary desegregation problems, a trial court which attempted to function in exclusively legalistic terms, confining its concerns to matters directly derivable from authoritative rule, could not speak effectively to the issue at hand, and hence could not vindicate the rights at stake in the controversy. A rigidly legalist judiciary tends to uselessness. We tend to forget just how adaptive the federal judiciary has been in finding a place for itself in the political maelstrom of altered circumstances. In desegregation cases the newly perceived relationship between institutional restructuring and the undoing of discrimination, and the concomitant necessity for framing remedies extending beyond racial mixing, indicate judicial adaptiveness.

The court, however, can not assume *any* posture or confront *any* question, as long as the outcome promises to be efficacious, for then there would be neither place nor need for majoritarian government, no distinction whatsoever between principle and politics. Hence the core question: how can the judiciary reconcile the need to act effectively with the importance of retaining those qualities which distinguish it from the co-ordinate branches of government?

While no clear line demarcates the activities of courts, judicial decision-making is distinctive in two respects. The decisions them-selves emerge from interchange between the judge and those directly affected by the issue; they derive from actual controversies, and not from the desire to undo imagined mischiefs. And those decisions find their substantive predicate not in the judges' beliefs but in the positive law.

Consider the problems in preserving these distinctions in desegre-gation cases. The very sweep of the cases makes the actual partic-ipation of all those affected a practical impossibility; that is why 'classes' are represented not by all their members but by named individuals. Even within the courtroom, the idea that representative participation is preserved amounts to scarcely more than a conceit.[32] The entire class, usually the minority students of the school district, is never formally notified of the litigation. The named plaintiffs are essentially figureheads with little or no control over the course of the litigation. Discordant voices within the larger class – those who might be interested in securing black separatism, for example – are discouraged, for they introduce complications not readily resolved in the adversarial setting. Nor does the interchange between the judge and those directly affected include all those affected (children and parents of white, black and other minority children, teachers, taxpayers). And the artificial class offers the opportunity for a case to reflect the interests of lawyers and ideologues, not actual parties. The judge can not escape a political role – recognising legitimate participants and giving them a place in the negotiations over the strategic elements of remedy. Judges should recognise that the substantive basis for decision – here, quality – is very much in flux and, where consensus is itself a good, the effort to assure oppor-tunities for participation further enhances the legitimacy of the outcome.[33] Within constitutional bounds, equality means what those affected concur that it means. The meaning of justice evolves with changes in circumstances and with altered understandings of the core value of equality.

The role of the courts has been somewhat less substantial with respect to language minorities. Because the *Lau* decision pointedly did not rest on the constitution but instead relied on a narrower statutory predicate for its assertion that non-English speakers are entitled to some special assistance, it has not been that charter of reform that *Brown* proved to be; indeed, differences between the two decisions nicely symbolise the distinction between the activist Warren Court and the more cautious Burger Court. Nor has *Lau* been followed by other Supreme Court decisions expanding the rights of the non-English speaking.

'Do *something*' is the stance of *Lau*, and that seems a sensible prescription. That there was legislation upon which the Court could base its judgment has kept this issue from being over-legalised and depoliticised, and that too seems a sensible course. But vagueness at the Supreme Court level has its price in variability among the trial courts. Some federal courts have given short shrift to the claim that the law requires bicultural as well as bilingual instruction, while others have intruded as schoolmasters, reviewing in unbecoming detail the pedagogics of the programme. One district court, stretching the law beyond its apparent limits, treated black English as a language, requiring the school district to provide special bilingual instruction to teachers in order to overcome blacks' alleged incapacity to use standard English.[34] A better course for the trial courts, I would argue, is to insist that some serious effort be made, while deferring to school district expertise in determining the educational particulars.

The roles of the legislative and executive branches

During the mid-1960s, the legislative and executive branches of the federal government joined with the courts to undo Southern school segregation. By contrast, since 1970 Congress has warred with the executive branch and more recently with the courts over the scope of the federal presence. Over 100 bills and constitutional amendments have been introduced in Congress during this period, each intended to constrict the authority of the judiciary, the Office of Civil Rights, and the Justice Department. The war continues, with the most serious effort to limit the courts' capacity to order the busing of students mounted in 1982.

The present Congressional posture disappoints because it embodies a default in leadership, an ability to specify only what is not wanted, without any sense of a usefully positive federal presence. Returning to the activism of an earlier time would be neither appropriate nor imaginable, for the civil rights issues which need to be resolved are different, as is our sense of what Washington can usefully do. There remains a significant and useful federal role, however, if the political branches choose to assert it. Congressional and executive support for uniform minimum standards of the sort propounded by Justice Powell in *Keyes* would strengthen their political as well as constitutional legitimacy. Washington can also raise and redistribute substantial sums of money to encourage local experimentation with diverse approaches. The Emergency School Aid Act (ESAA), the one modest source of federal funds at present available to aid school districts in the throes of desegregation, has been at least a minor success in this regard.[35]

The federal government can, in addition, offer technical assistance directly to school districts. It might consider borrowing from Britain the idea of an education inspectorate which collaborates closely with professionals in the field, sharing ideas which have worked elsewhere and helping to implement new programmes. Such undertakings have not fared well in the history of American education. The Department of Education does not fancy itself as a helpmate. Since the Great Society era, federal education officials have sought to impose their priorities on local officials, using the federal authority to promote compliance with federal directives that specify how decisions are to be reached and the information which must be made available. Threatened cut-offs of federal funds have been used for the same purpose.

Where rights are at stake, compliance is indeed what is wanted: if the uniform minimum standards are established national rules, they ought to be followed nationally. Beyond the minima, an orientation to compliance as distinguished from assistance to fellow professionals makes little sense. But the alternative is not policy abdication, as the Reagan administration believes. Washington can encourage state and local educators, working within their own political frameworks, to resolve questions of race and schooling by selecting among the numerous alternatives an approach attuned to local needs.

The political history of bilingual education is in many respects comparable. Through the mid-1970s, efforts to aid those presumed in need of bilingual education were widely supported, within the three branches of government and across party lines in the Congress. That broad bipartisan support has more recently deteriorated. Educational experts now question the value of most bilingual educational offerings: students who needed least help were apparently getting the most, and what they were getting had no evident impact on achievement.[36] A *Wall Street Journal* editorial decried bilingualism as an effort 'designed to produce illiterates in both languages'.[37] Moreover, the civil rights rhetoric that had powered the initial successes of the movement no longer rang true.

The decline in financial support and civil rights enforcement tell the story. Funding for bilingual instruction, which grew from $7.5 m. in fiscal year 1969 to $191 m. in fiscal year 1980, has been trimmed to $142 m. in fiscal year 1982. Congress has expressed a preference for efforts aimed at returning students to the educational mainstream, an apparent shift from its earlier stance. The administration has proposed eliminating special funding for bilingual instruction, and may have its way in 1984, when the present Bilingual Education Act expires. Civil rights enforcement by the executive has almost ceased, a casualty of the Reagan administration's general indifference to minority claims.

Washington's posture concerning the non-English-speaking ought to parallel its stance with respect to blacks in important respects. The federal government has a responsibility to the non-English-speaking, particularly to those newcomers – Cuban, Vietnamese, Mexican – who have with national acquiescence settled here in considerable numbers. Their *minimum* entitlement is to programmes which offer effective entry into the educational system: these Washington should help support. As with racial issues, the national government's primary emphasis should be on the provision of technical assistance to school districts, including bringing together local officials to pool knowledge and jointly develop new initiatives. No single programme will work, for no single programme fits the needs of the diverse language minorities and varied communities in which they have settled. Myriad solutions can be tried under Washington's stewardship.

Prospects for racial and ethnic equality in the 1980s

The critical question remains: Will attention to racially or ethnically rooted inequities in an arena of decision that has been increasingly open to minority participation persist in the 1980s? The portents are disturbing. There is detectably diminished enthusiasm for reforms designed to bring about greater racial or ethnic equality or a fuller measure of equal educational opportunity. In fact, the success of the drive for racial equality may have dampened prospects for further government-initiated reforms. In 1976, 63 per cent of white Americans believed that the position of blacks in the society had changed greatly during the past few years; twelve years earlier, only 39 per cent held that view. Consequently, many whites resist further civil rights initiatives as mere special pleading. When questioned about the propriety of the federal government's making 'every possible effort to improve the social and economic position of blacks', just 15 per cent were strongly supportive in 1978, a decline from 20 per cent in 1970.[38]

Scepticism concerning the effectiveness of federal intervention may also contribute to an unwillingness to rely on federal intervention. Fewer than one-third of the white population believes that the '1960s programme' actually helped minorities: 60 per cent thought this initiative had either no impact or made things worse.[39] Support for government policy designed 'to insure integration' reached its highest point in 1972, when 41 per cent of the white population favoured it; by 1978 the ranks of the strong pro-integrationists had thinned to 34 per cent.

Blacks perceive a different world with different possibilities. In 1964, three-fifths of the black population reported substantial change in the position of blacks. But even as continuing progress was made, black scepticism increased. By 1976, only 32 per cent believed that considerable change in their status had occurred recently. While blacks remain far more enthusiastic than whites about government efforts to integrate the schools – 55 per cent favour this policy – they seem to share disillusionment with government efforts generally. Support among blacks for integration declined from 77 per cent in 1964 to 55 per cent in 1978.[40] Blacks now more frequently associate equality in education with successful black schools and have apparently less interest in an integrated system of public education.

Public education has become a beleaguered institution, and this too has significant implications for racial and ethnic concerns. During the liberal social reformist period of the 1960s and early 1970s, support for schooling increased dramatically at every level of government.[41] Between 1960 and 1975, expenditures on public schools grew from 3.8 to 4.6 per cent of the gross national product. During the same period, per pupil expenditures doubled (taking inflation into account).[42] With the decline in enrolment, communities are selling off their schools, not building new ones. Between 1971 and 1976, only half as many school bond issues – designed to finance new programmes, usually construction – were put before the voters as during the 1961–6 period, and voter approval rates fell from approximately 70 per cent to about 50 per cent. Voters in a number of states have approved ceilings on local tax rates and state expenditures.[43] Taking inflation into account, per pupil expenditures declined slightly between 1975 and 1978, an event without modern precedent.[44] Public schools were not the chief target of taxpayers' unhappiness, yet the schools have been among the major losers in the wake of the taxpayers' revolt.

The ideas of racial and ethnic equality and educational reform have been closely intertwined, and consequently cutbacks in expenditures have affected both bilingual education and race and schooling policy. When financial support for schools was rapidly growing, it seemed easy enough to add the claims of the non-English-speakers to those of other groups who sought more from the schools. The expanded federal effort was more than matched by state initiatives in such places as Massachusetts and California. Today, with resources at a premium, these special programmes like other race-specific policies become a source of resentment, exacerbating differences between the newcomers and the rest of the society. Budget-trimming potentially encourages institutions to rethink their mission – not a bad idea in the case of the schools – but there is little evidence of this now happening. It is hard to attend to racial or ethnic equality when the maintenance of the institution can no longer be taken for granted.

A resurgence of political interest in education was required to modernise the public schools. The emergence of the race and school question played a key role, for 'the heightening of black consciousness which began with the Supreme Court desegregation decision' has been 'the most unalloyed example of "democratic surge" ' in our nation's history.[45] But it was not just civil rights groups whose involvement was critical. The willingness of long-quiescent individual citizens and interest groups to contribute what Albert Hirschman terms 'voice' – to speak out to influence policy – animated this institutional transformation.[46] Such participation strengthens the political order by legitimating the process of decision-making. (There is no real parallel in the ethnic context. The claims of the non-English-speaking rarely galvanised broad-based support, save in particular communities.) But this citizen involvement proved fragile and tenuous. Signs point to a slackening of shared commitment, diminished interest in racial equality, and a focus on narrower self-interest. In the school context, this entails 'exiting' – moving to a more homogeneous community or removing one's children from the public schools.

The 'exit' option has always been available; and since the 1950s some parents have transferred their children to private schools to avoid racial mixing, and a steady stream of white and middle-class families has left the cities for the suburbs. More recently the pace of exit has quickened. Affluent parents now choose private schools, or seek out public school systems in which their children may be expected to learn more,[47] or isolate themselves in the remaining havens of excellence in big city systems. Race is pivotal here. Studies of whites who have left desegregating districts reveal that they moved because they opposed busing, resisted submitting their own children to the policy, and had the money to go elsewhere; self-interest tinged with racism motivated their actions.[48] Only where school systems enjoy an effective monopoly over education because they serve an entire metropolitan area has substantial exit not occurred, and even in those instances private alternatives such as fundamentalist Christian academies have expanded, affording havens for whites fleeing from desegregation.

The racial schism separating city and suburban schools means that the community which makes policy decisions grows even narrower, more clearly a congregation of the like-minded, more evidently divided by race and class, indifferent to the plight of outsiders. Four of the largest ten school districts in the nation, sixteen of the largest thirty, had a majority white enrolment in 1968. Just eight years later, only eight of the biggest thirty and one of the largest ten were majority white.[49] The line dividing city from suburb is treated as impenetrable by suburbanites who deny any responsibility for the fate of central cities. 'A lot of people moved out here because they didn't want to live in the Houston district', a suburban school board member observed, explaining why the community he represented wanted no part of any metropolitan-wide desegregation initiative. 'Now why don't they just leave us alone.'[50] Yet if the suburbs *are* left alone, if they are not induced to open their schools to blacks living in the neighbouring city, increased racial separation is inevitable. The black majority central city will represent not just one conception of racial fairness – not an option – but an inevitability. That eventually impoverishes the idea of racial equality.

A quarter-century ago, American public schools were effectively run as a two-track system, with whites predominating in the upper track and blacks peopling the lower track. That equilibrium, shattered by the protracted campaign for racial equality, has in some respects been restored. The two tracks are again in place, with blacks and whites now separated between as well as within school systems. Yet in contrast to the earlier era, blacks exercise political and administrative dominion over the lower track. The importance of exercising that sort of control should not be minimised, but one may still ask whether this represents the best we might hope for. Language minority students find themselves in much the same situation, spending time in programmes for the limited-English-speaking which are efficiently run by their elders, but this pattern raises similar questions.

An urban school system that has become predominantly non-middle class and non-white no longer resembles the common schools of historic memory and symbolic moment. Such a transformation jeopardises our sense of the public school as an institution critical to the nation's well-being, which we maintain out of enlightened self-interest. Urban public schools may instead come to be regarded as a welfare service, provided as largesse to the less favoured members of the society. The perception of public schools as charity schools was strongly resisted by American educators a century and a half ago. With good reason: if this view becomes widely held, it can only hasten the decline of the institution.[51]

The quest for equality: process and substance

It is easier to suggest in broad sweep what is wanted than to imagine how it might be pursued: a commitment to an understanding of equity, in education as elsewhere, which 'gives all persons a sense of fairness and inclusion in the society and which promotes a situation where . . . people *become* more equal so that they can be *treated* equally',[52] and a willingness to assume significant responsibility for defining the task of the schools. The courts can explicate core constitutional values and police the political process, but they cannot impose detailed solutions – at least not without a radical revision of our understanding of democratic institutions. The professionals need to rethink their mission, to learn from what has worked elsewhere how to nurture a 'climate of institutional expectation'[53] and not treat failure as inevitable. The influence of the professionals is most salutary if it coexists in healthy tension with legalist and political impulses. A return to the politically quiescent days of the 1950s, when the professionals dominated the apparatus of policy, is neither imaginable in the light of subsequent history, nor especially desirable, for professional hegemony encourages a narrowing of vision very much at odds with what is presently needed. The largest hope is that restructuring the governance of schools becomes not an end in itself, but instead a means of redesigning the schools in order to better the lives of children. In this conception, process and substance interact to secure a richer understanding of racial and ethnic fairness.[54] That seems at once a very tall order and a very important order.

'The spirit of a commercial people', John Stuart Mill wrote, 'will be . . . essentially mean and slavish, whenever public spirit is not cultivated by extensive participation of the people in the business of government in detail'.[55] So too with the furtherance of justice for minorities. In this respect present prospects are not cheering. Yet this is a decidedly short-run perception. The past quarter-century has been marked by almost continuous attention to racial and ethnic minority matters, and a period of respite and consolidation may be in order. In any event, the issue will not vanish. The American quest for equality is an ancient one, the end elusive, the dilemmas deep and likely to endure.

Notes

This paper draws heavily on the author's *Just Schools: The Idea of Racial Equality in American Education*, (Berkeley: University of California Press, 1982). The research assistance of Beth Firstman, who collected data concerning issues of ethnicity and education, is gratefully acknowledged.

1 Henry Steele Commager, *The American Mind*, (New Haven: Yale University Press, 1950), p. 10. See also Robert Wiebe, 'The Social Functions of Public Education', *American Quarterly* Vol. 21, 1969, p. 147.

2 Horace Mann, *Twelfth Annual Report of the Board of Education, Together with the Twelfth Annual Report of the Secretary of the Board* (1849), quoted in Lawrence Cremin, *The Transformation of the School: Progressivism in American Education, 1876–1957*, (New York: Knopf, 1961), p. 9. For discussions of these differing ends of education, see David Tyack, *The One Best System: A History of American Urban Education*, (Cambridge; Mass: Harvard University Press, 1974); Patricia Graham, *Community and Class in Urban Education*, (New York: Wiley, 1974); Raymond Callahan, *Education and the Cult of Efficiency*, (Chicago: University of Chicago Press, 1962); Frances Fitzgerald, *America Revised: History Textbooks in the Twentieth Century*, (Boston: Atlantic-Little, Brown, 1979).

3 347 U.S. 483 (1954).

4 Gunnar Myrdal, with Richard Sterner and Arnold Rose, *An American Dilemma: The Negro Problem and Modern Democracy*, (New York: Pantheon, 1972 ed.).

5 *Green v. County School Board*, 391 U.S. 430 (1968).
6 Eugene Rostow, 'The Democratic Character of Judicial Review', *Harvard Law Review* Vol. 66, 1952 pp. 193, 208.
7 Howell Raines, *My Soul Is Rested: Movement Days in the Deep South Remembered*, (New York: G.P. Putnam, 1977).
8 *Lau v. Nichols*, 414 U.S. 563 (1974).
9 See, for example, Peter Roos, 'Bilingual Education: The Hispanic Response to Unequal Educational Opportunity', *Law and Contemporary Problems* Vol. 42, No. III, 1978; Francesco Cordasco, 'The Continuing Controversy over Bilingual Education', *U.S.A. Today*, 30 September 1981.
10 See Frank T. Read, 'Judicial Evolution of the Law of School Integration Since *Brown v. Board of Education*', *Law and Contemporary Problems*, Vol. 39, No. 7 1975; Michael Namorato (ed.), *Have We Overcome? Race Relations Since Brown*, (Jackson: University of Mississippi Press, 1979).
11 See David Kirp, *Just Schools: The Idea of Racial Equality in American Education*, (Berkeley: University of California Press, 1982).
12 Compare *Guadalupe Organization, Inc. v. Tempe School District No. 3*, 587 F.2d 1022 (9th Circuit 1978) with *Cintron v. Brentwood Union Free School District*, 455 F. Supp. 57 (E.D.N.Y. 1978).
13 See generally, John Hart Ely, *Democracy and Distrust*, (Cambridge, Mass.: Harvard University Press, 1980).
14 Daniel Bell, *The Cultural Contradictions of Capitalism*, (New York: Basic Books, 1976), p. 185.
15 See the discussion of 'public values' in Owen Fiss, 'Foreword: The Forms of Justice', *Harvard Law Review*, Vol. 93, No. 1, 1979.
16 The survey data are collected in Philip Converse, *American Social Attitudes Data Sourcebook, 1947-1978*, (Cambridge, Mass.: Harvard University Press, 1980) and Tom W. Smith, *A Compendium of Trends of Social Survey Questions*, (Chicago: National Opinion Research Center, 1980).
17 Michael Kirst, 'Loss of Support for Public Secondary Schools: Some Causes and Solutions', *Daedalus* Vol. 110, 1981, p. 45.
18 See, for example, Nathan Glazer, *Affirmative Discrimination: Ethnic Inequality and Public Policy*, (New York: Basic Books, 1975) and Lino Graglia, *Disaster by Decree: The Supreme Court Decisions on Race and Schools*, (Ithaca: Cornell University Press, 1976).
19 See, for example, Ray Rist, 'School Integration: Ideology, Methodology, and National Policy', *School Review* Vol. 84, 1976, p. 417; Gary Orfield, *Must We Bus? Segregated Schools and National Policy*, (Washington, DC: The Brookings Institution, 1978).
20 Charles Lawrence, ' "One More River to Cross" – Recognizing the Real Injury in *Brown*: A Prerequisitive to Shaping New Remedies', in Derrick Bell (ed.), *Shades of Brown: New Perspectives on School Desegregation*, (New York: Teachers College Press, 1980), pp. 48, 53.
21 See, for example, Abigail Thernstrom, 'E Pluribus Plura – Congress and Bilingual Education', *Public Interest*, Vol. 60, No. 8, 1980; Francesco Cordasco, 'The Continuing Controversy Over Bilingual Education,' *Education Today*, Vol. 31, September, 1981.
22 Grant McConnell, *Private Power and American Democracy*, (New York: Vintage, 1970), p. 360.
23 These cases are reviewed in J. Harvie Wilkinson, *From Brown to Bakke: The Supreme Court and School Integration*, (New York: Oxford University Press, 1979).
24 402 U.S. 1 (1971).
25 See, for example, Owen Fiss, 'The Charlotte-Mecklenburg Case – Its Significance for Northern School Desegregation', *University of Chicago Law Review*, Vol. 38, 1971, p. 697.

26 413 U.S. 189 (1973).

27 These cases are discussed in David Kirp and Mark Yudof, *Educational Policy and the Law*, (Berkeley: McCutchan, 1982) chap. 5; see also Steven Barrett Kanner, 'From Denver to Dayton: The Development of a Theory of Equal Protection Remedies', *Northwestern University Law Review*, Vol. 72, 1977, p. 382.

28 *Keyes v. School District Number 1, Denver*, 413 U.S. 189, 226 (1973) (Powell, J., concurring in part and dissenting in part). In subsequent opinions, Justice Powell reverts to a narrower, intent-focused standard, implicitly rejecting his *Keyes* opinion.

29 Compare Frank Goodman, 'De Facto Segregation: A Constitutional and Empirical Analysis', *California Law Review*, Vol. 60, 1972, p. 275.

30 Nathan Glazer, 'Should Courts Administer Social Services', *Public Interest*, Vol. 50, 1978, pp. 64, 67.

31 See, for example, Robert Nagel, 'Separation of Powers and the Scope of Federal Equitable Remedies', *Stanford Law Review*, Vol. 30, 1978, p. 661; Alexander Bickel, *The Morality of Consent*, (New Haven: Yale University Press, 1975); Gerald Frug, 'The Judicial Powers of the Purse', *Pennsylvania Law Review*, Vol. 126, 1978, p. 715.

32 See Derrick Bell, 'Serving Two Masters: Integration Ideals and Client Interests in School Desegregation', *Yale Law Journal*, Vol. 85, 1976, p. 470; Steven Yeazell, 'From Group Litigation to Class Action, Part II: Interest, Class, and Representation', *UCLA Law Review*, Vol. 27, 1980, p. 1067.

33 See Laurence Tribe, 'The Emerging Reconnection of Individual Rights and Institutional Design: Federalism, Bureaucracy and Due Process of Lawmaking', *Creighton Law Review*, Vol. 10, 1977, p. 433.

34 See *Martin Luther King Jr. Elementary School Children v. Michigan Board of Education*, 451 F. Supp. 1324 (E.D. Michigan 1978); Nathan Glazer, 'Black English and Reluctant Judges', *Public Interest*, Vol. 62, Winter 1981, pp. 40–54.

35 20 U.S.C. §491 *et seq.* For evaluations of ESAA, see Ann MacQueen and John E. Coulsen, *Emergency School Act Evaluations: Overview of Findings from Supplemental Analyses*, (Santa Monica: System Development Corporation, 1978); Stephen M. Smith, *An Assessment of Emergency School Aid Act Program Operations: The Targeting of ESAA Grants and Grant Funds*, (Washington, DC: Applied Urbanetrics, Inc., 1978).

36 See Thernstrom, *op. cit.*; Noel Epstein, *Language, Efficiency and the Schools: Policy Alternatives for Bilingual-Bicultural Education*, (Washington DC: Institute for Educational Leadership, 1977); Melinda Burns, 'The Ax Falls in Bilingual Education: Fostering a Generation of Illiterate Kids', *Los Angeles Times*, 26 August, 1981.

37 'Beyond Hispanic Stereotypes', *Wall Street Journal*, 15 May, 1981.

38 Philip Converse, *American Social Attitudes Data Sourcebook, 1947–1978*, (Cambridge, Mass.: Harvard University Press, 1978), p. 75.

39 Kathleen Maurer Smith and William Spinrao, 'The Popular Political Mood', *Social Policy*, Vol. 11, March-April 1981, p. 37.

40 Converse, *op. cit.*, p. 61.

41 On this period, see generally Dale Mann, *Making Change Happen*, (New York: Teachers College Press, 1978): Edith Mosher and Jennings Waggoner (eds), *The Changing Politics of Education*, (Berkeley: McCutchan, 1978); Paul Peterson, 'The Politics of American Education' in Fred Kerlinger and John Carroll (eds), *Review of Research in Education*, (Itasca, Illinois: Peacock, 1974), p. 348.

42 Eric Hanushek, 'Throwing Money at Schools', *Journal of Policy Analysis and Management*, Vol. 1, 1981.

43 On the impact of Proposition 13, and similar efforts in other states, on education, see Peter May and Arnold Meltsner, *Strengthening Local Governance in a Post-Proposition 13 World*, (Berkeley: University of California, Graduate School of Public Policy, 1979). Interviews with school board members in San Francisco, Berkeley, and Oakland confirm this perception.

44 See Paul Peterson, *Federal Policy and American Education* (report prepared for the Twentieth Century Fund, 1981).

45 Peter Steinfels, *The Neoconservatives: The Men Who Are Changing America's Politics*, (New York: Basic Books, 1979), p. 263.

46 Albert Hirschman, *Exit, Voice and Loyalty: Responses to Decline in Firms, Organizations, and States*, (Cambridge, Mass.: Harvard University Press, 1970).

47 See, for example, Harvey Rosen and David Fullerton, 'A Note on Local Tax Rates, Public Benefit Levels, and Property Values', *Journal of Political Economy*, Vol. 85, 1977, p. 433; Gerald McDougall, 'Local Public Goods and Residential Property Values: Some Insights and Extensions', *National Tax Journal*, Vol. 20, 1976, p. 436.

48 See Michael Giles and Douglas Catlin, 'Mass-Level Compliance with Public Policy: The Case of School Desegregation', *Journal of Politics*, Vol. 42, 1980, p. 722.

49 Diane Ravitch, 'The Evolution of School Desegregation Policy, 1964–1979' in Adam Yarmolinsky, Lance Liebman, and Corinne Schelling (eds), *Race and Schooling in the City*, (Cambridge, Mass.: Harvard University Press, 1981).

50 Quoted in *New York Times*, 2 December, 1978, p. 68.

51 See David Kirp, 'Poor School System?', *Times Educational Supplement* (London), 15 August, 1980.

52 Daniel Bell, *op. cit.*, p. 113.

53 Ronald Edmonds, 'Effective Education for Minority Pupils: *Brown* Confounded or Confirmed' in Derrick Bell, *op. cit.* See generally William Brookaver, Charles Beady, Patricia Flood, John Schweitzer, and Joe Wisenbacker, *School Social System and Student Achievement: Schools Can Make a Difference*, (New York: Praeger, 1979); Edward McDill and Leo Rigsby, *The Academic Impact of Educational Climates: Structure and Process in Secondary Schools*, (Baltimore: Johns Hopkins University Press, 1973).

54 On the relationship between governance and policy outcomes, see Judith Gruber, 'Authority and Exchange in the Control of Public Bureaucracies', paper prepared for the National Institute of Education (1981); Frank Levy, Arnold Meltsner, and Aaron Wildavsky, *Urban Outcomes* (Berkeley: University of California Press, 1974).

55 John Stuart Mill, 'M. de Tocqueville on Democracy in America', in Marshall Cohen (ed.), *The Philosophy of John Stuart Mill: Ethical, Political, and Religious*, (New York: Modern Library, 1971) p. 141. See generally Glenn Tinder, *Community: Reflections on a Tragic Ideal*, (Baton Rouge: Louisiana State University Press, 1980).

7 Educational Opportunity in Multi-ethnic Britain
Bhikhu Parekh

This chapter sets out to summarise the current state of our knowledge of the under-achievement of ethnic minority children in British schools, to examine some of the more popular explanations of under-achievement, and to argue for remedial measures that are both feasible and appropriate.[1] There are nearly 6 per cent of West Indian and Asian children in British schools. Concern about the educational performance of the former was expressed as long ago as the early 1960s. Dozens of surveys conducted since then have established that the vast majority of them perform extremely badly.[2] The evidence on Asian children, who have not been much studied, is less clear cut. However, it would seem that their general performance is much better than that of the West Indians and in some cases is equal or even superior to that of indigenous white children.

The most extensive survey on the comparative performance of West Indian, Asian and white children so far was carried out by the Department of Education and Science on behalf of the Rampton Committee of Inquiry into the educational problems of ethnic minority children.[3] The DES Statistics Branch in its school-leavers survey for 1978–9 decided to ask a question on the ethnic origin of the school-leavers to all maintained secondary schools within six local education authorities covering nearly half of the school-leavers from the ethnic minorities settled in Britain. Some of the figures published in the Rampton Report are worth a careful look.

According to the Report, in CSE and 'O' level English, 9 per cent of West Indians scored higher grades, compared with 21 per cent of Asians, 29 per cent of other school-leavers in the six local education authorities surveyed, and 34 per cent of all maintained school-leavers in England. In CSE and 'O' level mathematics, the figures were 5 per cent, 20 per cent, 19 per cent and 23 per cent respectively. In CSE and 'O' level examinations, only 3 per cent of West Indians obtained five or more higher grades, compared with 18 per cent of Asians, 16 per cent of other school-leavers, and 21 per cent of all maintained school-leavers in England. The picture is equally bleak so far as 'A' level examinations are concerned. Only 2 per cent of West Indians gained one or more 'A' level passes compared with 13 per cent of Asians, 12 per cent of other leavers, and 13 per cent of all maintained school-leavers in England. The situation is no different so far as admission to the universities and further education courses is concerned. Only 1 per cent of West Indians went on to study at the university compared with 3 per cent of Asians, 3 per cent of other school-leavers in the six local authorities surveyed and 5 per cent of all maintained school-leavers in England. Again, only 1 per cent of West Indians went on to do full-time degree courses in further education compared with 5 per cent of Asians, 4 per cent of other leavers in the same areas, and 6 per cent of all the maintained school-leavers in England.

The Rampton Report provides the first ever definitive, comprehensive and comparative statement of the achievement figures of West Indian, Asian and white children in British schools. Since the figures have been subjected to some strange interpretations, three points need to be made.

First, the Report does *not* show that *all* West Indian children achieve poor results, only that the bulk of them do. As we saw, 3 per cent of the West Indian children did achieve five or more higher grades at CSE and 'O' level; 2 per cent of them achieved one or more 'A' level passes and 1 per cent of them went on to university. The Report also shows that while the majority of West Indian children failed to secure five or more higher grades at CSE and 'O' level, the majority of those who did went on to secure good results at 'A' level. In other words, once they overcame the initial hurdle at 'O' level, they experienced relatively little difficulty in crossing the subsequent hurdles.

Second, the Rampton Report does *not* show that *all* Asian children in British school are doing well, and that their educational performance does not provide a cause for concern. It is true that Asian children performed better than West Indians in some areas; however, it is also true that they did less well in others. In CSE and 'O' level English, 32 per cent of Asians secured no graded result compared with 30 per cent of West Indians, 30 per cent of school-leavers in the six local authorities concerned, and 21 per cent of all maintained school-leavers in England. Again, in CSE and 'O' level examinations, 19 per cent of Asians either failed to secure a graded result or to take the examination compared with 17 per cent of West Indians, 22 per cent of other school-leavers in the six local authorities, and 14 per cent of all maintained school-leavers in England. It would seem that while the bright Asian children generally did better than most ethnic minority and even white children, the less gifted as a rule performed worse. In lumping all Asians together, the Rampton Report obscured the wide variations in the levels of educational achievement of the constituent sub-communities, and gave rise to the wholly mistaken belief that all Asian children do *equally* well. Although no figures are available, there is some evidence to suggest that while the middle-class Indian and Pakistani children generally do quite well, their working-class compatriots do less well, and the Bangladeshis and Turkish Cypriots perform even worse than the West Indians.

Third, the Rampton Report compares the educational performance of West Indian and Asian children with that of the whites in the maintained schools. If one took into account the achievement figures of the public schools as well, where the non-white children are grossly underrepresented, and worked out the national average, the West Indian and Asian achievement would appear ever poorer.

Some explanations of under-achievement

In the light of the findings of the various surveys, especially the one commissioned by the Rampton Committee, it is evident that the West Indian children in British schools perform far below their white peers. During the past few years considerable discussion has taken place concerning why this should be so. Several explanations have been offered and different factors have been held responsible. Of these the following are widely canvassed.

First, the low attainment of West Indian children is, according to some commentators, easily and adequately explained in terms of their genetic intellectual inferiority. This view of Eysenck and others is far more widely held than is realised and is favoured by conservative writers. They argue that since the West Indian children's IQ is several percentages lower than that of the whites, their low attainment is not surprising or worrying, and should not be considered a problem about which remedial action should or indeed could be taken. They argue further that *low* attainment by West Indian children should not be called *under-achievement* as is generally the case, for the latter term rests on the unsubstantiated assumptions that the children have a greater *potential* than their actual attainment suggests and that the potential is *equal* to that of their white peers.

A second explanation accounts for West Indian children's low attainment in terms of the structure of their family.[4] According to this the West Indian family is marked by an inconsistent pattern of discipline, acute inter-generational conflict, lack of commitment to and willingness to make sacrifices of time, energy and money for children's education, and failure to provide a supportive environment. It is argued that the West Indian parents do not take adequate interest in their children, encourage and put pressure on them to do well, read to or with them, discuss school work, visit schools and so on. Some proponents of this explanation go even further and maintain that the West Indians simply do not have a family in the usual sense of word, but only a loose association of a man and a woman living together and rearing children of whom one of them may not even be a parent. In their view, it is therefore hardly surprising that the West Indian children should grow up lacking the incentive, ambition, drive and self-discipline so necessary for educational success.

Third, some commentators explain the fact of low attainment in terms of the materially and culturally disadvantaged West Indian home.[5] While the previous explanation blames the parent and the traditional structure of the family, this one blames their economic conditions and the character of the wider social structure within which the family functions. It is argued that the majority of West Indians are relatively poor, ill-educated, engaged in low-paid, dull and unskilled jobs, working at odd hours and living in over-crowded houses. A large number of West Indian women have to go out to work; 68 per cent of them compared with 42 per cent of whites.[6] As a result, many West Indian children are looked after by untrained child-minders and grow up lacking linguistic and conceptual abilities. For these and other reasons, they miss sustained and relaxed contact with their parents, have extremely limited access to children's magazines and books, receive little guidance from adults, are left to spend an unusually large amount of time with their peers, are poorly motivated and so on, and grow up lacking adequate and linguistic stimulation and training.

Fourth, some explain West Indian children's low educational attainment in terms of racism both in society at large and in the school.[7] In their view, racism in society at large demeans and degrades the child, destroys his enthusiasm, weakens his motivation, distorts his psyche and makes him feel that educational success, however considerable, will not secure him a good job or enable him to improve his prospects. They argue, further, that institutionalised racism in the school in the form of biased textbooks, culturally loaded tests, ethno-centric curricula, low teacher expectations, the all-white ethos of the school, and so on, alienates the West Indian child from the entire educational system. What is more, he internalises the low image of his group and therefore of himself, and develops insecure self-identity (his conception of who he is) and low self-esteem (his opinion of who he is).

Fifth, some hold the structure and ethos of the school responsible for West Indian children's low educational attainment.[8] In their view, black children fail to achieve their full potential because many a school has renounced its traditional task of educating its pupils and helping them achieve basic intellectual skills, in favour of dabbling in social work and psychotherapy. Seduced by the allegedly 'progressive' ideology of 'romantic liberalism' and child-centred education, they base their teaching on personal 'relationships' and the child's 'self-realisation' and underplay the value of formal methods of teaching, hard work and self-discipline. As a result of all this, little effort is made to train and stimulate the mind, and like many working-class children, West Indian children receive little by way of education.

Sixth, some explain the low attainment of the West Indian child in terms of the failure of the educational authorities to identify and meet his basic educational needs.[9] Until only a few years ago, the educationalists naively assumed that Creole was English, or at least a dialect of it, and made no provision to teach standard English to West Indian children. Unlike the Asians whose lack of English was too obvious to be missed, the West Indian children therefore went through school without acquiring even the minimum linguistic competence, and predictably came to grief. When the educational authorities eventually came round to realising their mistake, they swung to the other extreme and frowned upon and even punished the use of Creole in the school. Predictably this provoked anger and hostility, especially as Creole had by then come to be seen as a symbol of West Indian cultural identity, a means of resisting the assimilisationist pressure and a protective mechanism against white racism.[10] Not surprisingly, the West Indian children not only developed resistance to learning English but also became alienated from the entire educational system.

In addition to the above, several other explanations are also advanced from time to time. They have not been systematically articulated and are largely hinted at or merely assumed. Some commentators hold the West Indian culture responsible, but disagree about the aspects of it that allegedly hold back the West Indian child. Some argue that, unlike the Asian, the West Indian culture values not educational success but excellence in such activities as sports and music; for some others it does not sufficiently emphasise the qualities of self-discipline, individuality, competition, ambition and hard work so crucial to academic success; yet others contend that as the West Indian version of Christianity, the character of social relations, and the vocabulary and syntax of Creole demonstrate, West Indian culture is sensuous, concrete and articulated in terms of images, and inherently incapable of developing the capacity for abstract and conceptual thinking, the necessary precondition of higher intellectual activities.

Some commentators argue that teachers feel threatened and insecure in the presence of the tall, aggressive, noisy, cliquish and somewhat 'unintelligible' West Indian children, and are as a result never able to establish a meaningful relationship with them. Some others maintain that the modes of communication employed by West Indian children fall outside the 'cultural competence' of most of their white teachers and create 'cultural dissonance'. As a result the relations between the two are marred by confusion, misunderstanding and hostility, and teachers are unable to relate to and give them necessary help and support.[11] Some have even suggested that West Indian children do not *want* to attain educational success either as a protest against the capitalist system whose skilled manpower they refuse to provide, or because success leads to integration in white society and isolation from their ethnic group.[12]

The underlying assumptions

Much of the current educational and political debate on the West Indian child's low educational attainment centres around the explanations sketched above. Although the debate has been lively, has thrown up interesting ideas and sometimes opened up fruitful lines of enquiry, on the whole it remains unsatisfactory.

First, the debate is vitiated by what I might call the fallacy of the single factor. The participants tend to look for one specific factor, be it class, racism, West Indian family, West Indian culture, the school or educational system, to explain the fact of under-achievement. This is obviously an inherently impossible enterprise. Not even a relatively simple natural phenomenon like the falling of an apple or the dropping of a stone can be explained in terms of a single cause. What is more, a cause is effective only within the context of a specific set of conditions whose causal efficacy cannot therefore be disregarded. Such highly complex phenomena as the individuals failing or refusing to realise their full potential obviously require highly complex and multi-factoral explanations. One needs to show how, within the framework of specific patterns of social conditions, various factors, which cannot themselves be easily disengaged, interact and modify each other and give rise to a specific form of behaviour. Any explanation that falls short of this minimal theoretical requirement is inherently suspect and cannot be taken seriously.

Second, the debate is led astray by two false assumptions, namely, that all West Indian children fail and all Asian children succeed in the English educational system. Thanks to these assumptions, some have argued that the reasons for West Indian children's under-achievement *cannot* be found in the factors they share in common with the Asians, and further that they can *only* be found in those that are distinctive to them. Thus racism, either in the society at large or in the school, is dismissed as an important factor on the ground that otherwise we would not be able to explain Asian success. By contrast, the structure of the family, the sub-culture of rebellion, and the pattern of behaviour towards the teachers, which allegedly distinguish the West Indians from the Asians, are held responsible for West Indian under-achievement. This whole mode of reasoning is invalid. It is based on the assumptions that all West Indians under-achieve and all Asians achieve well. As we saw, the assumptions are false. It is invalid also because it wrongly assumes that the same factor must always produce the same results. Racism, for example, affects both West Indian and Asian children, but may have less deleterious effects on the latter because of the protective mechanism provided by the Asian sense of cultural superiority, or the greater Asian experience of living in hostile lands. It would therefore be wrong to conclude that since racism does not have a shattering effect on the Asians, it does not have a similar impact on the West Indians either.

Third, much of the debate is conducted at too abstract a level to connect with the reality of the school or the child, or to permit sensible discussion, or to have clear policy implications. The Marxists, for example, talk about the capitalist exploitation of black workers, but do not explain how this is translated in the school, how it affects the child and his relations with the teacher, why there is such a difference in the achievements of West Indian and Asian working class children, why some West Indian children do well and what we are to do until the arrival of classless society. The social psychologists glibly talk about the West Indian child's insecure self-identity and low self-esteem, but do not analyse these highly complex concepts, produce necessary evidence for their generalisations, explain how self-identity is constructed or destroyed, and self-esteem fostered or undermined, nor indicate what educational authorities can do in the matter.

Fourth, with few notable exceptions, the participants are deeply committed to specific theories and either ignore others or dismiss them with a bundle of sweeping generalisations. They make little attempt to arbitrate between conflicting explanations on the basis of a critical evaluation of the available experiential and research evidence, or to explore what new information is needed to throw light on specific areas of disagreement and how it can be obtained.

Fifth, as we would expect, a debate on so sensitive an issue as the educational failure of the majority of black children can hardly remain apolitical. By its very nature every explanation of it points an accusatory finger at a particular target and calls for a specific course of action. For example, an explanation in terms of genetic inferiority, the structure of the family or lack of cultural depth, fastens the blame on the West Indian community; an explanation in terms of the West Indian child's low self-esteem, ethnocentric curriculum, racist textbooks and the ethos of the school lays the blame at the door of the school and the educational system; and one that stresses racism and economic inequalities puts the responsibility upon the white society. Not surprisingly, the group which suspects that it might be blamed and asked to change its ways tends to marshal whatever arguments it can against the threatening explanation, or to demand impossible standards of proof and conceptual rigour from it while not bothering to provide these for its own alternative explanation, or to impugn the intellectual judgement and honesty of its advocates. Like every political debate, the debate on the West Indian child's low educational attainment has an ideological character, and is characterised by a certain amount of intellectual dishonesty.

Given the character of the debate and the lack of clarity and consensus on the reasons for the low educational attainment, it is hardly surprising that little should have been done to tackle the problem, or that what has been done so far should have remained so ineffective and irrelevant. Most schools, local authorities and successive governments have sought ideological shelter behind the unsatisfactory character of the debate and used it as an excuse for inaction, arguing against every proposed course of action that the factors involved are not the only ones, the evidence is not conclusive, and so on. Some schools and local authorities have, no doubt, appreciated the magnitude and urgency of the problem and sincerely tried to cope with it. However, their policies have been aimed at wrong targets, or have not been implemented, or have lacked focus and co-ordination. They have appointed multi-cultural advisers, involved black parents in the work of parent-teacher associations or the management of the school, introduced multi-religious assemblies, recruited and promoted black teachers, introduced non-racist books, broadened the curriculum, celebrated ethnic minority festivals, and so on.[13]

These and other initiatives have had some impact, but not much, and while they have to some extent changed the atmosphere in some schools, they have hardly affected the reality of low attainment. For example, the multi-cultural advisers remain outsiders to schools, lack authority, have no recognised place in the educational system, do not generally enjoy the support of the teachers and do not generally have clear objectives and strategies. Parent-teacher associations are largely ornamental and have little influence on the school's policies and practices. Multi-religious assemblies are often dull and uninspiring, have little meaning for the Christian West Indians, and bear little relevance to their basic problems. Being generally very few in number, black teachers have little chance to shape the school's policies, are constrained by its structure, and at times find themselves forced to act as its apologists.

Assessing the competing explanations

We outlined earlier some of the important reasons why the debate on West Indian under-achievement is unsatisfactory. We observed that it rests on dubious assumptions, that the participants tend to talk past each other, and in their commitment to large social theories ignore the available experiential and research evidence. It would therefore be useful briefly to assess the cogency of, and arbitrate between, the explanations offered. Obviously, if it is to be satisfactory, such an exercise would have to be far more detailed than is possible here. What follows should therefore be seen as merely a sketch of such a critique.

The first explanation which emphasises the intellectual inferiority of the West Indians is the least persuasive. The IQ tests have been subjected to so much criticism that they can hardly be accepted as unproblematic. The champions of the tests have never clearly explained what they mean by intelligence, whether it is trans-cultural as they take it to be, whether it can be equated with and identified by means of 'reasoning', be it verbal, numerical or of some other variety, whether it can be quantified and measured, how it is related to the learning ability, and so on. Even assuming that the IQ tests have some validity, no comprehensive tests have so far been conducted on all the British children to demonstrate the alleged inferiority of those of West Indian origin. On the contrary, the few tests conducted so far have suggested that there is no significant difference between the black and white children.[14] Further, the ability to learn is educationally far more significant and relevant than an indeterminate and undifferentiated ability called intelligence. The tests conducted in this area show little difference between white and black children.[15]

There are also other grounds on which the first explanation deserves to be rejected. As we saw, some West Indian children do perform as well as and even better than their white peers. Although their number is relatively small, it is not so small as to make it a 'freak' variation, and hence the assumption of genetic inferiority does not hold water. Besides, West Indian children in the West Indies do not seem to perform significantly differently from the white children in the West Indies and Britain in their Senior Cambridge (A-level) and other examinations. Further, the performance of West Indian children in England improves considerably as a result of their attendance in supplementary schools. What is more, as we shall see, the educational performance of middle-class West Indian children is far superior to that of white working-class children, and almost equal to that of white middle-class children. In short, the explanation of the under-achievement of West Indian children lies not at all in their allegedly low IQ, but elsewhere.

As for the second explanation, the family is obviously an important factor. The educational significance of parental pressure, encouragement, support, etc., is widely acknowledged and need hardly be argued. It is not, however, appreciated that the importance of the family can be exaggerated. Rutter's research, to be outlined later, demonstrates that the school is as important as and sometimes even more important than the family.[16] The high scholastic achievements of many of the boarding school boys and girls, in whose education the family plays a relatively small part and certainly smaller than the school, proves the same point.

As for the structure of the West Indian family, much of what is said is either mistaken or unrelated to education. It is obviously not like the nuclear Western family, but nor is the Asian family. To say that it is *therefore* not a family at all, or somehow defective, is ethnocentric nonsense. Further, the West Indian family cannot be as crucial as is sometimes suggested, for, as we saw, it produces successful as well as unsuccessful children. What is more, since the structure of the family does not seem to harm the educational performance of West Indian children in the West Indies, there is no justification in holding it primarily responsible for their poor performance in Britain. Again, it is true that the West Indian family is increasingly showing signs of inter-generational conflict. However, this is no less true of the Asian and white British families. What is more, there is no evidence that the generational conflict is directly or indirectly related to any significant extent with children's educational achievement, for otherwise the Asians would have paid a heavier price.

As for the socio-economic conditions of the family, they are of crucial importance. The achievement levels of white children show that those coming from the middle and upper classes generally do much better than those of humbler social origins. There is no reason why this should not also be true of the West Indian. Further, it is striking that the West Indians occupy the lowest rung of the economic hierarchy and that their children's educational performance is also the poorest. Much research, not all of it conducted by the socialists, has shown that the educational performance of West Indian children tends to vary with the class of their parents, that it improves as one goes up the class hierarchy, and that there is no significant difference in the performance levels of middle-class West Indian and white children.[17] That the relationship between class and educational achievement is not a mere or even a striking coincidence but signifies a causal connection is easily established by articulating the mechanism by which class influences education. A social class is associated with specific levels and types of economic, social, psychological, cultural and other opportunities. Many, though not all, of these are educationally relevant and significant, and cannot but shape the child's education.

While class is thus an extremely important factor, it is not all-important. Notwithstanding their economic and cultural disadvantages, working-class West Indian and Asian children do well when fully stretched or adequately encouraged by their teachers. Conversely, middle-class West Indian and Asian children do not perform well when discouraged by their teachers, or if the school lacks discipline and academic ethos, or when they are subjected to racist pressures by their peers, or if educational achievement entails isolation from their ethnic group. Further, like the school too, racism mediates and modifies the influence of class. It is therefore hardly surprising that the performance of working-class West Indian children should be significantly lower than that of the similarly disadvantaged white working-class children.[18]

Like class, racism is an extremely important factor. Racism in society at large influences parents' economic and social opportunities, and for reasons considered earlier, these influence their children's education. Its direct impact on the children is also significant.[19] The failure to get appropriate jobs over time diminishes the motivation to acquire relevant qualifications. The absence of blacks in positions of authority weakens ambition and dampens enthusiasm. Racist remarks on the street, in the media and so on, provoke anger, bitterness, hatred, frustration, despair, and so on. These in turn shatter the inner calm, weaken the integrity of the self, throw the personality off-balance, encourage self-pity or mad hatred of the world, generate listlessness and lack of concentration, and pave the way for low attainment.

While the impact of racism in society at large upon the educational achievement of the black child is somewhat diffused and difficult to assess or demonstrate, that of racism in the school is not. Racism in the school can take many forms, for example, low teacher expectations, placing black pupils in lower streams and remedial groups without adequate assessment, racist insults and attacks, social ostracism by white pupils, racially discriminatory structure and practices of the school, and the racist character of the covert and overt curriculum. Not all of these educationally specific forms of racism are equally damaging. Some affect children far more than others. For example, the impact of the ethnocentric curriculum and textbooks is not as great as is sometimes suggested by those who have made them their chief targets. There is no evidence to show that they have held back black children, nor, conversely, that the so-called multi-cultural curriculum has improved their performance. Further, the racist bias of books is easily laughed off and may provoke amusement rather than indignation when the teachers are non-racist, the school is tolerant and respectful of racial minorities, the pupils have access to non-racist books, or possess self-confidence and ethnic pride.

Of the factors mentioned above, the impact of teacher expectations and attitudes seems to be the most powerful. This has been amply demonstrated by several surveys in Britain and America. Rosenthal and Jacobson showed how teacher expectations become self-fulfilling prophesies.[20] The studies by Ray Rist and by Rubovits and Maehr have shown the enormous influence of teacher expectations and attitudes.[21] Maureen Stone's and Peter Ratcliffe's work reinforces the point.[22] Though not wholly reliable, Giles' research points in a similar direction.[23] The HMIs' report in 1980, based on five years of inspection, concluded 'These schools frequently blame their pupils' background for the poor results. This is largely unjustifiable. The fault lies in low teacher expectation'.[24] The researches by Brittan, Sally Tomlinson, Peter Ratcliffe and many others, have shown that teachers, who are otherwise reluctant to classify pupils, have little hesitation in making glib and unfavourable generalisations about those of West Indian origin.[25] They have also shown that teachers generally expect West Indian children to be intellectually inferior and slow in learning, place them in lower streams and discourage them from taking 'O' and 'A' level examinations. Children accept the teachers' assessment of them, aim low, rarely stretch themselves, divert their energy and attention to sport and music and leave school without much success.

While racism is thus an extremely important factor, it would be wrong to view it as the only factor responsible for West Indian under-achievement. As we saw, class too is a very important factor and mediates the impact of racism. Further, although we do not have statistics about West Indian children based on their islands of origin, there is some evidence to suggest that the Barbadians, who too are subject to racism, perform better than the Jamaicans whose educational achievements seem to be the lowest of all the West Indian children. Again, the impact of racism is less shattering if the victim has a vigorous culture to sustain his pride and confidence, or has over time acquired the ability to live in an alien and hostile society and negotiate his way past racial indignities and discrimination. The East African Asians who have a tradition of migration have developed these skills, whereas their compatriots from the sub-continent have not, and are therefore less affected by racism.

The ethos and structure of the school is obviously an extremely important factor. Among the various studies which have demonstrated that the school is not a passive recipient of external influences but an active agent exerting considerable independent influence, one by Rutter and his collaborators is the most relevant.[26] The researchers investigated a sample of 3,485 children from twelve comprehensive schools in the inner London area with a view to finding out why there were differences between schools in terms of various measures of their pupils' behaviour and attainments, and to discovering how schools influence children's progress. The findings were revealing. Even when factors such as pupil ability at entry and social and home background were taken into account, there was considerable evidence to show that the individual schools dramatically affected their pupils' achievement. What the pupils achieved or did not achieve hinged very much on the set-up in the school. Thus pupils were found to make better academic progress and to behave better in schools which stressed academic achievement.

Although the ethos of the school is an extremely important factor, its importance should not be exaggerated. Its influence is modified by the type of children studying in it. If they lacked the home background capable of sustaining the intellectual pressures of the school, they would over time either drop out or force the school to lower its standards. Again, black children would only benefit from the academic ethos of the school if the teachers required the same standards of them as of the white children and did not under-estimate or dismiss them as inferior. In short, the socio-economic conditions of the child, racism, etc., exert independent influence on the school, and foster or frustrate its academic ethos.

As for the sixth explanation, it makes an important but limited point. It is true that West Indian children have suffered greatly as a result of the educational authorities' failure to identify their linguistic needs. Lacking the basic linguistic skills, they were unable to make much progress in the subjects requiring the use of English. It is also true that the recent enthusiasm to teach them standard English by forbidding and even punishing the use of Creole has proved counter-productive. However, none of this can adequately account for the overall West Indian under-achievement. It cannot explain why the West Indian children perform badly in mathematics and the sciences, are as a rule assumed to be intellectually inferior, placed in lower streams, discouraged from taking 'O' or 'A' level examinations, and so on. One also needs to explain *why* their linguistic needs were not identified and the initial mistake allowed to continue for so long. Surely much more than negligence must be at work.

We noted above several other factors sometimes believed to be responsible for the West Indian child's educational under-achievement. Since they have not been adequately theorised and systematically articulated, we cannot comment on them in any detail. The explanations in terms of such general and indeterminate concepts as the culture and character of a group are inevitably vague, rarely backed up by adequate evidence, lack focus and promise far more than they can deliver. There is no evidence that the West Indian culture does not value education. To the contrary, it puts enormous premium upon it and views it as the only way to upward mobility. It is also false to say that it does not foster individuality, ambition and competitiveness, for without these qualities a group cannot excel in sport as most West Indian children do, or in education as some of them do. Further, since every culture and language inevitably involves abstraction, it both requires and develops abstract thought.

Like the explanation in terms of West Indian culture, the one in terms of 'cultural dissonance' does not wash either. The cultural dissonance is no less operative in the relations between the teachers and their Asian pupils, and yet it does not seem to damage the latter. Further, the dissonance would not arise if the teachers made sympathetic attempts to understand their West Indian pupils' mode of communication, and one needs to ask why they do not make the attempt. What is more, the modes of communication deployed by West Indian children are often intended to protest against as well as to defend themselves against what they regard as their teachers' racist attempts to keep them down. They are therefore not *sui generis*, and their significance must be sought in the wider context of the school and society at large.

Conclusions

We outlined and commented above on the explanations offered for the educational under-achievement of West Indian children. As we saw, the explanations are not all equally cogent. Some are patently false, some are unsupported by evidence, some are superficial, whereas some others are persuasive. Our brief examination of the available evidence would seem to suggest that the socio-economic conditions, racism in the school, and the academic ethos of the school are the three most important factors responsible for West Indian children's educational under-achievement. To be sure, none of them by itself is enough; nor do all of them collectively account fully for the under-achievement of *all* the children, for human beings vary greatly and are influenced by different things in different degrees. Even when the three factors account for the bulk of the West Indian children, they cannot *wholly* explain their under-achievement, for the other factors noticed above do exert some influence. All that our analysis implies is that the three factors in their complex interaction explain to a *considerable* degree why the *bulk* of West Indian children under-achieve. At the theoretical level such a conclusion is obviously unsatisfactory and calls for further research. In the realm of social policy and action, however, it provides as much knowledge as is necessary and possible and constitutes an adequate basis for action. We need, of course, to know a lot more than we do at present as to why children under-achieve. In the meantime, we have to deal with urgent and explosive human problems. In this area, as in others, we can only act on the basis of well-considered judgements grounded in the best available knowledge.

If our conclusion is correct, the line of action is reasonably clear. In order effectively to tackle the problem of the educational under-achievement of the ethnic minority children in general and the West Indians in particular, both the local and central government must devise policies capable of achieving a threefold objective. First, helping the West Indian parents improve their social and economic conditions; second, combating racism in society at large and, especially, in the school so that black children can relax, feel confident and be encouraged and helped to bring out their best; third, ensuring that while they should be sensitive to their pupils' personal problems and needs, the schools devote their energy and attention to their primary task of giving them basic intellectual skills. Unless appropriate and effective strategies are devised to realise these objectives, the problem of under-achievement is bound to get even worse.

Notes

1   I am grateful to David Halladay for discussing with me some of the basic ideas of this paper.

2   For a useful summary, see Sally Tomlinson, 'The educational performance of ethnic minority children', *New Community*, Vol. VIII, no. 3, 1980.

3   Committee of Inquiry into the Education of Children from Ethnic Minority Groups, *West Indian Children in Our Schools*, Cmnd. 8273, (London: HMSO, 1981).

4   This is the favourite theory of the liberals, and can be glimpsed even in such excellent works as J. Rose *et al.*, *Colour and Citizenship*, (London: Oxford University Press, 1963).

5   See John Rex's interesting critique of the Rampton Report in *Times Educational Supplement*, 7 August 1981.

6   *West Indian Children, op. cit.* p. 15.

7   Bernard Coard, *How the West Indian child is made educationally subnormal in the British school systems*, (London: New Beacon Books, 1971); also R. Giles, *The West Indian Experience in British Schools*, (London: Heinemann, 1977).

8   Maureen Stone, *The Education of the Black Child in Britain*, (London: Fontana, 1981).

9   See Rampton Report, pp. 18ff, and the articles by V.K. Edwards in *Educational Research*, Vol. 18. no. 2, 1976, and *Educational Review*, Vol. 30, no. 1, 1978.

10   H. Rosen and T. Burgess, *Languages and Dialects of London School Children*, (London: Ward Lock Foundation, 1980); and V.K. Edwards and D. Sutcliffe, 'Broadly speaking', *Times Educational Supplement*, 13 October 1978.

11   G. Driver, 'Cultural Competence, Social Power and School Achievement', *New Community*, Vol. 5, no. 4, 1977, and G. Driver *Beyond under-achievement* (London: Commission for Racial Equality, 1980).

12   Farrukh Dhondy, 'Teaching young blacks', *Race Today*, May 1978. See also J. Mack, 'West Indians and School', *New Society*, 8 December 1977.

13   For a good discussion of how such decisions are made, see Ken Young and Naomi

Connelly, *Policy and Practice in the Multi-racial City* (London: Policy Studies Institute, 1981), chap. 7.

14 For a good discussion see Monica Taylor, *Caught Between: A Review of Research into the Education of Pupils of West Indian Origin* (London: NFER-Nelson, 1981), pp. 60ff.

15 *ibid*, pp. 93f.

16 M. Rutter, B. Maughan, P. Mortimer and J. Ouston, *Fifteen Thousand Hours*, (London: Open Books, 1979).

17 See Rex, *op.cit.*.

18 See Taylor, *op.cit.*, pp. 102 and 227.

19 *ibid*, p. 168.

20 R. Rosenthal and L. Jacobson, *Pygmalion in the Classroom*, (New York: Holt, Rinehart and Winston, 1968).

21 Ray Rist, 'Student, Social Class and Teacher Expectations', *Harvard Educational Review*, Vol. 40, no. 3, 1970; P.C. Rubovits and M.L. Maehr, 'Pygmalion Black and White', *Journal of Personality and Social Psychology*, Vol. 25, no. 2, 1973.

22 Maureen Stone, *op.cit.*

23 R. Giles, *The West Indian Experience in British Schools*, (London: Heinemann, 1977).

24 Many white teachers and black parents stressed this point in their evidence to the Rampton Committee.

25 E. Brittan, 'Multi-racial education: teacher opinion on aspects of school life', *Educational Research*, Vol. 18, nos. 2 and 3, 1976; S. Tomlinson, 'West Indian Children and ESN Schooling', *New Community*, Vol. 6, no. 3, 1978.

26 Rutter *et al.*, op.cit.

8 Public Policy and Employment Discrimination in the United States
Richard B. Freeman

An employer is said to discriminate against workers of a given ethnic group when, faced with equally competent applicants for a job (or promotion) from that group and other groups, he selects members of the given ethnicity in disproportionately low numbers. If relatively many employers have such discriminatory attitudes, members of the group discriminated against will be forced to take lower wages (worse jobs) than their peers or to suffer from unemployment. Their lower wages/worse jobs can be viewed as a means of compensating employers for prejudiced attitudes in the context of the theory of compensating differentials.[1]

In the light of this definition of employer discrimination, consider the comparative evidence on the ethnicity of successful job applicants in the United States and the United Kingdom in the late 1970s displayed in Table 8.1. The figures in this table are taken from two roughly comparable US and UK studies in which firms were mailed bogus applications of persons with equivalent credentials but differing ethnicity, and the treatment of the applications compared. While there are some differences between the studies (the US study sent blind letters to firms from master lists of the Office of Federal Contract Compliance (OFCC), whereas the UK study sent letters in response to job advertisements in the press), the basic procedures were the same.[2] As is readily apparent in the table the results are not. The US study found no evidence of discrimination against the 'bogus' black job applications, and indeed the ensuing debate in the journal focused on the possibility of reverse discrimination;[3] in the UK study, by contrast, there is remarkable differentiation in the success of applications among ethnic groups. While we lack a comparable US study for an earlier period, or for companies who are not federal contractors and thus not required to take 'affirmative action' in favour of minorities and women workers in addition to being subject to anti-bias employment laws, it is highly unlikely that the US firms showed the same colour-blindness in treatment of applicants thirty or forty years ago,[4] and may indeed have looked more like their British peers.

Table 8.1 Percentage of bogus job applications that are successful US and UK

Nationality	UK responses to advertisement 1977–78		Ethnic	US blind letters to employers 1977
Great Britain	85		Black	30
Australia	75		White	24
France	68			
Africa	53			
India, Pakistan	44			
West Indies	48			

Source: UK; Michael Firth, 'Racial Discrimination in the British Labour Market', *Industrial and Labor Relations Review*, Vol. 34, No. 2 (January 1981) pp. 265–72; Table 1, p. 268.
US; Jerry M. Newman, 'Discrimination in Recruitment: An Empirical Analysis', *Industrial and Labor Relations Review*, Vol. 32, No. 1 (October 1978) pp. 15–23; Table 1, p. 20.

To what extent is the absence of employer discrimination among US firms with federal contracts, at least at the level of responding to applicant letters, mirrored in aggregate statistics on incomes/occupational attainment by ethnic group? How great has been the improvement in the economic position of blacks, the major minority discriminated against in the US? To what extent can the evidence of non-discrimination in Table 8.1 and changing patterns of aggregate labour market position be attributed to US public policy? In the light of the wide array of laws and policies in the US, what if anything can be said about the effectiveness of specific public policy tools?

Aggregate labour market performance
Table 8.2 summarises the change in the earnings, income, and occupational position of black workers over the entire postwar period, detailing the years 1964 (when Title VII of the Civil Rights Act of 1964, which made employment discrimination illegal, was passed in Congress), 1969, a 'peak' economic year, and 1979. The final column of the table records changes in the relevant ratios from 1964 (or closest year) to the most recent year.

The table tells a clear story. Virtually every indicator of positions shows a marked improvement in the economic status of employed

Table 8.2   Progress in Black Earnings, Income and Occupational Status

(a) Black Earnings as a proportion of White Earnings, 1949–79

	1949	1959	1964	1969	1979
MALES					*Change*
1. *Median Wages and Salaries*					*1964–79*
All workers	.50		.59	.67	.72	.13
Year-round and full-time workers	.64 (1955)		.66	.69	.76	.10
2. *Median or usual weekly earnings*	–		.69 (1967)	.71	.78	.09
3. *Median income, by age, all workers (1949) and year-round full-time workers (other years)*					*Change 1959–79*
20–24	.66	.64		.82	.80	.16
25–34	.60	.61		.72	.80	.19
35–44	.55	.59		.68	.85	.26
45–54	.54	.55		.68	.67	.12
4. *Median income or mean earnings, by years of education*					*Change 1959–79*
High school graduates	.68	.69		.68	.73	.04
College graduates four years or more*	.60	.60		.63	.76	.16
FEMALES					
5. *Median wages and salaries*					
All workers	.40		.58	.79	1.02	.44
Year-round and full-time workers	.57 (1955)		.69	.82	.94	.25
6. *Median usual weekly earnings*	–		.80 (1967)	.83	.95	.15

Source: US Bureau of the Census as listed below. Lines 1 & 5 take the ratio of black and other races' earnings to whites. Lines 3 & 4 the ratio of blacks to all other workers in 1949 and 1959.

1949: *Census of Population 1950; Special Reports: Education*, Table 13.
1959: *Census of Population 1960; Subject Reports: Educational Attainment*, Table 6.
1964: *Current Population Reports*, Consumer Income Series P-60, No. 47, Table 33.
1969: *ibid*. No. 75, Table 45 & 59 (lines 1, 3, 6) and Table 47.
1979: *ibid*. No. 129, Tables 51 and 62.
Lines 2 & 6: *Monthly Labor Review*, various issues. 1979 figure is for 1978.
* College graduates four years only in 1959.

(b) Ratio of percentage of all non-whites in occupations to percentage of all whites in occupations

	1950	1959	1964	1969	1979	Change 1964–79
MALES						
Professionals	.39		.45	.48	.54	.09
Managers	.22		.22	.28	.37	.15
Craftsmen	.41		.58	.68	.81	.23
Managers, college graduates only	.42		.41	.49	.75	.34
FEMALES						
Professionals	.47		.60	.70	.75	.15
Clerical	.15		.33	.55	.79	.46

Source: US Bureau of Labor Statistics, *Educational Attainment of Workers*, Special Labor Force Reports No. 240, Table K, p. A–21; No. 125, Table J, p. A–29; No. 53, Table J, p. A–14. 1950 employment from *Census of Population 1950, Education* P–E No. 5B, Table 11, pp. 88–94 (figures for 15 and over).

black workers, with – as has been widely noted by various analysts – gains concentrated among women, highly educated or skilled men, and young men. Virtually every indicator of positions also shows a marked acceleration in the economic status of employed black workers after 1964, when the US anti-bias effort intensified as a result of Title VII of the Civil Rights Act of that year. Despite the poor performance of the economy in the 1970s there is no evidence of a decline in the relative black positions in that period. The continued positive trend in the face of cyclical forces operating against blacks[5] suggests that the earnings and occupational progress of the post-1964 era are persistent rather than transitory developments. Detailed analyses of the changing patterns of progress of individuals and cohorts confirm this conclusion.[6]

The time pattern of the upswing in the labour market position of black Americans is analysed in greater detail in Table 8.3, which examines whether or not there is, other factors held fixed, a time series relation between the post-1964 improvement in the relative economic position of blacks and the upswing of anti-bias activity in the period. The dependent variables, measured in logarithmic form, are: the median wage and salary earnings of non-white workers relative to white workers from 1947 to 1975; the median wage and salary earnings of non-white workers employed full-time year-round to the earnings of comparable white workers from 1955 to 1975; the ratio of the fixed weight index of the occupational position of non-white workers to the index for white workers from 1958 to 1975.

The explanatory variables are:

TREND, a time trend which takes the value 1 in the first year of the regression and increases by one unit in each succeeding year. This variable is designed to control for overall trends in the relative earnings of non-whites.

CYCLE, a business cycle indicator which is obtained as the deviation of the log of real gross national product from its trend level.

EEO, real cumulated expenditures by the equal employment opportunity agency per non-white worker, measured in log units, with the value 1 used for the period prior to the Civil Rights Act of 1964 and as

Table 8.3   *Regression coefficients and standard errors for the effect of variables on the log of the ratio of non white to white earnings and occupational position, 1948–75[a]*

Measure of relative economic position	Constant	TREND	CYCLE[b/]	EEO	RED	R^2	d.w.
Male workers							
1. Median wages & salaries, 1948–1975	– .55	– .001 (.002)	.42 (.23)	.08 (.01)		.83	2.3
2. Median wages & salaries of year-round & full-time workers, 1955–1975	– .49	.003 (.002)	– .40 (.17)	.03 (.01)		.87	2.1
3. Occupation index, 1958–1975	– .33	.003 (.002)	.10 (.05)	.02 (.004)	.08 (.14)	.99	2.3
Female workers							
1. Median wages & salaries, 1948–1975	– .96	.022 (.002)	.34 (.32)	.13 (.02)		.97	1.8
2. Median wages & salaries of year-round & full-time workers, 1955–1975	– .70	.019 (.004)	– .48 (.27)	0.05 (.02)		.96	1.3
3. Occupation index, 1958–1975	– .97	– .001 (.005)	.12 (.10)	.07 (.01)	.66 (.25)	.99 +	2.0

[a]Dependent variables are the log of the relative economic status of nonwhites to whites.
[b]CYCLE obtained as residual from regression: GNP = 6.14 + .035T; R^2 = .99 where
(.0001)

GNP = log of GNP in 1972 dollars.

Source: R. Freeman in Sherwin Rosen (ed.), *Studies in Labor Markets* (University of Chicago Press, 1981). Tables 8–10, pp. 272–3.

cumulated real spending per non-white plus 1 in later periods. This variable is essentially a post-1964 trend variable, which has the value 0 until 1965, when the Act became effective and which has an upward trend thereafter. It is to be viewed as an indicator of the shift in demand for the period and *not* as a measure of the effectiveness of the Equal Employment Opportunity Commission or of any specific governmental activity. If in the future the pattern of demand changed due, say, to court rulings reducing the efficacy of the affirmative action effort, a more complex variable would be required.

RED, the ratio of the median years of schooling of non-white workers to the median years of schooling of white workers, entered to control for the increased educational attainment of non-white relative to white workers. Because this variable has a very strong trend, however, its effect cannot be readily distinguished from the trend. It is entered only in a limited number of equations.

The coefficients in the equation tell us the effect of the various independent variables on the measures of relative economic position of blacks. For example, the coefficients in line 1 show that there was a slight negative trend (–.001) in the log of the ratio of black to white median wages and salaries. The coefficient .42 on CYCLE shows that when GNP deviated positively from its trend (indicative of a boom year) the relative position of blacks improved while the converse is true when GNP deviated in the negative direction from trend. The standard error reported beneath the variable measures the precision of the estimate: when the coefficient is large (roughly two or more times) relative to the standard error the estimated impact is statistically significant; when the standard error is large relative to the coefficient, the estimated impact is not statistically significant.

The key variable in the equations is EEO, which reflects the possible impact of policy. As can be seen, in each case it obtains a sizeable statistically significant impact, which dominates the equations for males and has a major impact in the female equations as well. What this means is that in the period when the government was making an effort to improve the position of blacks via EEO activities there was indeed an otherwise unexplained improvement in the relative black economic status. A simple post-1964 time trend would, it is important to note, do about as well. The calculations do not 'prove' any policy effect but they do show a change in pattern in the period of time unexplained by other factors.

The data in Tables 8.2 and 8.3 should not be taken as measures of extant discrimination in the US labour market, as they do not control for various earnings-related characteristics which may differ between ethnic groups. If one performs a multiple regression of the logarithm of earnings on various characteristics one obtains a crude indicator of overall differences in pay due to race, other factors held fixed (I use the word crude because of the lack of very fine measures of characteristics in standard data sets). Such calculations for 1978 show relatively modest difference in the pay of blacks and whites with both men and women included in the data set, even with very limited controls (see Table 8.4).

At the same time as there has been a marked movement toward equality of earnings between employed blacks and whites, however, there has been a distressing deterioration in the likelihood of blacks having jobs, particularly among the young. In 1964 the black male civilian employment/population ratio stood at .73; in 1969, it was .73; in 1979 it was .64. By contrast, for white males, the ratio went from .78 (1964) to .78 (1969) to .75 (1979). Equally striking, the youth joblessness problem of the decade was one of increasing relative worsening in the black youth position, for reasons that no one has yet satisfactorily explained.[7] The aggregate data thus tell two stories: improvement for the employed but a reduction in the overall employment rate, especially in the 1970s.

Thus far, we have presented evidence on employer behaviour and aggregative labour market performance. What about perceptions of discrimination (or reverse discrimination) by labour market participants? If, in fact, labour market discrimination has become less of a problem in the United States in recent years, one might expect to find

Table 8.4   *Impact of being non-white on the log of average hourly earnings for employed private sector non-agricultural wage & salary workers, May 1978*

	Regression coefficient	t Statistic[a]
Constant	.555	—
Non-white	− .069	8.32
Education	.070	71.35
Female	− .415	82.89
Experience (age − schooling − 6)	.038	69.22
Experience squared	− .00064	54.73
R²	—	.351
n = 35, 816		

[a]The t-statistic is the ratio of the regression coefficient to the standard error of the estimated coefficient. When it is large (roughly greater than 2), the coefficient is statistically significant. All of the estimates in the table are highly significant.
Source: Tabulated from May Current Population Survey Tapes.

only a moderate proportion of blacks reporting discrimination and to find that proportion declining over time.

Table 8.5 summarises evidence on perceived discrimination from a variety of surveys. While there are differences among the surveys, there does appear to be a downward trend among blacks in reported discrimination (17 per cent (1969–70) to 14.9 per cent (1977) in the Michigan PSID: 5.9 per cent (1971) to 5.0 per cent (1976) in the National Longitudinal Survey) with at most 15 per cent of blacks reporting racial discrimination at work by the late 1970s. Again, we lack historical comparative data, but I think it is reasonable to believe that three or four decades ago one would have obtained much higher rates of reported discrimination.

In sum, the various pieces of evidence suggest a substantial reduction in labour market discrimination by race in the US and rather striking differences vis-à-vis the UK. While discriminatory differences may not have disappeared, they have become of sufficiently reduced magnitude to lead one important analyst (William Wilson) to make 'the declining significance of race', the title of his recent book.[8]

Table 8.5   Wage and salary workers who report racial discrimination at work on national surveys

Survey	% Reporting race discrimination	
	Non-whites	Whites
Michigan Survey Research Center Surveys of working conditions/ Quality of employment		
1969–70	17.0	1.3
1972–73	14.6	2.4
1977	14.9	5.3
National Longitudinal Survey		
Men, 1971	5.9	0.9
1976	5.0	1.4
Women, 1972	6.0	0.9
Young women, 1972	8.3	0.8
Young men, 1971	11.4	1.4

Source: Tabulated from the relevant surveys.

Role of public policy

To what extent can the changes in the economic position of black Americans and the apparent absence of employer discrimination in some aspects of market behaviour be attributed to public policy designed to eliminate overt market discrimination? This is a highly controversial question, as it raises important political and ethical issues in a society dedicated to equality of opportunity but not of outcomes. Some have concluded that public policy in the form of anti-discriminatory regulations has had an impact on the economic position of minorities; others have expressed more sceptical views.

In terms of actual pressures on companies to engage in non-discriminatory employment practices, the main thrust of the law is in the form of 'affirmative action' requirements under Executive Order 11246 and of court suits and consequent judicial decisions with respect to charges of discriminatory acts. Most large companies in the US have sufficient dealings with the federal government to be liable to affirmative action regulations. Indeed, the companies in the US blind letter study were, as noted, taken from the master list of the Office of Federal Contract Compliance in the Department of Labour. As a result of affirmative action and anti-bias laws the personnel practices of US companies are quite sensitive to issues of equal treatment of workers by race (see Table 8.6). Indeed, one of the major complaints about the affirmative action requirements placed on federal contractors is the expense it places on companies. While it is difficult to measure the 'full cost' of the affirmative action to the company, estimates of the direct administrative cost by accounting firms for the Business Roundtable suggests magnitudes of the order of $78 per employee per year, or roughly 1 per cent of profits.[11] As any observer of American corporations can attest, there is a significant effort being made by most companies to comply with (or, more cynically, to appear to comply with) affirmative action requirements.

Civil Rights Act of 1964, Title VII   Prohibits discrimination on the basis of race, colour, national origin, sex or religion. Enforced by EEOC. Procedural mechanism is change-oriented. In 1975 EEOC spent $55 m. and handled 77,000 cases.

Executive Order 11246   Prohibits discrimination by contractors doing business with federal government. Enforced by OFCC. Affirmative Action (AA) plans heart of programme. AAP requires employers to analyse racial/sexual composition of workforce, identify areas of under-utilisation and project goals and time tables for correcting problems.

State and local statutes   Many states have Fair Employment Practice laws much like Title VII and agencies to administer the laws. The EEO defers to state agencies. In 1975 about $34 m. was spent by the agencies or about 60 per cent as much as by the EEOC.

In the American legalistic society court decisions necessarily play a

Table 8.6 *Evidence of changes in personnel practices due to equal employment opportunity*

	% of companies
Have *Formal* EEO Programme	86
Including Affirmative Action Plan	96
(of those subject to OFCCP regulations)	
Have had investigation or other action under Title VII	63
Changes in selection procedures for EEOC reasons:	60
testing procedures	39
revised job qualifications	31
application forms	20
recruiting techniques	19
Special recruiting programmes	
for all minority workers	69
for minorities in professional/managerial positions	58
Programmes to insure EEO policies are implemented	
communications on EEO policy	95
follow-up personnel or EEO office	85
training sessions on EEO	67
periodic publications of EEO results	48
EEO achievements included in performance appraisals	33
Special training programmes	
For entry-level jobs	16
For upgrading	24
For management positions	16

Source: Bureau of National Affairs Personnel Policies Forum, *Equal Employment Opportunity: Programs and Results,* PPF Survey No. 112, March 1976
line 1, 2 table 9, p. 15; line 3, table 3, p. 4; line 4, table 1, p. 2; line 5, table 6, p. 9; line 6, table 5, p. 8.

major role in the actual impact of EEO legislation. Between 1964 and 1981 more than 5,000 suits dealing with discrimination under title VII were decided in the Federal District Courts.[12] Nearly a third of these were class action suits, in which statistical evidence pertaining to disparities now play a significant role in deciding guilt or innocence.

A class action discrimination suit has a major impact on company behaviour. In cases with which I am familiar companies invariably show an improvement in their treatment of minorities *after* the first major suit of this nature. The suit requires them to examine long-standing personnel practices which, possibly inadvertently, have limited the employment prospects of minorities within firms. It is also noteworthy that companies invariably seek to limit statistical analyses to their performance after 1 July 1965 (when the 1964 Civil Rights Act took effect), since the data invariably show marked improvements after the effective date of the law. Before July, 1965, discrimination

Table 8.7   *Percentage distribution of court discrimination suits,*
1966–9 and 1980

	1966–69 (n–22) %	1980 (n = 35) %
Result (Metric for computing average score)		
Relief of plaintiff (100)	27	26
Motion to dismiss denied (75)	47	11
Intermediate judgement (50)	9	6
Motion to dismiss partially granted (37.5)	9	6
Judgement for defence, case dismissed (0)	14	51
Average Score	65.6	39.5

Source: Richard E. Lung, 'A statistical Analysis of Title VII, Employment Discrimination Court Cases', Harvard University thesis, April, 1982. See p. 7 for coding used by Lung; pp. 15–20 for data.

on the basis of race, sex, and so forth was legal under federal law, though not under some state laws.

In the late 1960s court decisions regarding discrimination seemed relatively favourable to plaintiffs. As the most egregious forms of discrimination have disappeared, however, the likelihood of plaintiffs winning discrimination suits has fallen. Table 8.7 documents this claim for discrimination suits in five circuit courts from 1966–9 to 1980, using data from Richard Lung's analysis of 314 cases in the courts from 1966 to 1980. The table shows a striking increase in the proportion of judgements for the defence, from 14 per cent in the former period to 51 per cent in the latter, though no decrease in the fraction of cases in which plaintiffs won relief. Scoring the outcomes on a range from 0 to 100, with 0 least favourable to the plaintiff and 100 most favourable, the average discrimination suit in the five major circuit courts scored 65.6 in 1967–9 compared to 35.9 in 1980. In a statistical regression, with numerous controls for the type of suits, Lung obtained a significant downward trend in the extent of plaintiff's victory comparable to the change in mean figures cited above. Over the period covered, there was a one-half standard deviation shift in the outcomes, *against plaintiffs*,[13] which Lung attributed to the striking change in the nature of suits being brought, from those involving blatant discrimination to more subtle forms. As an example of an early court of appeals case, Lung cites *Gillin v. Federal Paper Board*, 479F 2d 100 where the judgement noted

He advised Gillin when she expressed her interest in the position that it was not suited to a woman and was more suitable to a man.

He indicated to the EEOC investigator that he would have placed the job newspaper advertisement in a column specifically directed to males, had such been available. On trial while he conceded that a woman might handle the job under special circumstances, he adhered to the view that the traffic manager's position was a 'man's' post. He stated that '(i) it would be an extreme case that a woman could ever take on a truck fleet operation and do it properly.' He further testified:

Q. So you are satisfied that Miss Gillin's femininity hurt her and also her qualifications weren't there, right?
A. Correct.
Q. All right. And that had her qualifications been there her femininity still would have hurt her?
A. Yes, it might have.'

One does not find such overt practices in the court cases of the 1980s.

Economic studies of the effectiveness of affirmative action and court activities

Two types of evidence have been offered with respect to the impact of the legal anti-bias effort on the gains of blacks shown earlier: time series data, focusing on the timing of the observed changes (see figure 8.1); and time series/cross-section comparisons of the performance of sectors of the economy/firms more or less pressured by the law.

With respect to the time series, while alternative possibilities have been suggested to explain the post-1964 upward trend in the position of blacks, the impact of anti-bias laws and regulations remains the most plausible explanation. Efforts to relate the trend to changes in attitudes[14] and in black labour force participation[15] have not eliminated the post-1964 shift shown in Figure 8.2.[16] This does not, of course, imply that the time series provides strong evidence that public policy was effective, only that it is consistent with such an explanation.

A complementary mode of examining the impact of public policy, with potentially more insight, is to contrast the performance of companies/sectors of the economy with/without affirmative action regulations or government compliance pressures and with/without significant court suits. Several studies were conducted in the early 1970s examining the apparent impact of the affirmative action contract compliance effort on company performance.[17] Three of these studies found evidence that black employment increased more rapidly in companies facing severe federal pressure than in other companies. One did not find such effects. These studies, however, dealt with

Table 8.8   Estimated effect of the number of Title VII class action suits decided in Federal District Courts on the 1978 proportion of employment by occupation, 1966–78[a]

	MEAN 1966	MEAN 1978	Percentage Change 1966–78	Percentage Change in Proportion due to a change in number of cases per firm	Change in standard deviation of proportion due to a standard deviation change in number of cases
1. Black proportion of all employment	.081	.120	33	3.6[b]	.093
2. Black male proportion of male employment	.085	.112	32	3.0[b]	.084
3. Black female proportion of female employment	.056	.135	141	14.0[b]	.229
4. Black proportion of all white-collar employment	.011	.042	282	14.0[b]	.169
5. Black male proportion of male white-collar employment	.010	.034	240	12.3[b]	.164
6. Black female proportion of female white-collar employment	.012	.060	400	25.3[b]	.236
7. Black proportion of all professional and managerial employment	.005	.029	480	31.4[b]	.246
8. Black male proportion of male professional &					

Table 8.8 (con'd)

	MEAN 1966	MEAN 1978	Percentage Change 1966–78	Percentage Change in Proportion due to a change in number of cases per firm	Change in standard deviation of proportion due to a standard deviation change in number of cases
managerial employment	.005	.026	420	29.2[b]	.241
9. Black female proportion of female professional & managerial employment	.011	.048	336	30.8[b]	.278
10. Black proportion of all blue-collar employment	.104	.150	44	3.1[b]	.086
11. Black male proportion of male blue-collar employment	.109	.144	32	2.5[b]	.073
12. Black female proportion of female blue-collar employment	.082	.174	112	11.5[b]	.216

[a] Estimated from regressions for 555 state by industry cells in manufacturing, with 1966 proportion of blacks in relevant category, and federal expenditures per capita held fixed.

[b] = significant at 1% level.

Source: Data from EEO-1 forms. Analysis by Jonathan Leonard, *op. cit.*

OFCC activity at an early stage in its history, before major administrative changes were made. Since the early studies, absence of publicly available data has precluded further work in the area until recently.

The impact of court decisions and suits on company performance, while extremely important in the eyes of those who have witnessed first-hand the effect of suits on behaviour, has also not received the statistical study it merits until very recently.

Both gaps in our knowledge of the apparent role of public policy on the observed changes in the black labour market position have been remedied by a recent doctorate thesis at Harvard University by Jonathan S. Leonard.[18] This dissertation provides what is perhaps our best statistical answer to questions regarding the impact of the two main thrusts of the law – court suits and affirmative action.

The Leonard dissertation results

Leonard's dissertation tests separately for the effect of court suits and affirmative action pressures on growth of employment of minorities, identifying the impact of policy on employment by linking policy in a period of time to growth in employment over time.

Table 8.8 summarises the results of Leonard's analysis of the effect of class action suits per non-white worker on minority employment. Leonard's 'experiment' is to relate the 1978 proportion of black workers in a segment of industry in each state to the 1966–78 cumulated number of equal employment opportunity suits per firm in that cell, to the proportion of blacks in the cell in 1966, and to various control variables. To perform this analysis he coded over 1,000 cases by industry and state; his data set contains 555 observations. If court cases have an impact on employment of minority workers one would expect a positive coefficient on the case variable, and this is what he finds.

Columns 1 and 2 of the table record the proportion of blacks in 1966 and 1978, while column 3 gives the changes in proportion, which are always positive, in part due to the rising black share of the US population. Note, however, the markedly larger percentage increase in the proportion of blacks in the white-collar and professional-managerial occupations than in the blue-collar occupations.

The positive significant coefficients on the court case variable in column 4 indicate that the growth of the black proportion of workers was not random across cells, but rather was largest where there was more court activity. The regression coefficients in column 5 show that a one standard deviation change in the number of suits per non-white worker raised the black proportion of workers in a state-industry cell from .09 to .25 standard deviations, depending on the specific proportion under consideration. The greatest effects were found for the more skilled male occupations and for black females in nearly all occupations. From these calculations Leonard concludes that EEO suits have an impact on the employment practices of American industry.

This does *not*, of course, mean that large numbers of black workers have been involved in court suits. They have not. What appears to be the case is that companies 'get their act together' in various areas of minority employment following a suit.

Turning to the impact of affirmative action, Leonard has obtained information on the black share of employment in 18,000 establishments, 72 per cent of which are federal contractors required to have affirmative action plans and 28 per cent are non-contracting establishments, for the period 1974–80. In addition, he has information on the number of 'compliance reviews' (formal examination of the effort to comply with affirmative action plans by federal compliance officials). To evaluate the impact of affirmative action on establishment employment of black workers he calculates the percentage changes in the black proportion of workers in contractor and non-contractor establishments from 1974 to 1980 and the percentage changes in the black proportion of workers in reviewed and non-reviewed contractor establishments over the same period. *If* the affirmative action effort was significant one would expect greater increases in the black share of employment in non-contractor establishments and greater increases in the black share of employment in reviewed than in non-reviewed establishments.

Table 8.9 presents Leonard's preliminary findings for black workers *in toto* and in professional and managerial occupations, and for black male workers *in toto* and in those occupations. Panel A treats establishments by contractor status while panel B treats contractor establishments by review status.

The figures in panel A show uniformly larger (and statistically significant, given the sample sizes) *increases* in the black share of workers in contractor than in non-contractor establishments. The differentials are moderate but noticeable for all employees but quite large in the professional and managerial areas, which have attracted much affirmative action pressure due to low 'utilisation' of minorities. The difference in the annual rates of change given in the final column to the right suggest *that the relative demand for black workers in contractor firms grew by 1–3 per cent per year more rapidly than in non-contractor firms* (depending on the particular group).

The data in panel B suggest that much of the 'better' performance of federal contractors is a result of compliance reviews. In all of the cases, contractors who were reviewed show greater percentage increases in the black proportion of employees than do contractors who were not reviewed. Unfortunately because of differences in the samples drawn, however, it is not possible at this time to contrast the reviewed/not-reviewed establishments with non-contractor

Table 8.9   The changing percentage of workers who are black in establishments by affirmative action status and pressure, 1974–80

A.   By Contractor Status[a]

Occupation/demographic group	Federal contractor			Noncontractor			Difference in compound annual growth
	1974	1980	%Δ	1974	1980	%Δ	
1. All occupations							
Both sexes	.088	.107	22	.092	.107	16	0.8
Male employees[b]	.083	.098	18	.091	.104	14	0.7
2. Professionals							
Both sexes	.020	.035	75	.022	.034	55	2.0
Male employees[b]	.017	.025	47	.018	.022	22	3.2
3. Managers							
Both sexes	.025	.043	72	.032	.048	50	2.3
Male employees[b]	.024	.038	58	.026	.039	50	0.9

B.   Compliance Review in 1978[c]

	1974	1980	%Δ	1974	1980	%Δ	
4. All occupations							
Both sexes	.106	.129	22	.084	.097	15	1.0
Male employees[b]	.095	.112	18	.081	.090	11	1.0
5. Professionals							
Both sexes	.015	.032	113	.020	.053	65	4.0
Male employees[b]	.013	.024	85	.017	.024	41	4.6
6. Managers							
Both sexes	.022	.043	95	.019	.031	63	3.0
Male employees[b]	.022	.039	77	.018	.028	56	2:1

[a]Sample size: 12,918 federal contractor establishments
           5,082 non-contractor establishments
[b]Figures report percentage of men who are black.
[c]Sample size: 272 reviewed establishments
           2,073 never-reviewed establishments.
Source: Tabulated from OFCC computer tapes by Jonathan Leonard.

establishments: as can be seen in the table, the proportions in panels A and B are not consistent; when Leonard completes a full analysis of *all* establishments, we will have a better picture of behaviour. As it stands, however, the panel B data strongly suggest that contractor firms respond to pressures generated by a review of their affirmative action plans, with relative demand for black labour rising by 1–5 per cent per annum as a result of the reviews.

In addition to looking at the growth in the black share of employment, Leonard has also compared the black share of new appointments and promotions with the share of employment, on the hypothesis that appointments and promotions represent the firms' margin of adjustment. In 1976 his data show that whereas (in companies facing compliance reivew) 1.6 per cent of professionals were black men, 3.2 per cent of new appointments to professional jobs were black men, and 2.5 per cent of promotions among professionals were given to black men – a rate 56 per cent above their share of the stock of workers. Similar patterns are observed for other white-collar occupations but not necessarily for blue-collar jobs where blacks are relatively well represented.[19]

In short, the Leonard dissertation results suggest that both court suits under Title VII and affirmative action under Executive Order 11246 contribute to employment of minorities.

From micro employment studies to macro earnings patterns

The reader will notice that Leonard's (and earlier studies) of the effect of policy on black economic progress analyse employment, whereas the aggregative data show improvements in earnings and occupational status. One way of relating the two pieces of evidence is to treat the micro changes in employment as representing the effect of *shifts* in demand, which, given relatively fixed supplies of black labour, cause increase in black wages. From this perspective the key link between the micro analysis and the macro earnings patterns is found in the elasticity of demand for black labour: the less elastic is the demand curve, the greater will be the impact of any shift in demand on the relative wages of black workers.

As a first approximation to relating the micro to the macro-analysis, I have developed a simple two-sector model to analyse the potential impact of the observed 1–2 per cent annual increase in the black share of employment in companies with affirmative action plans. This model, contained in Appendix A, relates the growth of wages of black workers relative to white workers to the growth of employment in the contractor sector on the assumption that the sector must increase wages to attract additional workers. On the assumption that the relative supply of black and white workers does not change, the model yielded the following equation for the relative wages of black workers:

Percentage change in relative wages of black workers	=	⎡ Percentage growth in demand for black workers relative to white workers in non-contractor sector	+

Contractor share of employment	×	Differential growth of employment for black relative to white workers in the contractor sector versus the non-contractor sector	÷	elasticity of demand for black relative to white workers

According to this equation the observed growth of relative employment in the contractor sector per annum will raise the wages of blacks by the ratio of the contractor share of employment to the elasticity of demand for black as opposed to white workers. Assuming for simplicity that demand elasticity is unity and that the contractor share is .60, we see that every 1 per cent increase in relative employment in the contractor sector will raise demand by .6 per cent. Over the six years covered, a 1–3 per cent annual increase in relative employment due to affirmative action pressures would translate into a 0.6 per cent increase in the ratio of black to white wages. An increase of 1–2 per cent per year would raise relative wages by 6–12 percentage points over a decade, a magnitude *consistent* with affirmative action playing a major role in improving the ratio of black to white earnings in the economy. As Leonard's estimates of the growth of the black share of employment in companies facing affirmative action pressure are comparable to those found in three of four earlier studies[20] it seems reasonable to conclude that the micro establishment work is consistent with an explanation of black economic progress that puts great weight on public policy.

Conclusion

This paper began with a comparison of the employment practices of American and British firms with respect to ethnic/national groups. It found American firms to be roughly colour-blind; it then went on to document what is by now the widely accepted finding regarding the diminished significance of race in the US labour market. With respect to the highly controversial issue of the impact of public policy, the paper summarised the newest research in the area, which finds a sizeable role for court suits and for affirmative action compliance activity. While US public policy in the area of equal employment has its faults, particularly with respect to administrative paper work, it has apparently done what it was meant to do: substantially remove employer discriminatory barriers to minority economic progress.

Appendix A: Formal model relating the shift in the black share of employment to macro changes in wages

Let: $\dot{E}_1$ = percentage change in the black share of employment in the contractor sector of the economy

$\dot{E}_2$ = percentage change in the black share of employment in the non-contractor sector

$\dot{X}_1$ = percentage growth in demand for black share of workers in non-contractor sector of the economy

η = elasticity of demand for black share of workers, assumed the same in both sectors

$\dot{W}$ = percentage change in wages of black workers relative to other workers, assumed the same in both sectors.

Then, the change in demand for black workers in the economy as a whole is:

$$(1) \quad \alpha\dot{E}_1 + (1 - \alpha)\dot{E}_2 = \alpha(\dot{X}_1 - \eta\dot{W}) + (1 - \alpha)(\dot{X}_2 - \eta\dot{W})$$
$$= \dot{X}_2 + \alpha(\dot{X}_1 - \dot{X}_2) - \eta\dot{W}$$

where α = 'share' of employment in contractor sector.

Setting the change in demand equal to the assumed zero change in supply yields the following equation for wage changes:

$$(2) \quad \dot{W} = \frac{\dot{X}_2 + \alpha(\dot{X}_1 - \dot{X}_2)}{\eta}$$

But, given the same elasticity of demand in the two sectors, the relative employment will grow more in the contractor sector according to the equation

$$(3) \quad \dot{E}_1 - \dot{E}_2 = \dot{X}_1 - \dot{X}_2$$

i.e. only if the shift in demand is greater in the contractor sector.

Substituting (3) into (2) yields:

$$(4) \quad \dot{W} = \frac{\dot{X}_2 - \alpha(\dot{E}_1 - \dot{E}_2)}{\eta} \quad \text{, the equation given in the text.}$$

Notes

1 The compensating differential theory of market discrimination was first developed by Gary S. Becker, *The Economics of Discrimination* (Chicago, Chicago University Press, 1971), second ed. For further theoretical work see K. Arrow, 'The Theory of Discrimination' in Orley Ashenfelter and Albert Rees (eds), *Discrimination in Labour Markets* (Princeton, NJ, Princeton University Press, 1973).

2 The UK study sent seven letters to 282 employers advertising in the press for accountants and financial executives. The US study sent two letters to 207 companies on the OFCC list. The difference in the acceptance rates represents the difference between letters sent to employers with a definite vacancy and those without. Michael Firth, 'Racial Discrimination in the British Labour Market', *Industrial and Labor Relations Review*, Vol. 34, No. 2, January 1981, pp. 265–77, and Jerry M. Newman, 'Discrimination and Recruitment: An Empirical Analysis', *Industrial and Labor Relations Review*, Vol. 23 No. 1, October 1978, pp. 15–23.

3 See *Industrial and Labor Relations Review*, Communications, Vol. 33, No. 4, July 1980, pp. 543–99.

4 Recall that prior to July 1965 companies could indeed discriminate blatantly without breaking federal law.

5 That black earnings and occupational position tend to be pro-cycles has been found in numerous studies. See, for example, R. Freeman, *The Changing Labour Market for Black Americans, 1948–1973* (Washington DC, The Brookings Institution, *Brookings Papers on Economic Activity*, Summer 1973).

6 See R. Freeman, *Have Black Labour Market Gains Post-1964 Been Permanent or Transitory?* (Cambridge, Mass., National Bureau of Economic Research, Working Paper No. 751, September 1981).

7 The employment/population rates for black youths aged 18–19 fell from 52 in 1964 to 37 in 1977 while the ratio for white youths actually rose from 58 to 65 over the same period. See R. Freeman and D. Wise, *the Youth Labour Market Problem: Its Nature, Causes and Consequences* (Chicago, University of Chicago Press, 1982).

8 William Wilson, *The Declining Significance of Race* (Chicago; University of Chicago Press, 1978).

9 R. Freeman; Charles Brown, *The Federal Attack on Labour Market Discrimination: The Mouse That Roared*? (Washington, DC; National Bureau of Economic Research, Working Paper No. 9, May 1961); Jonathan L. Leonard, 'Does Affirmative Action Work?' PhD Dissertation, Harvard University, 1982; P. Burstein, 'Equal Employment Opportunity, Legislation and the Income of Women and Non-whites', unpublished paper, Yale University, August 1978.

10 R. Butler and J. Heckman, 'Government's Impact on the Labour Market Status of Black Americans: A Critical Review' in Industrial Relations Research Association, *Equal Rights and Industrial Relations* (Wisconsin, 1977), pp. 235–81.

11 Arthur Anderson, *Business Roundtable Study of Costs of Regulation*.

12 This figure was tabulated from the LEXIS computer file of court cases. District courts handle only a selected set of cases. While their case load is not random, there is no reason to expect it to bias our results, as the nonrandom component has nothing to do with our analysis.

13 See Richard Lung, 'A Statistical Analysis of Title VII Employment Discrimination Court Cases', Harvard University thesis, April 1982.

14 Burstein, *op.cit.*

15 Butler and Heckman, *op.cit.*

16 Brown, *op.cit.*; Freeman, *op.cit.*

17 George Burman, 'The Economics of Discrimination: The Impact of Public Policy', PhD thesis, University of Chicago, 1973; Orley Ashenfelter and James J. Heckman, 'Measuring the Effect of an Anti-Discrimination Program' in Orley Ashenfelter and James Blum (eds), *Evaluating the Labour Market Effects of Social Programs*, (Princeton, NJ; Industrial Relations Section, Princeton University, 1976); James J. Heckman and Keenneth Wolpin, 'Does the Contract Compliance Program Work? An Analysis of Chicago Data', *Industrial and Labor Relations Review*, 29 July 1976, pp. 544–64; Morris Goldstein and Robert S. Smith, 'The Estimated Impact of the Anti-Discrimination Program Aimed at Federal Contractors', *Industrial and Labor Relations Review*, 29 July 1976, pp. 523–43.

18 Leonard, *op.cit.*

19 See Leonard, Table 3–1 from seminar paper 'Does Affirmative Action Work?' at Harvard University labour workshop, April 1982.

20 Ashenfelter and Heckman, *op.cit.*; Heckman and Wolpin, *op.cit.*; Burman, *op.cit.*; the exception being Goldstein and Smith, *op.cit.*

9 The Promotion of Employment Equality in Britain
Susan Ollerearnshaw

The extent of racial discrimination in employment

Discrimination on the grounds of race, colour, nationality and national and ethnic origins affects employees and job applicants in a number of different ways. These include access to initial employment; the level at which employment is offered; promotion and training opportunities; general treatment at work, for example in terms of benefits, facilities, industrial relations and personnel procedures; and dismissal, including redundancy.

The reasons for such discrimination will be examined in the second part of this paper but it is useful to describe the extent of discrimination that faces black people in their employment experience in some detail here. The majority of the statistical data that have been collected in the United Kingdom relates to access to employment, levels at which ethnic minorities are employed, and unemployment levels.[1] Research carried out over the past ten-year period shows high levels of discrimination against ethnic minority job applicants and employees and there is no indication that these levels are decreasing.

Research carried out by PEP in 1974 showed that Asian and West Indian applicants for unskilled and semi-skilled jobs faced discrimination in 46 per cent of cases when enquiring at the factory gate. In responding to advertisements by telephone for skilled jobs, applicants from these groups faced discrimination in 20 per cent of cases. In written applications for advertised non-manual jobs, discrimination occurred at the first stage in 30 per cent of cases.[2]

The experience of the Commission for Racial Equality, confirmed by more recent studies carried out in specific areas, indicates that these levels have not significantly changed. In Nottingham, for example, a study of applicants for white-collar jobs in 1980 showed that over half of young black job seekers faced discrimination at the initial stage of application.[3] A study of black and white school-leavers in the London Borough of Lewisham in 1977 showed that black school-leavers were three times as likely to be unemployed as their white peers and that those in employment had taken longer to find work, had made more applications and had been to a greater number of interviews than their white contemporaries.[4] These findings compared young people with similar qualifications and ability. This experience of a longer search for employment applies generally to black job seekers and is a demoralising and destructive form of discrimination.

Despite this discrimination, and despite rising levels of unemployment, the majority of black people are in employment. This raises the question of whether the levels at which they are employed are comparable with those at which white employees with similar qualifications and experience are employed. The difference between the overall distributions of job levels between the various ethnic minority groups and white employees is considerable and cannot be explained by differences in qualifications. Smith's study found that 79 per cent of white men with degree standard qualifications were in professional/managerial jobs, whilst 31 per cent of Asian/Afro-Caribbean men with degree standard qualifications are in such jobs. Eighty-three per cent of white men with 'A' levels were in non-manual jobs, compared with 55 per cent of Asian/Afro-Caribbean men with 'A' levels in these jobs.[5]

There is no evidence of a significant reduction in discrimination where second and third generations are concerned. Industrial tribunal cases often concern young black people born and educated in this country and the research described above showed that those with the same educational background and qualifications as their white peers face much the same sort of discrimination as their parents faced.

Statistical data on the comparative treatment of ethnic minority employees in terms of promotion, access to benefits and facilities and so on, and dismissal, have not been collected in any systematic way. Statistics, for example the National Labour Force Survey, census data, and the National Housing and Dwelling Survey, showing the disproportionately low numbers of black supervisors, combined with evidence of the long work experience of many of the black groups in the UK, confirm the convictions of the groups themselves that discrimination in selection for promotion is a major issue. Alleged discrimination in access to benefits has been the subject of a number of individual disputes and the dismissal of black workers, whether for performance reasons or redundancy, is an increasingly prominent issue in industrial tribunal cases.

Reasons for discrimination

The discrimination that faces ethnic minority employees and job applicants can be divided very broadly into two categories – conscious and unconscious – and these types overlap the Race Relations Act's definitions. Direct discrimination is largely a question of conscious discrimination, although it can be argued there are degrees of awareness on the part of those who discriminate in this way. If an applicant is turned down because of the sterotyped assumptions of the interviewer, he or she will have suffered direct discrimination, but the interviewer in this case is less aware of the act of discrimination than the one who does not want to employ black applicants simply because of hostility towards these groups. Examples of conscious, direct discrimination are regularly found in cases before industrial tribunals and research evidence such as the PEP studies confirms its widespread nature.

Indirect discrimination is, in many cases, unconscious in that the discriminatory effect of longstanding, traditional selection and other criteria on particular racial groups is often not recognised, generally because it has not been questioned. In a number of cases, however, discrimination in selection criteria may be used by employers consciously deciding to restrict the numbers of black applicants. A recent study of apprenticeship entry in Birmingham found evidence of employers in mainly white outer city areas restricting their catchment areas for applicants to the outer city, thus effectively barring many black applicants from the inner city areas of high black population.[6] Inner city employers, on the other hand, widened their catchment areas to the outer city. The researchers did not seek conclusive proof that such practices were intentional but their parallel findings of pressure from white employees against black recruits (see below) and of stereotyped assumptions on the part of those recruiting suggest that in some cases at least the discriminatory effect was recognised by the employer. In a Liverpool industrial tribunal case the employer made it clear to the Careers Office that youths from the inner city, predominantly black area, would not be considered because of alleged problems of regular visits from their friends and the distractions this could cause. This 'selection condition' was found to be indirectly discriminatory.[7]

Although direct or conscious discrimination often results solely from the prejudiced, hostile views of the person who makes the selection decision, this is not always the case. A personnel manager or supervisor may be instructed by a senior to discriminate, for a variety of reasons, or pressure from existing white employees or clients may encourage him or her to discriminate. Industrial tribunal cases have shown examples of pressure from above and below and the CRE's formal investigation of British Leyland illustrates clearly a case in which white employees passed a union resolution barring black recruits and made this known to the personnel manager who had interviewed a black applicant.[8] The researchers who carried out the Birmingham study of apprentice entry gathered further evidence of such pressure from white employees from managers and training group personnel in such statements as 'the management wants them but they know they can't force a black in'.[9]

Finally there are many cases in which the person who selects employees is unknowingly influenced by the views and actions of staff at an earlier stage of the selection process. For example, gate-keepers, receptionists or junior personnel may assume that the company will not want to employ black applicants or make stereotyped assumptions about the ability of particular applicants to speak English or carry out certain tasks. In this way significant numbers of black applicants can be discounted at the initial sifting stage and thus effectively barred from the main selection process.

Employer resistance to changes in practice
Employers are often unwilling to take action to prevent discrimination for a number of reasons, and it is important to examine these before assessing how promotional work can change their practices and policies. They include misplaced confidence, a lack of commitment, and ignorance.

A great many employers argue that they are confident that discrimination is not occurring in their establishments. They frequently cite as reasons for this confidence the existence of sophisticated selection procedures and criteria designed to eliminate the 'subjective' elements from selective decisions; the quality and experience of their managerial and supervisory staff; the wide knowledge and acceptance of the company's philosophy on such questions as equal opportunity; the practice of informing all managers of key employment legislation, including the Race Relations Act; and the existence of numbers of black staff in the organisation. Such confidence that discrimination is not occurring may be genuine, or may be stated in order to convince the enquirer, particularly if there is no available evidence from which to assess the position.

Such reasons for confidence were manifest in the statements made by the Civil Service at the start of the Tavistock study into equal opportunity provision in selected government departments.[10] Although the study did not set out conclusively to identify discrimination or its absence, the report identified a number of serious 'hazards to fairness' despite the Service's conviction that no significant mistakes were being made. In addition, the researchers found that the memoranda setting out the Civil Service's equal opportunity policy were not known of by senior managers in a position to select or to influence selection decisions.

One significant category of employers includes those who are not confident that their organisations are free of discrimination, or who are well aware that such discrimination occurs but are reluctant or unwilling to change their practices for a number of reasons. In some cases the employer or senior manager with overall influence has prejudiced views about ethnic minorities, or about a particular ethnic minority group, and is not prepared to recruit them as employees. In other cases, the employer is aware of the stated objections of white employees or customers to the employment of black staff and is not prepared to go against these. Similarly, perceived or feared hostility may influence the employer whether or not it exists or has been tested. In other cases, the employer may simply not view action to prevent discrimination as a priority, particularly if pressing industrial relations problems, redundancies or general management problems or other pressures are demanding attention. In all the above cases, the absence of external or internal pressure from ethnic minority employees, from agencies designed to promote equal opportunity and eliminate discrimination, and from central government compounds the view that no specific measures are necessary.

Finally, there are a number of industries and workplaces in which action to prevent discrimination would mean overturning longstanding arrangements. Major examples of this category are those occupations in which trade unions have traditionally played a key role in recruitment or where job opportunities are most likely to be circulated among friends and relatives of those already employed. Where the workforce is already entirely or mainly white, the opportunities for black applicants to be selected, or even to hear of vacancies is therefore very low indeed. The CRE's formal investigation of Broomfields Ltd describes the effect of this practice.[11]

Reluctance by employers to react to indirectly discriminatory practices is widespread and is to some extent due to the very high levels of ignorance among managers of the existence or implications of the indirect discrimination provisions of the Race Relations Act. Evidence of employers' lack of awareness on this issue is constantly shown during discussions with individuals at conferences and training sessions and in correspondence with those requesting advice. This lack of understanding is aggravated by the low number of cases in which industrial tribunals have defined the circumstances in which criteria which disproportionately affect ethnic minorities are not justifiable. In addition to the high level of ignorance, many conditions and criteria which are potentially discriminatory are long established and extensively used across industries, often following lengthy trade union negotiations. The incentive to employers to examine their criteria for indirect discrimination and change them if they are found to be discriminatory is therefore extremely low.

The reasons for employers' reluctance or refusal to change their practices was summarised in a study carried out by the Institute of Personnel Management staff with the co-operation of the Community Relations Commission. The authors concluded that:[12]

> In the 22 organisations visited, a commonly encountered initial pronouncement was 'we have no racial problems here'. Further investigation often revealed that this opening statement could be given a different or extended interpretation. Sometimes it turned out to mean, 'we do have problems but we don't like talking about them', or 'we do have problems but we are ignoring them', or 'we have no problems because there is no protest', or 'we don't have problems but our black employees do' . . . It would be misleading to give the impression that all the managers consulted adopted such stances. In a substantial proportion of the organisations visited management was well aware that racial problems and discriminatory practices were occurring on the firm's premises. Some of the managers had concluded that it was impossible or inadvisable for them to take action but others were determined to curtail discriminatory practices in the company. However, the overwhelming impression gained during the visits to organisations was of a disturbing lack of awareness in the face of obvious discrimination or severe disadvantage.

There appears to be an important difference between the response of employers and the general public in the USA and those in the UK to race relations legislation. Experience suggests that British employers take the law less seriously than it is taken in the US and show considerable reluctance to accept responsibility for improving race relations and eliminating discrimination in employment.

The legislative differences and the resulting penalties are doubtless responsible in part for the difference in reactions. But it is argued here that two additional factors play an important part. First, employers in the UK seem to differ from those in the US in their response to employment legislation generally, perhaps because such legislation is more extensive in this country and they will therefore only take an active interest in that which appears to be the least easily avoided. Combined with the fact that the compensation payments awarded by industrial tribunals to victims of discrimination have often been negligible and that most complaints of discrimination are not upheld, this selectiveness places the 1976 Race Relations Act very low on the list of priorities. Second, ethnic minority groups in the UK are still regarded by many of the white public as immigrants who belong elsewhere and are not 'truly British'. This justifies in employers' minds their low allocation of resources to measures to eliminate discrimination and their reluctance to offend their white majority workforce by appearing to favour black employees. This attitude persists despite the existence of second and third generations of ethnic minority groups in the country, with even more longstanding populations in some areas.

The methods and objectives of promotional work

The first part of this paper stressed that discrimination occurs for a number of reasons and that employers' motives for not taking action can vary considerably. In addition, the low priority which many employers give to the legislation means that promotional work is particularly important if the results of industrial tribunal cases and formal investigations are to have full impact and influence, and, more generally, if discrimination is to be eradicated.

The existence of industrial tribunal cases and accounts of these in management and professional journals are often not in themselves adequate to persuade other employers that they need take action to avoid breaches of the law. Similarly, the completion of a formal investigation into a major company will not of itself persuade employers in the same industry or locality that they should also follow the recommendations made in the report to the subject of the investigation. Separate approaches are needed, in order to put pressure on other employers and advise on the adaptation of the recommendations to their particular circumstances. The results of industrial tribunal cases and investigations are also given wide publicity through the CRE's own channels, and incorporated in the training programmes for groups of employers and trade unionists carried out by the Commission's staff and by other groups. In these training sessions and individual discussions there is clear evidence that very many personnel managers have not thought it necessary to study the law in any detail, or to examine industrial tribunal cases and formal investigations and assess their implications for their own practices. Most important, they have clearly not been pressed to do so at Director or Board level and have not felt it essential in terms of justifying their own potential. The practice which exists in a number of American companies, by which managers' records of recruiting, promoting or otherwise treating minority group employees is a significant factor in their annual appraisal, is not only virtually unknown in the UK, but would also be met with incredulity by many managers.

Although the low compensation figures awarded by industrial tribunals mean that employers do not regard the risk of lack of action to avoid such cases as seriously as they might if the penalties were more severe, there are other factors which can influence them. Many employers find it damaging to their reputation if they are found to have discriminated, particularly if they are among the 'household names' in the country or have substantial interests in Third World countries. Industrial tribunal cases and formal investigations can also show that an employer's overall personnel or industrial relations practices are outdated, inefficient and unprofessional and this too can be damaging to the reputation. Promotional approaches therefore make full use of these arguments and examples in urging changes in practice. The promotional work carried out by the Commission is, however, more than an adjunct to law enforcement and has a more general role in tackling discrimination. A number of approaches have been developed in order to deal with the causes of discrimination and the absence of remedial action.

As has already been stressed, a great deal of discrimination cannot be accounted for simply in terms of genuine ignorance and misunderstanding. In most employing establishments discrimination is occurring because of all the factors described in the previous paragraphs, ignorance and misunderstanding being part of an overall pattern of apathy and low priority, prejudice and hostility. Where it exists, however, ignorance and misunderstanding can be met by information and educational approaches and if there is a will or an interest on the part of employers, change can be achieved in this way. Guidance papers have therefore been published on a variety of topics, including equal opportunity in employment, monitoring, religious observance by Muslim employees, and ethnic records.

The CRE's draft Code of Practice has consolidated many of the issues described in the guidance papers and provides detailed recommendations to employers, trade unions, individual employees and employment agencies on steps which should be taken to prevent discrimination and to promote equal opportunity at the workplace. A quarterly journal is also published, containing information on new examples of good practice and equal opportunity development and operation, trade union training and information programmes, projects to assist unemployed youth, the progress of formal investigations and industrial tribunal cases.

In addition, staff participate in or provide training sessions for groups of personnel managers or for key staff in individual organisations. One example is the two-day course provided by the Oxford University Department of External Studies with CRE co-operation which gives detailed training sessions for personnel and training managers, including case studies on discrimination, how it occurs, good management practice in terms of dealing with it, methods of informing and training employees in the development of an equal opportunity policy, and discussion of indirect discrimination and its various occurrences.

In these sessions emphasis is placed both on the legislation and on relating equal opportunities to good business or personnel practice. Out-dated selection criteria which adversely affect particular racial groups are unlawful if they cannot be shown to be justifiable. But in order to get this across to the personnel manager in terms of the professional need to change such criteria the wider implications of using these criteria can usefully be drawn on. One London borough, for example, recognised that its recruitment and selection procedures for apprentice entry were indirectly discriminatory – in that recruitment was largely confined to relatives and friends of existing craftsmen, all of whom were white. The procedures were changed so that vacancies were advertised and all suitable applicants interviewed and given a selection test which related to the requirements of the skills to be learnt. The new procedures resulted in a 30 per cent intake of black apprentices – but the effects were wider still. The quality of apprentices in this new intake was found to be considerably higher than in previous years and the youths demonstrated this by winning awards in their external training courses.

Stereotyped views of the abilities and characteristics of particular racial groups, and generalisations to this effect, are a major part of prejudice and lead to a considerable amount of discrimination – particularly in selection for employment. This area is one of the most difficult to tackle. In each selection decision there is inevitably an element of subjectivity, no matter how carefully the selection process is structured to the requirements of the job. Equally, if prejudiced views influence the assessment and the applicant is turned down for this reason, it may be very difficult to prove that discrimination has occurred unless the selector examines the views and admits to them. If a pattern can be shown, in which suitable Asian or West Indian applicants are invariably turned down, discrimination may be proved, but without such a pattern and with no other distinguishing factors, it is not easy to prove that the interviewers' 'feelings' that one person would be more suitable for the job than another are due to racial discrimination. The line between one manager's view 'that this individual did not seem to quite fit the needs of the job' and another manager's view that 'they just don't fit in' is a narrow one to distinguish if the reasons for rejection are not honestly stated.

Approaches have been developed which provide training in 'racism awareness' to deal with such prejudices and stereotyping, but these are not yet widely used in the United Kingdom. The concentration of promotional and advisory work has generally been on changing behaviour rather than attitudes on the grounds that, in the short term at least, this will produce the most immediate results.

The approach which emphasises changed behaviour requires the top management of the organisation to make clear to all employees that breaches of the Race Relations Act and of company policy will be treated as disciplinary offences, to develop a policy of information and training which ensures that company policy is carried out, and to *monitor* the effectiveness of the policy on a regular basis. This is the fundamental position of the CRE in its guidance papers and draft Code of Practice where detailed recommendations are to be found.[13]

Indirect pressures on employers

In addition to direct approaches to employers, a number of indirect approaches are also used. These include work with central, professional and industrial organisations such as the Confederation of British Industry, Institute of Personnel Management, and the Industrial Society in order to persuade them to put pressure on their own members to adopt policies and practices consistent with the CRE's recommendations. Work is similarly carried out with the Trades Union Congress and individual trade unions, both to encourage their members to negotiate and co-operate with equal opportunity policies at the workplace and to stimulate the development of educational and training programmes for trade union members in avoiding discrimination in their own industrial relations procedures, conditions of membership, negotiations etc. Comprehensive policy statements, in line with the CRE's recommendations have been adopted and published by several organisations, including the CBI, the TUC and the IPM. These three organisations also each have panels or committees which consider race relations issues on a regular basis and initiate policy development among members. The TUC has developed a race relations module in its basic shop stewards training course and a number of unions have developed their own race relations training or training particularly designed for shop stewards in particular racial groups where there are language or other special training needs.

As an essential part of its work, the CRE plays an important role in providing financial and practical assistance to ethnic minority and other groups so that their own approaches and campaigns can be strengthened and developed. Joint projects are often developed between the CRE and such groups. For example, a joint study of the employment and training needs of the Bengali population in the Tower Hamlets area of East London[14] led to the strengthening of a local training group and action by the Clothing Industry Training Board to encourage employers to change their practices. While this emphasis on the work of enabling and facilitating external groups and agencies to carry out promotional projects is increasing, it is not discussed here in detail.

The scope for positive action

Action to improve the opportunities of ethnic minority employees in occupations or grades in which they are significantly under-represented is allowed by sections 37 and 38 of the Race Relations Act. These sections allow employers to encourage only members of particular racial groups to apply for work, or to train employees to help fit them for particular work where they have been under-represented over the previous twelve months. Training groups can offer similarly selective training and encouragement, although many categories of training group are required to apply to the Department of Employment for 'designation' before this can be done. Trade unions and employers' associations can use parallel measures to increase membership and representation in full-time and lay posts within their organisations. In such cases, discrimination on grounds of race, colour etc is not allowed at the point of selection for work.

Despite the moderate nature of these provisions, and the clear need for such action in many occupations and job levels, very little use has been made of them by employers, training bodies and other groups. Where 'positive action' under these sections has been taken, it has most often been confined to encouragement to apply for work or membership, for example through advertisements in the ethnic minority press, approaches to black self-help and community groups, or emphasis on schools and state Job Centres in areas of high ethnic minority population. A very limited number of employers and training groups have provided training courses for existing employees to help fit them for promotion to supervisory or other higher grades and this has usually occurred where there has been the easily identifiable training need of language proficiency.

The reasons for the near total lack of action in this area have already been described in relation to the prevention of discrimination and provision of equal opportunity, but reaction against use of 'positive action' is even more pronounced. Whereas employers will reluctantly admit to the need for action to prevent discrimination against ethnic minority groups (while not necessarily accepting that such action is needed in their own organisations), selective encouragement and training is seen as discrimination *in their favour* and rejected for a number of reasons. These include fear of a backlash from white employees, lack of resources, low priority and failure to recognise that without positive action of this sort equal opportunity will not be achieved for many groups, and in many industries. This is an area in which only promotional approaches are possible under the current legislation.

Industrial tribunal and formal investigation reports can *recommend* positive action but cannot require it and progress is therefore dependent on persuasion and example. The last two years have seen significant improvement, in that several local authorities have adopted positive action programmes, a major employers' training group has instituted a training course for black potential managers, and a number of media training groups are setting up courses. These projects are being used as models to persuade others to follow suit and progress in this field is a major priority in the CRE's promotional work. Mention of the need for positive action in Lord Scarman's report[15] on the Brixton disorders in 1981 has promoted discussion on radio and television and among professional bodies, and this increase in interest is being exploited in efforts to increase take-up of this part of the Act. In addition, the CRE is currently reviewing the operation of the Race Relations Act and this is one area which is being given careful attention.

In addition to the specific provisions enabling 'positive action' to be taken by any employer, local authorities also have a duty under Section 71 of the Race Relations Act to carry out their various functions 'with due regard to the need to eliminate unlawful discrimination and to promote equality of opportunity and good race relations between persons of different racial groups' and therefore have a major role to play in promoting equal opportunities and eliminating discrimination. First, they are always a major employer in their locality – often *the* major employer, and their employment policies affect considerable numbers of employees. Similarly they have a role in influencing other employers locally both by providing models of good practice and encouraging others to follow suit, and by using the contracts they offer to suppliers of materials and services as a lever to encourage equal opportunity development in those organisations. Over 30 local authorities now have equal opportunity policy statements and a number of these state in their job advertisements that they are 'Equal Opportunity Employers'.

A smaller but significant number of local authorities now have fully developed equal opportunity policies which are monitored through analysis of the ethnic origin of job applicants and existing employees. Considerable emphasis has been laid on work with local authorities in order to develop examples of good practice and, in general, the existing comprehensive equal opportunity policies follow the basic principles of these recommendations, at least in intention. Staff have also participated in and advised on the development of training programmes to inform and guide local authority staff in the legislation and to develop awareness of the potential for discrimination in selection and other employment procedures. In these cases, local authority policies have been developed in close consultation with the local Community Relations Council and here CRE staff have generally been involved in joint approaches to the local authority in order to ensure a co-ordinated approach.

A number of local authorities have developed the concept of 'targets', as a means of ensuring that the process of equal opportunity development is related to the proportions of ethnic minorities in their population. Although under the Race Relations Act, quotas are illegal, some local authorities have used the comparison between the low percentage of black employees in their workforce with that in the local population as a base from which to urge that more black employees should be recruited to the organisation, as long as this can be done by legal means, and have adopted targets for this purpose.

A small number of local authorities have also adopted policies by which those firms which are given contracts to provide services and materials for local authority programmes are required to state or show that they are equal opportunity employers. Practice in this area is still at a very early stage of development but there is considerable scope for using such contracts as an effective lever in encouraging equal opportunity development at the local level.

The role of central government

The influence of central government on the commitment of employers and others to eliminate discrimination and provide equal opportunity in their organisation cannot be underestimated. Central government's influence has a number of different facets. First, it has the role of legislator and in this respect the Race Relations Act of 1976 represents in a narrow sense the extent to which government is prepared to support measures to eliminate discrimination. More important than this, however, is the extent to which government is prepared to demonstrate its commitment *in practical terms* to the concept of equal opportunity and thereby make clear to employers and others that compliance with the legislation is a serious requirement. Throughout its existence the CRE has constantly asked central government to show its unequivocal commitment to the legislation and to the general principles of equal opportunity through its public statements and its own actions. In particular, in the employment field, the government has been urged: to develop a full equal opportunity policy for its own employees, and to monitor this policy in order to assess its effectiveness; to review the existing race relations clause in government contracts and require compliance with the clause; and to approve a strong Code of Practice on race relations and employment – as drawn up by the CRE.

On the first point, despite strong representations from the CRE and others to the joint management/union Working Party set up to discuss Civil Service policy following the Tavistock study,[16] progress has been slow. In the autumn of 1981, a modest pilot survey of existing staff and applicants according to ethnic origin was announced to be carried out in one area in order to assess whether the exercise could be extended Service-wide. The survey was drawn up to cover only the main grades below the level of Executive Officer and did not therefore include the 'career grades'. This was partly due to resistance at that time to the recording of information on ethnic origin among the members of the trade union which represents higher grades of civil servants.[17] No such resistance has been shown by the trade union which represents those at the level below Executive Officer.

On the second point, the Home Office has made clear that there is no prospect of a review of the race relations clause in government contracts in the foreseeable future. On the third point, there has been no decision to date (October 1982) on the CRE's draft Code of Practice which was submitted to the Department of Employment ministers in December 1981. Before the Code can be brought into operation the Secretary of State's approval, followed by that of parliament, is required. If the Code is finally approved it will be admissible in evidence before industrial tribunals and they will take its recommendations into account when considering a question to which they are relevant.[18]

In addition to the representations made to central government by the CRE and by race relations and ethnic minority organisations, a number of reports have recently recommended action to improve equal opportunities in employment and stressed the urgent need for priority attention to be given to this. In his report on the Brixton disorders Lord Scarman made the following comments and recommendations:[19]

> What is required is a clear determination to enforce the existing law, and a positive effort by all in responsible positions to give a lead on the matter. Eliminating discrimination will undoubtedly take time. It would be disastrous, however, if there were to be any wider doubt than at present exists among the ethnic minorities about the will of Government, employers, trade union leaders and others in positions of authority to see this through. There are already signs among some black youths, despairing of an end to white discrimination, of a disturbing trend towards a total rejection of white society and the development of black separatist philosophies.

The House of Commons Home Affairs Select Committee's report on racial disadvantage made a number of recommendations to government on employment issues including the following:[20]

The [then] decision not to undertake ethnic monitoring in the Civil Service should be re-examined and training programmes for administrators reviewed; All employers should consider declaring themselves equal opportunity employers; Larger firms should give serious consideration to ethnic monitoring; Employers and employees should together work out the best means of eradicating discrimination; Indirect discrimination in apprentice intake should be given careful examination.

In the government's official response to the recommendations concerning the Civil Service the limited pilot monitoring exercise referred to above was announced. The already qualified recommendations to private employers were qualified still further:[21]

The Government believes that if equality of opportunity and treatment are to be achieved in the workplace it is essential that employers, unions and workers themselves set aside racial prejudice and preconceptions and develop a more constructive approach to working relationships. The Government agrees with the Committee that equal opportunity policies have a part to play in advancing this objective; with its recommendation that employers should consider making a declaration that they are equal opportunity employers; and with its view that for such declarations to have value they need to be backed up by action to give practical effect to them in the working situation.

The Committee has rightly pointed out – and it is important to emphasise – that such declarations do not imply discrimination in favour of ethnic minority workers (which would be unlawful under the Race Relations Act 1976) and that they will not lead to the imposition of racial quotas. The Government would strongly resist any pressure in that direction.

The evidence received by the Committee has shown a wide diversity of views among employers, trade unions and employees of the possible benefits to be gained from monitoring the ethnic origins of employees as a means of advancing equality of opportunity in employment. In the absence of a clear consensus within industry the Government considers that the right course is to leave it to individual firms to decide whether, when and in what form ethnic monitoring can, in their own particular circumstances, contribute to the advancement of racial equality and harmony. Small firms will often not have the administrative organisation or the resources to undertake systematic monitoring, although they may find it possible to assess the distribution of employees from personal knowledge and visual identification. For larger firms the administrative and cost implications could also be an important consideration. The Committee recognises this and foresees that the collection of statistics may need therefore to be limited to selected areas.

The need for full and active commitment from central government to the elimination of racial discrimination and the promotion of equal opportunities in employment is essential to the CRE's promotional work. Industrial tribunal cases, formal investigations and research studies show clearly that discrimination is occurring and provide examples for other employers of the effects of continued inaction and apathy on race relations issues. But if central government does not firmly counter the argument that racial discrimination is not, after all, such a major transgression and that the race relations legislation has a lower priority than other industrial or social laws, the incentive to avoid discriminating will continue to be absent. Although government may stress the importance of equal opportunity in its public statements and ministerial speeches, its own practices and policies will inevitably stand as a major example from which other employers, large and small, will take their lead. In discussion with private employers, for example, CRE staff have often been told 'the Civil Service doesn't have an equal opportunity policy or carry out comprehensive monitoring. Why should we?' Employers who have followed the draft Code of Practice through its stages of preparation and consultation have declared that they will adopt equal opportunity policies and monitor them *if* the Code is put into operation. Implicit in these statements is the acceptance (however reluctant) of the need to change policies and practices if government endorses this by approving the Code. In effect, such employers are taking the position that they will not take practical steps to avoid racial discrimination unless government encourages them to do so, despite the requirements of the Race Relations Act. In promoting equal opportunities in employment therefore, central government's role is crucial and its actions will inevitably speak louder than words.

Notes

1 David J. Smith, *The Facts of Racial Disadvantage*, PEP Report 560 (London: PEP, 1976).
2 N. McIntosh and David J. Smith, *The Extent of Racial Discrimination*, PEP Report 547, (London: PEP, 1974).
3 Jim Hubbock and Simon Carter, *Half a Chance?: A Report on Job Discrimination Against Young Blacks in Nottingham*, (Nottingham: CRE in association with Nottingham and District Community Relations Council, 1980).
4 *Looking for Work: Black and White School-leavers in Lewisham*, (London: CRE in association with Lewisham Council for Community Relations, 1981).
5 D.J. Smith, *Racial Disadvantage*, *op.cit.*, p. 67.
6 Gloria Lee and John Wrench, *In Search of a Skill: Ethnic Minority Youth and*

Apprenticeships, (Birmingham: CRE in association with Birmingham Community Relations Council, 1981).

7 *Mr Mark Musa Hussein v. 'Saints' Complete House Furnishers, Paradise St, Liverpool 1.*

8 *BL Cars Limited: Report of a Formal Investigation*, (London: CRE, 1981).

9 G. Lee and J. Wrench, *In Search of a Skill, op.cit.*

10 Tavistock Institute for Human Relations and Civil Service Department, *Application of Race Relations Policy in the Civil Service*, (London: HMSO, 1978).

11 *F. Broomfield Limited: Report of a Formal Investigation*, (London: CRE, 1980).

12 Keith Carby and Manab Thakur, *No Problems Here? Management and the Multi-racial Workforce*, (London: Institute of Personnel Management in co-operation with CRE, 1977).

13 *Draft Code of Practice for the Elimination of Racial Discrimination and the Promotion of Equality of Opportunity in Employment*, (London: CRE, 1982).

14 Patrick Duffy, *The Employment and Training Needs of the Bengali Community in Tower Hamlets*, (London: CRE and Manpower Services Commission, 1980).

15 *The Brixton Disorders, 10–12 April 1981: Report of an Inquiry by Rt. Hon. The Lord Scarman, OBE*, (London, HMSO, Cmnd 8427 1981).

16 *Application of Race Relations Policy in the Civil Service, op.cit.*

17 The SCPS Annual Conference in 1982 reversed this decision and monitoring is now accepted.

18 The House of Commons Employment Committee examined the draft Code in March 1982. They took evidence from the CRE, followed by small firms' organisations, several ethnic minority organisations and the Advisory, Conciliation and Arbitration Service (ACAS). They concluded on balance that recommendations such as those contained in the Code were necessary if employers were to progress on equal opportunity development and endorsed the principle of monitoring equal opportunity through statistical information. They recommended, however, that the Code should not apply in the first instance to firms employing less than 200 and that safeguards for information on ethnic origins of individuals should be guaranteed.

19 *The Brixton Disorders, op.cit.*

20 House of Commons, *Racial Disadvantage: Fifth Report from the Home Affairs Committee, Session 1980–81.* (London: HMSO, 1981).

21 *Racial Disadvantage: Government Reply to the Fifth Report from the Home Affairs Committee*, Cmnd. 8476, (London: HMSO, 1982).

10 Race and Housing in Britain: The Role of the Major Institutions
Valerie Karn

Housing policy and practice in both the United States and Britain have proved particularly resistant to equal opportunities legislation. In Britain, if there was ever a belief that such legislation could eradicate racial inequality in housing, the last decade has destroyed it. Even the Commission for Racial Equality acknowledges that it is one thing to put pressure upon an individual landlord or estate agent, it is quite another to grapple with the large and powerful institutions in the housing system – the local authorities and the building societies. In these institutions enquiries about the impact of policy and practice upon ethnic minorities are frustrated by the lack of monitoring of the outcomes of policies, rules and day-to-day decisions, the widespread use of discretion and the self-protective view of senior management that, if there is no specific policy to discriminate, no discrimination occurs. These features combined have constituted a massive resistance to the achievement of equal opportunity. In this chapter I hope to illustrate some of the mechanisms through which the major institutions in the housing system protect white privilege against black incursions.[1]

The reaction of most major institutions to discussions of the possibility of racial discrimination within them is that, if it exists at all, it must be the product of the behaviour of a few racially prejudiced individuals. Research has not supported this line of argument.[2] Its main weakness lies in the fact that it regards racial discrimination as the behavioural consequence of rigid, dogmatic, irrational thinking about race. While such a conceptualisation may help one to understand the activities of those associated with extreme right wing organisations such as the National Front, as David Wellman has shown,[3] it does not get us very far in explaining why those who do not share these extreme views frequently engage in racially discriminatory behaviour. Furthermore, the conceptualisation of racially discriminatory behaviour and practices as prejudice does not help us to understand how it is possible for resource distributing agencies to engage consistently in racially discriminatory allocations, in spite of changes in the particular individuals who perform allocation duties within those agencies. Nor does it help us to explain why, as research demonstrates,[4] authorities with very different procedures, some highly discretionary, others very structured, produce the same product in terms of allocations.

This chapter therefore adopts a rather different conceptualisation of racial discrimination, namely that it is 'culturally sanctioned, rational responses to struggles over scarce resources'.[5] As such, racial discrimination and its attendant justifications are products of the structural inequality which obtains in society as a whole. Racial discrimination can be understood as a mechanism to protect perceived race interests, just as class discrimination is a mechanism for protecting class interests. If, then, instead of discussing black disadvantage and racial discrimination, we turn the issue round and look at the mechanisms through which white advantage is maintained, it becomes apparent that it is not just white advantage but gender advantage, class advantage and the advantage of particular interest groups within broader classes that we have to consider. Or, to take it from the individual upwards, there is self-interest, family interest and the sort of indirect self- and family-interest which expresses itself in support for groups with which one identifies. Seen from this angle it is possible to explain behaviour which fairly systematically puts black people at a disadvantage, without postulating dislike of black people or irrational ideas about them. It is possible to see why an ethnic group may be considered a threat in one time and place when in another it is not.[6]

The question of the protection of interests becomes more complex when we move from the level of individual reaction (say, the reaction of a white tenant to the arrival of a black tenant on his estate) to the level of institutional decision-making. In housing departments and building societies, for instance, officers are making decisions not on their own behalf but on behalf of their organisation, within the rules set by that organisation. Yet people do not shed their class and ethnic origins or political attitudes when they come into an office. They are bound to continue to identify with some people more than others. How much play this sympathy is allowed to have depends on the boundaries imposed upon their job by institutional management, by the interests of the institution itself, and by professional ethics. In addition, personal, class and race interests derived from the outside society are, within institutions, overlaid by further sets of personal interests, notably those of the individuals in their roles as officers of the institution. To complicate matters the institution may have conflicting aims; in the case of building societies, for instance, giving a safe return to existing investors versus attracting new savers by an expressed willingness to lend easily; in the case of housing authorities, typically the need to minimise vacancies and at the same time to meet tenant preferences. Officers too, within the bounds of the discretion allowed them, may be torn between actions which would maximise their chances of internal promotion, make their name in the external world of their profession, give them the least trouble with the public or appear to be most morally defensible, make the most profit, or reduce risk on expenditure.

The officer in an institution therefore finds himself making decisions which are subject to a whole range of pressures whose optimal outcomes may or may not coincide. In these circumstances, even the most intense social pressures to preserve the advantageous position of whites is unlikely to produce an entirely consistent pattern of decisions. In particular, we would expect the ethos of the institution to have a very considerable impact. It should not be forgotten, however, that many institutional aims and rules are themselves very likely to favour dominant interests in society and are unlikely to be sacrificed in the interests of racial equality, unless this is made an explicit and strongly stressed aim of policy. As a result, explicit debate of race issues is likely to be impossible in many local authorities 'without transgressing the norms of discussion' in that authority.[7]

Race and the British housing system

The British housing market is now dominated by two tenures, home-ownership (54 per cent) and local authority renting (31 per cent). Of the other tenures, private renting is dwindling rapidly and does not now constitute a life-time tenure. Its role now tends to be as a provider of accommodation for single young people and for couples who are saving for home-ownership or waiting for an offer of housing by their local authority. The provision of non-council rental housing on a longer term basis is increasingly passing into the hands of the only other significant tenure, namely the housing associations (non-profits). This is especially true in the inner areas of those cities where West Indians and Asians are concentrated. In the sorts of housing associations which specialise in rehabilitating inner city property a very large proportion of the tenants are West Indian. At present little work has been done on housing associations and race, and so I do not consider them in this chapter. However, this is an increasingly glaring gap in our knowledge, the more so in that the growth of housing associations introduces another set of fairly large organisations into the housing market, with their own values, allocation priorities, and modes of operation. They are replacing a rental sector which is very different, being characterised, except in parts of London, by individual small landlords rather than large organisations.

The private rental sector

Private renting represents the sector of housing which is based most clearly on individual relationships. The experience of racial discrimination in this sector is therefore mainly of an encounter between two private individuals, though sometimes mediated by an estate agent. Apart from the inadequately enforced provisions of the Race Relations Act and landlord/tenant law, landlords do not have to be publicly accountable for their actions. At the same time, as private individuals, they may be particularly likely to come under pressure from other tenants and neighbours to discriminate. These may be some of the reasons why private landlords and agents dealing with private landlords have, according to research findings, had a poor record on racial discrimination. In 1966–7, before housing was included in Britain's anti-discrimination legislation, PEP carried out a series of tests in which a West Indian, a Hungarian and a white tester applied in person and by telephone for rented accommodaton which had been advertised. They excluded advertisements which specified 'no coloureds'. In the telephone tests West Indians faced discrimination in 62 per cent of cases and in the personal tests in 75 per cent of cases.[8] In 1973, telephone tests were repeated, this time including Asian testers as well. In these tests 27 per cent of West Indians and Asians experienced discrimination.[9]

The fact that the private rental sector is run by a very large number of individuals means not only that some of these will discriminate but also that some will be favourably disposed to minorities. This, of course, is likely to be the case if the landlords themselves are members of an ethnic minority. The importance of this point is brought out by Smith in the 1974 PEP study when he demonstrates that members of minority groups tend to adopt strategies that avoid their being exposed to discrimination.[10] In the private rented sector this means that many apply only to landlords who are known not to discriminate, which frequently means having a landlord from one's own ethnic group. This behaviour is not necessarily with the specific intention of avoiding discrimination. It is most common amongst Asians with poor fluency in English and amongst the lower socio-economic groups whose dependence on their own community is strongest. But perhaps the most discouraging feature of the experience of discrimination in the private rental sector is that it is felt most acutely when members of minority groups try to move upmarket and in doing so have to move outside their own community to seek rented accommodation. Especially if their English is poor they are very likely to experience discrimination. As Smith says, 'in this way their confinement within their own communities is justified and reinforced'.[11] This in turn reinforces the view of the white population that ethnic minorities are very unwilling to move away from their own community areas.

In many ways the private rented sector is the one for which the Race Relations Acts are most suited. The identification of direct racial discrimination in private renting, though not easy, has nothing like the complications involved in addressing discrimination in council allocations or building society lending. Since there are not bureaucratic rules of allocation, the thorny issues of what constitutes 'indirect' discrimination and whether or not it can be legally defended on grounds of justification do not arise. The two PEP studies suggest that the legislation has substantially reduced levels of discrimination in this sector. Nevertheless, it is clear that the major 'solution' to the problem has not come from legislation or the white community changing its attitudes but from avoidance strategies by the minority groups, notably the use of landlords from their own community, and a movement into owner-occupation and council renting. The first two strategies, which have been particularly adopted by Asians, have resulted in the creation of sub-markets in the private rental and owner-occupied sectors dominated by Asian landlords and Asian home-owners respectively.

Local authority housing administration differs from private renting in the nature of the landlord/tenant relationship and in the accountability of local authorities both to a local electorate via elected members and to central government. Local authorities have a legal responsibility for providing rented housing for those in need and usually formulate rules upon which allocations have to be made. The building societies (which are comparable to savings and loan associations in the USA) can be seen as midway between the two. They are institutions, not individuals, but they are not as publicly accountable as local authorities. Building societies are accountable, and then in a limited way only, to their members and to the Registrar of Friendly Societies. They have no legal responsibility to provide loans in any one area or to emphasise the needs of poorer buyers. Yet because of their origins and their formal charitable non-profit status, plus the tax concessions they receive, building societies do profess a degree of social responsibility. Do these distinctions between the types of organisation have any real effect on their mode of operation in the housing market and in particular on their approach to ethnic minorities? Or are there basic similarities between these housing institutions which modify or override these distinctions? To examine these questions I propose to look first at local authority housing allocation processes and then to compare these with the allocation of mortgages by building societies.

Local authority housing

Local authority (public) housing accounts for about 30 per cent of all housing in Britain and 65 per cent of the rental stock. Within this very large housing stock, developed over more than sixty years, there are, of course, huge variations in quality and in popularity. Popularity relates to a large number of variables: the age of the stock, its location, its type (flats versus houses), its size and its physical and social environment and amenities. In every housing authority some estates and some types of property are the subject of fierce competition, while others are difficult to let. The allocation system has to find some way of judging between applicants, on a justifiable basis. The allocation process is, by its very nature, one of discrimination between one applicant and another, or one class of applicants and another, in the distribution of a scarce resource of good council housing. The formal allocation system of points for housing need or a date order queue can provide only general guidance and is, in any case, only one of the factors which determine the nature of allocations.

Other variables tend to be introduced into the allocation process to help to differentiate between applicants or even to disqualify some competitors completely. Some of these rules are the subject of official council policy. They are typically the exclusion or differential treatment of groups who are regarded as less in need of housing (commonly, for example, single people and ex-owner occupiers) or of those who are regarded as being less deserving of priority (again, commonly new arrivals to the district and those judged to have poor housekeeping standards or such groups as unmarried co-habitees). At the officer level, judgements of the applicant's 'worth' and 'respectability' are also brought in, both as factors in their own right and in combination with judgements about the applicant's acceptability to other tenants. Officers tend to ask about a good property, 'What sort of applicant deserves the property?' and about a bad property, 'What sort of applicant would accept it?' As Niner says, 'It is normal practice, if a "very good" standard applicant and a "less good" one are competing for a very good vacancy, to allocate the property to the higher standard applicant. Such a policy is seen to enhance estate management'.[12]

But tenant 'suitability' is only one of the factors which ultimately enter the allocation process. Housing officers have to weigh up a series of conflicting aims of the housing department and have to exercise discretion as to which of these aims they should pursue in each individual case. The aims of allocation processes include: prompt letting of properties in order to avoid rent losses and vandalism and to rehouse people rapidly; meeting people's preferences for properties and areas so far as possible; avoiding subsequent management problems arising from tenant complaints or rows between neighbours; observing the allocation rules (points system) concerning the priority to be given to various types of applicant and discouraging 'queue jumping'; avoiding wasteful expenditure of management time and staff resources; preserving the physical quality of the stock.

Let us take an example of such conflicting aims. Say, for instance, a two-bedroomed flat on an unpopular estate is to be let in an authority which operates a points system. If the allocation officer observes the points system strictly he will allocate this property to the person with the most points at the top of the two-bedroom queue. However, if the area is particularly unpopular, a family with high points and hence high priority for housing is likely to refuse it. To offer it to this person therefore entails a waste of time and staff resources, prevents prompt letting, and runs counter to the aim of meeting preferences. In practice, because of the overriding importance of rapid lettings, what is likely to happen is that an allocation officer offers this property to someone he thinks is likely to accept. This is likely to be someone who is desperate for somewhere to live, a homeless person for instance, or one who has not accumulated sufficient points for an early allocation of good property. Alternatively, the property may be offered to someone who is expected not to mind living in that area or to deserve no better. This is where ideas and stereotypes about different groups come into operation.

Where there are conflicting aims of this type, officers tend not to notice that the degree to which they emphasise particular criteria or institutional priorities varies from case to case. In effect, allocations then become a very discretionary exercise even when the system is described to the public as 'computerised'. All that the computer does is store the data upon which decisions are based. In addition, even in departments with computerised allocations, considerable information is kept about applicants in personal files and this too is available to those involved in the allocation process. An initial decision to allocate a property may be reversed when the applicant's personal file is inspected. These discretionary allocation processes are random neither in the criteria they use nor in their outcome. Combined with the tendency of the 'respectable' to refuse poor properties or poor areas, they tend to result in the letting of the worst estates to desperate applicants, 'potentially difficult' tenants or those whom other 'respectable' tenants would not welcome, and in the best property or estates being offered as a reward to the respectable. The end result of the whole series of decisions is that public housing allocations take on a pattern which is far less egalitarian than either the professed aim of council housing or the publicly stated allocation rules would lead us to expect.

So one of the crucial distinctions for housing officers is that between the 'respectable' and 'disreputable' working class or the 'deserving' and 'undeserving'.[13] People's life-styles offer bureaucracies certain cues or codes through which they can be classified as 'respectable' or 'disreputable'. The most important cue is probably family structure, for instance, being a single parent family, an unmarried couple or a very large family. Other cues are unemployment and more specific factors such as housekeeping standard, quality of furniture and rent paying record.[14] In using these cues an officer is, in effect, classifying an applicant or tenant along a disreputable/respectable dimension. The importance of the cues lies in the meaning attached to them; not the meaning of each individual one but rather the composite picture of applicants which housing departments and officers derive from a combination of cues.

How, then, does race fit into this picture? Given the use of 'respectability' as the key to access to the best housing, race is one of the 'cues' by which housing managers assess this respectability. Rex and Tomlinson quote a Birmingham housing visitor who unconsciously demonstrates the way in which race triggers attitudes similar to those held about the 'disreputable' white working class:[15]

> We can't hide the fact that people have different standards of housekeeping. We don't want to offend people. We try to put people in neighbourhoods where they won't conflict. After all, some of the Asians may be just getting out of the stage where they made curry patties on the floor. It's like the English working class – they kept coal in the hall and donkeys in the kitchen when some of them were put in council houses in the twenties. It takes education to raise standards.

The significance of 'respectability' measures, including 'race', in the allocation process is that they facilitate the rationing of a scarce resource of unequal quality. Housing officers are currently trapped into running an inadequate service with the result that even the most liberal adopt coping strategies that unconsciously reflect the priority given to white 'respectable' interests. It is useful to the housing service to adopt a practice of separating the interests of the respectable from those of the disreputable. By this means it can cope with shortage, not by expanding or improving the service but by rationing it. This happens at all levels, through both rules and discretionary decisions. For the individual officer the adoption of these criteria enables him to justify to himself or others what otherwise must appear arbitrary and often harsh decisions. Without such rationalisations the job would probably be intolerable. So officers, and indeed councillors, categorise and stereotype in the cause of 'occupational survival'.[16] If one can assure oneself that single parent families prefer flats, then it usefully disguises the fact that a family with children has been housed in high-rise. Or if an Asian is allocated a run-down pre-1919 terraced house, it is useful to believe that Asians prefer these sorts of inner city properties. These attitudes have some elements of truth which make it possible to justify them, but in the process half-truths are inflated into whole truths and stereotypes produced.

Measures of respectability have the added advantage as criteria for rationing scarce resources that they are publicly supported. They are drawn in fact from views held by the majority of the public, who believe that the disreputable should change their ways before they are helped. Class discrimination and, via the same process, race and gender discrimination, are then an integral part of what is regarded as good housing management practice. They meet the interests of the majority of tenants and the requirements of management.

I will now outline very briefly certain features of allocations which show how race and respectability classifications become introduced into and intermingled with the allocation process, either formally or informally. There have been a number of studies of public sector housing and race,[17] which have had broadly similar findings, namely that racial minorities are disadvantaged in three respects. First, they have had more difficulty in gaining access to any council housing at all; second, they have often received worse quality property, particularly older flats; third, they have become concentrated on certain estates, usually those of the poorest quality in inner areas of cities. At the same time that these studies have identified unequal outcomes for ethnic minorities, they have found that certain social groups, notably large families and one parent families also tend to receive inferior treatment. In addition they have pointed out that the worst allocations are made to those applicants in whom the 'disreputable' class and race codes coincide.[18]

What are the mechanisms through which these outcomes are produced? Very broadly, there are three ways in which the 'respectable' and 'disreputable' are differentially treated in the allocation process. The first is that some 'respectable' families receive abnormally good treatment, sometimes according to rules which reward 'good behaviour', sometimes by discretionary decisions which are actually in breach of the rules. The latter type may take a variety of forms. For instance, 'respectable' homeless families may be allocated brand new flats, while properties normally reserved for the homeless are ignored. Similarly, in authorities which will not accept ex-owner occupiers on their waiting lists, some white owner-occupiers may be allowed to enter council housing via the waiting list, while no Asians and West Indians are permitted to do so.[19] Finally, 'respectable' families may be given additional help by interviewers, visitors, and so on, in obtaining an offer of housing.

The second type of differential treatment is abnormally bad treatment for 'disreputable' families, again either through rules or discretion. I will give two instances of this approach to allocation. The first is the use of formal grading of housekeeping standards to assess suitability for a good property. Studies have revealed extremely strong relationships between low grading and size of family. Large families tend to receive very low grades and so do families moving out of slum clearance. Low grades have also very frequently been given to ethnic minorities, particularly Asians.[20]

Grading is very important because there is a strong correlation between grading and the quality of accommodation allocated, but racial differences emerge here too. In one study is was found that amongst white tenants the highest graded were the most likely to get the age of property for which they were graded, whilst the lowest graded often received newer property than that for which they were graded 'suitable'.[21] Amongst West Indians, however, the lowest graded were much less likely to be given newer property and were twice as likely as whites to be given pre-1919 acquired property. But it was Asians who showed the most remarkable difference, because they were likely to be allocated pre-1919 property whatever their grading. So they suffered even more than West Indians, both by being given low grades in the first place and then by being given property older than that for which they were graded. The same study found that when the formal grading system was dropped there was little change in the character of allocations to the types of households that received low gradings before. This was probably because 'cues' such as family size, race and origins in a clearance area which contributed heavily to the construction of the gradings continued to be easily identifiable. Here we have a clear example where the presence or absence of an explicit policy or practice may be irrelevant to the outcome, given a philosophy behind allocations which consistently produces the same effect through informal decisions.

Besides the suitability grading system, there are other mechanisms through which 'disreputable' applicants are filtered to 'suitable' vacancies. Even where allocations are initially identified from computerised data, it is usually possible for an allocation to be 'blocked' when the information in the applicant or tenant's file is checked. This information normally includes comments by visitors, the rent paying record, the state of decoration of the property, a record of the applicant's contact with the department, reasons for the refusal or withdrawal of previous offers, plus letters from outside organisations, such as social workers, councillors or other tenants. The file therefore gives a much more complete picture of the 'respectability' of the family, on which the type of allocation to be made can be based. In any allocation system these data are normally checked before an offer of housing is made.

In all this, race is also likely to be a factor. Area officers are generally acutely conscious of the pressure on them from the public, and many white tenants are very resistant to having black people moved to their street. It has been all too easy to adopt a policy of avoiding trouble by allocating blacks elsewhere. This has seemed all the more justifiable because white opposition to black tenants on council estates has not remained at the level of complaints to housing officers or councillors. Violent harassment of Asian tenants in particular has surfaced as a major problem.[22]

The third way in which 'race' and 'respectability' influence allocations is through the stereotyping of people's preferences and expectations. The dominant day-to-day activity of a housing department is not finding houses for people but ensuring that properties are let promptly. Empty properties mean lost rent revenue, vandalism, complaints from neighbours and no one housed, so it is in no one's interest that they stand vacant. However, the need to let property promptly leads to officers having to make judgements about the likelihood of property being accepted and these judgements inevitably involve stereotypes about the areas and types of property different groups will take. As a result, it appears that Asians, West Indians and whites are most likely to have their estate preferences matched with an allocation if they request an area which is usually popular with their own group[23].

Despite housing authorities' statements about wanting racial mix, and despite some adopting 'dispersal' policies, the tendency has been for allocations to concentrate racial groups even more than their preference would have predicted.[24] Clearly there is a dilemma for such authorities. White tenants almost invariably want suburban allocations. Most West Indians and Asians still opt for the inner areas but a growing minority are now wanting suburbia. If black tenants also want suburbia, how are the inner city properties to be let? In spite of the talk about dispersal, it is clearly in the day-to-day interests of both management and white applicants that West Indians and Asians should retain their demand for the inner city, despite the costs that the latter will pay for this in terms of poorer quality of dwellings. Though not officially recognised, current allocation practice thwarts rather than encourages the tendency of a minority of Asians and West Indians to move to white estates. One of the ways in which this happens is through limited discussion of alternatives. Many housing visitors have communication problems with Asians. With other applicants, visitors usually discuss the areas that they have applied for and suggest other estates on which they might have a greater opportunity of an allocation. With Asians this type of negotiation seldom occurs and, partly as a result, they name a very much more restricted range of estates, often in the inner city. These areas are not popular with white applicants who it is assumed will reject them. Indeed, the current preference of Asians and West Indians for inner city property is very useful to authorities facing a massive suburban movement by whites.[25]

These are, then, some examples of the ways in which a variety of (often conflicting) management aims interact with generally shared attitudes about race, class, gender and desert, to produce an unequal distribution of council housing between white and black, and between 'respectable' and 'disreputable'. Though the geographical segregation and poor housing conditions experienced by West Indians and Asians and the poorest white families are much more acute in the private than in the public sector, the potential of a large publicly owned housing stock for achieving greater equality of opportunity is not being realised.

To sum up then, our examination of the actual operation of housing departments has shown how central judgements of 'respectability' are to their allocation processes even when allocations are officially based on a points system of 'housing need'. We have traced how class and race attitudes in the wider society become invested with official or semi-official status as they are absorbed into the housing authority's rationing processes, both of a formal and an informal nature. In fact, as in the case of the discontinued 'suitability' gradings there is really no distinction between formal and informal practices. In addition, it is virtually impossible to disentangle decisions made on the basis of racial categories and stereotypes from those based on class and gender.

While these allocation processes run counter to the interests of Asians, West Indians and to some extent those of 'disreputable' whites, the principles on which they are based receive wide public support. Moreover, even if the 'respectable' are offered a representative range of estates and properties on a random basis, they reject the worst and wait for a better offer, or opt out of the public sector altogether. Here we see a major dilemma. In egalitarian terms we need to run council housing in the interests of those for whom the private sector provides least well. Yet moves in this direction would make council housing less attractive to the better-off working class, would lead to their leaving and would make council housing even more a 'welfare' tenure, with all the problems of a stigmatised service with intensified segregation of the poorest. This is the route that American public housing took, to its ultimate ruin.

Home-ownership, race and the role of the building societies

Our examination of the ways in which building societies relate to race must of necessity be more superficial than the section on local authorities for the good reason that no building society has allowed researchers to examine its operations. Severely though one may fault the local authorities' reception of criticisms, it is also true that a considerable number of them have opened up their files to independent examination. In the building society field, lack of this type of direct research material forces us to rely on four types of evidence. The first is situation testing by PEP. The second is evidence from interviews with officers of building societies and with estate agents. The third is survey evidence of the incidence of building society lending and applications. The fourth is material on building society management unrelated to the race issue.

In the same PEP studies in which discrimination in the private rental sector was examined, situation testing was carried out on home-owners' contacts with estate agents. It was found that in contacts with estate agents about house purchase West Indians were discriminated against in 64 per cent of the tests.[26] In a third of these discriminatory situations, it was the availability of mortgages which was the subject of the discrimination. In another third there was 'steering', that is, a different list of addresses of properties for sale was offered to the West Indians. A repeat of the tests in 1973, after the 1968 Race Relations Act had been in force five years, showed a marked drop in this type of discriminatory behaviour by agents.[27] In 1973, in 12 per cent of cases the West Indian or Asian testers were given inferior treatment and a further 17 per cent were given different treatment. So, as with similar results in the US, it was found in 1973 that discrimination by agents about house purchase appeared to be less than for renting. However, the procedures for buying a house are long and complex and only the initial stages of the transaction were being tested, namely approaches to an agent. Most important, situation testing has not been carried out on building societies. To know the true level of discrimination one would have to add on to initial agent behaviour any subsequent discriminatory acts which occur in the process of buying. There are so many opportunities; the valuation (appraisal) of the property, the terms of the loan offered, the priority in the mortgage queue, the requirement of savings with the building society and so on. We are still far from knowing the full impact of lenders' attitudes towards black buyers and black areas, but we are accumulating more and more evidence that leads us to question whether black buyers and black areas of cities receive equal treatment from building societies.

A number of studies have included interviews with building society managers and surveyors and from these have drawn the conclusion that building society managers typically have doubts about the soundness of investing in black areas.[28] There are also very big differences in the sources of finance for house-purchase between the general population of owners, and West Indians and Asians.[29] Amongst a national sample of owners in 1973, 73 per cent of whites with outstanding mortgages had borrowed from a building society, as compared with 51 per cent of West Indians and 43 per cent of Asians. The problem about interpreting national data is that one is not comparing like with like. Building societies are known to lend less willingly on older property in inner areas, yet this is precisely where most Asians and West Indians have bought. To isolate a 'race' effect, one therefore has to look at white and black buyers in inner cities. My own evidence for householders who bought in inner Birmingham in the periods 1972–4 and 1975–9 is striking.[30] Very few Pakistani or Indian buyers had a building society mortgage, though more Indians had them in 1975–9 (14 per cent) than in 1972–4 (5 per cent). In comparison, 36 per cent of white and 46 per cent of West Indian buyers had building society mortgages. These figures, though telling, still did not demonstrate racial discrimination against Asians because they were on the whole buying older cheaper housing than either whites or West Indians. Moreover, one needs to know how many of the Asians had actually applied for a building society mortgage and been refused. Analysis of applications to building societies by the buyers in 1975–9 showed that Indians and West Indians had particularly high refusal rates, 53 per cent and 51 per cent respectively, as compared with 39 per cent for the whites.[31] It was also found that white buyers tended to receive more help from solicitors and estate agents while black buyers normally obtained building society loans only if they were fully qualified in terms of savings.

Further evidence on the incidence of mortgages in white and black areas of inner cities and the patterns of borrowing among Asians, West Indians and whites, comes from Leeds, where three pairs of areas were selected for study, two in the innermost area, two in the middle ring of the inner city and two on the outer edge of the inner city.[32] In each pair, there was one white area and one mixed. A survey of buyers in these areas gave the following findings. Excluding the innermost areas, where there were no building society loans, only 76 per cent of the black buyers in racially mixed areas obtained a building society mortgage, compared with 88 per cent of white buyers in racially mixed areas and 85 per cent of white buyers in white areas.[33] Since building societies say they require people to save with them as a condition of lending, the possibility was explored that this was the crucial factor. It emerged that lack of savings was not the determining factor. On the contrary, the treatment of applicants without building society savings turned out to be yet another area of differential treatment; taking only those buyers without building society savings, 45 per cent of white buyers obtained loans from a building society compared with only 25 per cent of black buyers. Of those with building society savings, 81 per cent of whites and 78 per cent of blacks obtained a building society mortgage. So despite building societies' frequent statements that they cannot lend to non-savers, it appears, as in the Birmingham study, that black buyers are expected to meet these savings requirements in full, while white buyers are frequently given more lenient consideration. This is a repetition of the sort of 'positive discrimination' in favour of whites that we already experienced in the public sector.

The authors of the Leeds report also found that black buyers with savings were less likely to obtain a loan from their own building society; 33 per cent of black building society savers had had to approach a different society from the one they saved with, as compared with only 19 per cent of white savers. In general they had had much greater problems in obtaining their loan. The authors of the Leeds report conclude that:[34]

> Far from presenting an explanation of differential lending, an examination of the presence or absence of savings reveals yet another aspect of the differential treatment of white and mixed areas and of black and white buyers. In particular it exemplifies the very important point that discrimination is likely to take place at building society branch office level, where decisions are made with the manager exercising his discretion and where rules can be interpreted either favourably or unfavourably. In this study it is possible to see a pattern emerging in which white non-savers were more likely to have the rules interpreted in their favour. However, when an individual black buyer is told he cannot apply for a loan because he has no savings with that particular building society, it is impossible for him to make a case that racial discrimination has occurred since this is stated to be a general rule applied by building societies.

One of the explanations of the more favourable treatment of white buyers appears to be that they receive more help from estate agents and solicitors in obtaining building society loans. This in itself requires examination, as the PEP evidence about discrimination by agents indicated. But the racial bias of agents is not the total explanation. Several studies including that in Leeds, have shown that black buyers, and indeed all buyers in racially mixed areas, tend to be refused loans more frequently, even when they are referred by the local authority through the special Support Lending Scheme designed to help buyers of inner city properties.[35]

Another explanation given for low levels of lending in black areas is that the property tends to be given a low valuation by surveyors.[36] The Birmingham studies found low valuations particularly associated with West Indian buyers who were moving up-market a little.[37] However, it is not possible to separate the attitudes of surveyors from those of building societies.[38] Nor is there uniformity in the attitudes of different surveyors, different building societies or, more pertinently, different branches of the same building society towards any one buyer of any one property in a racially mixed or inner city area.

Building societies themselves frequently maintain that their poor lending record in inner cities is because people do not apply for mortgages. It is certainly the case that many people and especially Asians fail to apply but it is also clear that the lack of success experienced by many applicants to building societies not only has an effect on their own subsequent behaviour but also creates a more general expectation of failure amongst purchasers in inner cities. Given the fact that there are close informal contacts between low-income buyers within ethnic communities, it is not surprising that news of this type spreads rapidly and that low expectations of building societies become common knowledge.

The building societies therefore themselves help to create the climate in which people fail to apply for their mortgages. This is produced not only by the actual refusal but also by the manner of that refusal to many applicants. The reasons given often seem little more than excuses not to lend. The impression remains that building societies are very unenthusiastic about inner city lending and have plenty of business elsewhere to absorb their available funds. So applicants are given convenient reasons for a refusal. If they are non-savers they are told they have to save for two years. If they are savers their refusal has to be on grounds of age and condition of the property or that the price is too high. Without the expert help and special pressure that solicitors and estate agents are able to bring to bear upon building societies, individual buyers can only accept these refusals at face value.

In addition to the adverse effect that the failure to lend has upon the market and values in minority areas of the inner city, there is a very strong inference that this failure, coupled with a willingness of the banks to give short-term loans, is increasing racial segregation. This happens as follows. Most whites and West Indians will not buy at all if no conventional length mortgage is available. They, perfectly legitimately, do not want to take the risk, or make the extreme sacrifices in other aspects of their living standards, that high monthly payments on short-term loans imply. So, faced with refusals from conventional mortgage lenders they will either, if they can afford it, buy in a suburban area where mortgages are more readily available or they will rent instead. The results of this are that there will be a concentration in inner city areas of those people who are willing to take out short-term loans in order to buy in the inner city. Because West Indians and whites are less likely to consider short-term loans, it appears that lack of conventional lending is a factor in producing the very marked concentrations of Asian buyers in inner areas of, say, Birmingham. In some parts of that city they now constitute four-fifths of all the buyers.

As in the analysis of local authority responses to black and 'disreputable' tenants, it is possible to classify building society discriminatory treatment into three types: abnormally bad treatment of black buyers and black areas; abnormally good treatment of white buyers and white areas; and stereotyping of minorities' and indeed white buyers' preferences. In the category of abnormally bad treatment come the high refusal rates for black applicants and for sales in the black areas. White privilege is reflected in the willingness to lend to white non-savers, against the publicised criteria of the societies, and this is compounded by the greater help afforded to whites by solicitors and estate agents. The stereotyping of preferences sustains the expectation that Asians and West Indians will only want to buy in areas where their community is concentrated, and that no whites will want to buy there or remain living there. These stereotypes magnify half-truths into whole truths and lead building societies to believe that there will be 'no demand' for housing in certain parts of the inner city. This in turn leads to an expectation of falling values and hence a reluctance to invest in property there. The prophecy is likely to be self-fulfilling if potential demand is stifled by lack of mortgages.

The problems that black buyers have in obtaining loans parallel the type of discrimination which occurs in local authority allocations. As with the public sector, the process of discrimination against areas and against ethnic groups arises at the level of day-to-day, informal decisions. This allows the building societies to believe that because there may be no overt intention to discriminate, no discrimination exists. It also means that it is very difficult for black buyers and for the Commission for Racial Equality to prove discrimination against any one individual. The building societies continue to maintain that 'every case is taken on its merits', yet there is a consistency about the views held by exchange professionals, including building society managers, concerning what constitutes a 'bad risk', which means that 'every case on its merits' is a misnomer for what actually occurs.[39] There is, then, a clear need for much greater fairness, accountability and openness on the part of building societies, estate agents and solicitors about the processes through which building society mortgages are obtained and housing secured.

Conclusions

The evidence discussed in the previous sections of this chapter indicates important parallels in the ways in which the major institutions in the British housing system handle their allocation processes. Both local authorities and building societies have a scarce resource to allocate and a professional interest in maintaining demand for their product; both seek to manage this demand by means of rationing. The allocation process in both sectors is characterised by widespread discretionary activity, in the building societies at branch office level. The 'centre' tends in both cases to deny the existence of this, except in a positive sense of being able to show flexibility to applicants. Moreover, there is in both cases a failure by the 'central office' to monitor the activities of the 'branches'. This is not just inefficient management. It has a positive function in that it enables the 'liberal' position voiced by the centre to remain unexplored empirically and actual practices to remain unchanged.

Housing managers and building society branch managers tend to be technically trained rather than professionally educated. Their 'professions' have not up to now had any strong 'social' element in their training. So their ideas about race, class, gender, and so on tend to be 'common-sense' ones shared by other white, middle class males. They therefore include strong elements of racial (as well as class and gender) stereotyping. Both employ few, if any, black people in positions of real power.

Just as the ideal letting is one that gives no further trouble, the ideal loan is one that involves no risk of default. Higher management does not reward risk-taking in these respects, but it does punish failure. There is as a result a tendency in branch managers and housing officers to seek to identify in advance and avoid those applicants who are likely to produce trouble. In doing this, whole groups become labelled as problematic. In building societies areas of cities are also involved. In both building society and local authority decisions race and class attitudes are indissolubly linked with what is seen simply as prudent management.

Because neither a local authority nor a building society is centrally concerned, as for instance banks are, with maximising profit, if an activity is troublesome it will be avoided rather than exploited at a higher cost to the recipient. For instance, despite demand, local authorities avoid running furnished lettings. Similarly, building societies avoid inner cities rather than, say, charging higher interest for lending there.

Both institutions are centrally concerned with the maintenance of the condition and value of the housing stock within their area of activity. This emphasis leads to harder attitudes towards consumers who may be expected to damage the condition of the property or undermine the status or value of the area. Both are paternalistic in their approach to consumers. Both have an image of the ideal consumer, the steady, reliable good payer. Both tend to talk about 'standards having dropped' in this respect.

Though neither building societies nor local authorities are private market institutions, they operate within a private financial market. As a result the activities of both are, at the end of the day, determined by economic considerations. This is particularly obvious at the moment when local authority housing expenditure is being made a prime target for public expenditure cuts as part of government's economic strategy. In practical, day-to-day terms these pressures emerge in the emphasis by local authority officers on letting property rapidly and in the deterioration of the worst estates, those allocated to the 'undeserving poor'. In the building societies, economic pressures emerge in the fact that the branch manager has to concentrate on attracting investors, particularly via solicitors and estate agents.

The contrasts between the two sectors, while real, are less significant. Building societies' allocation criteria are far less overt and clearly defined than those of the public sector and it is probable that discretion plays a greater part than in local authorities. The crucial symbiotic relationship with solicitors and estate agents has no equivalent on the local authority side and makes it particularly difficult to identify the stage at which discrimination occurs.

Local authority housing departments are clearly housing institutions, but building societies regard themselves as being savings institutions first and foremost. Their housing function is subordinate to the interests of savers. In this building societies have clearly moved away from their origins, when they were founded precisely to provide housing and when investors and borrowers were the same people. The allegiance of building societies to suburban lending is closely related to the dominance of the suburbs as a source of investors. Similarly, the role of solicitors and agents in assisting applicants relates directly to their role as producers of investment funds. Building societies themselves have no obligation to lend. They also accept no responsibility for the fate of those applicants and those areas which they neglect. There are therefore no 'costs' imposed on them for their cautious approach to risk.

Local authorities tend to reap the ill-effects of their own actions, including management problems on 'sink' estates, tenant hostility and rising rates of homelessness. The fact that a local authority is accountable to the local electorate probably both intensifies the pressure on it to meet the interests of the white majority, and also restrains the degree to which minority interests can be neglected.

It appears, then, that the similarities between these two major sets of housing institutions are more numerous and more telling than the contrasts. In addition the common features that they exhibit help to explain how it is that both recreate a pattern of white privilege out of innumerable, small, day-to-day decisions. In both cases the decisions are part of mainstream management practice, not some aberration. As Townsend says: 'The housing market must be perceived as an institution which is doing far more than mediating housing supply and demand. It reproduces and indeed creates inequality within society.[40]

Notes

1 This chapter, especially the discussion of local authority housing, draws substantially upon ideas developed by Jeff Henderson, Bill Brown and myself in the course of our research. (See J. Henderson, V. Karn and W. Brown, 'Improving the Opportunities of Ethnic Minorities in Council Housing, unpublished report to Department of Environment 1981, and J. Henderson and V. Karn, 'Race and the Allocation of Urban Resources: the case of public housing in Britain', *Urban Studies* (forthcoming).)

2 For example, D.J. Smith and A. Whalley, *Racial Minorities and Council Housing*, (London: Political and Economic Planning, 1975.)

3 D. Wellman, *Portraits of White Racism*, (Cambridge: Cambridge University Press, 1977.)

4 e.g. D. Smith and P. Whalley, *op.cit.*.

5 D. Wellman, *op.cit.*, p: 4.

6 *ibid.*

7 K. Young and N. Connelly: *Policy and Practice in the Multi-racial City*, (London: Policy Studies Institute, 1981) p. 159.

8 W.W. Daniel, *Racial Discrimination in England*, (Harmondsworth: Penguin 1968.)

9 N. McIntosh and D.J. Smith, *The Extent of Racial Discrimination*, (London: Political and Economic Planning, 1974) p. 19.

10 D.J. Smith, *The Facts of Racial Disadvantage* (London: Political and Economic Planning, 1976).

11 *ibid*, p. 160.

12 P. Niner, *Transfer Policies: A case study in Harlow*, Research Memorandum 79, Centre for Urban and Regional Studies, University of Birmingham, 1980, p. 12.

13 D. Matza, 'The disreputable poor', in R. Bendix and S.M. Lipset, *Class Status and Power*, (London: Routledge and Kegan Paul, 1967); C. Valentine, *Culture and Poverty*, (Chicago: University of Chicago Press, 1968); J. Douglas, *Deviance and Respectability*, (New York: Basic Books, 1970).

14 See for instance O. Gill, *Luke Street: Housing Policy, Conflict and the Creation of a Delinquent Area*, (London: Macmillan, 1972) pp. 28–29.

15 J. Rex and S. Tomlinson, *Coloured Immigrants in a British City: a class analysis*, (London: Routledge and Kegan Paul, 1979) p. 141.

16 C. Satyamurti, *Occupational Survival* (Oxford: Basil Blackwell, 1980).

17 e.g. J. Parker and K. Dugmore, *Colour and the Allocation of GLC Housing*,

182 Ethnic Pluralism and Public Policy

Research Report 21, Greater London Council, London, 1976; J.G. Stunnell, *An Examination of Racial Equity in Points Scheme Housing Allocations*, Research and Information Report, London Borough of Lewisham, London, 1975; A. Power, *Racial Minorities and Council Housing in Islington – Is the Borough being fair?*, North Islington Housing Rights Project, 1977; London Borough of Lewisham, *Black People and Housing in Lewisham*, 1975 (unpublished report), 1980; R. Skellington, 'How Blacks Lose Out in Council Housing', *New Society*, 29 January 1981, p. 189, A. Simpson, *Stacking the Decks: A Study of Race, Inequality and Council Housing in Nottingham*, (Nottingham: Nottingham and District Community Relations Council, 1981); H. Flett, 'Bureaucracy and ethnicity: notions of eligibility to public housing,' in S. Wallman, *Ethnicity at Work*, (London: Macmillan, 1979), p. 135–54, and H. Flett, *Black Council Tenants in Birmingham*, Working Paper No. 12, SSRC Research Unit on Ethnic Relations; J. Henderson, V. Karn and W. Brown, *op.cit.*, D.J. Smith and A.P. Whalley, *op.cit.*,

18 cf. Parker and Dugmore, *op.cit.*; Skellington, *op.cit.*,

19 J. Henderson and V. Karn, *op.cit.*, forthcoming.

20 E.Burney, *Housing on Trial*, (Oxford: Oxford University Press, 1967;) R. Skellington, *Council House Allocation in a Multi-racial Town*, Occasional Paper Series, Faculty of Social Sciences, The Open University, 1980; Rex and Tomlinson *op.cit.*

21 J. Henderson and V. Karn, *op.cit.*, forthcoming.

22 Home Office, *Racial Attacks*, 1981; London Borough of Brent, *Final Report of Working Party on Racial Harassment on Local Authority Housing Estates*, 1982; London Race and Housing Forum, *Racial Harassment on Local Authority Housing Estates*, (London: Commission for Racial Equality, 1981); N. Fielding, 'Racial Harassment', *Roof*, May–June 1982; London, Borough of Hackney, *Racial Harassment on Council Estates*, Housing Management Committee, London Borough of Hackney, 1981.

23 J. Henderson and V. Karn, *op.cit.*, forthcoming.

24 London Borough of Lewisham, *op.cit.*

25 Power, *op.cit.*,

26 W.W. Daniel, *op.cit.*, p: 171.

27 N. McIntosh and D.J. Smith, *op.cit.* p. 19.

28 C. Lambert, *Building Societies, Surveyors and the Older Areas of Birmingham*, Working Paper No. 38, Centre for Urban and Regional Studies, University of Birmingham, 1976; S. Duncan, 'Self-help; the allocation of mortgages and the formation of housing sub-markets', *Area*, Vol. 8, No. 4. (1977) pp. 302–316; M. Boddy, *The Building Societies*, (London: Macmillan, 1976); K. Bassett and J. Short, 'Patterns of building society and local authority mortgage lending in the 1970s', *Environment and Planning A*, Vol. 12, pp. 279–300.

29 D.J. Smith, *op.cit.*,

30 V. Karn, 'The financing of owner-occupation and its impact on ethnic minorities', *New Community*, Winter, 1977/8; V. Karn, J. Kemeny and P. Williams, 'Home-ownership in the Inner Cities', (unpublished report to Department of Environment, 1982).

31 V. Karn, J. Kemeny and P. Williams, *op.cit.*

32 L. Stevens *et al, Race and Building Society Lending in Leeds*, (Leeds: Leeds Community Relations Council, 1982).

33 *ibid.*

34 *ibid.* p. 53.

35 *ibid.*; M. Harrison and L. Stevens, *Ethnic Minorities and the Availability of Mortgages*, Social Policy Research Monograph, Department of Social Policy and Administration, University of Leeds, 1981.

36 Stevens *et al, op.cit.*, 1982.

37 V. Karn, J. Kemeny and P. Williams, *op.cit.*

38 C. Lambert, *Building Societies, Surveyors and the Older Areas of Birmingham*,

Working Paper No. 38, Centre for Urban and Regional Studies, University of Birmingham, 1976.

39 The Housing Monitoring Team, *Building Societies and the Local Housing Market*, Research Memorandum 90, Centre for Urban and Regional Studies, University of Birmingham, 1982; Lambert, *op.cit.*,

40 P. Townsend, *Poverty in the United Kingdom*, (Harmondsworth: Penguin 1979) p. 505.

Riots and Representation

11 Racial Violence in the United States
Donald L. Horowitz

The urban riots of the 1960s in the United States generated a spate of theorising that had a scope far beyond the parochial concerns of the United States. In tandem with the Vietnam insurgency and to a lesser extent the African coups of the 1960s, the riots rekindled interest in the whole question of collective violence. The result was a vast outpouring of literature on the riot process, on the relations of grievances to violence, on the police, and on minority attitudes, not to mention the small industry that concentrated on the amorphous field of 'urban problems' or the wider network of analysts concerned with the interrelations of protest, spontaneous violence, terrorism, and guerrilla warfare. Theoretical schemes were elaborated, the correlates of aggression were studied in experimental laboratories, and aggregate data were deployed to seek out hitherto unsuspected relationships between violence and other variables. One significant impact of the riots was not on those who experienced them but on social science scholarship, which has never been quite the same since.

Given American pluralism, it was inevitable that an array of competing theories would emerge to explain the violence. An official commission concluded that the Watts riot was the work of a relatively few socially marginal members of the community, whereupon others rejoined that the violence was an act of articulate protest against identifiable grievances. Alternative interpretations focused on unfulfilled aspirations for economic wellbeing and social mobility; outright discrimination, police repression, and political neglect; the expression of youthful exuberance by the disproportionately young population of black urban areas; rapid communications and the contagion of one incident from another; deprivation relative to key reference groups; aggression as the result of repeated frustration or as the result of rising and then declining satisfactions. Even so diverse a list hardly does justice to the outpouring of retrospective theory.[1]

Empirical testing has followed somewhat more slowly and has been in any event only partial. Nevertheless, there is now at least some evidence to go on. Do we have the tools to explain the riots? Can we draw significant conclusions about their forms and patterns: where they occurred, what was attacked, who participated? How do we explain non-rioting, quiescence in the face of the earlier violence? And what of the riot conceived not merely as an effect but as a cause? Things happen as a result of riots, as a result of efforts to make them subside, and as a result of efforts to prevent their recurrence. The consequences of the riots have further implications for the future of ethnic and racial relations and for the social and political systems in which those relations are embedded. Do we yet know the impact of the violence? Such questions frame the present inquiry.

Despite the limited evidence available, it is already fairly clear that most of the theories, so glibly and occasionally self-righteously advanced, do not fare very well. This is as true of the relative deprivation theories as it is of the marginality and riff-raff theories they quickly eclipsed. As we immerse ourselves in the materials, it will become increasingly clear that riots, like all episodic events, strain our capacity for explanation. They come and go, and many of the variables that are adduced to explain their occurrence are, it turns out, also present before they occur or after they subside or where they did not occur. To explain riots, it is necessary to ask both time and space questions: Why now and not then? Why here and not there?

Three forms of racial violence
In the twentieth century, the United States has experienced three forms of racial violence.[2] From the 1880s to the late 1930s, lynching was a common form of anti-black violence in the Southern states. From the turn of the century to about 1920, and sporadically up to mid-century, another form of violence occurred. It was characterised by white mobs attacking black victims, largely in Northern cities. The riots of the 1960s, also mainly in Northern cities, took a different form: attacks by blacks on property owned by whites and on symbols of public authority. Each form of violence reached a peak, declined suddenly, and trailed off slowly thereafter. Since the early 1970s, collective racial violence has, with a few notable exceptions, been absent.

The three forms of violence correspond to three different stages in the evolution of black-white relations: the vigorous reassertion of white supremacy after the abolition of slavery and the occupation of the South; the large-scale black migration to the North, with its promise of economic advancement and greater freedom; and the growth of a mass movement toward full equality. However different these stages, it is important to underscore that the three forms of violence were related to each other and indeed overlapped each other in time.

Racial lynching was an adaptation of a frontier technique for dispensing a rough brand of justice where criminal courts were not functioning or were considered inadequate for community needs. The lynch mob was typically a vigilante group that apprehended an accused offender, conducted a summary trial, and dispensed punishment, often death for more serious offences. The practice of lynching had begun on the Southern frontier in the eighteenth century and moved westward with the pioneers.[3]

Even before the Civil War, lynching had moved from the West back to the South, where it was occasionally employed to deal with abolitionists or those accused of aiding runaway slaves. It was, however, after Reconstruction that lynching reached its apogee in the service of white supremacy. Partly in response to the biased behaviour of carpetbagger governments in the South and partly in an effort to put the regime of rigid segregation on a firm footing, the lynch mob went into action in the last decades of the nineteenth century.[4]

According to the best counts available, from 1882 to 1931, some 4,589 victims met their death through lynching. The 1890s were a particularly virulent decade, with an average of 154 victims per year. From that point on, lynchings steadily declined, but those that occurred were increasingly located in the South, and they increasingly involved black victims. The punishment was death, frequently preceded by torture. By the 1920s, more than 95 per cent of all lynchings took place in the South, and 90 per cent of all the victims nationwide were black. Virtually every victim in the South was black.

The black lynching victim was typically accused of some crime against a member of the white community or a breach of the *mores* of segregated race relations (in the latter case, most often insulting a white woman). The crimes ranged from homicide to rape to robbery and theft. Frequently, the accusation was false or the lynching victim was not the perpetrator, but often there was a sham trial conducted by the mob before the execution, which usually partook of brutal mutilation.

The lynching was a hybrid between a crude criminal proceeding and an exercise in collective racial violence. Great care was not always taken in selecting the individual victim. None the less, the existence of the alleged offence as a pretext for the violence was important to its legitimacy. The objective was to reinforce the rules of segregation by punishing putative breaches of them. The punishment function imparted to the lynch mob the self-justifying status of agents of the community.

Many lynchings were made possible by the acquiescence or connivance of local sheriffs and police officers. In the rare cases where indictments were later returned against members of lynch mobs, juries generally acquitted them. The support of the white community made lynching possible. When that support declined in the 1920s and 1930s, so did lynching.

The absence of retribution by the black community also facilitated lynching. Rates of lynching were 50 per cent higher in counties where the population was less than 25 per cent black than in counties where it was more than half black.[5] It has been speculated that economic variables account for this difference. The need for plantation labour in the counties with black majorities was incompatible with the fright and flight that might result from lynchings. In counties with small black populations, poor independent farmers, white and black, competed with each other, lending a special edge to race relations. Equally likely, however, is the absence of a fear of retaliation where whites were a strong majority.

The phenomenon of lynching thus contains three elements that are important constituents of racial violence in general. The first is the element of legitimacy. In the aftermath of abolition, it was important that the violence visited upon blacks be justified as criminal punishment. The second is social support. Official and unofficial elite condonation is a recurrent feature of collective violence cross-nationally. In addition to its legitimising impact, social support simultaneously provides immunity from punishment. The third is an assurance that retaliation by the class of victims will not be forthcoming. The propensity to racial violence is much affected by the absence of a fear of retribution by authorities and victims.

The second form of racial violence – the white mob attacking randomly chosen black victims – had a number of points of contact with lynching. Sometimes it was a direct substitute for a lynching that had been thwarted by the action of authorities who managed to spirit the objects of the mob out of town or of judges who refused to give way to vengeance inside the courtroom. This was the pattern of several such riots in the first decade of the twentieth century.[6]

The relationship to lynching bears on a much later debate. After the riots of the 1960s, there was a great deal of concern that the United States had always been a violent (and therefore 'sick') society, that violence was so deeply rooted in American culture, going back to the frontier, that it was naive to expect an absence of violence. Although it now appears that these concerns were greatly exaggerated, for in the United States, as elsewhere, violence is an episodic phenomenon, nevertheless there are connections to be made between frontier vigilantism, lynching, and the anti-black riots of the first two decades of this century.

The connection is made clearer by the character of the precipitants of the violence. Sometimes these appeared to be challenges to the norms of segregation, and sometimes they were, as in most lynchings, alleged crimes by blacks, usually assaults that were rumoured to have taken place.

Despite the connection, the riots were not merely a transplantation of lynching. After about 1910, the riot in lieu of a thwarted lynching was less common. Moreover, riots tended to occur, not in areas where the black population was sparse, but where it had been enlarged by recent migration: Northern or border cities like Springfield, Illinois, East St Louis, Chicago, Philadelphia, and Washington, DC. The concentration of black population made it feasible to organise for self-defence, and in such riots there were sometimes retaliatory killings.

Rather than involving attempts to reinforce the subordinate position of blacks in a rigid system of ethnic stratification, these riots involved attempts to avert dramatic changes resulting from the migration of black labour into the Northern industrial world. Indeed, there was an element of territoriality discernible in these riots. They were sometimes set off by black encroachment on a territorial boundary, and they were usually fought in a 'contested area' of the city, a neighbourhood between black and white residential areas.[7] The riots were sometimes accompanied by expressions of a desire to rid the area of its black population, something much less frequently heard in the South, with its historic dependence on black labour. Victims were chosen anonymously and randomly. No longer was it necessary to identify, however spuriously, a black victim with some specific offence. And, with the end of the criminal-trial dimension of the violence, one victim was no longer enough. The incidents became fewer, but when they occurred they were of far greater magnitude than lynchings. Large mobs of whites gathered to wage brief race wars in which between 15 and 40 people might be killed and several times that number injured. Violence had passed from the South to the North, from sparsely-settled rural areas to larger cities, from individually-identified victims to victims identified solely by group membership. The race riot had arrived.

By the time of the first World War, it was in full swing. By one count, 22 such riots, all of them involving white aggressors and black victims, occurred between 1915 and 1919.[8] By the 1920s, this form of violence had declined, although it recurred occasionally in the 1930s and 1940s.

By then, however, the third form of violence had appeared. The black riot became familiar in the 1960s, but it actually began in New York City in 1935 and again in 1943. As was common in the 1960s riots, the 1935 and 1943 Harlem riots were precipitated by white police action in a black area, followed by inaccurate rumours about what the police had done. The mob – this time a black mob – reacted by burning, breaking, and looting.

Again, there was overlap in time between two forms of violence. It has been suggested that the pattern of black mob retaliation that characterised the anti-black riots of the first World War period was 'a transition to the numerous riots of the 1960s that found blacks initiating and dominating the violence'.[9]

In spite of the connection, however, there was again a major difference. The objective of the earlier riots was assault, often deadly assault, on people. In the riots of the 1960s, this was at best a minor feature. The overwhelming attention of the rioters was concentrated on destruction and theft of property. Whites who happened to find themselves in a riot area were occasionally assaulted but less frequently killed. Police and National Guard personnel were attacked, but there were many more deaths among rioters than among agents of control. In Newark (1967), for example, 21 of 23 deaths were of blacks. In one study of 75 riots in 67 cities, there was a total of 83 deaths, all of them in only 12 of the riots and 80 per cent of the deaths in just two riots: Newark and Detroit.[10] The property damage wrought by participants in the riots was enormous (in hundreds of millions of dollars), partly because there were so many participants. Estimates of participation run to many thousands for major riots, such as Watts, Detroit, Newark, Grand Rapids, Dayton, and New Haven.[11] It is therefore all the more remarkable that from 1963 to 1970 in more than 500 total disturbances, major and minor, fewer than 300 people were killed. Indeed, in only 6 per cent of the 578 riots covered by one study of the 1967–71 period was anyone at all killed.[12] The deaths in all of the hot summers of the 1960s add up to about the same number of people who were lynched in the worst single year of the 1890s.[13]

As this account suggests, the three forms of racial violence in the twentieth-century United States grew out of each other. Like other forms of social behaviour, violence is related to antecedent patterns of behaviour. Given the relationship of the riots of the 1960s to earlier violence, it is inconceivable that whites could have participated significantly in the 1960s riots except as occasional victims, unlike Brixton or Handsworth, for example, where the crowds, though disproportionately minority, contained small but significant numbers of whites.[14] The American riots are embedded in a tradition – or at least a wider pattern – of overt interracial violence largely absent in Britain, with the exception of a series of anti-black riots in 1919.[15]

Explaining the riots

Social scientists seeking to confirm pet theories of violence in the riots of this century would do better to look elsewhere. For many theories there is no confirming evidence, and for others there is already disconfirming evidence.

Efforts to distinguish between cities that experienced and did not experience anti-black riots earlier in the century have generally come to little. At best, there are only fragments of evidence that, where blacks were attacked, they seemed to have average incomes slightly closer to average white incomes than in cities where they were not attacked, thus suggesting the threat of social mobility was the key to the violence.[16] Beyond that – and the tacit approval of the violence by police and other officials[17] – riot cities were not much different from non-riot cities.

The data are better for the riots of the 1960s, but the theories fare as poorly. Indicators of black disadvantage do not predict either the location of the riots or the severity of the violence when it occurs.[18] Riot cities are difficult to distinguish from non-riot cities. As I shall suggest later, however, the distinction between riot and non-riot *regions* is more fruitful.

Not only are linear relationships of this sort absent, but so are curvilinear ones of the kind embodied in the so-called J-curve. Here the key variable is not location but timing. The J-curve theory postulates that periods of progress create expectations of further progress, which will eventuate in violence if progress is followed by a short, sharp period of decline that thwarts optimistic expectations.[19] However they are manipulated, the data on black economic progress do not seem to fit the theory. The ratio of non-white to white median income increased steadily during the riot years.[20] In the preceding decade, there had been fluctuation, with no particular pattern.[21] More sophisticated measures of non-white economic satisfaction, such as non-white-to-white ratios of family income per year of schooling, are equally unavailing. These do bear some resemblance to a J-curve, but the curve turns downward in the early 1950s, a period of notable quiet, not the 1960s. By the time of the riots, it was on its way back up.[22] Alternative indicators of economic satisfaction have been constructed, but they do not produce any J-curve; rather, they produce fluctuations, ups and downs.[23]

Efforts to distinguish rioters from non-rioters fare no better than efforts to distinguish riot cities from non-riot cities. To begin with, rates of participation in riots varied from city to city, but nowhere was a major riot the work of merely a small number of atypical malcontents. In most cases, estimates of participation run between 10 and 20 per cent of ghetto residents. Theories of marginality, which suggest rioters were disoriented recent migrants to the city or unemployed, uneducated members of the underclass, are now fairly well discredited.[24] Rioters were significantly more likely than non-rioters to be born in the North and to be natives and long-term residents of their cities.[25] In Los Angeles, level of education was not related to rates of participation in the violence; in Detroit and Newark, rioters may have been slightly better educated than non-rioters.[26] The figures from Washington, DC, are particularly well documented.[27] Three-fourths of those arrested had lived in Washington more than five years, and more than half had lived there 15 or more years. Educational levels were high: the median arrestee had had 10.8 years of schooling, close to the national black average. And 80.6 per cent of those arrested were employed. On all these dimensions, rioters were not unrepresentative of ghetto males in their twenties and thirties.

Yet another set of explanations focuses on the precipitants of the violence, which, in the majority of cases, involved the police. In Watts, for example, it was a routine traffic arrest that got out of hand; in Newark, it was the same; in Detroit, it was a raid on an after-hours bar. From precipitating events of this sort it was frequently concluded that the riots were the product of police brutality, of endemically hostile relations between the police and minority communities, or at least of heavy-handed, unsophisticated policing.

There is no question but that minority communities had grievances against the police before the riots broke out, though some of the grievances related as much to under-policing as to over-policing. Despite the grievances, there is ground to think that the police precipitants of many riots do not provide the best clues to the etiology of the violence.

For one thing, diverse approaches to policing the ghetto do not seem to have produced very different riot outcomes. The police in Newark were harsh; they thus provoked a riot. The police in Detroit were restrained; they permitted a riot to develop.

For another thing, the psychology of aggression provides ample reason to associate the police with an outbreak of violence that has only a superficial relationship to grievances against the police. Cueing is an important part of channelling responses to frustration in an aggressive or non-aggressive direction. In the process of channelling, there is evidence that observation of an aggressive model, together with frustrating conditions, is likely to produce more aggression than either component alone.[28] Since the police are instruments of force and indeed use force in the precipitating incidents, it is not surprising that this action should increase the likelihood of violence.

Moreover, the rumours that typically follow in the wake of such precipitating incidents have a significance beyond that which is ordinarily attributed to them. Their character is highly patterned. A person who has been injured will be said to have been injured by the police. A person who has been injured by the police will be said to have been killed. A person shot by the police while fleeing will be said to have been shot while surrendering. A person who has been killed by the police will be said to have been killed wantonly and in cold blood. The pattern holds for the 1935 and 1943 riots in Harlem, for the 1981 riots in Brixton, and for many of the American riots of the 1960s. In cross-national perspective, rumours of aggression are the most common last precipitant before inter-ethnic violence begins.

There are many reasons for this pattern. One of the most important, however, is that such rumours reduce the ambiguity that characterises the pre-violence situation. They suggest a clearcut, malevolent interpretation of events. The rumour of aggression already accomplished also gives the upper hand to those in the crowd who are most inclined to violence. The 'fact' that an atrocity has already occurred has the effect of closing alternative channels of peaceful redress. Of what use are the ordinary processes of politics when the other side has already abandoned them? Most important of all, the rumoured acts of violence remove inhibitions that derive from moral precepts. If there are doubts about the propriety of violence in ordinary times, self-defence is regarded as a justifiable motive. Consequently, a report that first blood has already been drawn by the other side legitimises the course advocated by the most extreme, renders the fainthearted disloyal, and arouses the anger of the remainder to a higher level. In all of this, the police play an important catalysing role.

This analysis ought to suggest two conclusions. First, it mattered to those who engaged in the riots that their action be justifiable. Second, something prior in time to police activity provided the impetus for the rioting.

On the first point, there is evidence that, long after the riots subsided, substantial fractions of ghetto residents believed them to be justified. Black respondents in post-riot surveys frequently felt sympathy for the rioters. In Detroit, 46 per cent reported at least 'some sympathy'; in a fifteen-city survey, 54 per cent expressed sympathy.[29] In the late 1960s, between 12 and 31 per cent of black respondents were willing to advocate violence as 'the best' or a 'necessary' means to equality.[30] While these are, of course, *post facto* expressions of opinion, they do suggest that the violence was not utterly devoid of legitimacy in the communities in which it occurred.

What was devoid of legitimacy was killing. Survey after survey reported that black respondents believed the riots were useful in calling attention to ghetto grievances and ultimately in arousing white sympathy for problems faced by the black community – this despite a completely contrary pattern of white responses to the same question.[31] Most of the questionnaires did not distinguish between violence against property and violence against people, but there is some evidence that the black community itself made this distinction. Aberbach and Walker interpret their Detroit survey results in precisely this way:[32]

> Many blacks . . . believe the civil disorders in Detroit in 1967 were an understandable reaction to several injustices and expressed some sympathy for the individuals who took part in the disorders; but there was little approval given the sniping and firebombing that took place. Extreme violence of this kind was considered a legitimate or useful expression of grievances by only a small minority of blacks in Detroit . . .

These findings are corroborated by the sheer absence of themes of revenge and violence-as-an-end in survey responses by blacks nationwide.[33]

On the second point, the directions of a general explanation of the violence are suggested by three pieces of evidence we have already identified. The propensity to violence, we have seen, was not a function of characteristics peculiar to cities in which riots occurred, for efforts to discriminate among cities on this basis have been unavailing. Moreover, the idiosyncratic events that precipitated the outbreak of violence functioned more to lower inhibitions on the expression of violence than to serve as the source of anger. And, finally, subsequent explanations of the violence by ghetto residents focused on protest against general conditions rather than on purely parochial circumstances. All of these argue against an explanation based on local sources of grievance.

To make sense of the riots, it is necessary, then, to place them in the context of national currents. Needless to say, the major development of the time was the emerging civil rights movement. In the early and mid-1960s, that movement was centred in the South, for, as the sit-ins and freedom rides made clear, it began as a drive to eliminate segregation. The movement focused on Albany, Georgia, in the summer of 1962, moved to Birmingham, Alabama, in 1963, to Mississippi in 1964, and to Selma, Alabama, in 1965. It was carefully planned and highly organised. It involved demonstrations in which white law enforcement officers in the South acted out, before national news media, their role as oppressive instruments of racial subordination.

For a variety of reasons, the movement could not be transplanted readily to the North. Its organisational infrastructure, the black church, was a more cohesive force in the South. Law enforcement officers would be less likely to play their appointed part in the North if confronted merely with orderly demonstrations. And the moral force of outside opinion was located in the North and would be lost if the movement reconstituted itself there. In the nature of things, the strategy and techniques chosen by the movement had a certain regional specificity.[34]

During the first phase, therefore, Northern blacks were observers of the civil rights struggle. But they were by no means unaffected by the morality play being performed in the South. Minority representatives in the North accelerated their activity dramatically during this period. In south-central Los Angeles, there were 250 black protest demonstrations in the two years preceding the Watts riot.[35] According to one study of New York City, 'disruptive acts' (protests of various kinds) by minority groups increased from 40 in 1962 to 547 in 1963; and in this same period there was a marked change in patterns of communication with authorities, from co-operative to conflictual.[36] What this change signified was both a redefinition of conditions from inevitable to remediable and an emerging struggle to organise the black communities in the North. Data are not available on how widespread the surge of demand was, but it seems likely Los Angeles and New York were not alone in experiencing it. So great an increase in protest would have taxed even the most responsive political systems, which a good many Northern city governments were not.[37]

The first riots in Harlem in 1964 were more or less spontaneous outbursts, very much affected by the outrages inflicted in Alabama and Mississippi. And as Harlem followed Mississippi, a year later Watts followed Selma. As in many of the later riots, the precipitant in both cases was a violent act by a policeman. The added significance of this can be appreciated once the central and malevolent role of the police in the Southern demonstrations is understood, for it cast the Northern police officer in the role of a Bull Connor, the man who had used dogs and waterhoses on peaceful demonstrators.[38] Thus, the Northern riots were a counterpoint to the Southern demonstrations – except that, where the movement in the South was carefully planned and organised (especially in preparing demonstrators to respond peacefully to police abuses), and was therefore non-violent, the disorders in the North were neither carefully planned nor organised. What small element of protest demonstration there was to one or two of them in the first instance quickly dissolved into violence.

It is not surprising, therefore, that the riots of the 1960s were concentrated in the northeast quadrant of the United States.[39] The South was not entirely left out of the riots, but it was vastly underrepresented in them. This is an important clue to the origins of the violence.

The events in the South thus had a variety of effects in the North. They provided a model for conflict and a prototype of its participants. In the first instance, they seem to have stimulated demand levels in

Northern cities. Thereafter, they provided a focus for antagonism: the police and local authorities. The profound impact of the Southern demonstrations on the Northern riots helps explain why police precipitants were so important (for they were the focal points of civil rights activity in the South) and why there was so little interpersonal violence against white targets. By the time the riots got going, the conflict was cast in the same bipolar terms as in the South: the black community against the authorities.

To relate the Northern riots to the Southern demonstrations is to render far more comprehensible the subsequent interpretation of what started out as wholly unorganised disorders as coherent protest action. For, if the Northern riots were not protests, except *post hoc*, the Southern demonstrations surely were. What the events of the 1960s show, above all, is how homogeneous and interconnected the United States had become. Despite the different conditions of the North and South, despite federalism, despite varying local arrangements and wide disparities in the receptivity of local authorities to black grievances, the events of the 1960s in the North and South were part of a single phenomenon.

To view the riots in this way is not to denigrate the existence of real grievances in Northern cities. There were squalid living conditions, police harassment, and high rates of unemployment. But, in explaining violence, recourse to constants is not adequate; variables are required. The riots of the 1960s occurred at a time of rising black income and education,[40] major increases in the availability of welfare assistance – up 31 per cent, 1960–64[41] – and increasing legal recognition of civil rights, not only in judicial decisions but in passage of the comprehensive Civil Rights Act of 1964 and the Voting Rights Act of 1965. To understand why the riots occurred thus requires much more than identification of intolerable conditions. It requires either a theory that relates improvement to impatience or that rejects straightforward stimulus-response relationships between objective conditions and violent behaviour, in favour of a deeper understanding of the changing political context.

The impact of the riots
The national character of the problems highlighted by the riots is underscored by the nature of the response to them. One might have supposed that cities that experienced severe or repeated violence in the 1960s would have made the most determined efforts to take measures to avert a recurrence. Yet studies of municipal expenditures after the riots turn up only minor differences between riot and non-riot cities. The major difference is in the area of expenditures related to riot

control – principally police and fire protection – where riot cities did increase their expenditures. In health and public welfare expenditures, differences between riot and non-riot cities were not statistically significant; and in education, non-riot cities increased their expenditures more than did riot cities.[42] In terms of general measures of minority socio-economic welfare (income, unemployment rates, occupational mobility, and housing), evidence of changes that would differentiate riot cities from non-riot cities is equally weak.[43] More precise analysis based on census tracts produces the same result. On four of five indicators measured in 1960 and again in 1970 (unemployment, white-collar jobs, housing crowding, and children living with both parents), no differences are detectable. On a fifth, median family income, riot tracts showed less gain than non-riot tracts, but this difference washes out with a slight change in the method of analysis.[44] When black riot areas are compared with black non-riot areas, the latter, mainly containing more affluent black communities, show significant gains between 1960 and 1970.[45] The riots had no clear impact on social conditions in riot cities or riot areas of cities.[46]

One difference does show up in the expenditure data, however. When riot and non-riot cities are disaggregated by local political arrangements, these appear to bear on the nature of the response to the riots. In particular, cities that elect their councils by an at-large method were somewhat more responsive to demands for both increased social welfare and riot control measures than were cities that elect their councils on a ward basis.[47] This may be a function of the more centralised character of decision-making in the at-large cities or of the greater responsiveness of at-large councils to demands from all sectors of the population, since all members of such councils are elected by the city-wide electorate. (If it is the latter, the conclusion runs contrary to current conventional wisdom in the civil rights community, which is hostile to at-large elections for alleged unresponsiveness to minority communities.) The mediating impact of local political arrangements may well have a bearing on the quiescence of riot cities since the early 1970s.

Overall, however, the major policy response to the violence was carried out at the national level. Civil rights legislation is perhaps the earliest and most visible result, but the hostile reaction of whites to the riots, compared to their sympathetic reaction to the civil rights demonstrations in the South, suggests that the latter, more than the former, were responsible for favourable action in Congress. More closely related to the riots was federal assistance for upgrading local and state police capacities. The Law Enforcement Assistance Administration was enjoined to give special attention to aid for riot prevention and control, and it provided hundreds of millions of dollars for training and equipment.

Indeed, there is good evidence that police forces at various levels took careful note of the riot process and the failings of the police in coping with them. In the late 1960s and early 1970s, far more attention was given than ever before to innovative conceptions of policing, ranging all the way from minority recruitment and community relations to family crisis intervention to improved data retrieval, accelerated response time, and appropriate technology. In a curious way, there was a good fit between these measures and observed differences in riot behaviour, for the one variable that seems to discriminate between high-intensity and low-intensity riot cities is the probability of arrest of riot participants. In general, the introduction of the state police into a riot situation had a positive effect on riot intensity, while the introduction of the National Guard tended to reduce riot intensity.[48] The state police typically increased the provocation to the rioters without really overpowering them; the National Guard brought overwhelming force to bear. It seems appropriate that one consequence of the riots should be police forces that are both more sensitive to minority interests and more effective in coping with disorder. And it is also consonant with the psychology of aggression that police forces with a community service orientation, rather than merely an enforcement orientation, might cue aggressive responses in crowds somewhat less readily.

The other major area of policy change was the 'Great Society' programmes of the Johnson Administration: the War Against Poverty, the Model Cities Program, food stamps, the minority business programme of the Small Business Administration, and so on. The Johnson Administration took rather seriously the warning of the Kerner Commission that, if drastic steps were not taken, the United States would become 'two societies', one white and one black, and it embarked on the effort to ameliorate ghetto conditions with a sense of mission.

Before very long, however, many of these programmes had been overtaken by the expenditure demands of the Vietnam War and by the rather short time horizon of elite publics in the United States, which were willing to declare defeat in the War Against Poverty as rapidly as they were willing to declare the war itself. In this they were abetted by some endemic distributive tendencies of the American political system, which make it difficult to target expenditures to points of greatest need or to achieve results in accordance with the intentions of central decision-makers. With the relatively trivial exception of the VISTA volunteer programme, one study found no association between riot frequency or intensity, on the one hand, and later increases in federal aid programmes, on the other.[49] A good example of the reason for this is the Model Cities Program, initially conceived as a comprehensive attempt to concentrate resources on a few cities to see whether and how the innovative use of substantial federal resources could revive slum areas.[50] Politics did not permit the execution of this conception. In Congress, representatives demanded a more broadly-based distribution, and by the end of 1968 fully 150 cities had already been awarded planning grants. At the local level, political forces unleashed in the 1960s set out to capture the programme funds, with the result that local implementation of the programme was largely the product of that competition.[51] Consequently, while the major policy responses to the riots were national, the results were neither uniform nor centrally directed.

Violence and quiescence

It would seem unlikely that the riots ended by the early 1970s as a result of any specific policy response to them, with the possible and partial exception of changes in police practices, composition, and equipment. But the riots certainly did end. No doubt the police deliberately avoided some previously provocative behaviour. Yet if I am right that police precipitants called forth violence that primarily had other roots, changes in police behaviour are probably not sufficient by themselves to explain the decline of the violence.

Where, then, should we look? It goes without saying that the proof of negatives is a notoriously hazardous and unsatisfying enterprise. Why people do not riot, once they have previously rioted, is not a readily researchable question. Still, if anything other than randomness is responsible, we should like to know it, and so speculation is justified.

One area of change that seems unhelpful in accounting for the decline of violence, just as it is unhelpful in accounting for the occurrence of violence, is black income. During the 1960s, the time of the riots, black income increased relative to white income. From 1959 to 1964, median black family income as a percentage of median white family income rose from 51 to 54. It continued to rise throughout the 1960s, to 58 per cent in 1966, 59 per cent in 1967, 60 per cent in 1968, and 61 per cent in 1969. And then it stagnated; by 1976, it had declined to 59 per cent and by 1977 to 57 per cent.[52] So the violence coincides with an increase, and the non-violence coincides with a decrease, further confounding deprivation theories.

For the black poor, there are signs of some special hardships that coincide with the end of the riots. Black unemployment, especially youth unemployment, rose in the late 1960s and early 1970s. For the age 16–19 male group, it was 23.3 per cent in 1965 and 26.9 in 1973; for the age 20–24 male group, it was 9.3 per cent in 1965 and 12.6 in 1973.[53] And just as this was happening, the real value of welfare grants appears to have declined in about half the states, from 1965 to 1972.[54] Rapid economic progress does not show much promise as an explanatory variable for the absence of violence. Quite the contrary: one could construct a very handsome J-curve, turning down in the early 1970s, the time of maximum quiet in the cities.

What did change for the better in this period was political participation. Black voting rates nationwide increased dramatically. In the South, the Voting Rights Act produced a massive enfranchisement of blacks. Georgia, Louisiana, and Mississippi have all been above the national average in voter registration for more than five years. Alabama, South Carolina, North Carolina, and Virginia all hover around the national average. Before the Act, none of these states was at the 50 per cent mark in black registration. Alabama was at 23 per cent of eligible black voters, and Mississippi was at 6.7 per cent. Nationwide in 1956, 77 per cent of eligible whites said they voted; 35 per cent of eligible blacks did. In 1976, these figures were 73 per cent and 65 per cent.[55]

Perhaps more to the point, between 1968 and 1980, the number of black elected officials in the United States increased tenfold.[56] In 1967, the first black mayors were elected in major cities: Cleveland, Ohio, and Gary, Indiana. They were followed before very long by mayors in Detroit, Los Angeles, Atlanta, New Orleans, and Newark. The increase was sharp and steady, from a mere 29 in 1968 to 81 three years later and to more than double that number by 1978, as Figure 11.1 shows. Overall, there were four times as many black elected officials at the municipal level in 1981 as there had been when the riots came to an end around 1970.

The impact of these changes at the local level was considerable. In Newark, for example, black groups coalesced to capture control of the new patronage opportunities made possible by federal programmes; 'blacks perceived these programs to be theirs'.[57] The election of a black mayor in 1970 was the culmination of this campaign, which involved a significant mobilisation of energy toward a political process previously inhospitable to black aspirations. Much the same happened in Detroit, and the attitudinal impact was striking. As of the early 1970s, Aberbach and Walker report:[58]

> Detroit's black community has been growing steadily and is on the verge of gaining political dominance in the city. Although there were several setbacks and disappointments for the blacks during 1967–1971, they remained more likely than whites to report memberships in community groups, more likely to discuss public

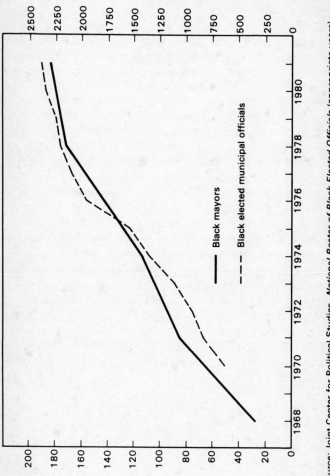

Source: Joint Center for Political Studies, *National Roster of Black Elected Officials* (appropriate years)

Figure 11.1: Black mayors in the United States, 1968–81, and black elected municipal officials in the United States, 1970–81

affairs, and more closely identified with labour unions and political parties; they felt better represented in matters pertaining to race relations and had stronger feelings of political efficacy.

These remarkable findings, if replicable in other Northern cities, would go a long way to explain the absence of violence. What they suggest is that urban political institutions were finally performing for the black community the functions they had historically performed for white immigrant groups, integrating them into a previously alien political system by means of patronage, the exchange of tangible benefits for votes, or simply by the more reliable delivery of basic municipal services: fire and police protection, garbage collection, street repairs, and the like. And this even in the face of – and perhaps in a small way to mitigate – generally more difficult economic conditions for the black community.

There is another side to political participation that is suggested by the Aberbach and Walker findings but is more difficult to document in hard data. Along with the political mobilisation that took place in the 1960s there was a general growth of organisational involvement. Black organisations were no exception. Although membership rosters of the major civil rights organisations fluctuated in the 1960s, the principal organisations had more members in 1972 than they had in 1961,[59] and their memberships were blacker than they had been.

The relevance of this observation ought to be clear from the earlier contrast of the South in the 1960s with the North. Save for a very few disorders, the South, well organised as it was, was given over to black protest, not riots. With the growth of organisation in the North, presumably strategies of protest were better developed and more smoothly executed. Furthermore, with the background of violence in Northern cities, protest strategies, which depend on the threat (but not the use) of violence, would probably be more effective. All of this is made more plausible by the finding of a positive correlation between black protest and black representation at the municipal level: 'blacks protest especially in those cities where they have been able to gain formal proportional representation'.[60] As black representation and organisation increased, it would be reasonable to expect an increase in protest and a decline in violence.

Important as organisation and participation are, they are unlikely to be the complete explanation for the absence of rioting after the early 1970s. Some part of the explanation probably rests with the end of the great civil rights confrontations in the South that had earlier called forth so much resonating passion in the North. Another part probably relates to the 'lessons' rioters drew from the riots. One likely lesson is that the violence was futile. Satisfying though it was as an expression of anger, it produced no immediate changes, save increases in inconvenience (businesses serving the ghetto having been burned and looted) and in police repression. There is evidence that the severity of disorders declined as a function of the number of prior outbreaks in a city,[61] a finding consistent with diminishing interest on the part of prospective participants. The benefits of an outburst, particularly in terms of emotional satisfaction, presumably seem greatest in the early stages; the costs come home later. An alternative lesson, which fits together only uneasily with the first, is that, in response to the riots, the political system was making efforts – modest, clumsy, fitful, halfhearted efforts, no doubt – to change in order to accommodate black interests. This conclusion, of course, is consistent with the optimism expressed by ghetto residents in post-riot surveys that the riots would awaken white opinion to the need for change. It is also quite compatible with the message being sent by black leaders, who, I have indicated, saw it very much in their strategic interest to hold a threat of violence in reserve.

The American riots in comparative perspective

In several respects, the American riots of the 1960s were markedly different from ethnic violence that took place around the world during the same decade. Most notable was the small number of people killed by the rioters. There were occasional white victims, but most of the violence was targeted at property, and security forces accounted for many more killings than did rioters. Although exact figures are lacking, the riots in Kuala Lumpur in 1969 probably involved about the same number of deaths as did all the ghetto riots of the 1960s taken together. The 1966 riots in Northern Nigeria took perhaps ten times that number of lives. Equally significant – and no doubt related to the casualty pattern – was the absence of threats from an antagonist ethnic group as the precipitant of the violence. These were not, as most ethnic riots around the world are, riots reflecting inter-group hostility so much as riots reflecting aspirations to be included in the political and social system on its own egalitarian terms. Then, too, the locale of the riots was not where discrimination and deprivation were at their worst (the South) but where the hope for amelioration was at its highest. This is also different from most ethnic riots, which typically occur where ethnic relations are perceived to be most desperate. Finally, the effects of the riots of the 1960s were far more benign than the effects of such violence elsewhere. No separatist movements emerged from them, as they sometimes did elsewhere, no terrorism, no civil war, not even any ethnic political parties. What emerged, rather, was a renewed effort, albeit a spotty effort, to redress black grievances.

In general, ethnic conflict in countries such as Canada, Belgium, Switzerland, Britain, and Spain has involved much less interpersonal violence than the equivalent phenomenon in Asia and Africa – save, of course, the terrorism in Northern Ireland and in the Basque country. For this there are a good many reasons: the overarching level of national identity in the established states of the West; more strongly-held conceptions of indigenousness in some Asian and African countries to which immigrants have come; the existence of religious, class, and regional identities in the West that compete for attention with ethnic identities and ethnic conflict; and the generally more open, democratic systems of the West. On these grounds, there is some reason to identify a generally milder Western pattern of ethnic and racial conflict and a generally more severe non-Western pattern.

The riots of the 1960s in the United States and of the early 1980s in Britain clearly exemplify the former pattern. In comparative perspective, they were very mild affairs. In Britain, as in America, the objective was not to kill ethnic antagonists but to throw stones and Molotov cocktails at the police and to burn and loot property. Casualties were comparatively light: no one was killed in Brixton.

The British riots occurred, as the American riots did, at a time of improvement in the condition of minorities. In housing, employment, and income, there were discernible trends in Britain toward convergence between the minority position and that of the general population. The minorities were still worse off, but they were significantly better off in 1980 than they had been, for example, in the mid-1970s, when there were no riots.[62] In spite of this, minority perceptions of race relations in Britain were far more pessimistic in the period immediately before the riots than they were in the mid-1970s.[63] Like the American data, the British evidence suggests the need to distinguish between objective racial *conditions* and subjective racial *relations*. Discontent and violence may go hand in hand with improving conditions if the political setting provides evidence of continuing inhospitality to minority interests or of outright discrimination and abuse.

The meaning of Miami

Before we conclude from the relative mildness of the American riots and the quiescence of a decade that there is no cause for alarm, some features of the American situation carry special significance. The first is the long history of ethnic and racial violence from which the riots of the 1960s sprang. I have taken some pains to show connections between the 1960s riots and earlier anti-black riots and lynchings. In fact, the American violence goes further back. Before black-white conflict eclipsed intra-white conflict, there was a significant period of nativist hostility to immigrants, punctuated by anti-Irish violence in the North and more general anti-foreigner violence in the South around the middle of the nineteenth century. In Louisville, for example, on election day in 1855, 22 people were killed in an anti-foreigner riot. It is too soon, I suspect, to conclude that violent wellsprings so deep have run dry.

That they have not may be inferred from the Miami riot of 1980, consideration of which I have deliberately deferred so as not to commingle it with the riots of the 1960s. For Miami was not quite the same. As in the 1960s riots, there was a great deal of looting and property destruction, some $100 m. of it. But, in addition, there were brutal killings: three young whites dragged from a car and stomped to death, a Cuban man pulled from a car and mutilated, an elderly Cuban burned alive. In all, eighteen people died. The Miami riot had elements of both the 1960s riots and the anti-black riots of the earlier part of the century, except that the ethnic identity of the victims was reversed.[64]

As in the 1960s riots, there was wide support in the black community for the riot as a response to grievances.[65] As in the 1960s, participation in the riot was not the preserve of a marginal or deviant few. Participation rates were substantial; participants appear to have been slightly better educated than non-participants; and the occupational profile of the two groups was similar. The only evidence of deviance is that participants were more likely to have had prior arrests than non-participants.[66] Like the 1960s riots, too, the Miami riot took place against a background of relative income improvement rather than decline. In 1960, median black family income was 63 per cent of overall median family income in Miami. In 1970, it was 65 per cent. By 1980, it was up to 74 per cent.[67] In all of these respects, the Miami of 1980 can be compared to the Watts, Detroit, or Washington of 12 or 15 years before.

In another respect, there is an important difference. The Miami riot had an aspect of inter-ethnic threat that the riots of the 1960s really did not have. The threat is reflected in the brutality of the killings and in the dual ethnic identity of the victims: Cubans as well as non-Hispanic whites. Cubans comprised 41 per cent of Dade County's population in 1980. Surveys conducted before the riot show high levels of anti-Cuban resentment on the part of blacks, as well as strong perceptions of Cuban economic competition.[68] Cuban income was significantly higher than black income. Median family income for Hispanics (which includes generally poorer Puerto Ricans as well) was 86 per cent of the overall family income for Miami. Not surprisingly, the survey responses speak of opportunities usurped by newcomers.

Miami may be unique, or it may be portentous. The evidence for interpreting it as an exceptional event is substantial. For one thing, the riot was preceded by an unusually long succession of alleged police abuses and failures of the criminal justice system that alert authorities might have intervened to redress.[69] They were precisely the sort that, since the 1960s, many police forces had learned to avoid. Equally important, the violence was preceded by an extraordinary growth of Cuban population. In 1970, Dade County had 218,000 Cubans. Throughout the 1970s, this number was augmented by a continuing flow, both from Cuba and from other cities in the United States, culminating in an influx of 125,000 Cubans – the so-called Mariel boatlift – within a few weeks in early 1980. As it happens, those few weeks coincided with the trial and acquittal of white police officers for the killing of a black suspect, and it was their acquittal that provided the immediate precipitant for the violence. The numbers of Cuban immigrants were so large, the rates of influx so rapid, the Mariel boatlift so concentrated and so fortuitously timed, that the resulting violence hardly seems to be a harbinger of developments elsewhere. On the contrary, one could almost derive a perverse comfort from the isolated character of the Miami riot and the fact that, compared to the 1960s riots, it took so much provocation to produce it.

It seems unlikely, then, that Miami augurs either a resurgence of 1960s-type riots or a spate of more directly interpersonal, inter-ethnic riots. Nevertheless, the killing of Cubans and non-Hispanic whites in Miami raises questions about the shape of ethnic conflict in the United States. There is good comparative evidence that the cumulation of grievances against more than one competitor ethnic group may produce especially strong hostility.[70] If Miami does not portend a new round of riots, it may none the less signify an emerging pattern of tensions in which the large-scale immigration the United States has experienced since 1965 provides the cutting edge for ethnic conflict.[71]

Notes

1 The literature on the riots is prodigious. For a sampling, see Joe R. Feagin and Harlan Hahn, *Ghetto Revolts: The Politics of Violence in American Cities*, (New York: Macmillan, 1973), Chapter 1.

2 I follow here the conventional American practice of denominating colour-group differences as 'racial', despite the evidence that the relationships between such groups are not analytically different from relationships between ethnic groups demarcated by other indicators of identity. See Donald L. Horowitz, 'Three Dimensions of Ethnic Politics', *World Politics*, Vol. 23, 1971.

3 Richard Maxwell Brown, 'The History of Vigilantism in America', in H. Jon Rosenbaum and Peter C. Sederberg (eds), *Vigilante Politics*, (Philadelphia: University of Pennsylvania Press, 1976).

4 Arthur F. Raper, *The Tragedy of Lynching*, (Chapel Hill, NC: University of North Carolina Press, 1933) and *The Mob Still Rides: A Review of the Lynching Record*

1931–35. Pamphlet. (Atlanta: Commission on Interracial Co-operation, 1936).

5 Raper, *Tragedy of Lynching, op.cit.*, pp. 27–8.

6 A useful collection covering this and later periods is Joseph Boskin (ed.), *Urban Racial Violence in the Twentieth Century*, (Beverly Hills: Glencoe Press, 1969). An excellent case study is Elliot Rudwick, *Race Riot in East St. Louis, 1917*, (Carbondale: Southern Illinois University Press, 1964). See also Hugh Davis Graham and Ted Robert Gurr (eds), *Violence in America: Historical and Comparative Perspectives*, (Washington DC: Government Printing Office, 1969).

7 Allen D. Grimshaw, 'Urban Racial Violence in the United States: Changing Ecological Considerations', *American Journal of Sociology*, Vol. 66, 1960.

8 Richard Maxwell Brown, 'Historical Patterns of Violence in America' in Graham and Gurr, *op.cit.*

9 Richard Maxwell Brown, *Strain of Violence: Historical Studies of Violence and Vigilantism*, (New York: Oxford University Press, 1975), p. 214.

10 National Advisory Commission on Civil Disorders, United States, *Report* (Washington DC: Government Printing Office, 1968), p. 66.

11 Feagin and Hahn, *op.cit.*, pp. 280–81.

12 Jane A. Baskin *et al.*, *The Long Hot Summer? An Analysis of Summer Disorders 1967–71*, Pamphlet. (Waltham, Mass.: Lemberg Center for the Study of Violence, Brandeis University, 1972), p. 7.

13 Raper, *Tragedy of Lynching, op.cit.*, p. 480.

14 Rt. Hon. Lord Scarman, *The Brixton Disorders: Report of an Inquiry*, (London: HMSO, Cmnd 8427, 1981), pp. 29–32; Simon Field and Peter Southgate, *Public Disorder: A Review of Research and a Study in One Inner City Area*. Home Office Research Study No. 72. (London: HMSO, 1982), p. 43.

15 Field and Southgate, *op.cit.*, p. 4.

16 Stanley Lieberson and Arnold R. Silverman, 'The Precipitants and Underlying Conditions of Race Riots', *American Sociological Review*, Vol. 30, 1965; cf. Milton Bloombaum, 'The Conditions Underlying Race Riots as Portrayed by Multidimensional Scalogram Analysis: A Reanalysis of Lieberson and Silverman's Data', *American Sociological Review*, Vol. 33, 1968.

17 Grimshaw, *op.cit.*

18 Seymour Spilerman, 'Structural Characteristics of Cities and the Severity of Racial Disorders', *American Sociological Review*, Vol. 41, 1976 and 'The Causes of Racial Disturbances: Tests of a Theory'. Discussion paper. (Madison: University of Wisconsin Institute for Research on Poverty, 1969); Marian Lief Palley and Howard A. Palley, 'Social Welfare Indicators as Predictors of Racial Disorders in Black Ghettos'. Paper presented at annual meeting of the American Political Science Association, 1969.

19 James C. Davies, 'The J-Curve of Rising and Declining Satisfaction as a Cause of Some Great Revolutions and a Contained Rebellion', in Graham and Gurr, *op.cit.*

20 Feagin and Hahn, *op.cit.*, p. 23.

21 *ibid.*

22 Abraham H. Miller, Louis H. Bolce and Mark Halligan, 'The J-Curve and the Urban Riots: An Empirical Test of Progressive Relative Deprivation Theory', *American Political Science Review*, Vol. 71, 1977.

23 *ibid.*, pp. 968–70.

24 cf. Joan M. Nelson, *Migrants, Urban Poverty, and Instability in Developing Nations*, (Cambridge, Mass.: Harvard University Center for International Affairs, Occasional Paper No. 22, 1969).

25 David O. Sears and John B. McConahay, *The Politics of Violence: The New Urban Blacks and the Watts Riot*, (Boston: Houghton Mifflin, 1973), pp. 29, 31; Feagin and Hahn, *op.cit.*, p. 10.

26 Sears and McConahay, *op.cit.*, pp. 23–4.

27 H.C. Strasel and Paul G. Larkin, *Rioters in Washington: A Study of People and Employment*, (Falls Church, Va.: Software Systems, Inc. 1968), pp. 23, 30–31.

28 Ladd Wheeler and Anthony R. Caggiula, 'The Contagion of Aggression', *Journal of Experimental Social Psychology*, Vol. 2, 1966. See also Leonard Berkowitz, 'Some Aspects of Observed Aggression', *Journal of Personality and Social Psychology*, Vol. 2, 1965; Leonard Berkowitz and Russell G. Geen, 'Film Violence and the Cue Properties of Available Targets', *Journal of Personality and Social Psychology*, Vol. 3, 1966; Leonard Berkowitz, 'The Study of Urban Violence: Implications of Laboratory Studies of Frustration and Aggression', in Louis H. Masotti and Don R. Bowen (eds), *Riots and Rebellion: Civil Violence in the Urban Community*, (Beverly Hills: Sage Publications, 1968).

29 Joel D. Aberbach and Jack L. Walker, *Race in the City*, (Boston: Little, Brown, 1973); p. 57; Angus Campbell and Howard Schuman, *Racial Attitudes in Fifteen American Cities*, (Washington, DC: Government Printing Office, 1968), p. 55.

30 Feagin and Hahn, *op.cit.*, p. 277.

31 See *ibid.*, Chap. 6.

32 *op.cit.*, p. 218.

33 See Gary T. Marx, *Protest and Prejudice: A Study of Belief in the Black Community*, (New York: Harper & Row, 1967), p. 33.

34 See the interesting analysis of Howard Hubbard, 'Five Long Hot Summers and How They Grow', *The Public Interest*, No. 12, 1968, on which this and the preceding paragraph are based. See also Peter H. Rossi, 'Urban Revolts and the Future of American Cities', in David Boesel and Peter H. Rossi (eds), *Cities Under Siege: An Anatomy of the Ghetto Riots 1964-1968*, (New York: Basie Books, 1971), pp. 412-13.

35 Robert M. Fogelson, *Violence as Protest: A Study of Riots and Ghettos*, (Garden City, NY: Doubleday, 1971), p. 111.

36 David J. Monti, 'Patterns of Conflict Preceding the 1964 Riots: Harlem and Bedford-Stuyvesant', *Journal of Conflict Resolution*, Vol. 23, 1979, p. 59.

37 There is at least some evidence that policy responsiveness is reduced when protest groups adopt militant stances. See Paul D. Schumaker, 'Policy Responsiveness to Protest-Group Demands', *Journal of Politics*, Vol. 37, 1975.

38 'This is just like Selma', shouted a bystander at the rough handling and arrest that precipitated the Watts riot. Quoted in Milton Viorst, *Fire in the Streets: America in the 1960s*, (New York: Simon and Schuster, 1979), p. 331.

39 For 1967 figures see National Advisory Commission on Civil Disorders, *op.cit.*, p. 114. For 1967-71 figures see Baskin *et al.*, *op.cit.*, pp. 4-5.

40 In 1940, black men aged 25-29 had an average of 6.5 years of education, 4.0 years below the average for whites. In 1962, it was 11.0 years, only 1.5 years below the white average. See Sears and McConahay, *op.cit.*, p. 37.

41 Robert P. Albritton, 'Social Amelioration through Mass Insurgency? A Reexamination of the Piven and Cloward Thesis', *American Political Science Review*, Vol. 73, 1979, p. 1005.

42 Susan Welch, 'The Impact of Urban Riots on Urban Expenditures', *American Journal of Political Science*, Vol. 19, 1975.

43 William R. Kelly and David Snyder, 'Racial Violence and Socioeconomic Changes Among Blacks in the United States', *Social Forces*, Vol. 58, 1980.

44 William R. Berkowitz, 'Socioeconomic Indicator Changes in Ghetto Riot Tracts', *Urban Affairs Quarterly*, Vol. 10, 1974.

45 *ibid.*, pp. 79, 83.

46 The argument that the riots produced a massive expansion of welfare rolls (which undoubtedly did occur in the 1960s) has now been rebutted. See Albritton, *op.cit.*

47 Welch, *op.cit.*, pp. 756-7; Feagin and Hahn, *op.cit.*, pp. 255-7; Harlan Hahn, 'Civic Responses to Riots: A Reappraisal of Kerner Commission Data', *Public Opinion Quarterly*, Vol. 34, 1970. cf. Schumaker, 'Policy Responsiveness', *op.cit.*

48 'An Economic Analysis of Riot Participation,' *Economic Inquiry*, Vol. 13, 1975, Chalmers and Shelton also conclude that socioeconomic variables explain little or none of the variation in riot intensity once probability of apprehension and levels of enforcement are taken into account. James A. Chalmers and Robert B. Shelton, *ibid.*, p. 334.

49 The study, by James Button, is reported in Feagin and Hahn, *op.cit.*, pp. 242–3.

50 For the background and early operation of the programme, see James L. Sindquist, *Making Federalism Work*, (Washington DC: The Brookings Institution, 1969), Chap. 3.

51 Such conflicts are described in Donald L. Horowitz, *The Courts and Social Policy* (Washington DC: The Brookings Institution, 1977), Chap. 3.

52 *Ebony Handbook*, (Chicago: Johnson Publishing Co., 1974), p. 299; William Julius Wilson, 'The Black Community in the 1980s: Questions of Race, Class, and Public Policy', *The Annals*, Vol. 454, 1981, p. 34.

53 Wilson, *op.cit.*, p. 33.

54 Albritton, *op.cit.*, p. 1009.

55 Samuel P. Huntington, *American Politics: The Promise of Disharmony*, (Cambridge, Mass.: Harvard University Press, 1981), p. 198.

56 Joint Center for Political Studies, *National Roster of Black Elected Officials*, (Washington, DC: Joint Center for Political Studies, 1981).

57 Fred Barbaro, 'Newark: Political Brokers' in Peter H. Rossi (ed.), *Ghetto Revolts*, 2nd ed. (New Brunswick, NJ: Transaction Books, 1973), p. 302.

58 *op.cit.*, p. 217.

59 This is made clear by contrasting figures in the third and seventh editions of the *Encyclopedia of Associations*, (Detroit: Gale, 1961 and 1972). CORE, for example, reported 70,000 members in 1972, compared to 16,000 in 1961.

60 Peter K. Eisinger, 'The Conditions of Protest Behaviour in American Cities', Discussion Paper. (Madison: University of Wisconsin Institute for Research on Poverty, 1972), pp. 18, 22 (emphasis omitted).

61 Spilerman, 'Structural Characteristics', *op.cit.*, p. 780.

62 See Simon Field *et al.*, *Ethnic Minorities in Britain: A Study of Trends in Their Position Since 1961*, Home Office Research Study No. 68, (London: HMSO, 1981).

63 Commission for Racial Equality, *Race Relations in 1981: An Attitude Survey*. Pamphlet. (London: Commission for Racial Equality, 1981), p. 14.

64 For useful accounts, see Manning Marable, 'The Fire This Time: The Miami Rebellion, May, 1980', *The Black Scholar*, July-August 1980; *The Economist*, 24 May 1980, pp. 35–6.

65 Robert A. Ladner *et al.*, 'The Miami Riots of 1980: Antecedent Conditions, Community Responses and Participant Characteristics', in Louis Kriesberg, (ed.), *Research in Social Movements, Conflicts and Change: A Research Annual*, Vol. 4, (Greenwich, Conn.: JAI Press, Inc., 1981).

66 *ibid.*

67 The 1960 and 1970 figures are drawn from Commission on Civil Rights, *Confronting Racial Isolation in Miami: A Report*, (Washington, DC: US Commission on Civil Rights, 1982), p. 20. The still-unpublished 1980 figures were made available through the co-operation of Mr G. Patterson of the United States Bureau of the Census.

68 Ladner *et al.*, *op.cit.*, p. 198.

69 Commission on Civil Rights, *op.cit.*, pp. 229–42.

70 Donald L. Horowitz, 'Direct, Displaced, and Cumulative Ethnic Aggression', *Comparative Politics*, Vol. 6, 1973.

71 In this connection, it is probably significant that a much milder riot in Miami at the end of 1982 was brought on by the shooting of a young black man by a Cuban police officer.

12 After the Riots: Police and Minorities in the United States, 1970–1980
Lawrence W. Sherman

The 1960s were years of struggle between American police and minorities. The police were the most visible and accessible symbol of white society in black neigbourhoods, so they became a focal point for the full range of racial conflict. Police conduct was blamed as the 'precipitating event' in the majority of the riots studied by the National Advisory Commission on Civil Disorders.[1]

From 1970 to 1980 the conflict subsided. The routine contacts of police with minority youth, always the prime source of conflict, seemed less often to be emotional confrontations and more often to be coldly hostile, but business-like, encounters. The number of riots, or even major demonstrations, involving the police declined substantially. One issue, police use of deadly force, refused to go away; it became more visible because the other issues of harassment and brutality had faded. But for the most part, police-minority relations substantially improved throughout the 1970s.

How can we account for this improving climate? What exactly was the nature of the problems in the first place? What lessons, if any, can be applied from this experience to the current conflicts between minorities and the police in Britain? None of these questions can be answered with much precision, but various hypotheses about each can be either supported or rejected.

The nature of police-minority conflicts
Police minority tensions have three separable elements: police behaviour toward minorities, minority crime and disorderly behaviour, and minority behaviour toward the police. Of the three, the greatest change has occurred in police behaviour toward minorities. Some change has also occurred in minority behaviour toward police.

Police behaviour toward minorities
The history of police behaviour toward minorities of any sort in this country is not pleasant. One leading account of the establishment of

American police departments in the mid-nineteenth century attributes their very existence to the influx of Irish and German immigrants. The net change in arrests after the creation of bureaucratic police agencies was not in felons brought to trial, but almost entirely in arrests of immigrant minorities for drunkenness and other minor public order offences.[2] Even after police departments became heavily staffed by immigrants, one of their major tasks remained the maintenance of order among minorities, by both legal and extra-legal means.

The extra-legal means for policing minorities included unjustified use of force, illegal searches, third-degree interrogations, and other methods attacked by President Herbert Hoover's blue ribbon crime commission.[3] These methods were particularly harsh against minority labour organisers in the North and blacks in the South. The labour movement became institutionalised, putting an end to police harassment of strikers. But the poor treatment of southern blacks at the hands of white police has had a lasting impact on police-minority relations. For as southern blacks migrated north to find industrial jobs, they took with them their expectations, fears, and anger towards the police. Northern police often justified these fears. In the early race riots in East St Louis (1917) and Chicago (1919), both begun by white (citizen) attacks on blacks, police were reported to have joined the white citizens in beating and killing blacks and burning black homes. At the very least, police failed to provide blacks with protection from rioting whites.[4]

The largest black migration northward began after the second World War, a period of economic growth. For the first time in a century, economic growth was not accompanied by large-scale immigration from abroad. Some blacks filled the immigrant labour role; others moved north without finding work. As blacks evolved from the position of being one among many groups of ethnic immigrant minorities to a position as the only large group of recent immigrants, police behaviour toward blacks became more of a public issue. It is not clear that police behaviour toward blacks changed in its nature, but it certainly increased in its visibility. With more blacks than ever before to police, there was greater potential for friction.

It seems clear that racist attitudes were widespread among the police, as they were elsewhere in American society. A survey of Gary, Indiana police in 1949 found 76 per cent of them to be strongly 'anti-Negro', with 44 per cent believing that 'the Negro is biologically inferior'.[5] A 1966 survey for President Johnson's Crime Commission found similar attitudes among police officers in Boston, Washington, DC, and Chicago.[6] The survey also found evidence that the attitudes were translated into discriminatory behaviour.[7] In systematic observations of police encounters with some 10,000 citizens, the

Crime Commission study found that police were more likely to arrest blacks than whites, for roughly similar offences and conditions.[8] A 1973 study in Dallas found the same pattern in field interrogations, with blacks more likely than whites (as a percentage of both the general population and the arrestee population) to be stopped and questioned.[9]

The most serious allegation of racist police behaviour is that they are more likely to kill blacks than whites. The raw statistics support this charge. Since the late 1960s, about half of the deaths officially recorded as due to 'legal intervention by police' have been of blacks and Hispanics, who comprise less than 20 per cent of the population.[10] The legal justifications for these killings range from self-defence by the police officer to shooting an unarmed juvenile burglary suspect in the back to prevent him from escaping arrest. Police explain the fact that the death rate of blacks in these cases is eight times higher than it is for whites by pointing to the similar disproportionality in serious arrest rates. In some cities the percentage of black arrestees for serious crimes matches the percentage of those killed who are black. But there are two problems with this explanation. One is that many killings emerge out of incidents that are not serious crimes, such as neighbourhood disputes. The other problem is that, nationally, blacks account for only 30 per cent of arrests, leaving a substantial portion of the killings unaccounted for by this argument.

The police killings issue summarises many other aspects of police-minority conflicts. Minorities view police behaviour as discriminatory. Police view their own behaviour as appropriate, given their perception that blacks are much more likely than whites to violate the law.

Minority crime and disorderly behaviour

Measured solely in terms of such street crimes as robbery, rape, and homicide, there is some evidence to support the police view. Both official crime records and victimisation survey data show disproportionately higher involvement in these crimes among blacks than among whites.[11] This does not mean that police are justified in committing what social scientists call the ecological fallacy: assuming that every member of a group carries the traits that characterise the group on average. Most blacks are not criminals and should not be treated as if they were. But as long as rates of street crime appear to be higher among blacks (or other minorities) than whites, police will be prone to stereotype blacks as criminals.

Perhaps more important than the actual rates of serious crime among minorities is the street behaviour that police, like most citizens, associate with crime. Hanging out on street corners, running around in groups shouting and cursing, publicly urinating, playing loud music, occasionally fighting with large audiences, and pan-handling are all offensive to the middle-class eye. Moreover, they engender fear of crime. Where such behaviour is reduced, general public fear of crime is reduced, regardless of what is actually happening to the crime rate.[12] The fact that whites exhibit the same behaviour in suburban shopping centres with similar conflicts with the police, is often forgotten. The density of inner city areas, combined with the perception of blacks as criminals, seems to make such behaviour more threatening, in urban settings.

Minority behaviour toward police

Partly because of the conflicts over manners within the black community, and partly because of the higher rates of street crime in poor black urban neighbourhoods, those neighbourhoods call on the police for assistance more often than white neighbourhoods. They are more likely to call on the police to settle interpersonal disputes. And when the police arrive, blacks are more likely than whites to demand a punitive, legalistic solution to a conflict, such as arresting an offender. (The police are also less likely to give black complainants what they ask for, but their partial responsiveness to the greater demands for arrest helps to account for the greater likelihood of black suspects being arrested. That leaves police with the choice of appearing to discriminate against black complainants or black suspects.)[13]

At the same time that blacks demand more of the police, the police also find blacks harder to deal with than whites. The Crime Commission observation study found that black suspects were more likely than whites to show 'antagonism' toward police, which may also account for the higher arrest rate of black suspects.[14] Black complainants, however, generally showed the same demeanour as white complainants.[15]

Blacks are also more violent towards police than whites, just as police are more violent towards blacks. About 58 per cent of the suspects in killings of police officers are reported to be blacks who comprise only about 12 per cent of the population. Just as police officers vary in their behaviour towards blacks,[16] of course, blacks vary widely in their behaviour toward police. The variation in behaviour is supported by variation in attitudes. As numerous surveys have demonstrated, there is striking evidence that black citizens generally hold positive views about police.[17] But there are substantial divisions by age and sex. Studies of the Watts area after the 1965 riot and of public attitudes in fifteen large cities showed younger black males to be highly critical of police abuse, harassment, and brutality. Older blacks of both sexes were much more sanguine in their view about police.[18] The major criticism older blacks seem to have is that there is not enough police protection: police response time is not fast enough, police are not tough enough on criminals, and there are not enough police assigned to black neighbourhoods.[19] This is hardly the complaint of a community that uniformly views the police, in James Baldwin's terms, as an 'occupying army' of the black ghetto.

What changed?

The reduction in police minority tensions over the 1970s can be attributed to all three elements described above, but in varying degree. There was little apparent change in minority crime and disorder, and only some discernible change in minority behaviour towards police. The biggest change appears to have occurred in police behaviour towards minorities.

The 1970s appear to have been a time of growing divisions among American blacks. Affirmative action in education and employment accelerated the upward mobility of middle-class blacks. Economic dislocations made poorer blacks less employable. Many middle-class blacks moved from city centres to suburbs, while black ghettos deteriorated as a result of arson and neglect.

But the divisions did not change the basic nature of minority crime and disorder as the urban police observed it, perceived it, and dealt with it. If anything, the growing stratification of blacks made minority behaviour among the poor all the 'worse', from the police standpoint. More unemployed black youths (to the degree we can measure their numbers accurately) meant more people hanging out on the streets and more rowdy behaviour for police to contend with. Black involvement in homicides has declined in some cities (notably Detroit), but there is no perception among police that blacks as a group have lower crime rates than a decade ago. It would be hard to point to any changes in the crime and disorder of blacks as a cause of a decline in police-minority tensions.

Minority behaviour toward police may have changed somewhat more. The frequency with which blacks (and whites) kill police officers has declined somewhat. It is my impression that black youths appear to be less openly rebellious in encounters with police. As one police chief claimed, the fact that 'afro' haircuts are shorter may indicate a decline in hostility. The number of demonstrations police must confront appears to have declined. Middle-class blacks seem more supportive than ever of police efforts to control crime. But poor blacks still place heavy demands on police for dealing with disputes and other personal emergencies.

The greatest change can be found in police behaviour towards minorities. The rate at which police kill blacks and other minorities has declined substantially in many cities, although specific incidents of outrageous killings can still provoke riots. The notorious Liberty City (Miami) riot of 1980 was precipitated by a jury's acquittal of several police officers charged with beating a black man to death after he had been subdued and taken into custody. The beating to death of one Joe Campos Torres after Houston police arrested him in a bar in 1977 also provoked minor rioting. The fatal shooting of Mrs Eulia Love by Los Angeles police intervening in a dispute over a utility bill did not provoke violence, but it did provoke a major crisis in police-minority relations and police governance lasting over a year. Milwaukee blacks staged a sit-in in the prosecutor's office to demand indictment of several police officers who killed a mentally disturbed black man after he was handcuffed. But these are dramatic cases that belie the trend. Los Angeles police shot half as many citizens (of all races) in 1980 as they did in 1977.[20] Kansas City, Atlanta, and New York police also cut their shooting rates substantially in response to directives from their chief police executives. In the 52 largest cities, the overall killing rate of citizens dropped slightly from .27 per 100 officers per year in 1975 to .25 in 1980.[21]

The killing data may be an easy-to-measure exception to the more general situation, but I doubt it. Impressions gleaned from riding in patrol cars in different cities regularly from 1971 to 1981 suggest that police have become less aggressive and less insulting in their behaviour towards blacks. What brutality remains seems far more circumspect, although there is much variation across departments on this issue. Major problems still exist, but there seems to have been some improvement.

Most important, the police seem to be doing better at managing the 'rowdiness' of young blacks. The methods have always been available, although the automobile cut off the police practice of talking in the streets which they need to maintain order effectively. It is not that police rediscovered the potential of foot patrols and methodical knowledge of small geographical areas.[22] Rather, they seem to have learned better how to avoid escalating conflicts through excessive legality.

Holyoke, Massachusetts in the early 1970s provides an example. An old mill town with a large black and hispanic population, Holyoke had a heavily Irish police department which enforced the town's Yankee Protestant laws fairly uniformly. One of those laws forbade drinking of alcoholic beverages from open containers while on a public street. Minority group males enjoyed doing precisely that on the front stoops of their houses on summer evenings after work. When police commanded them not to drink publicly, the clash of *mores* and law often erupted in violence. One police officer wound up stabbed in the stomach. But under a federally funded programme in neighbourhood team policing, the rigid law enforcement approach changed, and the violence subsided at least for a while. As the project's evaluators put it, in Holyoke's minority neighbourhoods the conception of policing shifted from enforcing the law to 'patching holes in the social fabric'.

Another example can be found in Oakland, California, once the classic example of a 'legalistic' police department.[23] After a major reform in the 1950s, the Oakland police made a point of enforcing all the laws they could against all violators, no matter what their social status – including police officers themselves. By the late 1960s this rigid posture led to increasing problems with the large minority community. A new chief and a painful change of direction (including a police union vote of no confidence in the chief) softened the legalistic stance. By the 1980s Oakland police were being asked to serve as advisers to hispanic youth groups interested in setting up their own businesses and were building on those relationships to manage conflict among the youth gangs.

This improved capacity to manage incivilities – or willingness to tolerate them, which may be a poor solution – was not accompanied by an end to differential rates of arrest for minorities. A multi-city observation study of police encounters in 1977 showed that the race of the suspect, controlling for all other factors, was still a significant factor affecting arrest decisions; blacks were more likely than whites to be arrested.[24] But this kind of discrimination, if that is the implication of the statistics, is not very visible. Overall patterns of arrest may have far less impact on police-minority relations than a highly publicised legalistic arrest or shooting stemming from a trivial public disorder incident. As long as the police avoid such incendiary racial cases, their relations with minorities are considered improved.

Some unlikely reasons for the change

Many hypotheses can be suggested to explain the apparent changes in police behaviour towards minorities. Three can be drawn from liberal solutions proposed to alleviate police-minority tensions in the 1960s: better training, recruitment of more police from the minorities, and more college-educated police officers. None can be conclusively rejected, but there are good reasons to be sceptical about their importance.

Training

Americans have great faith in the power of knowledge to shape behaviour. Where rational choices about personal self-interest are at stake, this faith may be warranted. Knowledge about tobacco and cholesterol has produced substantial reduction in the consumption of both substances, for example. But the effects of training in areas fraught with ideology and value judgements are far less clear.

American police, especially in the smaller cities, were exposed to far more training in the 1970s than they were in the 1960s. A 1967 study for the Crime Commission[25] found an average requirement of three weeks training of recruits in almost half the police agencies serving cities of over 250,000 people, and many smaller agencies required no training at all. By the mid-1970s a larger survey found that 24 per cent of the 998 police agencies surveyed (only 11 per cent of which served cities over 100,000 people) required more than five weeks formal recruit training, and almost 100 per cent of the agencies of all sizes required some formal training.[26] Massive amounts of funding from the (now defunct) US Law Enforcement Assistance Administration (LEAA) helped increase training even beyond these minimum requirements. Much of the training covered race relations issues or types of police work that often involved minorities. But it is doubtful that much of it did any good.

With growing union power and court cases giving police officers freedom of speech, a form of anarchy came to at least some police training classrooms. No matter what the subject or who the speaker, American police in the big cities often were able to read the newspaper, walk around the room, talk to the people next to them, or otherwise ignore what was going on. Courses on race relations, in particular, were subjects of police disdain, especially for in-service training. Often taught by speakers from civil rights organisations or universities, race relations courses provoked hostile questions, catcalls, and other disorderly behaviour. Courses of instruction turned into combative political debate. While it is possible that even such encounters helped to change police behaviour toward minorities, it seems doubtful.

Training in handling domestic disputes was a favourite for LEAA funding. Thousands of police officers were exposed to rather vague psychological principles for managing conflicts and counselling disputants. But none of the evaluations of these training programmes, except the initial pilot effort in New York, showed that police changed their approach to disputes after the training. The initial evaluation in New York even showed a higher level of violence in the experimental (trained officers) area in comparison to a control area.[27]

Riot training was also a popular way to spend LEAA funds. The errors of police responses to the racial disturbances of the 1960s had been well documented by blue ribbon commissions. Some useful training materials were produced from those reviews, and many police managers and field commanders were exposed to them. But by the time the training was delivered, the need for it had almost disappeared. Perhaps the training enabled police departments to keep minor disturbances from turning into major riots. But it seems more likely that it was the decline in disturbances, rather than initial police responses to them, that kept the 1970s virtually free from major racial conflagrations.

Minority recruitment

Nationally the percentage of minority police officers appeared to rise from 1967 to 1982, although there are no national figures by race on police personnel. A comparison of data compiled by the National Advisory Commission on Civil Disorders[28] with a more recent Police Foundation survey[29] showed that minority police in New York City doubled from 5 to 10 per cent of the force, in Atlanta they rose from 10 to 48 per cent, and in Detroit from 5 to 30 per cent. But some cities actually had a decline. Philadelphia, for example, declined from 20 per cent black officers in 1967 to 17 per cent black in 1982. Other cities made almost no progress. Chicago, for example, went from 17 to 19 per cent.

Police department efforts to recruit and promote minorities in the 1970s were valuable for their own sake. In some places, they corrected longstanding patterns of discrimination in employment and produced a more equitable distribution of the high-paying jobs police departments offer. Since police departments have never been able to develop selection procedures that accurately predict good performance, there was little trade-off of meritocracy for equality of opportunity for ethnic groups. In the absence of valid merit criteria, group membership has long been a major criterion for selecting police. The minority recruitment programmes in some, but not all, major cities simply added one more group to be included among the preferred list.

Whatever the merits of minority recruitment as an end in itself, it is easy to argue that the presence of more black officers can ease police relations with black communities. That was the premise of the various presidential commissions' recommendations that police departments recruit more minorities. The theory is that since black police are more likely to understand 'black culture' (assuming there is a monolithic 'black culture' that cuts across social classes), they would be more able than whites to police black communities without friction. If the white police are seen as an occupying army, then black police should be less likely to be brutal and oppressive. This theory presumes that the cause of poor policing is racism and that black police have little cause to be racist against their own race.

But this theory is full of holes. Even accepting it on its own terms, it ignores the lesson of colonial and reservation policing. If white police are an occupying army, they would be well advised to hire a staff of indigenous police who, history suggests, will be as harsh or harsher in policing their fellow nationals. The theory also ignores the power of the 'organisational culture' of policing to shape the behaviour of black officers, sometimes more powerfully than any racial allegiances they may feel. Black officers can suffer extreme conflicts of loyalty, but they know their economic security and social status is tied to their adjustment to the demands of the police organisation.[30]

The theory also disregards the diversity of perspectives among blacks. Black police officers are, by definition, middle class; the young males who are the greatest problem for police are lower class. Some black officers report that they are especially angry at the 'worthless bums' who hang out on street corners and reflect poorly on the race. Indeed, as late as the 1960s in Harlem, black officers had a reputation for being much tougher than white officers, since they had less fear of a citizen complaint for racist police conduct.

Whatever theory one accepts, the available evidence suggests little difference between blacks and whites as police officers. The 1966 Crime Commission study found that black and white police officers were about equally likely to use illegal and excessive force against prisoners who had already been subdued and taken into custody.[31] Black and white officers differed little in their interaction with citizens, although black officers were somewhat more likely to patrol aggressively and make arrests.[32] In New York City from 1971 to 1975 black officers were twice as likely to shoot as white officers, although the difference was almost entirely explained by the fact that blacks were far more likely to be assigned to or live in high crime neighbourhoods.[33]

One must be cautious, however, in generalising from differences at the individual level to group effects. The fact that, as individuals, black and white officers show little difference does not exclude the possibility that a department with more black officers behaves differently from a department with fewer black officers. The effects of proportions on groups are often subtle but powerful. As blacks comprise a larger portion of a police department, they may become less isolated and more influential in shaping the values and culture of the entire police department. Racist language, for example, may disappear in police locker rooms simply because there are too many black officers around to hear it. There may be – and have been – numerous incidents of violence between black and white police during the process of transition. But increasing the number of black police can change the internal organisational climate.

Even so, the question remains: does the internal organisational climate produced by a larger proportion of blacks change the way police generally behave towards minorities? This argument might be used to explain the declining use of deadly force in the Detroit and Atlanta police departments as the percentage of minority officers increased. However, other reasons for those changes (suggested later on) strike me as more plausible, although we simply do not know the answer.

Another question is what symbolic value a 'representative' police force may have in fostering the consent of the policed. Even if black police do not behave any better (or behave worse) than white police, it is possible that the black community believes they behave better. A situation perceived as real has real consequences, no matter how false the perceptions may be. Blacks may be less hostile generally to a police department with more black officers, even while they are hostile to individual blacks who become police officers. But once again, we lack any clear evidence. Available evidence tells us that individual black officers behave little differently from individual white officers. While it is possible that better minority recruitment has had some effects at the group level, we simply do not know. Minority recruitment may have been worth pursuing as an end in itself, but was probably not a leading factor in improving police behaviour toward minorities. Whether it helped improve minority behaviour towards police is unclear.

College-educated police

One of the reform proposals of the 1960s most favoured by intellectuals was that all new police recruits should hold a baccalaureate degree. Several theories supported this proposal. One was that college-educated people were simply better: smarter, more honest, less racially prejudiced, more creative, more hardworking. As better people, they should be better police. Another theory was that a college-educated police force would command more public respect, as the FBI does, especially since such a large portion of the public is now college-educated. A third theory was that a college curriculum focused on police work subjects would prepare police officers better for their work.[34]

The first two theories have been almost impossible to test, despite the fact that the federal government spent over $250m. subsidising college education for policing, despite the fact that the percentage of officers with some college courses increased from 20 per cent in 1960 to 46 per cent in 1974, and despite the fact that the mean level of education for police surpassed the level of the general public for the first time in recent history. None of these changes tested the theory or the reform proposal itself, since they did not produce police recruits who were college graduates. Instead, they resulted in people who were already police exposed part-time to college classes in classrooms that were often full of other police officers from the same department. Whether they represented recruiting the educated or educating the recruited, the percentage of officers who were college graduates increased to only about 10 per cent.[35] The number of police departments that require new recruits to be college graduates can be counted on one hand. American policing never acquired either the substance or the prestige of a profession requiring advanced education for admission.

The third theory behind this proposal was tested, although not in the way intended. Police-related subjects comprised the bulk of what police officers studied in their part-time college enrolment. But the subjects often duplicated what was taught in police training academies,[36] often by the same instructors moonlighting as college professors. The courses rarely added depth and breadth to discussions of policing, as history, philosophy, sociology, and ethics of police work might have done. Instead, they recapitulated many of the 'nuts and bolts' practical instructions, such as how to write an arrest report, how to conduct an investigation, or how to shoot. Since there was little change in the content of instruction, it is not reasonable to expect that the college courses produced a change in behaviour.

Only limited evidence, hopelessly flawed by inadequate methodologies, is available on the individual differences between officers with and without some college education. The findings are generally in conflict depending on the methodology each study employs.[37] The combination of the failure to implement the proposal properly and the lack of any clear evidence of change suggests a conclusion: college education of police had relatively little to do with improving police behaviour towards minorities in the 1970s.

This is not to say that the proposal to require college degrees would fail it if were properly adopted. Even if individual officers do not behave differently according to their level of education, there may be group effects from creating police departments fully staffed with college graduates. These effects might be especially likely to change police behaviour if the officers had studied a broad range of subjects, not just police-related topics. But despite the recommendation of at least three national commissions from 1962 to 1978, police departments do not seem likely to adopt this approach to upgrading police educational levels.

Some likely reasons for the change

Sociologists often discount any approach to changing institutions that is based more on the kinds of people in them than on the structure of their interaction. Training, minority recruitment, and college education for police are all 'people' theories rather than 'system' theories about police change. The evidence (or perhaps my sociological biases) seems to point to systemic changes as the more likely reasons for improved police behaviour toward minorities. Increasing black political power, tougher discipline of police, more restrictions on police discretion, rising litigation against police, and the 'cooling off' of black protest all strike me as important factors.

Black political power

As early as the 1960s it was clear that police behaved differently in cities whose mayors were relatively liberal on matters of civil rights and race. Often the most apparent difference was the visibility of police protests against efforts to control their behaviour towards minorities. The most famous example was the successful police union campaign for repeal of New York City's independent civilian complaint review board to investigate charges of police brutality and rudeness. The review board, a leading minority group solution to police brutality, had been a key plank in the platform of liberal Mayor John Lindsay. Using television advertisements that tied the review board to an impotent police force and rising crime, the union persuaded white voters in the referendum on the statute to repeal it.

Despite union resistance, the liberal mayors seem to have got their message across. In a study for the National Commission on Civil Disorders, Rossi and his colleagues measured controversial police practices.[38] They asked police in seventeen cities how often they stopped people to check their identification and frisk them, searched without a warrant, broke up loitering groups, and interrogated suspected drug users. These findings were confirmed by public opinion surveys asking citizens how often police did these things. The researchers also interviewed police to determine their backgrounds, including age, education, and race. Their analysis showed that the individual differences in officer backgrounds made little difference in self-reported frequency of using controversial police practices. What made the most difference was the city the officer worked in. That is, the differences in police practices appeared to be due to group effects of police department culture rather than the kinds of people the officers were.

The Rossi study also interviewed the mayors and police chiefs of the seventeen cities. The police chiefs' attitudes towards black people and black aspirations were largely determined by the mayor's attitude, which makes sense in cities where the mayor can hire and fire the chief. The more striking finding was that the attitudes of the mayor and the chief had a very strong effect on the frequency of controversial police practices. The more sympathetic the mayor and chief were to black aspirations, the lower the frequency of controversial police practices. The mayors' attitudes alone explained 40 per cent of the variance in police practices.[39] Combined with the degree to which police were acquainted with people in their precincts and the level of citizen hostility which police perceived, the executives' attitudes accounted for over half the variance – an unusually powerful explanation for social science.

This study, conducted in 1967–8, predated the rise of black influence in American city politics. Since then, black mayors have been elected in Detroit, Los Angeles, Newark, Atlanta, Washington, Cleveland, New Orleans, Oakland, and other major cities. No-one has attempted to document the impact of these elections on police practices. But the Rossi study suggests that the rise of black political influence may have had a dampening effect on the use of controversial police practices.

There is ample anecdotal evidence to support this view, much of it related to police use of firearms. In both Detroit and Atlanta in the early 1970s, police use of guns was rapidly increasing during the administrations of white mayors. Many of the shootings were controversial, provoking outrage in the black communities. In both cities, black mayoral candidates campaigned against the shooting practices. When they were elected, they appointed new police chiefs, and the frequency of police shootings declined sharply. In Los Angeles, a black mayor appointed new members of the Los Angeles Board of Police Commissioners, a body that had historically left control of the police in the hands of the civil service-tenured chief. Slowly but surely the new Board has taken over control of the department, setting new policies restricting police discretion and actively reviewing investigations of police misconduct.

In addition to the actual changes black mayors (or black city council members or other politically influential figures) may make in police management practices, they may also have an indirect influence on police behaviour for purely symbolic reasons. When blacks gain political power, police can no longer assume a culture of white supremacy in which police can get away with murder (as some have literally done). The black person a police officer deals with may look poor and powerless, but he may also be related to the mayor or an alderman. Officers have been transferred or disgraced in years past for offending relatives of white politicians. The election of black officials broadens the scope of that political sanction and adds one more note of caution to police interactions with blacks.

Tougher discipline

It is hard to convey to lay people the degree to which police misconduct once went unpunished. Some departments, such as Newark at the time of its 1967 riot, refused even to investigate citizen allegations of police misconduct. Others might as well have said no. Philadelphia, for example, throughout much of the 1970s rarely disciplined officers for excessive use of force. In the 1960s many big city police departments covered up for their officers, investigating the charges from the perspective of a defence lawyer seeking to justify the accused officer's conduct. But by the end of the 1970s this was probably less often the case.

A new generation of police chiefs was raised in the era of public dissatisfaction with police disciplinary procedures. By the end of the 1970s, they saw their own clear interest. Either the police department had to provide visibly tough discipline for misconduct, or there would be increasing pressure for removing control of discipline from the police department to place it in the hands of an external board. Police chiefs could lose their jobs for not being tough enough. Also police unions constantly attacked chiefs for other reasons, reducing the sense of loyalty and collegiality which chiefs had once felt toward the rank and file and which had limited the severity of punishment.

Another factor encouraging tougher police discipline was the US Supreme Court's expansion of citizen rights to sue police departments, and chiefs personally, for the misconduct of police officers. If a plaintiff could demonstrate that misconduct was an organisational custom or practice, then he could recover damages from the city's deep pocket. The best way to prove that misconduct was an organisational custom was to show that the officer (or other officers) had committed similar acts in the past without being punished. Such a finding would place the blame directly on the police chief.

While there are no systematic data available to measure changes in the severity of police discipline over the 1970s, my impression is that it increased. Although this view seems to be confirmed by discussions with police officers and chiefs from twenty or more departments, as well as empirical research in New York, Los Angeles, Louisville, Minneapolis, and several smaller police agencies, it may not be generally valid. It certainly may be wrong in the case of specific departments. But the factors encouraging tougher discipline were clearly increasing throughout the 1970s.

Did tougher discipline change police behaviour? Here again, the evidence is impressionistic. But the theory of deterrence is gaining support in other contexts. Police officers themselves increasingly complain that they don't do anything any more for fear that their actions in performing good police work will be disciplined. Since arrest rates per officer may be increasing while they make this complaint, we can only infer that the manner in which they deal with citizens is less aggressive than before, rather than that the frequency of their contacts is declining. And that may be precisely what the chiefs intended to achieve through discipline.

Restrictions on police discretion

Tougher discipline backed up another trend that may have improved police behaviour towards minorities: more restrictions on discretion. Police rulebooks have been very thick in some cities for many years. A new rule was added each time someone complained about some aspect of police behaviour. There are (or have been) rules against smoking on duty, going hatless in the patrol car, engaging in 'unnecessary conversation' with citizens, and being seen with 'known gamblers'. But until the 1970s few police agencies had explicit rules concerning police interactions with minorities.

One of the first restrictions to become commonplace was on language. Many agencies put out long lists of derogatory ethnic names that officers were forbidden to use. The lists were ignored until civilian complaints alleging use of the term 'nigger' or other such words were punished seriously. The apparent change in behaviour is instructive. Police officers still commonly use such abusive terms as 'asshole' when they wish to give a citizen a tongue-lashing, but the epithets are not racist. They are the same epithets police would use against whites – and that may be a positive change.

Another major area of restricted discretion is in the use of force. At the end of the 1960s few police departments even had a written policy governing the use of firearms. They relied solely on state laws, which were very broad. Over half the states still empower a police officer to use his gun if there is no other way to effect an arrest on suspicion of any felony. In the absence of police department policy, many officers used their legal powers by shooting unarmed fleeing burglary suspects in the back. These shootings, while perfectly legal, often outraged black communities. In response, many police departments adopted formal, written policies limiting far more strictly than the state law, the police officer's discretion to use his gun. Some departments went from policies as broad as 'never take your gun out unless you intend to use it' to 15-page, complex policies governing the use of warning shots, off-duty use of the gun, due care for not endangering innocent bystanders, shooting at automobiles, shooting at juveniles, and even the conditions under which officers could take their guns out of their holsters. The result, as noted earlier, has been a substantial decline in the rate at which people are killed by police. And in at least two cities examined empirically, this reduction in citizen lives lost has been achieved without an increase in police officers' lives lost or an increase in the serious crime rate.[40]

To be sure, police discretion is still very broad, as perhaps it ought to be. The power of arrest may be best used as one of many tools to negotiate conflicts and respond to problems of maintaining order, the most common task of the police. That tool is still abused in response to personal insults to police, or even failure to act sufficiently deferentially towards police. 'Contempt of cop' is often sufficient cause for arrest, which many blacks and whites interpret as harassment. No police executive has discovered a way to control this abuse, except through discipline of the rare cases that come to an executive's attention. Yet the beneficial side of police discretion is that it allows officers not to make arrests when an arrest could disrupt the maintenance of order.

Civil litigation

One of the worst aspects of police-minority relations in the 1960s was that there were almost no channels of complaint. In many cities, both the police chief and the mayor ignored citizen complaints against police. The FBI and the US Attorney usually claimed a lack of jurisdiction. And what may seem incredible in our modern litigious society, there was a time in many cities in which no lawyer could be found who was willing to represent a black person in a civil suit against the police department. Moreover, the legal basis for such suits was very limited, since courts at that time interpreted the doctrine of sovereign immunity broadly.

Two things happened in the 1970s to make civil litigation a major – and far more lucrative – avenue of protest against police practices. One was the rapid expansion in the supply of lawyers, with some 30,000 new law school graduates each year looking for legal business. This trend, in the context of the civil rights movement, greatly increased the number of lawyers ready and willing to represent minorities in suits against the police. The number of suits increased rapidly, from 1,741 in 1967 to 3,894 by 1971.[41] Many police officers even suggested that some offenders habitually filed civil suits each time they were arrested to give themselves additional leverage in plea bargaining. They could offer to drop the civil suit if the charges were dropped or reduced.

The other trend was the narrowing of the scope of sovereign immunity. By the late 1970s, the US Supreme Court had given citizens broad rights to recover damages from municipal governments for police officers' actions depriving citizens of their rights (for example, *Monell v. Department of Social Services*, 436 U.S. 658 [1978]). These decisions appear to have encouraged even more suits and perhaps increased the fairly low rate at which plaintiffs actually won their suits. The size of damage awards also increased, now reaching as high as $5.75m. in cases in which people are killed.

There is some reason to question the effectiveness of civil litigation in shaping police behaviour. A *Yale Law Journal* survey of federal suits against police suggested that police officers almost never are held personally liable for their actions.[42] And as long as the city pays the damages and the city or the police union pays the legal expenses, a lawsuit is not a financial threat to the officer or the chief. On the other hand, many police officers have described the personal stigma, shame, and stress they suffer from having court employees serve papers on them at their homes in front of their families, and the caution they use to avoid lawsuits.

Regardless of how much litigation has shaped police behaviour towards minorities, it seems to have diverted organised minority protest against police. Civil litigation provides incentives for individual action against police, not for collective protests. In that sense it may have had a 'divide and conquer' effect on organised minority efforts to shape police policy. But it may also have increased the sense of efficacy blacks have about seeking redress. By reducing their sense of powerlessness, civil litigation may have made blacks more comfortable in their dealings with police, leading to better relations between them.

Cooling off of blacks in other spheres
Since some of the improvement in climate must be traced to changes in minority behaviour toward police, we must account for that change as well. One reason may be at least a temporary reduction in the sense of powerlessness that middle-class blacks have had in American society. With better access to jobs, education, and housing, not to mention more frequent appearances by black actors and newscasters on television, racial discrimination in American society has visibly declined. It is still pervasive, but in more subtle ways. With less intense black anger over the cruder forms of discrimination, there is less hostility to focus on the police as the most visible representatives of a discriminatory social system. To the degree that middle-class blacks have been diverted from organised protests because of better opportunities to make a living, they have followed the general American trend toward placing personal concerns ahead of civic action. This is not due to anything that the police have done, but is a tendency that has probably eased police relations with minorities.

One can hardly claim, however, that lower class minorities have effectively 'cooled off'[43] their anger and protest by improved conditions and opportunities. If anything, they may become worse off in the 1980s than they were in the 1960s. The reasons they have suffered lie more in the economy than in civil rights policy. But in the irony of social life, declining economic opportunities may have reduced the expectations of poorer blacks, making them more angry at themselves for being unemployed and less angry at the system that makes them unemployable. In contrast, when the economy was expanding in the late 1960s, poorer blacks may have felt more confident in challenging the representatives of the social order.

From law enforcement to peacekeeping

Of all the reasons for the improvement in police behaviour towards minorities, one stands out. It is perhaps the hardest to measure, but it runs through every aspect of police activity. This trend is a change in the very philosophy of police work, away from a rigidly mechanistic conception of enforcement of every law to a more malleable conception of keeping the peace.

The difference between these two philosophies of law enforcement is subtle, but crucial. It arises not in the enforcement of laws against homicide, rape, or robbery, but in the less serious offences of noise violations, bar fights, neighbourhood disputes, domestic assaults, and sometimes even burglary. The difference is a distinction between ends and means. The law enforcement conception of police work views enforcement of the law as an end in itself, regardless of its consequences for the social order. The peacekeeping conception of police work views law enforcement as a means towards achieving an end: the highest possible level of public safety, order, and preservation of life and property.

Robert K. Merton many years ago observed the tendency of most bureaucracies to displace their basic goals with overwhelming devotion to the means provided for accomplishing the goals.[44] Police departments in the United States were created to maintain order, often because of dislike of new minority groups. If law enforcement was not the best way to keep order, then other methods were used – from brutality to political organising. As police departments became more professional and independent as 'crime fighters',[45] law enforcement began to take precedence over maintaining order and keeping the peace.

Even in the 1960s police departments varied widely in the degree to which they emphasised one philosophy over the other.[46] Many older, eastern cities still rarely used arrest to handle disputes or minor offences. The posture of some departments was passive, so much so that police would often leave the scene of what might appear to be a life-threatening situation (such as a domestic conflict) on the grounds that 'it's none of our business.' These departments would break up fights but rarely arrest the participants. They were not without their problems of corruption and brutality, but at least they did not create more problems.

The 'legalistic' departments of the 1960s, however, did create unnecessary problems. They lacked patience, tact, diplomacy, and balance. If a hostage was being held by a gunman, these departments might storm the location with a SWAT (Special Weapons and Tactics) team, killing the hostage as well as the kidnapper. A peacekeeping department like the one in New York City, on the other hand, developed a special hostage-negotiating team with trained psychologists and did not lose one hostage's life in hundreds of incidents over eight years.

The legalistic departments were always in a hurry to enforce the law and get on to the next call for service. That is the underlying reason, I think, for the Los Angeles Police Department's 1979 killing of Eulia Love over a utility bill dispute. The officers made no attempt to defuse the situation by delay. Instead, they forced an immediate confrontation with an emotionally upset person, who responded by attacking them.

With the rise of black political influence, police executives have used tougher discipline and more restrictions on discretion to reshape their officers' philosophy of police work. If heavy law enforcement presence at a block party where dope is sold might precipitate a riot, it is much less likely that police in 1982 will go ahead with such an enforcement operation than it was in 1968. If the only way to capture a black, 15-year-old burglary suspect is to shoot him in the back, it is much less likely that police in 1982 will shoot than it was in 1968. If a group of young black males loitering on a corner provokes a neighbour's complaint, police are much less likely in 1982 to break up the group forcibly than they were in 1968; today they are more likely to use talk.

The riots of the 1960s still provide a context for much of the policy-making of the police in the United States. We have seen the vision of urban anarchy, and we have learned what we must do to avoid it. The price of that avoidance is that some laws will go unenforced, but the law was underenforced before the riots anyway. We have discovered the paradox that in some situations more law enforcement may produce more crime. Less law may produce more order.

Implications for British policing

Not all of these observations are relevant to the current state of race relations in Britain, but some are. They have implications both for what won't work and for what might.

Britain in 1982 is much like the United States in 1968. It has suffered a long, hot summer of the worst rioting in memory, largely focused on the police. It has in the Scarman Report an official review and a set of proposals for dealing with the problem.[47] And it appears to have in its current philosophy and management of policing a major set of obstacles to any improvement. If this assessment is correct, it seems unlikely that many of the proposals in the Scarman Report will have much effect, even if they are implemented. Training and minority recruitment seem unlikely to ease the tensions for the reasons offered earlier, although they may be worth while for other reasons. The proposal to find better tests for screening out officers who might be racially prejudiced totally misses the social nature of the problem. Race prejudice is not a personal disease, like high blood pressure, for which individuals can be tested. It is a learned pattern of attitudes and behaviour. As long as the British police suffer from institutional racism, as the American police have done and still do, then the most unbiased police recruit will be likely to adopt a prejudiced viewpoint within a year or two.

The distinction between personal prejudice and institutional racism is crucial. The two may exist together, but not necessarily. It is possible for personally prejudiced police to behave in ways that are equitable towards minorities, as they often do in American cities controlled by black leaders. It is also possible for officers who are not personally prejudiced to behave in ways that penalise blacks more than whites for the same conduct. Institutional racism is far more subtle than crudely expressed personal prejudice, but its effects can be far more serious.

Institutional racism is a strong charge to make against any organisation but there is at least some evidence concerning British police. The 1976 Runnymede Trust study, showing the overwhelmingly disproportionate presence of blacks among those arrested for the crime of 'being a suspicious person', provides one piece of evidence.[48] The 1824 law (modified in 1981) allows police to arrest someone not for having committed a crime, but for looking as if they might be about to commit a crime. A police officer's judgement to that effect can lead to punishment of the suspect by a £100 fine or three months in jail. Blacks constitute about 42 per cent of arrests for being suspected of committing theft, even though they constitute only 5 per cent of the population and 11 per cent of those people arrested for actually committing a theft. Other evidence includes the many horror stories of harassment told by black leaders, as well as implicitly racist statements by British police leaders.

The institutional racism of the British police, like that of the American, will probably not be curbed until blacks gain political influence. Judging by present trends in English politics, that is not likely to happen soon. What could happen soon is that the police could shift their conception of policing from law enforcement to peacekeeping. And that could make a great difference in their relations with minorities. This idea runs throughout the Scarman Report, with reference to all of the concrete problems of English policing. Lord Scarman begins with the necessary philosophical statement of the three police missions: i) maintenance of public order, ii) effective law enforcement, and iii) the protection of life and property, 'public order is, in the last resort, the most important'.[49] He then shows how the peacekeeping goal would alter the general approach of 'hard policing' in high crime areas, such as the 'swamping' (saturation patrol) operation that helped provoke the Brixton riot. He recommends more consultation between police and black leaders and development of close ties between individual officers and the residents of particular beats.

Unfortunately, Lord Scarman's philosophy of peacekeeping may receive little support in policy-making circles. The current government appears to blame the problem largely on the minorities, without suggesting redirection of the philosophical basis of minority policing. More police aggressiveness to fight crime may be the policy result, rather than an alliance of middle-aged blacks and police working cooperatively to reduce crime among younger black males. Some mid-level police commanders and many 'home beat' officers may see things differently. But unless the British Government explicitly endorses Lord Scarman's preference for peace and order over rigid law enforcement, Britain may be headed for more of what America has already suffered.

The irony is that the British police pioneered the idea of policing by consent, of 'selling' the public the idea that policing was a good thing. Historically, they have been better at it than the Americans.[50] But policing a multi-racial society in the historical context of colonialism may have led to the abandonment of the consent idea, which Lord Scarman restates so clearly. If the British police are to remain the leading example of democratic police work, they would do well to recapture their original philosophy of peacekeeping by consent rather than law enforcement by coercion.

Notes

1 National Advisory Commission on Civil Disorders, *Report* (Washington DC: USGPO 1968).
2 Alan Levett, 'The Centralisation of City Police in the Nineteenth Century United States'. PhD dissertation, Department of Sociology, University of Michigan, 1975.
3 Zachariah Chaffee, W.H. Pollack and C.S. Stern, *The Third Degree* (Washington DC: National Commission on Law Observance and Enforcement, 1931).
4 Anthony Platt, *The Politics of Riot Commissions* (New York: Macmillan, 1971).
5 William Westley, *Violence and the Police* (Cambridge, Mass.: MIT Press, 1970), p. 100.
6 Donald J. Black and Albert J. Reiss Jr., 'Patterns of Behaviour and Citizen Transactions', in President's Commission on Law Enforcement and Administration of Justice, *Studies in Crime and Law Enforcement in Major Metropolitan Areas, Field Surveys III*, Vol. 2., sec. 1 (Washington DC: USGPO, 1967).
7 Robert J. Friedrich, 'The Impact of Organisational, Individual and Situational Factors on Police Behaviour'. PhD Dissertation, Department of Political Science, University of Michigan, 1977.
8 Donald J. Black, 'The Social Organisation of Arrest'. *Stanford Law Review*, Vol. 23, 1971, pp. 1087–1111; Friedrich, *op. cit.*
9 Robert Bogomolny, 'Street Patrol: the Decision to Stop a Citizen', *Criminal Law Bulletin*, vol. 12, No. 5, 1976, pp. 544–582.
10 Lawrence W. Sherman and Robert Langworthy, 'Measuring Homicide by Police Officers', *Journal of Criminal Law and Criminology*, Vol. 70, No. 4, 1979, pp. 546–60.
11 Michael J. Hindelang, 'Variation in Sex-Race-Age-Specific Rates of Offending', *American Sociological Review*, Vol. 46, No. 4, 1981, pp. 461–74.
12 Police Foundation, *The Newark Foot Patrol Experiment* (Washington DC: Police Foundation, 1981).
13 Donald Black, *The Behaviour of Law* (New York: Academic Press, 1976); Donald Black, *The Manners and Customs of the Police*, (New York: Academic Press, 1980).
14 Donald Black, 'Social Organisation of Arrest', *op. cit.*
15 Albert J. Reiss Jr., *The Police and the Public* (New Haven: Yale University Press) 1971, p. 52.
16 Federal Bureau of Investigation, *Law Enforcement Officers Killed Summary, 1981* (Washington DC: Federal Bureau of Investigation, n.d.), p. 19.
17 James Q. Wilson, *Thinking About Crime* (New York: Basic Books, 1975), p. 99.
18 *ibid.*, pp. 100–104.
19 *ibid.*, p. 104.
20 Marshall W. Meyer, *Officer Involved Shootings*, part four (Los Angeles: Police Department Board of Police Commissioners, 1980).
21 Kenneth Matulia. *Justifiable Homicide by the Police: a Study of Homicide by the Police in 57 US Cities* (Gaithersburg, Md: International Association of Chiefs of Police, 1981), Tables E–1 and F–1.
22 Egon Bittner, *The Functions of the Police in Modern Society* (Chevy Chase, Md: National Institute of Mental Health, 1970).
23 James Q. Wilson, *Varieties of Police Behavior* (Cambridge, Mass: Harvard University Press, 1968).
24 Douglas A. Smith and Christy A. Vishner, 'Street Level Justice: Situational Determinants of Police Arrest Decisions', *Social Problems*, Vol. 24, No. 2, 1981, pp. 167–177.
25 President's Commission on Law Enforcement and Administration of Justice, *Task Force Report: The Police* (Washington DC: USGPO, 1967), p. 138.
26 Elinor Ostrom, Robert B. Parks and Gordon P. Whitaker, *Patterns of Metropolitan Policing* (Cambridge, Mass.: Ballinger, 1978), p. 271.

27 Morton Bard, *Training Police as Specialists in Family Crisis Intervention* (Washington DC: USGPO, 1970).

28 National Advisory Commission on Civil Disorders, *Report, op. cit.* pp. 321–2.

29 Margaret Triplett, 'Survey of Police Agency Minority Representation', Unpublished manuscript, 1982.

30 Nicholas Alex, *Black in Blue* (New York: Appleton – Century Crofts, 1969).

31 Albert J. Reiss, Jr., 'Police Brutality' in Leon Radzinowicz and Marvin E. Wolfgang (eds), *Crime and Justice Volume 2: The Criminal In the Arms of the Law* (New York: Basic Books, 1972), p. 304.

32 Robert J. Friedrich, *op. cit.*

33 James Fyfe, 'Shots Fired: A Typological Examination of New York City Police Firearms Discharges', PhD dissertation, Graduate School of Criminal Justice, State University of New York at Albany, 1978.

34 Lawrence W. Sherman and the National Advisory Commission on Higher Education for Police Officers, *The Quality of Police Education* (San Francisco: Jossey-Bass, 1978).

35 *ibid.*, p. 186.

36 Lawrence W. Sherman and Maureen McLeod, 'Faculty Characteristics and Course Content in College Programs for Police Officers', *Journal of Criminal Justice*, Vol. 7, 1979, pp. 249–67.

37 Dennis C. Smith, *Empirical Studies of Higher Education and Police Performance*, (Washington DC: Police Foundation, 1978).

38 Peter Rossi, Richard A. Berk and Bettye K. Eidson, *The Roots of Urban Discontent* (New York: Wiley, 1975).

39 *ibid.*, p. 183.

40 Lawrence W. Sherman, 'Reducing Police Gun Use: The Effects of Administrative Policy' in Maurice Punch (ed.), *Control of the Police Organization* (Cambridge, Mass.: MIT Press, 1982).

41 Americans for Effective Law Enforcement, *Survey of Police Misconduct Litigation 1967–71* (Evanston, Illinois: Americans for Effective Law Enforcement, n.d.).

42 'Suing the Police in Federal Court', *Yale Law Journal*, Vol. 88, 1979, pp. 781–824.

43 Erving Goffman, 'On Cooling the Mark Out: Some Aspects of Adaption to Failure', *Psychiatry*, November, 1962, pp. 45–63.

44 Robert K. Merton, 'Bureaucratic Structure and Personality' in *Social Theory and Social Structure* (New York: Free Press, 1968).

45 Robert M. Fogelson, *Big City Police* (Cambridge, Mass.: Harvard University Press, 1977).

46 James Q. Wilson, *Varieties of Police Behaviour. op. cit.*

47 Rt Hon. Lord Scarman, *The Brixton Disorders, 10–12 April 1981* (London: HMSO, Cmnd 8427, 1981).

48 Bruce Porter, 'The British Riots: Hatred of the Police was the Common Thread', *Police Magazine*, Vol. 5, No. 1, 1982, pp. 6–18, 59–63.

49 Lord Scarman, *op. cit.*, p. 75.

50 Wilbur Miller, *Cops and Bobbies* (Chicago: University of Chicago Press, 1977).

13 Beyond Scarman: Police Accountability in Britain
Laurence Lustgarten

Identifying an issue in ethnic terms often has important practical implications. It may be taken more seriously by government and the media, receiving more attention and resources than would have been devoted to a problem seen as more diffusely and less emotively focused. Conversely, ameliorative responses may be more strongly resisted if ethnic animosities mean that the majority is unwilling to assist those it denigrates. However, the ethnic identification may also mean that more fundamental causes or relationships are obscured, that only the more flashy and explosive elements of a problem claim attention; the part is taken for the whole. Such has been the case with policing in Britain, which only burst on to the political centre stage with the riots of 1981. Yet the fundamental issues concerning the relationship between the police and the public range far more widely, and are even more intractable, than those specifically pertaining to ethnic minorities. The present paper attempts to document that conclusion, taking Lord Scarman's Report on the Brixton riots as both a target and a foil for a more comprehensive perspective.[1]

The contemporary political context
Fifteen years ago, issues of police accountability, let alone more radical demands for democratic control of the police, were wholly absent from the agenda of English politics. Some years previously, in response to a series of isolated incidents involving corruption and individual misconduct, a Royal Commission on the Police was established to examine questions of constitutional status, accountability and responsiveness to complaints. Its Final Report in 1962 recommended no major changes, and focused largely on questions of amalgamation of forces, centralisation and co-ordination, and efficiency generally.[2] The ensuing debate, measured in tone and never highly politicised, ended with the enactment of the Police Act 1964, whose major provisions are discussed below. Such questions then vanished from public attention.

Peripheral voices, such as those among newly-arrived immigrants from the West Indies complaining of crude bigotry, rampant discourtesy and occasional violence, and of CND demonstrators alleging harassment and assaults, went unheard by those at the political centre. To the great majority of the public, the police were personified by the traditional image of the benign local bobby – Dixon of Dock Green or even PC Plod. Unarmed, well-known to the people living on his 'patch', perhaps not overbright but full of commonsense, he was above all an individual who dealt with members of the public as individuals. He was not the anonymous representative of a distant bureaucracy. To use the two words most frequently applied to a police organisation, he was felt to be providing a service, rather than acting as part of a force.

Notwithstanding various ephemeral rows, in retrospect the mid and late 1960s now appear as the very end of the post-war era of political consensus and rising prosperity well described as the age of secular Anglicanism.[3] Fundamental political stability meant that the inevitable tensions between maintaining order and respecting personal liberties were minimised. Once the calm of the political waters became roiled, the police began to respond as Tom Bowden argued is inevitable in such circumstances: by emphasising their repressive functions and strengthening their capacity to combat the perceived threats.[4]

The early and mid-1970s were critical. A series of unrelated but very severe conflicts thrust the police into new roles, and into a new and more threatening posture vis-à-vis substantial segments of the population, seen now in terms of collectivities rather than individuals.

First, there was a dramatic rise in the scope and intensity of industrial disputes. These included a near general strike, mass picketing, and deployment of mobile 'flying pickets' on an unprecedented scale and effectiveness, and repeated invocations of emergency powers by the national government which twice promulgated three-day working weeks. The resulting strain on individual forces and their members, and the belief that much militant industrial action was politically motivated, led to Home Office co-ordination of enlarged and more sophisticated arrangements of 'mutual aid' among forces – 'flying police'.

Second, and concurrent with these developments, came the IRA bombing campaigns which stimulated greater use of informants and surveillance of suspected Republican sympathisers. After a bomb killed 21 people in a Birmingham public house in December 1974, hastily enacted legislation gave the police power to hold persons for questioning for up to five days on the basis of very slender evidence.[5] There have been numerous complaints of harassment of Irish immigrants.

Third, fear of other forms of terrorism, notably hijackings and the taking of hostages, led among other things to an increased emphasis on para-military training and armament. The unarmed bobby, the source of such pride, still predominates, but a vastly increased number of his colleagues now carry or have ready access to firearms, and training in their use is much more widespread.

Fourth, radical student activism, which flourished until the mid-1970s and produced spin-off political movements, resulted in a vastly increased number of demonstrations and a visibly greater hostility on the part of instinctively conservative-minded men to political 'extremists.' Meanwhile, ever-increasing racism in politics, embodied by the rise of the National Front, spawned demonstrations and counter-demonstrations which often turned into small battles. As they had done in the 1930s,[6] the police more often than not took the view that they would protect the right of racialist groups to march where they pleased, and give little protection to the rights – equal in law – of those who wished to demonstrate peacefully against them.

Fifth, sharply exclusionist immigration legislation, administered with hardening rigour by the Home Office and interpreted retrospectively by the courts, exposed greater numbers of people, many settled here for years, to liability to deportation. Increasingly the police conducted raids on factories with large immigrant workforces and arrested people in their homes. The ensuing practice of random checks on the immigration status of people, usually Asians, who had initiated contact with the police for other reasons (such as criminal victimisation) was, and continues to be, a source of great bitterness.·

Finally, the increased use of cannabis led not only to more arrests and confrontations with young people of the so-called counterculture, but also provided the opportunity for use of the powers of search under the Misuse of Drugs Act 1971 authorising searches on 'reasonable suspicion'. These powers, it has repeatedly been alleged, were often used against the long-haired or otherwise unrespectable, and against black youths gathered in large numbers.

Thus events of the last decade have thrown more strain upon the police, and placed them in a more actively antagonistic stance toward various segments of the population to an extent perhaps unrivalled in living memory. For despite the Blackshirts and the Public Order Act, the 1930s saw nothing like the same sort of sustained multiple and simultaneous bitter conflicts; perhaps the nearest parallel is the 1911–14 period of semi-syndicalist labour militance and suffragette demonstrations. None of these problems, however, involves what most people, and most policemen, would regard as 'ordinary', everyday policing: the prevention and detection of assaults and thefts. Yet this was the final turn of the screw. For 'ordinary' crime has been rising inexorably: see Table 13.1.

Table 13.1 *Serious offences recorded by the police (thousands)*

Offence Group	1969	1974	1979
Violence against the person	37.8	63.8	95.0
Burglary	420.8	483.8	549.1
Robbery	6.0	8.7	12.4

Source: *Criminal Statistics England and Wales 1979*, Cmnd. 8098, London: HMSO.

Even acknowledging all the obvious strictures about the unreliability of crime statistics and their openness to redefinition, misinterpretation, and deliberate manipulation, it takes a singular blindness to deny the reality of an increase, and the equally significant reality of a growing fear of crime. The latter has, however, been intensified by calculatedly hysterical media campaigns,[7] and it often seems that the fears, rather than the more mundane reality, are shaping the response of politicians and the public to the problem of crime.[8] Moreover, in the past few years the media have inflamed rational fears in a particularly vicious manner, deliberately emphasising the frequency with which West Indians are involved in street robberies. Symbolically and practically, fear of being unable to walk the streets safely is one of the heaviest strains of urban living, and it is not surprising that the police, particularly in London where West Indians are disproportionately concentrated, placed particular emphasis on crackdowns against 'mugging'. What is unclear is whether the Metropolitan Police were responding to popular and media pressure, or attempting to create a climate of opinion favourable to the unfettered exercise of their powers.[9] It is quite plain that the Met's release of crime statistics in March 1982 showing for the first time the racial breakdown of reported offenders for mugging – an offence unknown to the law – and for no other offence, was a shrewd attempt to put critics and advocates of greater control over the police on the defensive,[10] but one must be wary of the anachronistic fallacy.

One critical practical response to the increases in recorded crime was the growth of specialist squads, isolated from the bobby on the beat, and highly action-oriented and aggressive in their dealings with suspected criminals.[11] The Metropolitan Police Special Patrol Group (SPG) in particular has so often been accused of excessive use of force that the fact, though not the incidence, of misconduct of this kind must be taken as established beyond reasonable doubt. There is an important, and unresolved, dispute over whether they conduct their operations in an overtly racially discriminatory way[12] but even if they do not, their Action Man/Supercop approach and their concentrated deployment in black areas inevitably created resentment and widespread belief among young blacks of racial victimisation.

It is necessary to understand the developing political context of policing in the 1970s to appreciate the impact of the riots of 1981 and the nature of the demands for greater police accountability that have now begun to be taken seriously in government circles. The hardening of right-wing political attitudes among police spokesmen and their representative organisations, increasing fear of crime, and deteriorating relations between racial minorities and the police made some sort of major blow-up predictable.[13] It is easy, however, to distort the impact of the racial element. Whites were not attacked in Brixton, indeed many joined in the rioting and looting. In the thirty or so riots that broke out three months later (July 1981), black and white youths again participated together or in parallel, and several such outbreaks involved youths living in all-white areas. (The Chief Constable of Leicestershire reported that the first disturbance he had to counter involved one hundred young whites in Melton Mowbray, a staid market town best known for the making of pork pies). What was unmistakable, however, was the concentration of animosity upon the police.

Thus although the most severe riots occurred in black areas, and racism and cultural distance greatly intensified the hostility between a significant number of blacks and the police, it is important to avoid adopting the narrow view that reduces issues of the governance of the police to a sub-category of race relations. Lord Scarman, unfortunately, set the pattern. His appointment two days after Brixton erupted with a remit specifically directing him to inquire into the disorders there would inevitably have cast his findings and policy recommendations in this context, but his insistence – which won general approval on the Left – upon extending his brief to include a long excursus on racial disadvantage, gave this element undue prominence.

Subsequent political debate on policing has been similarly skewed. At the simplest level, this approach is politically self-defeating. In sharp contrast to the United States, not only is the total black population small (roughly 3 per cent), there is no political unit in which ethnic minorities are even close to a majority. Brixton, for example, is part of the London Borough of Lambeth, which in 1978 was estimated to contain a population 25 per cent black, only half of whom are West Indian or of West Indian descent. Even the five wards comprising Brixton itself were then nearly two-thirds white.[14] As Crewe argues at a more general level, simple political arithmetic dictates that change can only be brought about through multi-racial coalition politics. More fundamentally, we have seen how police practices and policies have created antagonism among several disparate categories of whites, and the moral and political issues raised by the manner in which the police have chosen to exercise their powers are of deepest concern to the community as a whole. A society which has at least temporarily lost the comfortable consensus of the post-War quarter century cannot expect its police to function uncontroversially and apolitically. The question of Who Governs? would not vanish even if the ethnic minorities were all magically bleached and absorbed into the pre-existing class structure.

Lord Scarman's report

In immediate practical politics, the Scarman Report has defined the narrow boundaries within which reform of policing is conceived and discussed in official circles; the bulk of public debate has centred around which of his specific recommendations should be implemented. It is therefore important to see how those proposals have been shaped or at least reflect the specific limits of his Inquiry, and also to test the rigour of the analysis supporting them.

Lord Scarman was appointed to conduct an Inquiry under s. 32 of the Police Act 1964, which speaks of a 'local inquiry'. He remained faithfully within that jurisdiction, concentrating almost wholly on Brixton with only brief side visits to the West Midlands and Liverpool, which contributed virtually nothing to the Report. The trouble is that Brixton, like the rest of the Metropolitan Police District, is subject to a structure of police governance quite unlike anywhere else in Britain. Over 80 per cent of the population live in areas where the relevant institution is a police authority. This is a committee consisting of two-thirds local (elected) councillors and one-third magistrates, drawn from the police area for which it is responsible.[15] Few aspects of police authorities have escaped criticism (see further below) but they are at least the rudiments of a mechanism of democratic local influence on police practices.

The Metropolitan Police Authority, by contrast, is the Home Secretary. He is in theory accountable to parliament, and indeed London MPs can table parliamentary questions about police activities within his jurisdiction, a facility denied to representatives of other constituencies for the policing of which the Secretary of State is not legally responsible. None the less, it is idle to pretend that a full-time politician commanding a department responsible also for immigration, nationality, prisons and race relations, along with a miscellany of functions that would be otherwise homeless, can exercise more than the most perfunctory supervision over a force of 26,000, even with the assistance of specialised civil servants. Successive Home Secretaries have been content to leave even formulation of policies with major political implications in the hands of the Commissioner – a complaisance which, as we shall see, is quite different from the attitude taken in late Victorian times. *A fortiori* they have abdicated any responsibility to ensure that what the SPG do in Notting Hill conforms to their view of priorities, still less that PC Armstrong behaves with due courtesy whilst patrolling the streets of Hackney, or at least that middle-level officers insist that he does. In practical terms of direct influence that Londoners may bring to bear on those who serve them, the Metropolitan Police are literally out of control.

It was this underlying political structure that led Lord Scarman to emphasise so heavily the role of police-community liaison committees. His account of the events leading up to the Brixton riots emphasises and describes at distended length the disillusion and dissolution of the committee that had been established in Lambeth, and one of his central recommendations was that liaison committees be established by statute at the level of the London Borough, and at Divisonal level outside London.[16]

Certainly the views of those represented on such committees would at least be formally conveyed to the police, who in turn would be under a statutory duty to consult and discuss with committee members policing policy and operational matters not involving specific investigations or security. How such bodies would be made representative, how they could be made to work effectively in terms of size and similar apparently mundane but actually essential points, Lord Scarman did not explore. How their function would mesh with police authorities, and in particular whether their existence could be used to undermine police authorities seeking to assert their statutory powers to demand information about police operations and to exercise more vigorously their responsibility for the 'efficiency' of their force, also received no attention. Beyond the flat assertion that 'There are good reasons for the national accountability of the Metropolitan Police',[17] the report ignored entirely calls for an elected London police authority which could exercise identical powers. Finally, the police would in no way be bound to act upon the sentiments expressed by a majority of the lay members, nor would there be any directions as to the appropriate response where there were sharp divisions of opinion. Depending upon one's view of the political realities (and perhaps also on one's temperament), Lord Scarman's proposal would create an ineffective talking shop, and possibly a distracting substitute for mechanisms of democratic accountability, or a valuable forum for dialogue.

There seem to be two key assumptions underlying Lord Scarman's emphasis on consultation and discussion. One is that some sort of generally harmonious relationship between the police and various sections of the public can be sustained. What bitterness exists, is not so great, nor are conflicts so deeply embedded in social structure, as to make broad agreement on policing impossible. Nor will the disagreements which inevitably emerge be so severe that the disputants will stop talking to each other. One may interpret this view as characteristic of a man who rose to prominence in the period of post-war consensus, or as the approach that must inevitably be taken by anyone in a semi-official position. Whatever the interpretation, any other assumption would imply a policy of reliance on open coercion.

The related assumption is that there is something to discuss. Scarman clearly rejected the view that the law is the law is the law. He noted criticisms that the police have not yet learned to enforce the law in ethnic minority areas 'with the same degree of discretion with which they are wont to enforce it in other parts of the country'.[18] He acknowledged that there will inevitably be conflict between enforcement of the law and maintenance of public order, and insisted that the latter is the supreme value. Resolution of the conflict was said to depend upon the wise exercise of discretion, upon which he loaded enormous weight:

> Indeed the exercise of discretion lies at the heart of the policing function. It is undeniable that there is only one law for all: and it is right that this should be so. But it is equally well recognised that successful policing depends on the exercise of discretion in how the law is enforced. The good reputation of the police as a force depends upon the skill and judgment which policemen display in particular circumstances . . . Discretion is the art of suiting action to particular circumstances. It is the policemen's daily task.

Unfortunately, what he has failed to see, or chosen to ignore, is that exercise of discretion is not simply and solely a matter of good old fashioned common sense exercised in everyday encounters between police and individuals. It exists at the levels of policy, of organisation and of allocation of resources. In its most important senses, it is a *political* act: one which favours certain values over others and consequently which satisfies some interests at the expense of others. Exercised candidly and systematically, it deprives the notion of 'one law for all' of much of its resonance, and those conservative commentators who understood Lord Scarman to advocate more responsive, and therefore in some ways more lenient, law enforcement practices in West Indian areas, could plausibly fault him for advocating 'one law for black and another for white'.[20] Yet their criticism depends upon the proposition that law enforcement is a mechanical, automatic process. This is obvious nonsense, but to defend his approach Lord Scarman needed to pray in aid arguments of a kind he clearly would have found unpalatable. One might be that both substantive law and traditional police practices are culturally biased against West Indians, and that the discretion he extols is a necessary corrective. A related, even more radical view would be that the bias is as much grounded in class relations as in cultural conflict. Those who do not possess sufficient property to be defined as respectable and to create effective institutions of privacy to screen their activities from the agents of authority inevitably receive a disproportionate amount of police attention;[21] where an ethnic group consists primarily of manual workers or the unemployed, this disproportion becomes so great that adjustments must be made if the whole group is not to be routinely treated as potential offenders.

A more traditional proceduralist argument is that a process involving choice among values ought, like any other political decision, to be undertaken democratically. This is a position whose implications must be faced squarely, for there are obvious dangers of, in Scarman's words, 'manipulations and abuse of the law, whether for political or private ends' if law enforcement simply reflects the working political majority of a given moment. Yet once the inevitability of discretion is admitted, there equally inevitably follows the question, who determines how it shall be exercised? Lord Scarman's answer is that this must be done by the police independently exercising their professional judgment, but accountable to the community.[22] Unfortunately his discussion of the issues involved is confined to two sentences stating abstract principles, and burkes all the difficult questions. These include analysing the reasons for the existence of discretion, differentiating between discretion exercised at the levels of policy formulation and operational planning and that occurring in street encounters between police and members of the public, and further distinguishing between the decision whether formally to invoke the law at all, and the nature of the proceedings to be taken if a prosecution does ensue.[23] Different kinds and circumstances of discretion may call for very different kinds and degrees of democratic participation and accountability, and it is confusing at best, and an abdication of power to the police at worst, to reify discretion into a sort of amorphous lump, like putty.

Another way of arriving in the same cul-de-sac is to accept uncritically the idea that policing decisions are matters of professional judgement. Scarman does this, invoking the analogy of the doctor or the lawyer.[24] Yet the analogy is surely faulty, or at any rate requires far deeper analysis and more extensive elaboration than he undertook. Apart from the suspicion that the claim of professionalism is a way in which occupational groups assert power in the sense of autonomy from public or government control – 'all professions are conspiracies against the laity', said Bernard Shaw – it requires a concept of professionalism that readily distinguishes its opposite. A defensible application of such a concept would have to explain why it extends to the police, in their early years deliberately recruited from the lower classes (those 'who had not the rank, habits or station of gentlemen'[25]), whose educational entry standards even today remain low and whose initial training in provincial forces lasts only ten weeks.[26] More fundamentally, it would require analysis of the quality of police decision making, to see whether policy level decisions primarily involve choice among values or allocation of resources, i.e. are political in the broadest sense, rather than technical and beyond the grasp of the untrained, as the notion of professionalism implies. At the level of contact with the public, policing decisions seem primarily to involve applications of rules, value judgments about behaviour, and sensitivity to intent and motivation; these are both difficult and extraordinarily important, but it is far from apparent that labelling them 'professional' advances understanding of the tasks involved, or usefully points the way to answering the question of accountability and control.

Moreover, the growing scepticism with which claims of self-regulation based upon professionalism are now greeted, whether from doctors, lawyers, social workers or planners, seems not to have reached Lord Scarman's ears. The human and social consequences of supposedly value-neutral decisions have become all too clear, whether in the context of enforced treatment or confinement of those labelled 'mentally ill', the impact of ambitious redevelopment schemes on those forced to live in them, or the effect on whole families when children are compulsorily taken into care. Law enforcement may arguably be different from all these types of activity, and the police might arguably be regarded as engaging in qualitatively different work from tax inspectors or social security fraud investigators, who are subject to much more direct administrative control, but it remains a matter of argument, which needs to be presented cogently. In any case, if one takes the critique of professionalism seriously, acknowledgement that certain work involves specialised knowledge or relevant experience is merely the beginning of the debate over which areas of work necessarily are removed from external supervision. As it stands, however, the invocation of professionalism by or on behalf of the police is a political counter, a weapon – specifically a shield – usable only by those who believe in the minimisation of democratic influence.

The analysis of discretion as exercised by the police, and of the notion of professionalism and its implications if validly applied to them, are two of the major analytical questions involved in the governance of police. I hope in forthcoming work to make some contribution to that analysis, and can do little more here than point to its virtual absence in Lord Scarman's influential report. More subtly, this silence has (perhaps inadvertent) political implications: to maintain the present degree of independence of the police largely intact by leaving its basis unquestioned.

Understandably in the light of his brief, Lord Scarman barely mentioned practices in other countries. This Anglocentrism may well be sensible in dealing with a subject so tightly stitched into the social fabric and in an exercise designed to produce recommendations for immediate implementation. However, it is possible that other societies which have faced similar problems may have devised transplantable responses; and a look at their experience might at least shed light from an unusual angle on whether the English approach has been unnecessarily culturally blinkered.

In this context, Professor Sherman's claim that relations between police and blacks in urban America have significantly improved since the riots of the 1960s, and his analysis of the factors that have brought about the change – and those which have been irrelevant – seem enormously important to this country.[27] I take his main findings to be that more and better training, increased exposure of policemen to higher education, and attempts in some cities to increase the percentage of blacks in the force, have all made little discernible impact on police behaviour, although they have been the object of enormous expenditure. The key factor seems to be the growth of black political power, manifested in the mayor's ability to hire and dismiss the chief of police; under such pressures, police officials have tightened discipline, and promulgated policies reducing discretion of individual officers and making them conform to standards more acceptable to black citizens, in matters ranging from manner of speech to the circumstances in which they may use their guns. The impact of this political power on the individual policeman was most pithily expressed by one of the contributors to this seminar in informal discussion: 'In these cities (where mayors depend on black electoral support) the word got around to patrolmen fast: the kid whose ass you kick may be the cousin of an alderman. To the cop who wants promotion – who doesn't? – that made all the difference'. Note that the impact of the shift in the political balance was not failure to enforce the law, the giving of preferential immunities to blacks or black leaders (any more than white influentials had traditionally been so treated) or any of the other disasters Lord Scarman apprehends. Rather it has reduced the incidence of some practices either specifically and illegitimately directed at blacks, for example racist verbal or physical abuse, or altered policies which had particularly harsh impact on blacks, both in a purely statistical and an emotional sense, as with the number of shootings of members of the public.[28] More fundamentally, in

Professor Sherman's words, deliberate political influence has brought about a change 'from law enforcement to peacekeeping . . . not in the enforcement of laws against homicide, rape or robbery, but in the less serious offences of noise violations, bar fights, neighbourhood disputes, domestic assaults and sometimes even burglary'.[29]

Some might see this process as simply another, more politicised way of bringing about what Lord Scarman meant when he said that in the event of conflict between enforcing the law and maintaining public tranquillity, the latter must prevail. Police spokesmen, too, are quick to emphasise their responsiveness to community feeling, though seldom being explicit as to how that feeling is articulated and received. Yet it is anything but certain that Lord Scarman's ordering of priorities will be accepted either in the abstract or by policemen taking rapid decisions on the ground, or that their perception of when that conflict arises will echo his, mine, the reader's or that of the community they purport to serve. There has also been a political counter-attack, typified by the episode of the selective release of crime statistics outlined earlier, whose thrust has been to emphasise hard-line crime control. There is no reason at all to be confident that, in the absence of institutionalised political control, the change in orientation and specific practices of policing that Lord Scarman wishes to see – let alone that more radical critics have in mind – will occur. It is therefore worth considering what obstacles exist in Britain to the use of political power to change policing as has occurred in the United States. In the interests of avoiding unnecessary anxiety and other strains of the modern age, it may be said at this point that those obstacles are, under present law, almost insurmountable.

The legal structure of police governance

The statutory structure of police governance is found in the Police Act 1964 which, apart from the provisions dealing with complaints, has remained unchanged in substance since its enactment. Much of it, indeed, merely consolidated earlier legislation. A police authority is placed under a duty to 'secure the maintenance of an adequate and efficient force' for the area it covers (s. 4(1)). In pursuance of this duty, it may – subject to the consent of the Home Secretary – provide, maintain and alter necessary buildings, structures and premises; ditto, subject to Home Office Regulations, for vehicles, apparatus, clothing and other equipment (s. 4(3) and (4)). It may appoint a chief constable, his deputy and assistant chief constables, and may call upon the chief constable to retire in the interests of efficiency, but only with the Home Secretary's approval (ss. 5 and 6). The latter may require the police authority to exercise this power, but only after an inquiry has been undertaken by someone not either a police or governmental official (s. 29).

The Home Secretary is given no direct administrative powers over provincial forces, but he is under a general duty to act to promote the efficiency of the police (s. 28), and his powers are wide indeed. He makes regulations governing the entire range of personnel and disciplinary matters in all forces (s. 33), he is the appellate authority in all cases of discipline imposed by chief constables on their subordinates (s. 37), he is responsible for the national inspectorate of police (s. 38), and may require any chief constable to submit a report to him on any matter connected with the policing of his area (s. 30). This latter power is also held by police authorities in relation to their chief constable; however, if the latter believes that such a report would require disclosure of information prejudicial to the public interest or unnecessary for the police authority to carry out its duties, he may appeal to the Home Secretary, who is the ultimate arbiter (s. 12). The financing of all provincial forces is divided evenly between the rates and the Exchequer, as has been the case since the 1870s.

This is an ill-woven patchwork of central and local control, with some powers overlapping, others ill-meshed and the resulting fabric full of holes. Power, like Nature, abhors a vacuum, and into the void have stridden the chief constables, who have staked out effective independence from both levels of government. To a considerable extent that has happened in a fit of absence of mind: ambiguity and absence of conflict allowed them simply to get on with it. But they have also been assisted by the reluctance of the Home Office to use its powers, augmented in 1964 relative to local bodies, in any significant visible way to control their actions. And in urban areas outside London, their position was significantly strengthened by the 1964 Act. They have taken over from police authorities powers of appointment and discipline within their force. Membership of these bodies now consists of one-third magistrates, who had previously only been members of county authorities and are generally regarded as unwilling to be critical of police actions.

Most police authorities have been supine creatures, serving as rubber stamps for their chief constables, or devoting their attention to matters such as the appearance of uniforms or the catering in police accommodation. It is unclear why this posture has been so common, for little is known about the selection of members or whether some may seek to exert influence on police practices behind the scenes.[30] But in the rare instances in which conflict between the authority and its chief constable has surfaced, the latter has been able to persist with impunity over opposition to his policies. Such disputes have occurred most spectacularly in Merseyside and Greater Manchester, and the latter's Chief Constable, James Anderton, has not scrupled to attack his critics as politically motivated. Since the conflicts have been over matters like the deployment of police to control pickets in a bitter strike, patrolling after outbreak of riot, and Anderton's well-publicised campaigns against pornographic bookshops and homosexuality in public lavatories, his attacks have stated a truth, if in inverted fashion. All these issues are in the broadest sense political, and most polarise opinion along Right-Left lines. The battles have occurred between police authorities with Labour majorities and (not always in an overtly partisan sense) conservative-minded chief constables, who know full well that the authorities have no formal policy-making powers, and that the extreme step of dismissing a chief constable requires the Home Secretary's approval. (Even in Greater Manchester the police authority were unwilling to go this far, so the Home Secretary was never involved.) Thus bereft of effective weapons, these police authorities have been engaged in struggles which, at least at the formal institutional level, they can only lose. It is hardly surprising that most authorities, constituted of members ideologically in harmony with their chief constables and seldom finding themselves caught up in dramatic events, have kept so low a profile as to have become invisible.

Nineteenth century roots
It was not ever thus. The notion that chief constables are independent of the control and direction of their police authorities is a twentieth century heresy. The Victorians, and still more their ancestors, would not have known what to make of it. Policing in the historically pre-eminent sense of maintaining tranquillity was the original duty of that peculiarly English institution, the Justice of the Peace. In 1885, Maitland, England's greatest constitutional historian, wrote of the JP: 'To keep the peace is the justice's oldest duty. It is now performed chiefly by means of orders given to police constables'.[31] He went on to show that even the establishment of the Metropolitan Police by Sir Robert Peel was inextricably tied to the reform of the magistracy, which had been tainted by the corruption of the 'trading justices' – men who grew rich from taking fees for the exercise of their powers of office. These offices had to be cleansed before the public would accept them as worthy of their controversial function of controlling the 'new police'. Peel indeed followed a pattern that had developed over the previous forty years, during which seven 'police offices' were at various times established by statute in the London area, each under the control of justices, one of whose chief duties was to appoint and control constables attached to each office. Peel's enactment simply

established one more police 'office' at Westminster to govern the whole Metropolitan district, to be directed by two JPs responsible to the Home Secretary. Only a decade later did these justices come to be called Commissioners; even today the Commissioner is sworn in as a Justice upon taking office.[32]

The Justice of the Peace was of course the key executive functionary of local government in the Shires, in charge of everything from poor relief to highway maintenance as well as public order. Not until 1888 was he replaced by popularly elected councils, to be left only with his judicial role as the trier of minor criminal charges. As Maitland shows, no-one ever questioned the propriety of his control over policing, and it is anything but obvious why such a question should be raised about his constitutional successor, the police authority. The answer may well be political in the most contentious sense: the JP was always a reliable member of the landed classes, who could be trusted to direct the police in a manner that would not threaten aristocratic rule. When the general movement toward elective democracy proved irresistible, the notion of the independence of law enforcement provided a useful check on popular influence, and certainly one likely to appeal to judges, in Britain drawn almost wholly from the upper and upper-middle classes. The analogy to the history of the Poor Law, in which democratisation of local government led rapidly to contraction of its functions,[33] is very suggestive, though, in the present state of knowledge, no more. Much more also needs to be known about the working of watch committees established in 1835 in the boroughs, which came immediately under middle-class control, and apparently did exercise considerable direction over their force.[34] It is certainly clear that under the old regime of local government no one doubted that the justices in their executive capacity could direct the operations of the police.[35] Modern policing may be more technical, but that merely argues for a relationship between the elected representatives of local government and the competent official they have chosen analogous to that which exists in any other complex field, like planning or social services.

In terms of accountability, one cannot plausibly distinguish between the relationship of the Metropolitan Police to the Home Secretary and that between provincial forces and police authorities. And it seems incontrovertible that virtually at the precise moment when rural government was at last being democratised, Home Secretaries took the view that the ultimate responsibility for the policies adopted by the Metropolitan Police rested firmly on their shoulders. The late 1880s were a bad time for London's police. Their handling of the Trafalgar Square riots, in which one demonstrator was killed on the first British 'Bloody Sunday', and their inability to run to earth the

Whitechapel killer later christened Jack the Ripper, subjected them to strong and widespread criticism – including a quietly barbed comment from the Queen.[36] When Commissioner Sir Charles Warren unsuccessfully sought the Home Secretary's support for any action, 'however illegal', and was denied authority to offer a reward for information relating to the murders, he resigned.[37] It is startling to realise that an 'operational' matter like offering a reward was one that even a notoriously high-handed Commissioner understood to require approval from his political superior.[38] His resignation occasioned a parliamentary debate, in which the Conservative Home Secretary Henry Matthews and his Liberal predecessor Sir William Harcourt were in full agreement on the fundamental principles. In Harcourt's words:[39]

> There cannot be any doubt about the matter. It is not a dual control at all . . . (T)he Commissioner of Police is no more independent of the Secretary of State than the Under Secretary of State for the Home Department . . . Of course the Commissioner is the man who knows the Force under him, what is its work, and how it can best be accomplished; but for the policy of the police, so to speak, the Secretary of State must be, and is, solely, responsible. For instance, whether public meetings are to be allowed or prohibited in the Metropolis, is not a question of police, but a question of policy, for the Secretary of State to decide.

Simultaneously but independently of this controversy came the introduction of elected representative government in London. The establishment of the London County Council had long been resisted by Conservatives, and one of the key questions was what functions it would be permitted to assume from central government. To the dismay of some of the radicals, policing was retained by the Home Office, and in March 1889 a Conservative writer thought the question sufficiently important to devote a long article to attacking the radicals' position.[40] For present purposes, the interest of his argument lies in what it does *not* question. The level on which he confronted his opponents was that of *who* should govern the police, not of the limitations on that power of governance. For he did not think any such limitations existed. He characterised the radical position in a purely descriptive sense as requiring that the Metropolitan Police 'should be placed in the same position to the London County Council as the constabulary bear to the County Council of (other major cities.) In these the chief constables will be appointed by the County Council, in *whose hands also the sole control and organisation of the police will be placed* . . . The question is thus reduced to the very simple one: whether the *absolute control* of the Metropolitan Police shall pass from the Secretary of State to a Council chosen by the electors of the Metropolis'[41] (emphasis added). And in passing he echoed Harcourt's view of the Home Secretary's powers to 'give direct instructions to the Commissioner of Police' in relation to mass meetings and public disorder.[42]

Thus whilst the location of ultimate political control was a matter of serious dispute, the existence and extent of that control over police policy and operations in contentious areas was not. A seriously neglected subject of research is how this strong consensus of the late Victorian period came to be eroded so that when the judiciary began to enter the field, the new-fangled theory of police independence could so quickly become orthodoxy.[43] For in the past half-century there has sprung full-blown from the judicial mind a doctrine of the independence of chief constables which is both analytically suspect and, as we have seen, historically baseless. Full diagnosis of its analytical frailties would involve greater technicality and, in view of their severity, greater length than is possible here, but it is necessary to look in detail at the key case, *Fisher v. Oldham Corpn.*,[44] decided in 1930. Though the decision of a single judge in the High Court (the court of first instance), it has been repeatedly cited by later judges, Royal Commissions and other authoritative sources as though graven on tablets of stone. Nearly twenty years ago it was subject to extensive penetrating and to my mind unanswerable criticisms by Geoffrey Marshall, which continue to repay careful reading,[45] but which unfortunately have made no impression at all upon the courts.[46]

The facts of the case were quite simple. Fisher, the victim of mistaken identity, was arrested under warrant in London and taken to Oldham to answer charges which, when the error was discovered, were promptly dropped. He instituted an action in tort claiming compensation for false imprisonment. Rather than sue the officers who arrested him – who presumably would have been unable to pay damages – he proceeded against their employer, the Oldham Corporation, on the well-established principle of vicarious liability of employers. The corporation denied liability, on the ground that the policemen acted on their own initiative, and that the relationship of master and servant necessary to ground liability did not exist.

In one critical respect, this case exemplifies a distinctive characteristic of English constitutional law. It was a civil action between two parties contesting private rights and liabilities, no different in form from what would have obtained if Fisher had sued for injuries sustained by the negligent driving of a police car. It was not heard before a constitutional court, nor of course did it involve interpretation of a specific legal instrument, nor was the ultimate question before the judge – is the defendant vicariously liable? – a question that would normally be regarded as raising constitutional issues. Dicey regarded this process of judicial creation of constitutional principle through private law litigation as one of the hallmarks, and strengths, of the British constitution.[47] Like so many Victorian self-panegyrics, this one may read less persuasively in less confident times. Is litigation dependent on the initiative of private individuals – in which other bodies which will be affected, and the public as a whole, are unrepresented; in which the skill of the formulation and presentation of argument are dependent on which barrister happens to appear; and in which (as may well have happened in this case) the opportunity of higher courts to pass judgement upon the issue depends entirely upon the parties' financial capacity – really the best way to establish principles of high constitutional importance? The judgement in the *Fisher* case, and still more its subsequent influence, certainly give one pause.

The holding of the case was that the corporation as police authority were not liable for a policemen's tortious acts. Although the defendant employed, paid and could dismiss the errant constable, they none the less did not stand in the relation of master to servant. The statutory powers of the Home Secretary described above created an even closer link between a constable and the Crown and – not entirely a *sequitur* – the former's oath of office said nothing about his relationship to the police authority, whilst it did bind him to serve his Sovereign. Several cases in England and the Commonwealth, all of them tort actions turning on the master and servant point, were cited by McCardie J. in support of his conclusion that 'a police constable is not the servant of the borough, but of the State, a ministerial officer of the central power, though subject, in some respects, to local supervision and local regulation'.[48]

On the face of it, this conclusion could have had extraordinary implications. Depending upon how 'servant' was used, the case might have been invoked to support the view that constables were subject to whatever degree of control and direction 'the central power' chose to exert – a position obviously untenable as a matter of history and cutting across the wide grain of tradition and ideology of local control which has much deeper roots than mere self-restraint by central government. What has in fact been deduced from Fisher's case is not only that the constable is not the 'servant' in the peculiar tort law sense of either local or central government, he is also independent of both in the constitutional sense. Further, a case involving law enforcement activity by a subordinate constable in relation to a specific suspect gave rise to a doctrine applied unthinkingly to chief constables. That the latter are engaged in formulating and administering broad policies of general application throughout their jurisdiction has not prevented this extrapolation, which has been assisted by the further constitutional fiction that the difference between the most junior constable and his chief is merely one of rank, not office.[49]

McCardie J. was indeed aware of the constitutional dimension to his decision. Having treated the case, quite appropriately, as one of tort law, at the close of the judgement he invoked public policy of a very different kind in support of his holding. If a police authority were held liable for improper arrests, he argued, they would logically be entitled 'to demand that they ought to secure a full measure of control over the arrest and prosecution of all offenders. To give any such control would, in my view, involve a grave and most dangerous constitutional change'.[50] This argument is most peculiar. 'Control' is quite ambiguous in this context.[51] Were the police authority held liable, they might indeed become more alert in exercising their powers to insist upon adoption of procedures to ensure that only persons reasonably suspected of crime were arrested. One would have thought this was precisely the sort of activity for which they were created. That is a very different thing from, let us say, using their 'control' to prevent the arrest of friends of members of the authority - an act plainly *ultra vires*, as well as criminal. The implication simply does not follow from the premise. Secondly, if the constable is the servant of the central power, by parity of reasoning, the Home Secretary could have been argued to have precisely the power McCardie J. feared in the hands of the local authority. That would indeed have been a grave constitutional change, but the judge remained blind to this seemingly unescapable corollary. Finally - although this is more a criticism of subsequent doctrine than of the decision itself - the incontrovertible need for insulation from political influence in the arrest and prosecution of individual suspects implies nothing at all about the proper role of elected officials in the framing of policy. What may be called the fallacy of the seamless web has reigned supreme in the debate over police governance.

Conclusion

Thus all the hard questions remain. Lord Scarman, in the footsteps of his fellow judges, has led us up a blind alley in which the answers to those questions have already been assumed. His proposed solutions implicitly reject democratic political control without even cursory analysis of the wide range of possibilities that would stop well short of corruption or tyranny. There is an urgent necessity, intellectually and as a matter of practical politics, to develop a theory of democratic policing. It would begin with an apparently simple question: What are the purposes of contemporary policing? If, as seems plausible, at least three answers emerge – maintenance of public order, suppression of crime, and provision of what may loosely be called emergency social services[52] – the real work begins. None of these aims can be treated, as Scarman did, as though their meaning is self-evident; in particular, the concept of public order or public tranquillity badly needs meticulous dissection.

Once the goals are defined, it must be determined whether they may conflict and, if so, how priorities should be ordered. The theory would then address the problems of discretion and professionalism discussed earlier. It would also incorporate criteria to distinguish those areas where independence of police from political authority is essential from those where it has become a shibboleth. It would take due account of the history of the control of policing and its relationship to local government, which has thus far been passed over in unremitting silence. Certainly Lord Scarman's Report, and the debate that has flowed along the channels he has dug, will take us very little beyond where we have started, and nowhere at all toward where we need to go.

Notes

1 I should like to acknowledge the valuable criticisms of Marian Gerrard on earlier drafts of this paper.

2 Report of the Royal Commission on the Police, 1962, Cmnd. 1728.

3 A. Marwick, *British Society since 1945*, (London: Allen Lane, 1982).

4 T. Bowden, *Beyond the Limits of the Law*, (Harmondsworth: Penguin, 1977), Chap. 5.

5 The Prevention of Terrorism (Temporary Provisions) Acts 1974 and 1976, which despite their name are routinely re-enacted annually, authorise the arrest of persons not suspected of any particular offence; it is enough that the police suspect they are somehow 'involved' with or in terrorism. In the first seven years of operation, proceedings were taken against only one-eighth of the people arrested under the Act. There is widespread belief that people are being held to enable the police to gather information about others, with no intention of bringing charges against those detained. See further C. Scorer, *The Prevention of Terrorism Acts 1974 and 1976: A Report on the Operation of the Law*, (London: National Council for Civil Liberties, 1978); Lord Shackleton, *Review of the Operation of the PTA 1974 and 1976*, Cmnd. 7324, (London: HMSO, 1978).

6 G. Lebzelter, *Political Anti-Semitism in England, 1918–1939*, (London: Macmillan, 1978), pp. 115–27, shows how the police provided extensive protection from Mosley's Blackshirts whilst prosecuting their opponents. The Metropolitan Police Commissioner repeatedly expressed dissatisfaction that his stern instructions on dealing with anti-Jewish agitation were ignored by the lower ranks.

7 See, for example, S. Chibnall, *Law and Order News*, (London: Tavistock, 1977); S. Hall *et al.*, *Policing the Crisis*, (London: Macmillan, 1978), Chaps. 3–5.

8 This seems particularly true of the way the Conservative Party chose to politicise the 'law and order' issue in its 1979 Election Manifesto and rhetorical appeal to the electorate. Advocacy of 'the short, sharp shock' for the young offenders, the promise of a parliamentary free vote on the reintroduction of hanging, accelerated implementation of a large pay rise for policemen and increase in their numbers were all part of a package thought politically attractive, and which was given great prominence in election addresses.

9 They may also have adopted this emphasis as part of a strategy to defend the so-called 'sus' law, a vagrancy provision dating from 1824 and used wildly disproportionately against black youths congregating on the streets. In the event they lost, for the 'sus' law was repealed by the Criminal Attempts Act 1981.

10 See the careful documentation of the co-ordinated timing of various newspaper articles highlighting mugging and black involvement before the release of the statistics by Pierce, *The Guardian*, 15 March 1982.

11 See D. James, 'Police-Black Relations: The Professional Solution' in S. Holdaway (ed.) *The British Police*, (London: Arnold, 1979) for a description based upon participant observation.

12 Compare James, *op. cit.*, with Hall *et al.*, *op. cit.*

13 One should also throw into the pot one economic factor: the steady increase in unemployment since the mid-1970s, which spiralled spectacularly following the election of the Conservatives in 1979. In the latest wave young people generally and young blacks still have been the hardest hit, and the black population contains roughly twice the national proportion of young people.

14 The Scarman Report, *Lord Scarman, Report of an Inquiry into the Brixton Disorders*, (London: HMSO, Cmnd 8427, 1981) para. 2.15.

15 This area is often different, and much larger, than the governmental unit with which the councillors are normally concerned. Thus a Coventry Councillor may serve on the West Midlands Police Authority, which covers the entire Birmingham conurbation as well. This is part of a more general problem which despite its importance cannot be discussed here: the sheer size of the police forces created by two decades of amalgamation, and the ensuing difficulties of internal as well as external control.

16 Scarman Report, paras. 5.55–5.71.

17 *ibid.*, para. 5.68.

18 *ibid.*, para. 4.51.

19 *ibid.*, para. 4.58.

20 Especially Sir Robert Mark, the former London Police Commissioner, in *The Observer*, 29 November 1981.

21 A. Stinchcombe, 'Institutions of Privacy in the Determination of Public Administrative Practices', *American Journal of Sociology*, Vol. 69, pp. 150–60.

22 Scarman Report, para. 4.59.

23 It must be remembered that in England there is no separate prosecutorial body for the overwhelming majority of cases (the Director of Public Prosecutions is involved in only a handful of difficult or controversial areas), and that some of the smaller forces do not employ full-time lawyers; often the police choose which charges to lay, and in minor cases may conduct the presentation themselves.

24 Scarman Report, para. 4.59.

25 Sir Robert Peel, quoted in T. Critchley, *A History of Police in England and Wales*, (2nd edn), (London: Constable, 1978), p. 52.

26 The Metropolitan Police had for years received 15 weeks training, which in response to Scarman was recently increased to 16. Scarman recommended six months for initial training of all police.

27 See the paper by Lawrence Sherman in this volume.

28 *ibid.*, pp. 227–8.

29 *ibid.*, p. 230.

30 The main exception seems to be M. Brogden, 'A Police Authority – The Denial of Conflict', *Sociological Review*, Vol. 25, 1977. See also M. Dean, 'The Finger on the Policeman's Collar', *Political Quarterly*, Vol. 53, 1982 for a very good account by a journalist, relying on anecdotal evidence, of the present inadequacies and potential responsibilities of police authorities.

31 W. Maitland, *Justice and Police*, (London: Macmillan, 1885), pp. 91–2.

32 *ibid.*, pp. 99–100.

33 See N. Branson and M. Heinemann, *Britain in the 1930s*, (London: Weidenfeld and Nicolson, 1971), Chapter 5 together with B. Keith-Lucas, 'Poplarism', *Public Law*, 1962.

34 Dean, *op. cit.*, p. 159 presents an interesting example from Birmingham in the 1880s, and G. Marshall, *Police and Government*, (London: Methuen, 1965) p. 27, provides examples of influence exerted by brewing interests on these bodies in the mid-nineteenth century.

35 See Geoffrey Marshall's firm conclusion, 'The compatibility of common law constabulary powers with administrative direction by police authorities and justices seems to have been assumed by all the statutory provisions for police forces in the nineteenth century'. He then provides supporting quotations from relevant English and Scottish statutes from that period. Marshall, *op. cit.*, pp. 28–29.

36 Critchley, *op. cit.*, p. 161.

37 *ibid.*, pp. 161–62. See also J. Pellew, *The Home Office, 1848–1914*, (London: Heinemann Educational Books, 1982), pp. 47–51.

38 Offering a reward from police funds is indeed an unusual measure, but the police today operate large funds with which they pay and, in extreme cases, help resettle informers. It has never been suggested that this practice required the approval of the Home Secretary.

39 330 Parl. Deb. (Hansard) 3rd ser., col. 1162–63.

40 H. Evans, 'The London County Council and the Police', *Contemporary Review*, Vol. LV, March, 1889.

41 *ibid.*, pp. 446–7.

42 *ibid.*

43 See Marshall, *op. cit.*, pp 34–4, for a collection of a series of authoritative twentieth century pronuncements to this effect. He notes that 'the majority of these opinions are merely self-reinforcing and stand upon a kind of inverted pyramid (of which) the apex is the opinion in Fisher v. Oldham Corpn.'

44 (1930) 2.K.B. 364.

45 Marshall, *op. cit.* Chap. 3.

46 For example, Lord Denning, MR, in the well-known case of *R.v. Metropolitan Police Commissioner, ex p. Blackburn* (1968) 2 Q.B. 118, 136, said of the chief constable, 'The responsibility for law enforcement lies on him. He is answerable to the law and to the law alone (i.e., to the courts). That appears sufficiently from *Fisher v. Oldham Corpn.* and (a later case echoing *Fisher*).'
The magnitude of the leap from what *Fisher* actually involved, and the lack of intellectual support for it, are quite breathtaking.

47 A.V. Dicey, *Law of the Constitution*, (10th ed. E. Wade), (Cambridge University Press, 1959) pp. 195–97. This book was originally published in 1885 and the relevant passage remained unaltered.

48 (1930) 2 K.B. at 371.

49 Again, Marshall's lucid summary of the doctrine he criticises cannot be bettered: 'For the doctrine that chief constables were not subject to control in law enforcement matters rested squarely upon the proposition that they were constables at common law; and the notion that constables at common law exercised independent powers rested in turn upon the doctrine that they were not in a master and servant relationship with anyone for purposes of civil liability.' *op. cit.*, p. 98.

50 (1930) 2 K.B. at 377–78.

51 As is 'full measure', which I take to mean complete and unrestricted. If it means anything less, then the argument is disingenuous, because the degree of change that would be involved is precisely what is unclear.

52 See further, M. Punch, 'The Secret Social Service' in Holdaway, *op. cit.* and E. Cumming *et al.*, 'Policemen as Philosopher, Guide and Friend', *Social Problems*, Vol. 17, 1964.

14 Representation and the Ethnic Minorities in Britain
Ivor Crewe

This chapter describes the participation of Britain's West Indian and Asian minorities in the country's formal system of electoral representation. It is primarily concerned to answer two questions. How effectively has that system of representation expressed the interests of the ethnic minorities until now? How effectively might it be got to do so in the future? Discussion of ethnic minority political participation could, of course, have a different focus. There are other paths to power and influence than those leading to Westminster and the town halls. An alternative route leads to Whitehall, to the politics of committees and contacts. Another doubles back into the local community, into the politics of what Rex terms 'defensive confrontation'.[1] The relative merits of these different strategies will not be examined here. They perform different functions, anyway, and are not strict alternatives. In the following discussion the usage suggested in Brown's chapter is adopted; the terms 'black' or 'ethnic minority' are taken to refer to non-white people of Afro-Caribbean or Asian origin.

The political context of minority representation

Any examination of black electoral power in Britain must begin with an obvious but curiously unfashionable truth. Electoral power depends largely on sheer numbers. As a proportion of the British electorate the number of black electors is tiny. Precise estimates vary according to year and definition[2] but it is almost certainly below 3 per cent. Table 14.1, based on self-declared ethnic identity in the 1981 Labour Force Survey, suggests that there are (in mid-1983) 357,000 electors of West Indian origin (0.9 per cent of the British electorate), 47,000 of African origin (0.1 per cent), 485,000 of Indian origin (1.2 per cent) and 183,000 of Pakistani and Bangladeshi origin (0.5 per cent). This total of 706,000 (2.7 per cent) should be adjusted upwards to include those unwilling to declare their Asian or West Indian identity in a survey, but then downwards again to exclude those not on the electoral register, despite being eligible. The figure will rise over the next two decades as the very small number of elderly Asians and

Table 14.1 The size of the ethnic electorate

Ethnic origin	Aged 0–15		Age 16 +	
	Thousands	%	Thousands	%
White	11,150	92.2	38,763	95.6
West Indian or Guyanese	162	1.3	357	0.9
African	18	0.1	47	0.1
Indian	234	1.9	485	1.2
Pakistani	127	1.1	156	0.4
Bangladeshi	25	0.2	27	0.1
Chinese	30	0.2	60	0.1
Arab	7	0.1	28	0.1
Mixed[b]	135	1.1	97	0.2
Other	45	0.4	132	0.3
Not stated	154	1.3	454	1.1
Total	12,088	100.0[a]	41,609	100.0[a]

[a] Three-quarters of this group were born in the UK.
[b] Rounded to one decimal place
Source: 1981 Labour Force Survey (N = about 83,000). Respondents to the survey were asked to select the ethnic group in a given list to which they considered they belonged; the groups listed are shown in this table. For further details see *OPCS Monitor* LFS 82/1, 11 May 1982.

West Indians who die are replaced by the much larger number who reach electoral age. But the increase will still be small: on *ceteris paribus* assumptions, barely over 500,000 – an extra 1.1 per cent of the electorate – by the year 2000. At the end of the century only one elector in 25 will be black.

It is true that the Asian and West Indian minorities are heavily concentrated in particular districts of certain, mainly large, cities. Thus in a few constituencies black electors between them constitute a substantial minority of the electorate. Again, however, one should be aware of how limited this concentration is. According to the 1971 Census, there were only 18 constituencies (out of 635) in which the proportion born, or with at least one parent born, in the New Commonwealth and Pakistan (henceforward 'NCWP-born') exceeded 15 per cent, and only five in which it exceeded 20 per cent.[3] The 1981 Census figures for parliamentary constituencies are not yet published, and with further immigration of Asians (for example from East Africa), better rates of registration and a second generation of black electors, the number of such constituencies will now be higher. Yet it is doubtful if blacks make up a third of the electorate in more than a handful of seats, or constitute a majority in any. (There are, however, a few local wards, for example Northcote in Southall, where they are now a majority.)

Moreover, it would be mistaken to lump together Asian and Afro-Caribbean electors as if they form a solid ethnic block. In religion, language, origins and culture they have little in common and political collaboration between the two groups is limited.[4] Indeed, reference to 'the Asian community' is also misleading. 'The various Asian communities' would be more accurate: Punjabi Hindus in Southall and Birmingham (Handsworth), Gujerati Hindus in Wembley and Leicester, Punjabi Muslims in Manchester and Birmingham (Sparkbrook), Mirpuri Muslims in Bradford, Bengali Muslims in the East End, and so on. Although these communities share a common experience of discrimination in Britain, they do not necessarily respond in concert to political events. It is not unknown for Asian voters to prefer a white candidate of the 'wrong' party to an Asian candidate of the 'right' party – but the 'wrong' origins.[5]

It is certainly possible to devise electoral institutions which will represent quite tiny minorities proportionately – sometimes disproportionately – in parliaments, councils and other elected bodies. A reserved electoral roll achieves proportionate representation for Maoris in New Zealand and more than proportionate representation for whites in Zimbabwe. 'List' electoral systems without thresholds or constituencies, of the kind found in Israel and the Netherlands, achieve the same effect for those of their minorities that vote solidly for their party list. Indeed, small minorities can be over-represented in the government if their party occupies a strategic position in the formation of coalitions, as the National Religious Party representing orthodox Jews does in Israel.

The position in Britain, however, is very different. It is hard to imagine a political system more ill-equipped to represent the specific concerns of small and unpopular ethnic minorities. For working against them are three defining and linked features of British electoral politics: the single-member, simple-plurality electoral system (henceforward SM-SP); the nature of two-party competition; and race and immigration as election issues. The implications of these features can be summarised as follows.

First, *the electoral system would discriminate against a separate ethnic party*. In translating votes into seats, single-member, simple-plurality electoral systems always reward the big parties at the expense of the small.[6] It is true that minor parties with concentrated support like the Welsh Nationalists or, presumably, a putative ethnic party, are less heavily penalised than those with evenly spread support like the Liberals.[7] None the less, a separate ethnic party, without white support, but facing Conservative, Labour and Liberal/SDP opposition, would only begin to have a chance – and then a most remote one – of winning those wards and constituencies in which either Asians or

West Indians formed at least a quarter of the electorate. As already pointed out, there are very few such places. To be sure, an ethnic party might win sufficient support to affect the prospects of the main parties – for example, by siphoning off Labour votes in marginal seats. But under Britain's electoral system it could elect only a handful of councillors and probably no MPs.

Second, *the electoral system offers the ethnic minorities very few 'prizes'*. The alternative to beating the main white political parties is joining them. Politically active members of the ethnic minorities can seek nomination as a candidate of one of the established parties. Unfortunately, Britain's electoral system offers few such prizes. One reason is, quite simply, the small number of posts subject to election. Comparison with the United States is instructive. Unlike Britain, its first executives – presidents, governors, mayors – are directly elected, as are auxiliary posts such as treasurer and sheriff; it has two directly elected legislatures, not one; and elections every two, not five, years. As a result, parties in the United States can easily absorb the growing political ambitions of an emergent minority – as the ethnically 'balanced ticket' of the big city Democratic machines testifies. British parties do not have the same opportunity. A second reason is that Britain's parliamentary constituencies are single-member. Here comparison with Western Europe (except France) is telling. On the Continent parties can cater for ethnic (or other) minorities by ensuring that their representatives are placed sufficiently high on the list (where party list systems operate) or are among the candidates in multi-member constituencies (as under the Republic of Ireland's single transferable vote system). These means of balancing the ticket are also closed to British parties. Instead, competition for party nomination in a winnable seat approaches a zero-sum game, with no consolation prizes, in which the slightest supposed drawback – like being black – makes the difference between a long parliamentary career and the political wilderness.

Moreover, incumbents of safe seats rarely fail to secure re-selection as candidates, and thus re-election as MP. Unlike the United States, there is no system of party primaries by which incumbents can be challenged by outsiders for party nomination. Recent rule changes in the Labour party have made the re-selection of its sitting MPs less automatic, but up to now only seven have been de-selected.[8] Thus at any one election the number of winnable seats for which West Indians or Asians can seek a party nomination is limited; in 1979, estimating generously, there were only 60 such prizes.[9]

Third, *under two-party competition the interests of minorities are ignored*. The ethnic minorities have other means of participating in, and securing a response from, the established parties than becoming their candidates. Active work in the local party organisation, including the holding of office, might be one channel of influence. Partly as a result of the electoral system, Britain is, in essence, a two-party system: despite the recent surge of support for the Liberal/SDP alliance and the presence of six parties in Parliament (setting aside the Irish parties), only the Conservative and Labour parties have a realistic chance of forming a government on their own. And two-party systems are structurally incapable of representing the particular, *exclusive* interests of small minorities. The electoral disincentive against emphasising the specific concerns of any one minority is always considerable, but overwhelming when that minority is also unpopular. Only in alliance with other interests can small minorities be represented in a party. In constructing a coalition of support a major party must paper over, not expose, the differences between its supporters. It normally does this by keeping its appeal broad, its policies fuzzy and its commitments limited. Under two-party systems the specific interests of small minorities might be 'aggregated'; they will not be 'articulated'.

Fourth, *under Britain's electoral and party system a tiny shift of votes can make or break a government*. Neither major party has entrenched itself as the natural party of government. In the eleven elections between 1945 and 1979 their share of votes and office has been almost exactly equal. Moreover, the SM-SP electoral system magnifies a tiny net shift in the vote into a large turnover of seats: every one per cent shift in the Conservative-to-Labour vote ratio makes a 30 seat difference to the majority of one over the other. To obtain office, therefore, the two parties will compete intensely for the marginal voter, usually by occupying the electoral (which is not always the same as the ideological) centre ground.

This is not their only option. Sometimes competition will take the form not of their relative positioning on one issue, but of the importance they attempt to invest in those issues which work in their favour (for example, unemployment for Labour, taxation for the Conservatives). Sometimes they will tacitly agree not to compete, as on Northern Ireland. Collusion of this kind, at least among the party leaderships, has occurred on issues of race and immigration in some elections, such as 1966 and February and October 1974. However, if either party seeks to make it a major matter of public concern, as in 1968–70 and 1978–9, *both* parties must move close to the median position of the electorate if they are not to lose votes.[10]

Fifth, *among British electors racists outnumber the ethnic minorities*. Attitude surveys consistently reveal that the median position of the electorate is far removed from that of the ethnic minorities. The typical British elector is implacably opposed to further coloured immigration, regards strict immigration control rather than inner city aid as the key to good race relations, and considers that action on behalf of racial equality has already gone far enough.[11] An overwhelming majority have always said, since the early 1960s, that 'too many immigrants have been let into this country', about half claiming to feel 'very strongly' on the issue (see Table 14.2). Support for repatriation is much lower, but none the less substantial: 20 per cent in 1970, 19 per cent in February 1974 and (in answer to a differently worded question) 30 per cent in 1979. The British public do distinguish between the issues of immigration and racial equality, being less rampantly racist on the second. Yet considerable traces of racism exist. The 1979 British Election Study found that at least as many felt that 'recent attempts to ensure equality for coloured people' had 'gone too far' (30 per cent) as had 'not gone far enough' (29 per cent).

It is not only in direction, but in its relation to party support that public opinion on these issues is significant. It cuts across party preferences rather than with them. On these issues Labour voters think no differently from the rest of the electorate.[12] In setting out its position on immigration and race the Labour party cannot ignore the hostility to the ethnic communities that exists among many of its own supporters, let alone the uncommitted. The brutal electoral fact is that racists easily outnumber Asians and West Indians combined among the electorate, and indeed among Labour partisans.

Sixth, *race and immigration can offer easy electoral pickings*. In company with crime and strikes, the issues of race and immigration are unusually emotive for substantial minorities of the electorate. The prominence of racial themes in grafitti, anonymous hate-mail, asides to survey interviewers[13] and unguarded conversation suggest a resentment of deep, but submerged, intensity. It will not always surface in voting figures and the opinion polls; but occasionally it does. Minor incidents, given prominence by the media and thus by politicians (or vice versa), can provoke sudden and major shifts in the public mood, with electoral repercussions. The spontaneous demonstrations of support for Enoch Powell after his 'rivers of blood' speech in April 1968 and the immediate jump in Conservative support in the opinion polls after Mrs Thatcher's reference to 'feelings of being swamped' in January 1978 are cases in point.[14] There are votes for the picking in fanning the flames of racial resentment, as the Conservative win at Smethwick in 1964 (against the national trend), the late swing to the Conservatives in 1970, and the surge of support for the National Front in the 1977 local elections all show. Unfortunately there are few extra votes to be won by dousing the flames.

Thus the political context in which the Asian and West Indian

Table 14.2 Attitudes to Immigration 1963–1979

Q. 'Do you think too many immigrants have been let into this country
or not? *If yes*: 'How strongly do you feel about this? Very strongly,
fairly strongly or not very strongly?'

column percentages

	1963[a]	1964	1966	1970	1974	1979
feels *very* strongly that too many immigrants		45	46	46	43	40
feels *fairly* strongly that too many immigrants	87	29	28	28	29	35
Too many immigrants but doesn't feel strongly		12	11	11	15	11
Not too many immigrants	13	14	15	15	14	14
Total[b]	100	100	100	100	100	100

Notes
[a] The follow-up strength-of-feeling question was not asked in 1963.
[b] Rounded. 'Don't knows' are excluded.
Source: Butler and Stokes, *Political Change in Britain*, p. 461; British Election Study,
1970-February 1974 panel survey and 1979 cross-sectional survey. The data for these
surveys are available from the SSRC Data Archive, University of Essex.

minorities seek more effective representation is not a favourable one.
The electoral prospects for separate ethnic parties appear slim. The
established parties have few prizes to offer by way of candidatures, or
an influential voice in party counsels. They are under constant pressure to appeal to, or at least not alienate, the marginal voters among
whom there are as many, probably more, racists than black electors.
The ethnic communities must cope with a system of electoral politics,
which, being shaped before they arrived in Britain, was not designed
to accommodate the interests of small minorities.

Strategies of electoral representation
The strategies of electoral representation open to the ethnic minorities
can be categorised according to whether they depend on (a) collective
or individual action, and (b) independence from, or involvement in,
the established white parties. This provides four alternatives.

	Collective Action	Individual Action
Independence	1. Separate ethnic party	2. Independent ethnic candidates
Involvement	3. Ethnic electoral power	4. Ethnic candidates for the main parties

A separate ethnic party?

So far the Asian and West Indian communities have not pursued a strategy of collective action outside the established party system. One option is the organised electoral boycott. This is sometimes used by the Catholic community in Northern Ireland, but has never been attempted by the ethnic minorities. On the contrary, ethnic community leaders have been at pains to urge the opposite. In the 1979 general election the Asian and West Indian press called on its readers to act as text-book citizens – not only to vote, but to compare manifestos and write to candidates.[15] However, the alternative option of establishing a separate ethnic party has not been attempted either. No organisation claiming to represent one or more of the ethnic minorities has fielded a set of candidates subscribing to a common programme. Ethnic associations such as the Standing Conference of Pakistani Organisations and the Indian Workers Association have advised their members how to vote, and local branches have occasionally campaigned actively on behalf of particular candidates, but they have not formed a party of their own. The absence of a separate party is puzzling. That it might be regarded as *electorally* pointless – for the reasons given earlier – is understandable. That it should be regarded as *politically* pointless is less so.

Independent ethnic candidates

The little independent electoral activity to have taken place has been on the initiative of individuals, acting almost completely on their own. At each general election a few Asians or West Indians have stood for Parliament without the nomination of an established, national party – nearly always as 'Independents' rather than as the candidates of an explicitly ethnic interest. Table 14.3 summarises their performance, which by any standards has been derisory. The number of such candidates has been surprisingly small, given the cheapness of the deposit (£150); and the fact that, Southall excepted, different constituencies have been involved at each election, suggests that these political initiatives are taken somewhat haphazardly. The vote for independent ethnic candidates has always been negligible and, incidentally, always below that of the National Front where it too has fielded a candidate.

Table 14.3 Votes obtained by West Indian and Asian parliamentary candidates standing as Independents or for a 'fringe' party

Year	Name	Constituency	Party	Vote	% of vote
1964	Ali Mohammad Abbas	Holborn & St. Pancras Sth	Ind.	226	0.8
1970	Dharam Dass	Wolverhampton SW	Ind.	52	0.2
1970	Saed-uz-Safar	Birmingham Small Heath	British Commonwealth	117	0.5
1970	Tonderai Makoni	Howden	Ind.	154	0.4
Feb. 1974	Balder Singh Chalal	Ealing, Southall	Anti-Helment	310	0.6
Feb. 1974	Tariq Ali	Sheffield Attercliffe	International Marxist	424	0.9
Feb. 1974	Sylvester Smart	Lambeth Central	Workers Revolutionary Party	337	1.1
Feb. 1974	Ekins Brome	Lambeth Central	Marxist-Leninist	107	0.3
Oct. 1974	Silvester Smart	Lambeth Central	Workers Revolutionary Party	223	0.9
Oct. 1974	Chandra Rao	Hampstead	Ind.	31	0.1
Aug. 1977	R. Ahsan	Birmingham Ladywood*	Socialist Unity	534	3.5
Aug. 1977	J. Hunte	Birmingham Ladywood*	Ind.	336	2.2
Aug. 1977	K. Gordon	Birmingham Ladywood*	Socialist Workers Party	152	1.0
Apr. 1978	J.A. Chase	Lambeth Central*	Socialist Unity	287	1.4
1979	S. Gupta	Ealing, Southall	Ind.	637	1.2
1979	Tariq Ali	Ealing, Southall	Socialist Unity	477	0.9
1979	S.S. Paul	Ealing, Southall	Ind. Businessman	115	0.2
1979	Ola Banjo	Paddington	Workers Revolutionary Party	117	0.3

* by-election.

The only occasion on which ethnic candidates standing outside the established parties have succeeded in making a more than minuscule separatist appeal was the Birmingham Ladywood by-election of August 1977. Here the combined vote for three ethnic candidates (one standing as an Independent, two for different far-left parties) amounted to 6.7 per cent of the vote, estimated to be about 12 per cent of the ethnic vote.[16] The claims at the time that this was an early sign of an emerging ethnic separatism exaggerated the significance of the figures. Birmingham Ladywood has the highest proportion of ethnic minority electors in the whole country. The by-election occurred in the midst of violent and provocative National Front campaigning and in the aftermath of the National Front's strong showing at the May 1977 local elections; as a result ethnic consciousness was particularly strong. The state of the economy made the Labour government deeply unpopular. Moreover, the ethnic candidates' vote was split three ways and below that obtained by the National Front. Birmingham Ladywood revealed the limits, not the potential, of ethnic separatism in British elections.

In local elections ethnic Independents tend to do slightly better, usually winning between 5 and 10 per cent of the vote, occasionally a little more. But there have been very few such candidates (for example, only twelve throughout Great Britain in 1979 and a mere five in 1980) and none have come near to being elected.[17] Clearly, if there is an electoral path to influence for the ethnic minorities it must take a different route.

Ethnic bloc voting

A more realistic option might be the organising of a separate ethnic *vote* which could be deployed, as Samuel Gompers sought to use the trade union vote, to 'reward friends and punish enemies'. Belief in the potential impact of an ethnic bloc vote took root among the ethnic minorities and the parties themselves in the mid-1970s and is now firmly established. It is based on two electoral facts.

The first is the residential concentration of Asian and West Indian electors in areas containing marginal constituencies. In 1975 the Community Relations Commission published figures, based on the 1971 Census and the results of the two 1974 elections, which identified 59 seats in which Asian and West Indian residents out-numbered the majority of the winning candidates at both elections. These included 13 of the 17 seats that Labour gained from the Conservatives in October 1974 when it secured a (bare) overall majority. The implication seemed clear: 'without the minorities' support Labour would not have won more seats than the Conservatives in February 1974 and would not have won an overall majority in October 1974'.[18] These conclusions were taken very seriously by the Conservative party. In early 1976 it set up an Ethnic Minorities Unit inside Conservative Central Office for the express purpose of winning the votes and active participation of the ethnic communities, especially Asians, by the time of the next election.[19]

The second basis for the belief in an ethnic bloc vote was the *prima facie* evidence that in the 1979 election, in contrast to whites, Asians and West Indians swung to Labour. As a result Labour held on to a number of seats which would otherwise have fallen to the Conservatives on the national swing:[20]

Two of the only 6 English swings to Labour in seats where Conservative and Labour shared first and second places occurred in Bradford West (-2.9 per cent) and Leicester South (-0.8 per cent), turning two pre-1974 Conservative seats into relatively safe Labour ones. Both have substantial Asian communities, as does Southall, which produced the lowest swing in the South-East (0.8 per cent) . . . in Birmingham the four most black constituencies, where the 1971 population contained more than one-sixth born in the New Commonwealth, had low swings (mean 3.0 per cent) whilst the remaining eight (all with less than one-tenth New Commonwealth born in 1971) had much higher swings (mean 9.0 per cent); there were signs of a similar pattern in some other parts of the West Midlands conurbation and also in Manchester and Leeds (in the Ardwick, Moss Side and Leeds North-East results).

Command over a large, independent, block vote in marginal consti-·tuencies would indeed be a powerful electoral weapon in the hands of the ethnic minorities. But do they, in fact, possess it?

For the exercise of ethnic electoral power the following conditions must all be met:

a) the *full electoral mobilisation* of the ethnic minority, i.e. high registration and high turnout;

b) an *ethnic bloc vote*, i.e. uniform support for one party, or at least against one party, in response to ethnic as opposed to 'normal' issues, which shifts *en bloc*;

c) a *strategic location* of this ethnic vote in marginal constituencies such that it has the potential to deliver seats to one party at the expense of another;

d) a net effect in terms of seats over the country as a whole that *outweighs that of the white anti-ethnic vote*.

Examination of each condition will tell us whether in fact the ethnic minorities have wielded, or could wield, electoral power. It will also reveal much else about their electoral behaviour.

As to the first, electoral mobilisation has been weak. For many reasons, including apathy, ignorance, language difficulties, fear of detection by the police or Inland Revenue, and complacent electoral registration officers the proportion of eligible ethnic residents not on the electoral register has always been substantial. In the 1960s under-registration was very marked – exceeding 50 per cent, even 80 per cent, in some areas at the 1964 election.[21] A small survey conducted a decade later by the Community Relations Commission reported some improvement: under-registration was 37 per cent among West Indians, 27 per cent among Asians—but only six per cent among their white neighbours.[22] Between 1974 and 1979 registration drives among some ethnic communities were organised by local authorities, parties and ethnic voluntary associations. A follow-up survey by the Commission for Racial Equality reported a further improvement by 1979 in registration rates, notably among West Indians, but none the less showed that considerable and disproportionate under-registration persisted: among whites it was 7 per cent, among Asians and West Indians 23 per cent and 18 per cent respectively. Moreover, very little of this difference could be attributed, as had been commonly supposed, to the presence of more movers and minors coming of age among ethnic than white households.[23] Under-registration clearly diminishes electoral power. If about one in five eligible ethnic residents are not in fact registered to vote it follows that the number of constituencies in which Asian and West Indian *electors* (as opposed to residents) exceeds the majority of the winning candidate in the most recent two or three elections must be less than the number suggested by the Commission for Racial Equality.

A common assumption is that some of the factors that have left a minority of Asians and West Indians off the register have also depressed the turnout rates of those on the register. Were this true, the potential electoral power of the ethnic communities would be diminished further. However, accumulating evidence suggests the opposite. Precise measurement of ethnic turnout rates is difficult. In the case of Asians a good approximation can be obtained by matching the polling card number of identifiable Asians entering the polling station against the electoral register, counting all obviously Asian names on that register, and expressing the first as a proportion of the second. Painstaking research of this kind in Bradford, conducted over many years, found that throughout the 1970s the turnout of Asians at local and general elections outstripped that of their white neighbours.[24]

The CRE applied the same technique on the day of the 1979 election and corroborated what had until then been a strictly local finding for a wide sweep of the country. In 18 out of the 19 constituencies in which polling districts were being surveyed the turnout of Asians exceeded that of their white neighbours. This was partly because white turnout was well below both the national and, usually, constituency level; but it was also because Asian turnout was always *above* the constituency level (73 per cent as against 70 per cent for the 19 constituencies altogether).[25] In some cases Asian turnout was astonishingly high and thus the contrast with white turnout very marked. For example, it was 91 per cent in the selected wards of Leicester South (compared with 61 per cent among whites) and 89 per cent in Manchester Ardwick (compared with 60 per cent among whites). These two clear instances of a full mobilisation of the ethnic vote were almost certainly responsible for Labour's successful stemming of the national Conservative tide in both seats.

The turnout of West Indians cannot be measured as precisely. Their anglicised names make an accurate count of West Indians on the register impossible, and thus preclude the estimation procedures adopted for Asian turnout. Close observers have usually concluded that West Indian voting rates fall below those of whites and Asians.[26] A near-total mobilisation of the West Indian vote, of the kind cited for Asians, has not been recorded at any election. However, some recent fragmentary evidence hints at a narrowing of turnout differences between West Indians and others. The jump in their registration rates is one clue; another is the 'exit poll' at the April 1978 by-election in Lambeth Central (where the ethnic minority is largely West Indian) which recorded very similar turnout rates between whites and blacks.[27] There are certainly grounds for expecting higher West Indian voting rates in the future. The facts that most members of the ethnic minorities cast a vote does not mean, however, that they are casting an 'ethnic vote'.

As to the second, it cannot be assumed that the ethnic minorities cast an 'ethnic bloc' vote. If Asians and West Indians supported the different parties in similar proportions and for similar reasons to whites one could speak of ethnic voters, but not of an ethnic vote. A 'true' ethnic bloc vote only exists if the party preferences of the ethnic minorities are i) – uniform, ii) – a response to ethnic as opposed to 'normal' issues, and thus iii) – shiftable *en bloc*.

The predominance of Labour voting among the ethnic minorities is long and widely established. An early study in Nottingham found that 93 per cent of the ethnic minority vote went to Labour in 1966.[28] By the mid-1970s, however, there was some speculation that Labour's dominance was temporary, especially among Asians, and was already beginning to crumble. One argument was that the two parties' treatment of immigration issues when in office was very similar; indeed the Conservative government's handling of the Ugandan Asian refugees in 1972–73 was more liberal than the Labour government's rushed and restrictive measures against Asian immigration from East Africa in 1968. Another argument was that past Labour support among ethnic minority voters had been based on class, not ethnicity. Among Asians, growing business and professional success and movement into the suburbs would lead increasing numbers to vote Conservative out of class interest. A third argument was that the values of Asian communities made them 'natural' Conservative supporters. The importance they attached to economic independence, 'getting on', education, traditional morality and a close-knit family would create an affinity for the party that most vociferously claims to stand for the same things. *Embourgeoisement*, instinctive conservatism, and an appreciation of the parties' records as opposed to rhetoric would encourage the Asian community to drift steadily rightwards, much as the Jewish community a generation earlier appears to have done.[29]

None of this, however, is supported by the survey evidence, which points instead to the persistence of a massive ethnic factor in black voting patterns. Thus in February 1978 support for the Labour and Conservative parties (voting intentions) split 44:56 among whites, but 95:5 among West Indians and 92:8 among Asians. Labour's staggering advantage among black voters, moreover, cannot be attributed to the fact that they are younger and more working-class than white voters. As Table 14.4 shows, social class had a major impact on the vote of whites but almost none on that of Asians and West Indians. Even the middle-class Asians and West Indians (occupational grades A, B and C) divided by at least 86:14 in Labour's favour, whereas among whites the split was 26:74. Similarly, age had a small impact on the white vote but almost none on the ethnic minority vote.

The survey just cited was conducted when reaction against the Conservative party in the ethnic communities might have been temporarily boosted as a result of Mrs Thatcher's notorious remarks about 'swamping' a few weeks earlier. The CRE's exit poll at the 1979 general election, however, revealed the persistence of an indubitably ethnic vote. Labour's support from ethnic minority voters remained overwhelming (see Table 14.4). It took 90 per cent of the West Indian vote, 86 per cent of the Asian vote but only 50 per cent of the white vote; its share of the two-party vote was 92 per cent, 91 per cent and 56 per cent respectively.[30] Moreover, comparison with the previous exit poll showed that the Labour vote had *risen* among the ethnic minority electorate, *especially Asians* (up 8 per cent since October 1974). While the white electorate was swinging hard to the right, the black electorate was moving to the left. There seems little doubt that strictly ethnic considerations lay behind this 'deviant' swing. (The coming on to the register of disproportionately unskilled and unemployed – and

Table 14.4 Labour share of two-party support, by class and age
within ethnic groups

	White %	West Indian %	Asian %
Social class			
A, B, C1	24	90	86
C2	49	94	93
D, E	63	99	97
Age			
16–34	48	96	90
35–54	43	92	93
55 +	40	100*	100*
All	44	95	92
(N)	(1,416)	(233)	(256)

* Number too small for statistical significance.
Source: NOP, 'Attitudes Towards Immigration', February 1978.

thus 'naturally' Labour – ethnic residents will also have played a part.)
When asked to say how important they considered each of 14 issues,
92 per cent of ethnic minority respondents, compared with 74 per cent
of white respondents, regarded 'improving race relations' as
'extremely' or 'quite' important. On this basis the issue ranked first in
importance for black respondents, but only twelfth for the whites.[31]
The conclusion seems obvious: by the late 1970s West Indians and
Asians were voting as a solid, ethnic, bloc.

True ethnic voting, however, requires something in addition: a
proven willingness by ethnic voters to 'reward friends and punish
enemies'. A reputation for overwhelming and unshakeable support
for one party would weaken, not strengthen, their electoral clout by
encouraging the favoured party to take them for granted and the other
parties to ignore their existence. There is some danger of that happening in years to come. The Conservatives demonstrated in 1979 that,
despite (perhaps because of) their tougher position on immigration,
they could win an election comfortably without the ethnic vote. The
ethnic minorities will only get to exercise electoral power in the future
by threatening to withdraw support from the Labour party – or at
least some local Labour parties – and by occasionally and con-
spicuously carrying out the threat.

It is probably too early to judge whether the ethnic communities
have the organisational capacity and willingness to go that far. A clear

opportunity has not arisen because since the early 1970s, when the ethnic communities first began to participate fully in elections, the two major parties have not radically altered their positions on race and immigration. The CRE has been at pains to argue that ethnic voters 'form part of the population of "floating voters" ' but the evidence it presents is not convincing.[32] Re-analysis of its published figures on voting movements between October 1974 and 1979 casts doubt on the proposition. Of those claiming to have voted at both elections, 18 per cent of whites but only 10 per cent of West Indians and 11 per cent of Asians changed parties.[33] The CRE's report also emphasises the variation of ethnic voting preferences from one area to another, but much of this variation must be interpreted very cautiously because of the tiny sub-samples involved.[34] One can point to a few clearly 'deviant' constituencies. In Rochdale, for example, the majority of the (mainly Asian) ethnic community appears to vote Liberal.[35] In Bradford West in February 1974 34 per cent of the (mainly West Pakistani) ethnic voters supported the sitting Conservative MP. This was partly because of his assiduous 'welfare' work on behalf of ethnic constituents, but also because he sided with West Pakistan in the Pakistani civil war of 1972–3. Only eight months later support for the Conservatives among Asian voters fell to 19 per cent. These two examples underline the potential for ethnic vote switching. None the less, one's impression is that it has not yet been exercised in a marked and disciplined way; in particular there are no known cases of the ethnic community withdrawing their support from Labour MPs who are not strongly committed to their interests.

Third, are ethnic voters strategically located? As already explained, the presence of ethnic voters does not entail an ethnic vote, and the exercise of an ethnic vote does not entail a specifically ethnic swing. It also needs to be appreciated that a specifically ethnic swing does not entail ethnic electoral power – that is, the capacity to take seats away from one party and deliver them to another. That capacity depends on a combination of circumstances: the size of the ethnic electorate, the marginality of the seat, and the size and direction of the specifically ethnic swing.

The size of the ethnic electorate and the MP's majority together impose logical constraints on ethnic electoral power. Where the ethnic electorate is less than half the MP's majority it is impossible for the pattern of ethnic voting, however extreme, to determine the result in that constituency. At the 1979 election exactly half the 88 seats with a black electorate of at least 5 per cent fell into that category. However, we cannot infer the opposite about the remaining 44 seats. The Commission for Racial Equality has made some play of the sizeable group of constituencies in which electors born in the New

Commonwealth and Pakistan (NCWP) outnumbered the MP's majority in all three elections between 1974 and 1979.[36] This tells one less than the Commission thinks. On the one hand, no ethnic group has a 100 per cent turnout for one party exclusively. On the other hand, in highly marginal seats, where less solid ethnic voting could in theory determine the result, all manner of groups – new electors, previous abstainers, defectors to the National Front – outnumber the narrow majority and thus have an equally strong claim to have clinched the result. To show that a party owes one of its seats (as opposed to the exact size of its majority) to the ethnic vote, it has to be established that, having taken account of vote switches by the rest of the constituency electorate (the 'non-ethnic swing'), it was vote switching or its absence among the ethnic group (the 'ethnic swing') which delivered the seat to one party rather than another.

Before the 1979 election I published an analysis demonstrating that a seat has to be *very* marginal, the differential ethnic swing *very* marked, and the ethnic group a *very* substantial proportion of the constituency, for that seat to be owed to the ethnic vote.[37] Only a tiny number of seats meets this exacting combination of conditions. Assume, for example, that in 1979 the national two-party swing of 6.5 per cent to the Conservatives (i.e. the change in the percentage ratio of Conservative to Labour votes) occurred evenly across the white electorate. In addition, assume that among the ethnic electorate the two-party swing was, by contrast, 10 per cent to Labour – a generous estimate which takes increased registration and turnout, as well as actual vote switching, into account. In 1979 ten Labour-held seats with an NCWP-born electorate of at least 5 per cent were vulnerable to a 6.5 per cent two-party swing among whites. Of these only two – Walsall South and Battersea South – could have been saved for Labour on the postulated ethnic swing (and did in fact stay Labour). Had the white swing to the Conservatives been more modest – 2.5 per cent, for example – the assumed ethnic vote again would have saved only two Labour MPs (in Leicester South and Huddersfield West). On a zero swing among whites the Conservatives would have lost, yet again, only two seats on the ethnic differential: Brentford and Isleworth and, possibly, Hornsey. Had the election gone decisively the other way, with a 2.5 per cent white swing to Labour, the ethnic increment would have harvested at most three additional seats for Labour: Birmingham Edgbaston, perhaps Croydon North East and just possibly Kensington. On any plausible combination of white and black swings, the ethnic vote appears incapable of making a difference of more than two or three seats. The alleged electoral power at the disposal of ethnic minorities in marginal constituencies is, in fact, a myth, albeit a benevolent one.

To this brutal electoral truth two qualifications should be made. First, the exceptional conditions required for the wielding of ethnic electoral power are more likely to arise at local than general elections. The ethnic electorate forms a more sizeable minority of local wards than parliamentary constituencies and is easier to organise into a disciplined bloc vote. There are already examples of ethnic voting making a decisive impact in some local wards.[38] Secondly, a major swing by ethnic electors *to the Conservatives* would make a substantial difference. The CRE's 1979 election report is right to claim that 'with an even distribution to the "ethnic vote" between the two parties, the Conservative party would have won that general election (i.e. in 1979) with an even greater majority than it did'.[39] But such a fifty-fifty split amounts to a 36 per cent two-party swing to the Conservatives – well beyond the bounds of plausibility for Asians and West Indians, or indeed any group, at a single election.

Finally, there is another side to the equation when calculating ethnic electoral power: *the white anti-ethnic vote*. Earlier in this chapter it was noted that in the British electorate white racists almost certainly out-number West Indians and Asians combined. White antagonism towards blacks could well have delivered more seats to the Conservatives than blacks have delivered to Labour.

Precise calculations are not possible because it is even harder to make an exact count of white racists than of ethnic minorities. However, an accumulation of scattered evidence strongly suggests that the Conservative party has benefitted as much, and probably more, from the anti-ethnic vote than Labour has from the ethnic vote. The unexpected Conservative gain of the hitherto solidly Labour Smethwick in 1964, against the national pro-Labour tide, is a celebrated example of the power of the anti-immigrant, white, working class vote. (Two other – admittedly very marginal – Labour seats, Birmingham Perry Barr and Eton & Slough, fell to the Conservatives for the same reason.) In 1970 white constituencies adjacent to areas of immigrant settlement, especially in the West Midlands, recorded swings to the Conservatives well above the national and regional averages.[40] In 1979 a further mixture of white fear and white flight appears to have had a similar effect, not only in the West Midlands (as noted on p. 268) but elsewhere. In Greater London the Conservatives benefitted from 'tactical racist voting': there was a strong association between the size of the pro-Conservative swing and the size of the National Front vote at the GLC elections two years earlier. The exceptional swings to the Conservatives, especially in the Northeast quadrant of London, included at least two unexpected Conservative gains from Labour (Hornchurch and Enfield North).

The relative impact of the ethnic and anti-ethnic vote needs to be judged over a series of elections, not just one. Over the long term, the post-war immigration of overwhelmingly pro-Labour West Indians and Asians must have helped the Labour party. But by how much? Ethnic minorities have increased the total British electorate by about 2.7 per cent. On the generous assumption that the ethnic minorities are fully registered, turn out to vote at the same rate as whites, and split 9:1 in Labour's favour, this ethnic increment has been worth a 1.1 per cent two-party swing to Labour. In 1979 that was equivalent to 12 seats, *over thirty years*. It is hard to believe that the white anti-ethnic vote has been worth less to the Conservatives over the same period. At one election alone, in 1970, the national impact of Enoch Powell's speeches on immigration was almost certainly greater. Estimates vary, but of the three published the most cautious assesses their effect as a 1.5 per cent swing.[41] Some of that effect will have stuck, and to it can be added the impact of the Conservative party's 'tough' stand on immigration in 1979. The concentration of ethnic electors in some marginal seats has almost certainly been outmatched by the spread of anti-ethnic electors across all marginal seats.

Selection and election as main party candidates

An alternative electoral strategy for the ethnic minorities is the election of some of their members, as candidates of the main parties, to Parliament and local authorities. The physical presence of Asians and West Indians on the floor of the Commons or Council Chamber, it is argued, would ensure the representation of the ethnic minorities' specific interests. Whether in fact a small number of coloured councillors or MPs could act – or would wish to act – as ethnic spokesmen is far from certain. Elected members of other minorities – Jews and 'Irish' Catholics, for example – do not generally act in this way. Most Jews in the Commons regard themselves as 'MPs who are Jewish', not as 'Jewish MPs'.[42] But no doubt the first black MPs would be treated willy-nilly as minority spokesmen. Even if the practical effects were modest, their election would probably raise the status of the ethnic minorities in the eyes of the country – and themselves. This strategy also has the attraction of apparent practicality. Election requires adoption as a candidate in a safe seat, and adoption requires the support of only a small number of people – a majority of the local party's selection committee. Selection for a safe local ward is usually in the hands of as little as a dozen or so people; selection for a safe parliamentary seat, especially a Labour seat, is in the gift of 60 to 80. Securing the votes of so few people should be within the capabilities of a well-organised ethnic community. Even without organised lobbying the tiny Jewish community, forming under one per cent of the electorate, provided 40 MPs and three cabinet ministers at the time of writing (September 1982).[43]

Yet since the war there have been no black MPs. Very few Asians and West Indians have ever been adopted as parliamentary candidates by the main parties, and those selected have usually had to contest hopeless seats. In 1979, a 'record' election for ethnic minority candidates, only five were adopted by the three main parties (out of 1,820 candidates). Two were Liberals in unpromising territory. Two were Conservatives, one in the unswervingly Labour Greenwich, the other in Glasgow Central, the thirty-ninth safest Labour seat in Britain (and the safest in Scotland). The fifth was the Ghanaian-born Labour candidate for the City of London and Westminster South, the fifty-ninth safest Conservative seat in the country. In October 1974 there were no black Conservative or Labour candidates. In February 1974 there was one – an Asian selected by Labour to fight East Fife, the third safest Conservative seat in Scotland. Only once, in fact, has a major party selected a black candidate for a winnable seat. In 1970 Dr Pitt stood for Labour in the marginal but normally secure Clapham – and lost.

This negligible selection of ethnic minority candidates will probably be repeated at the next election. So far only one black person has been adopted for a remotely winnable seat. Paul Boateng, born in Guyana, and a GLC councillor, has recently been adopted as prospective Labour candidate for the Conservative-held marginal of Hemel Hempstead. However, the adoption was fiercely controversial (for procedural not racial reasons), has deeply divided the local party, and is subject to appeal to Labour's National Executive Committee. Moreover, the seat has been won by Labour only once, in October 1974, and then with a tiny 0.7 per cent majority. In these circumstances, and given the current electoral standing of the Labour party, the odds are strongly against Paul Boateng becoming Britain's first black MP since the war.

Why are there so few black candidates, in particular for the Labour party which is so massively supported by ethnic minority voters? Prejudice on the selection committees is only a small part of the explanation. More important is the common assumption of selectors that a black candidate would lose votes,[44] although this does not explain why so few are adopted in safe or hopeless seats where a small forfeit of votes could not affect the outcome. Two other factors are more important still. The first is the negligible number of Asians and West Indians applying for selection. This is not surprising, as most have only started to take an interest in British party politics in the last ten years; their number is likely to increase in the future. However, it has to be related to the fact, mentioned earlier, that few safe seats are 'up for grabs' at any one election and thus the competition for adoption is very intense. The second reason is the criteria applied by selection committees when choosing a candidate. These criteria are complex and difficult to pin down. They vary from seat to seat, are not formally set out, and are only dimly discerned by the selectors themselves. In the Labour party, ideological position appears to count for less than local roots and certain personal qualities. The crucial personal qualities have to do with public 'presence' – especially speaking ability and informal sociability – and it is possible that the accents and other culturally distinctive attributes of Asians and West Indians are handicaps in this respect. 'Local roots' usually means many years of service as a local councillor, trade union official or party officer – or being the son or daughter of such a person. For obvious reasons very few Asians and West Indians have yet had the opportunity to serve such a long political apprenticeship.

However, the number is slowly rising and gives grounds for cautious optimism for, if not the next election, the one after that. By 1982 there were about 70 local councillors from the minority communities, mainly in London, including 13 in Brent, five in Tower Hamlets, and 4 each in Lewisham and Islington. The growth in the number of black councillors has been glacially slow and of course amounts to much less than the ethnic proportion of the electorate warrants. The position in the provinces is particularly bleak, with only three of Bradford's 90 seats, four of Birmingham's 117 seats and one of Leeds 100 seats held by Asians or West Indians.[45] None the less, the number will continue to rise as some of the black candidates selected for hopeless seats are 'promoted' to winnable ones.

Are ethnic minority candidates an electoral liability, as some selection committees suspect? The simple answer is 'yes'; the qualified, more realistic, answer is 'usually, but not that much, and anyway less than in the past'. A survey in October 1974 suggested that about a quarter of white Labour and Liberal supporters and two-fifths of white Conservatives were unwilling to vote for their party if it fielded a black candidate.[46] The Labour figure had been closely confirmed four years earlier, in the 1970 election, when Labour's West Indian candidate lost Clapham. In surrounding constituencies the pro-Conservative swing was 2.3 per cent, insufficient to wrest the seat from Labour; in Clapham it was 10.2 per cent. Labour's vote was 23 per cent below what a normal swing and change of turnout for that area would have produced. A similar if less marked pattern occurred in the safely Conservative East Fife in February 1974, where the Labour candidate was Asian. And Asian Liberal candidates have generally done particularly badly, even by Liberal standards.[47]

However, by 1979 the unwillingness of whites to vote for black candidates, while still present, appears to have diminished. In the two constituencies with Asian Conservative candidates the swing was close to the local average. In the City of London and Westminster South, where the Labour candidate was black, the pro-Conservative swing of 7.3 per cent was one of the largest in West London, and twice that in the two most similar adjoining constituencies (Chelsea and St Marylebone). But this time the black Labour candidate's vote was 84 per cent of what a normal swing and change of turnout would have produced, compared with 73 per cent in the case of Clapham in 1970; to that extent the electoral handicap of a black candidate was reduced. Using a different kind of calculation, Dr Le Lohe reports a parallel decline in the 'coloured handicap' in local elections since 1979.[48] In all probability the handicap will continue to diminish slowly in coming years.

Conclusion: reform and the future

Any realistic assessment of the political position of Britain's ethnic minorities makes for sobering reading. So far the electoral process has given them very little influence. A separate ethnic party is not a serious proposition. The ethnic communities cannot affect election results in more than a few constituencies, let alone the country as a whole. Only a handful of local parties have been 'captured'. Asians and West Indians are badly under-represented among the main parties' candidates, officers and officials. Not one MP is non-white. It is against this bleak background that the speck of optimism at the end of this analysis should be regarded.

The situation will not change quickly or dramatically. A few more local parties, especially in Bradford, Birmingham and parts of London will come to be controlled by predominantly black party workers. The number of Asian and West Indian candidates will slowly increase, first at the local and later at the parliamentary level. A few more brown and black faces will be found among the delegates at party conferences. There will eventually be a tiny number of black MPs, but probably not at the next election.

Can anything be done to accelerate this painfully slow rate of progress? The blunt answer is: precious little. The institutional reforms which would help most are unlikely to occur. A separate electoral roll for the ethnic communities would be the single most effective reform. It is also politically inconceivable: the very suggestion would provoke outright and unanimous rejection from across the ethnic and ideological spectrums. A change in the electoral system to some form of proportional representation, preferably a party-list system, would also help. But this will only happen if the Liberals and

SDP form a government, or succeed in making it the price for supporting a minority Conservative or Labour government. In this still unlikely event, moreover, the new electoral system would not be a party-list system, but some form of the single transferable vote – which is less helpful to the ethnic minorities. A reformed House of Lords, with guaranteed ethnic representation and enhanced powers (especially over constitutional matters) could be of protective value to the ethnic communities. But reform requires cross-party support which will not be forthcoming so long as Labour party policy is to abolish the Lords – and any other second chamber.

More modest progress might be achieved through some minor reforms, especially changes within the Labour party. Automatic inclusion of Asians and West Indians on the shortlist for candidacies, the affiliation of ethnic organisations to the Labour party, and reserved places for Asians and West Indians on the National Executive Committee have been canvassed.[49] So far the response from both white and black workers for the Labour party appears to have been lukewarm. Even if these changes were eventually implemented, they would not necessarily have much impact. The slender effect of having reserved places for women on Labour's NEC on the number of women Labour MPs and on Labour policy on women's rights is not an inspiring precedent.

The stark truth is that the ethnic communities must very largely rely on the commitment and goodwill of whites to dissolve prejudice, eliminate discrimination, guarantee legal and civil rights and abolish poverty. This chapter began by pointing out that the electoral process is only one means of helping to secure that commitment. It may not be the most effective. Rioting is certainly more likely to attract publicity, official inquiries and research. Whether it is any more effective in obtaining commitment and goodwill remains to be seen. This author doubts it.

Postscript

Since this chapter was drafted, further information has become available about the concentration of blacks in constituencies and the under-registration of blacks. Although the chapter's conclusions are unaffected, readers may wish to be kept up to date.

Concentration in constituencies: according to the 1981 Census there were 58 constituencies with more than 15 per cent of the population living in households with an NCWP-born head (see Office of Population Censuses and Surveys, *Parliamentary Constituency Monitors 1–12*, October–November, 1982). In 19 of these the black proportion exceeded one quarter; in 7 it was over one third. The highest proportions of all were in Birmingham Ladywood (48.1 per cent) and Birmingham Handsworth (45.8 per cent). In 1971 there were only 18 constituencies in which the proportion born, or with at least one parent born, in the NCWP was over 15 per cent. However, my original conclusion – that 'it is doubtful if blacks make up a third of the electorate in more than handful of seats' – still stands. The 1981 Census figures refer to the black proportion of the population. The black proportion of the *electorate* will be lower because, compared with whites, blacks are less likely to be 18 and over, or to be on the register (see below). Moreover, some of the constituencies with the heaviest concentrations of blacks will disappear as a result of the boundary revisions, which will almost certainly be in force by the next general election. This applies particularly to inner-city seats in London and Birmingham.

Under-registration: the most thorough investigation for over a decade of the accuracy of the electoral register found that 14 per cent of New Commonwealth citizens, compared with 3 per cent of those born in the UK, Ireland or the old Commonwealth lived at an address in April 1981 which was not on the electoral register. (See Jean Todd and Bob Butcher, *Electoral Registration in 1981* (London: Office of Population Censuses and Surveys, 1982).) These figures are somewhat lower than those reported by the CRE for 1979. However, the CRE's sampling points were mainly in inner urban areas whereas the OPCS survey covered the whole of England and Wales. A separate OPCS study of Inner London reported figures similar to the CRE's: 25 per cent of blacks compared with 12 per cent of whites were not on the register.

Notes

1 John Rex, 'Black militancy and class conflict', in Robert Miles and Annie Phizacklea (eds), *Racism and Political Action in Britain*, (London: Routledge and Kegan Paul, 1979.)

2 Office of Population Censuses and Surveys, 'Sources of statistics on ethnic minorities', *OPCS Monitor* PP1 82/1, 22 June 1982.

3 David Butler and Dennis Kavanagh, *The British General Election of October 1974*, (London: Macmillan, 1975).

4 For an illustration of their mutual antipathy, see Daniel Lawrence, 'Race, elections and politics' in Ivor Crewe (ed.), *British Political Sociology Yearbook* (Vol. 2: The Politics of Race) (London: Croom Helm, 1975). The recent formation of the Afro-Asian and Caribbean Alliance for Labour, however, may well be a precedent for closer collaboration in the future.

5 M.J. Le Lohé, 'Participation in Elections by Asians in Bradford', in Ivor Crewe *op. cit.*, *British Political Sociology Yearbook*.

6 Douglas Rae, *The Political Consequences of Electoral Laws*, (New Haven, Conn.: Yale University Press, 1967).

7 John Curtice and Michael Steed, 'Electoral Choice and the Production of Government: the changing operation of the electoral system in the United Kingdom since 1955', *British Journal of Political Science*, 12, 1982, pp. 249–98.

8 Patrick Seyd, 'The reselection of Labour MPs: grassroots democracy at work',

paper presented to the annual conference of the Political Studies Association, University of Kent, 1982.

9   This is the total number of Labour and Conservative seats which did not change party control in 1979 and where the sitting MP retired.

10 See Anthony Downs, *An Economic Theory of Democracy*, (New York: Harper and Row, 1957) for the classic statement of this political truth.

11 SSRC Data Archive, *Codebook for SN 1533: British Election Study May 1979 Cross Section*, University of Essex.

12 See, for example, A.D. Fox, 'Attitudes to Immigration: A comparison of Data from the 1970 and 1974 General Election Surveys', *New Community* IV, 1975, p. 7; and I. Crewe, 'The Labour Party and the Electorate', in D. Kavanagh (ed.) *The Politics of the Labour Party*, (London: George Allen and Unwin, 1982) Figure 1.6.

13 D. Butler and D. Stokes, *Political Change in Britain* (2nd edn.), (London: Macmillan, 1974).

14 In January 1978, before Mrs Thatcher's remarks were broadcast, only nine per cent mentioned immigration as one of the two 'most urgent problems facing the country' and support for the two parties (voting intentions) was level-pegging at 43.5 per cent each. In February 1978 21 per cent mentioned immigration and the Conservatives led Labour by 48 per cent to 39 per cent.

15 Muhammad Anwar, *Votes and Policies: Ethnic Minorities and the General Election 1979*, (London: Commission for Racial Equality, 1980), pp. 58–60.

16 Zig Layton-Henry and Stan Taylor, 'Race and Politics: The Case of the Ladywood By-election', paper presented to Conference on Racism and Political Action in Britain, SSRC Research Unit on Ethnic Relations, Bristol University, September 1977, p. 6.

17 M.J. Le Lohe, 'Ethnic Minorities' Candidates and Voter Discrimination in the Local Elections of 1980', paper presented to the Annual Conference of Political Studies Association, University of Hull, April 1981, p. 10.

18 Community Relations Commission, *Participation of Ethnic Minorities in the General Election October 1974*, (London: Community Relations Commission, 1975), p. 18.

19 Zig Layton-Henry, 'Race, Electoral Strategy and the Major Parties', *Parliamentary Affairs*, XXXI, 1978, pp. 274–5. The Conservatives also set up an Anglo-Asian Conservative Association and an Anglo-West Indian Conservative Association. The latter was never very active outside Haringay, but the former was more successful. Mrs Thatcher is President and such redoubtable right wing campaigners against immigration as John Biggs-Davidson and Juilan Amery are among its Vice Presidents.

20 John Curtice and Michael Steed, 'An analysis of the voting' in David Butler and Dennis Kavanagh, *The British General Election of 1979*, (London, Macmillan, 1980), pp. 398–9.

21 Nicholas Deakin (ed.), *Colour and the British Electorate 1964*, (London: Pall Mall Press, 1965), p. 7 and p. 100.

22 Community Relations Commission, *op. cit.*, p. 14.

23 Anwar, *op. cit.*, pp. 35–6.

24 M.J. Le Lohé, 'The participation of Asian candidates in the local elections of 1979', paper presented to the PSA Ethnic Minorities Study Group, University of Warwick, December 1979.

25 The CRE's turnout figures refer to selected polling districts, not the whole constituency. The comparison for the 19 constituencies is between the average (mean) Asian turnout in the selected polling districts and the average of the constituency turnouts. It suggests that Asian turnout was higher than white turnout in general – at least in these constituencies – but also that the turnout of whites living in Asian areas was lower than that of whites living elsewhere.

26 Layton-Henry and Taylor, *op. cit.*, p. 9; Deakin, *op. cit.*

27 MORI (Market and Opinion Research International), *Lambeth Central By-election Same Day Poll – The Tables*, prepared for Election Unit, BBC TV, 20 April 1978.

28 Lawrence, *op. cit.*, p. 71.

29 Geoffrey Alderman, 'Not quite British: the political attitudes of Anglo-Jewry' in

Ivor Crewe (ed.), *British Political Sociology Yearbook*, *op. cit.*, pp. 198, 204.

30 Anwar, *op. cit.*, pp. 43–4.

31 *ibid*, p. 20.

32 *ibid*, p. 42.

33 See also Stan Taylor, 'Is the ethnic vote a floating vote?', *New Community*, IX, 1981, pp. 278–81.

34 Muhammad Anwar, 'The ethnic vote: mountains and molehills', *New Community*, IX, 1981, pp. 281–3.

35 Community Relations Commission, *op. cit.*, p. 25.

36 The correct definition of a constituency in which the ethnic electorate could in theory affect the outcome is one in which they outnumber *half* the sitting MP's majority. The number of constituencies in this category is, of course, much greater than the 41 listed by the CRE.

37 Ivor Crewe, 'The black, brown and green votes', *New Society*, 12 April 1979.

38 Le Lohé, 'Asians in Bradford', *op. cit.*, pp. 103–16.

39 Anwar, *Votes and Policies*, *op. cit.*, p. 46.

40 Steed points out, for example, that 'in Birmingham the average swing in the five constituencies where immigrants provided more than seven per cent of the population was only 1.6 per cent compared with an average swing of 7.0 per cent in the five constituencies where immigrants provided under two per cent of the population; the drop in turnout in the two groups of seats was respectively 1.6 per cent and 6.2 per cent'. Michael Steed, 'The results analysed' in David Butler and Michael Pinto-Duschinsky, *The British General Election of 1970*, (London: Macmillan, 1971), p. 396.

41 William Miller, 'What was the profit in following the crowd? The effectiveness of party strategies on immigration and devolution', *British Journal of Political Science*, 10, 1980, p. 27; Donley Studlear, 'Policy voting in Britain: the coloured immigration issue in the 1964, 1966 and 1970 general elections', *American Political Science Review*, 72, 1978, p. 62; Douglas E. Schoen, *Enoch Powell and the Powellites*, (London: Macmillan, 1977), pp. 58–66. Estimates vary according to assumptions and methods of analysis. Miller's figure of 1.5 per cent is based on the difference between the national swing (3.0 per cent) and the swing that, according to his analysis, would have occurred had the election been fought on the immigration issue alone (4.6 per cent). This latter figure takes account of various 'stabilising influences' such as voters' tendency to assume that their party's position on immigration agrees with their own. Schoen is specifically concerned with the electoral impact of Enoch Powell (who had firm and popular views on subjects other than immigration, such as the EEC). He offers a series of tabular evidence to support his argument that Powell made a major contribution to the swing to the Conservatives, but offers no single summary statistic. Analysis of a 1966–70 panel shows that the pro-Conservative swing was 4.6 per cent among pro-Powell respondents – the identical figure to Miller's on the effect of the immigration issue. (The swing among anti-Powell respondents was only 1.8 per cent). Studlar concludes that the immigration issue was worth an extra 6.7 per cent of the vote to the Conservatives. This figure is based on a multiple regression analysis which included other variables related to attitudes on immigration, including aspects of social and partisan background, but which excluded the effects of other issues.

42 Valentine Herman and Gary Zimmerman, 'Jewish members of parliament: a profile', mimeo, University of Essex, 1977.

43 Since the war the number of Jewish MPs has never been lower than 17 (1951) i.e. 2.7 per cent of Parliament. The number has been at least 40 since 1966, and reached 46 in February and October 1974.

44 A recent survey of those attending Labour party selection conferences found that 51 per cent agreed that, other things being equal, CLPs should select more coloured candidates. A further 25 per cent only disagreed because they thought that making colour a factor in selection was itself discriminatory. However, being coloured was

one of the few characteristics regarded as electorally disadvantageous (although not as much as being English in a Scottish constituency!). Twenty-three per cent saw colour as a great disadvantage and 48 per cent thought it some disadvantage. See, John Bochel and David Denver, 'Candidate selection in the Labour Party: what the selectors seek,' *British Journal of Political Science*, 13, 1983, pp. 48–9.

45 *Runnymede Trust Bulletin*, No. 144, June 1982, p. 5.

46 Community Relations Commission, *op. cit.*, pp. 7–8.

47 See Steed, *op. cit.*, 1971, p. 408; Michael Steed, 'The results analysed', in David Butler and Dennis Kavanagh, *The British General Election of February 1974*, (London: Macmillan, 1974), p. 335; Michael Steed, 'The results analysed' in David Butler and Dennis Kavanagh, *The British General Election of October 1974*, *op. cit.*, p. 344; and Curtice and Steed, *op. cit.*, pp. 413–4. A telling illustration is provided by the constituency of Coventry South East. In February 1974 its Liberal candidate was an Asian. He was one of only four Liberals in the whole of England to lose a deposit. The white Liberal candidate in the neighbouring Coventry South-West received 20.0 per cent of the vote. In October 1974 the Liberal candidate was white. His vote rose and he saved his deposit, despite the regional and national decline in the Liberal vote.

48 M.J. Le Lohé, 'Ethnic Minorities' Candidates' *op. cit.*, p. 11.

49 'Labour plan to give black leaders greater role is set in motion by Mr. Wedgwood Benn', *The Times*, 10 November 1980; 'Black leaders critical of Benn appeal to fight for change by affiliating with Labour and unions', *The Times*, 17 November 1980.

Postscript

15 Ethnic Pluralism and the Policy Agenda in Britain
Ken Young

In 1976, Talcott Parsons wrote that 'ethnic pluralism on something like the American model [is] increasingly characteristic of modern societies'.[1] Since then, however, it has become clear that responses to multi-ethnicity in the very different historical context of Western Europe diverge from, rather than follow, the American model. In the case of Britain, the ambiguities of citizenship in a post-colonial era have been reinforced by the reversal of economic fortunes; problems of status, of rights and of social and economic inequalities arise in ways which are specific to that experience.

Ethnic pluralism has then a different resonance and evokes different responses in the United States and Britain. Few among us assume any convergence in outcomes; the limits to transplanting institutions are readily apparent. Much of the four-day meeting at which these papers were presented was taken up with the exchange of experience at both anecdotal and analytical levels, exchange which served to sharpen our sense that, as one participant put it, 'there is no one road to racial equality'.

While this conference was being planned, Nathan Glazer posed the question which in part it was to address: 'Is there anything someone from the New World, where this mixing of peoples into new societies has gone on more vigorously than anywhere else, and, I would argue, more successfully, has to say to the Old?'[2] In the event there was much. The American contributions tended towards the broader analysis, taking a philosophical and speculative tone appropriate to retrospective reflection on two decades of civil rights and anti-discrimination efforts. The British contributors, unsurprisingly, were more concerned to identify problems and kept closer to the specific issues of ethnic pluralism and racial discrimination in housing, education, and employment. The first group spoke of their experience; the second of their aspiration. Each therefore approached the relationship between ethnic pluralism and public policy from a different viewpoint.

In responding to the papers which we invited, I am struck by the points at which the respective concerns and the respective experiences diverge. Two points in particular deserve some attention. First, there is the relative insignificance of targeted programmes of race-related measures in Britain. Second, there is the entrenched resistance to any specific discussion of ethnicity within the British policy debate outside the arguably marginal area of curriculum reform. Ultimately, however, what emerge most strikingly from this comparative exercise are not programmatic but conceptual variations. I shall accordingly argue that, in comparison with the American case, the policy framework for multi-racial Britain has stalled at the agenda-setting stage. Ethnic pluralism, with all its ambiguities and conflicts of value, has yet to be reflected in the policy agenda.

The force of this is best seen in the uncertain status of black groups as beneficiaries under the two programmes (themselves marginal to mainstream funding) which aim to tackle 'racial disadvantage'. Cutting as they do across the discrete policy sectors of housing, education and employment, the Urban Programme and the grant-aid provided under Section 11 of the Local Government Act 1966 are treated only obliquely, if at all, by our British contributors. The American reader might be forgiven for remaining in ignorance of the special status of these programmes as, respectively, 'the major source of finance for voluntary sector schemes' and 'the major vehicle of central government financial support for local authority programmes' designed to combat racial disadvantage.[3] In practice, they are marginal to mainstream provision and have had little effect in shifting priorities within main programmes; moreover, there is a notable lack of agreement on the legitimacy of using either scheme to the *specific* benefit of black populations.

Weak targeting of programmes under conditions of ambiguity and ambivalence is a sure formula for evasion. The norms of British social policy tend to emphasise, on the one hand, universalistic programmes of benefit and, on the other, discretionary judgements fitted to the circumstances of particular cases. Alone among British social policies, the Urban Programme and Section 11 enable central and local policy makers to address, if they so choose, the distinct needs of minority ethnic groups. However, as we shall see, the stumbling block to the realisation of this potential is to be found in another of the well-established norms of British social policy: compensatory programmes are more acceptably aimed at *areas* than at *groups*.[4] At this point it is necessary to take a closer look at these two programmes in order to see how they are infused not only with ambiguity but also with characteristically British ambivalence about ethnicity, about groups, and indeed, about equality itself.

Ambiguity as policy: Britain's race programmes

Britain's Urban Programme was born to ambiguity and never quite managed to attain clarity in the successive stages of policy revision that followed its inception in 1968. On 20 April that year, opposition front-bencher Enoch Powell, then MP for Wolverhampton South-West, transformed the debate on immigration control and race relations with a series of populist anecdotes which, he claimed, summoned up for him a vision of 'the river Tiber foaming with much blood'.[5] The effect of the speech in unleashing overtly racist sentiments was immediate.[6] Fifteen days later, Prime Minister Harold Wilson responded with the announcement of 'a new and expanded Urban Programme' directed at the needs of distressed cities including those areas 'where there is virtually no immigrant problem'.[7]

The tone of Wilson's speech suggested the unveiling of a carefully prepared new initiative; the substance, an attempt to stem any gathering support for Powell among Labour's traditional white working class followers, was but the cue for hurried preparation and for a most curious episode in *post hoc* legislative development. Within two days an interdepartmental working party of civil servants had been established in Whitehall under Home Office chairmanship, charged with the production of a scheme for which the Wilson speech was virtually the sole guide.[8]

Thereafter it was the civil servants who effectively shaped the Urban Programme which emerged in the Local Government Grants (Social Need) Act, 1969. The working party operated in a political context in which a funding programme recognisably aimed to enhance the welfare of black communities might prove as politically explosive as the earlier inattention to developments in the inner cities. Ambiguity prevailed; officials questioned 'whether it might be possible to disguise the focus on immigrant areas by describing them as "urban areas of general social need" '.[9]

Thirty-four local authorities were invited to submit projects for funding under the new Act. The public criteria for the selection of these areas stressed, in markedly non-specific terms, overcrowding, large families, unemployment, poor environment, concentrations of immigrants and children in trouble or in need of care. In effect, however, the 34 'had been selected because they contained areas of high household density or an exceptionally high immigrant population'.[10]

The history of the Urban Programme over the next ten years is one of progressive extension and generalisation. For the second year, attempts to identify qualifying authorities were abandoned and 'special social need' had to be argued by the applicant. Initial schemes had been limited to nursery provision and children's homes; thereafter, the scope of the Programme was extended to take in a wide range of other social and, eventually, industrial and commercial projects. Initial grant-aid took the form of a 50 per cent Exchequer contribution; from the second year it was raised to 75 per cent. The eligibility of projects proposed to the local authority by voluntary organisations and community groups was mentioned in the 1969 circular; emphasis on this source of proposals has been increased with the passage of time. Expenditure also increased from £22m. in the three years 1969–72 to almost £100m. in 1978/9, the last year in which the Urban Programme took its original form.[11]

What, in the meantime, had happened to the ethnic element in the Programme? Specific provision for black citizens had indeed been implied in the launch of the scheme; however, as a 1980 review document noted:[12]

> it is only since 1974 that this aspect has been consistently and explicitly publicised. Two types of project may be said to be meeting this objective: schemes which are aimed directly at ethnic minorities and others which are directed at a wider group but have a high proportion of ethnic minorities among their clients.

Herein lies yet further ambiguity, for 'indirect' benefit has proved a claim of convenience in many areas where the local authority is unwilling to sponsor applications for distinctively ethnic projects. Moreover, in the 1980 review an attempt to evaluate performance under the Urban Programme enunciated several criteria: two, 'ameliorating a special social need' and 'operating in a deprived area' were deemed *fundamental* while five, of which the last was 'assisting ethnic minorities', were deemed *desirable*. Eighteen projects of the 54 studied were judged to benefit minority groups, nine because they formed a significant proportion of the client group, nine in more direct fashion.[13]

The Urban Programme had arisen in response to a conception of 'special social need' in which the presence of a substantial minority population loomed large. By 1980, after seven successive annual circulars stressing this aspect of urban deprivation, projects directly and specifically benefiting black populations were a subsidiary, though not an insignificant, component of total funding. Meanwhile, the Urban Programme had undergone a fundamental change. The deepening economic crisis of the older cities heralded a reversal in urban policy in 1977, when it was announced that henceforth special aid would be channelled to defined inner city areas under arrangements established soon afterwards in the Inner Urban Areas Act, 1978. Responsibility for the Urban Programme was transferred from the Home Office to the Department of the Environment. A far stronger emphasis was to be placed on industrial and commercial projects designed to secure economic regeneration.[14]

To this end, more money was made available under the 'Enhanced' Urban Programme, but by far the greater part of it was earmarked for seven specially designated 'Partnership' arrangements and fifteen 'programme' authorities.[15] In 1979/80 expenditure was set at £165m. of which only £26.6m. was *not* earmarked and was therefore subject to competitive bidding on the part of the remaining authorities. Of these, 121 received funding that year under what was now to be known as the Traditional Urban Programme (Trad UP) to distinguish it from the Inner Areas Programme (IAP).

The new arrangements introduced a further ambiguity, for a one-time social programme had now been given a strong economic policy slant. The status of ethnic groups under the Trad UP and the IAP was in clear need of redefinition when the Conservatives took office in May 1979. Despite ministers' strong predispositions to axe these programmes, both schemes survived their respective reviews and emerged with reduced funding. In their reprieved states, both the Trad UP and the IAP have become vehicles for the Environment Secretary to advocate greater support for wealth-creating schemes of an industrial nature, a priority which has been rather unevenly received among the local authorities themselves.

Thus, by 1980, black groups with an interest in social and community projects were at risk of being squeezed out of the urban programmes. However, in this most recent phase the ambiguity which has continued to characterise the Urban Programme proved an asset. The first riots in the black areas of the cities of Bristol and Leicester led to eleventh-hour adjustments of their Urban Programme bids to steer some tangible benefits towards the communities in question. The far more serious riots the following year in many cities, and in Brixton and Liverpool in particular, produced a dramatic re-awakening of interest in the Urban Programme as a vehicle for social measures in multi-racial areas. The government placed greater stress on the voluntary sector (where ethnic interests tended to receive greater attention) and consultation with local Community Relations Councils was enjoined more firmly; the 1981 ministerial guidelines to the Partnership authorities called for 'due priority' to be given to 'projects designed to benefit disadvantaged minorities such as certain ethnic groups, particularly through the provision of work and training'.[16] Funding for the total urban programme (Trad UP plus IAP) was dramatically increased, against the trend, to a 1982/3 level of £270 million.

Other developments served to sustain the momentum of this revival of the ethnic dimension to urban policy. The Secretary of State for the Environment acquired an unprecedented special responsibility for

Merseyside. The House of Commons Home Affairs Committee underscored the significance of the Urban Programme for tackling racial disadvantage, as did Lord Scarman's report on the Brixton disorders.[17] Sir George Young, a junior minister at the Department of the Environment, was given a special responsibility for those race related questions falling within the DoE's sphere of concern. A substantial proportion of British blacks live within the areas covered by the Partnership and programme authorities: DoE influence over earmarked IAP funds is all the stronger for the close consultative relationships that these authorities maintain with the DoE regional offices. The casual visitor to the cities in late 1982 can hardly fail to collect anecdotes testifying to the willingness of DoE officials to look favourably on projects which directly benefit the riot areas.

There can be little doubt that the riots of 1981 had a significant impact on an Urban Programme from which blacks had only recently risked virtual exclusion. The effects are particularly noticeable in the Partnership areas and in such cities as Bradford, where the pursuit of racial equality has come to the forefront of local Urban Programme discussions. Nationally, over 200 new 'ethnic projects' have been approved for 1982/3; in the Partnership authorities these are valued at £2m. (£0.77m. in 1981/2) while Traditional Urban Programme expenditure on 'ethnic projects' has increased still more sharply to £7m. (£2.7m. in 1981/2). It is estimated that £15 m. is currently being spent on ethnic projects under the urban programme.[18]

These are significant increases, the more so because the black community organisations themselves figure increasingly as sponsored applicants. Such projects are important not just in terms of the sums spent, but also as a mechanism for bringing local policy makers and the communities into a closer relationship, opening up the decision processes in ways which are likely to benefit black and white alike.[19] Moreover, while there are scant signs that the Inner Area Programmes have had much success in their intention to change the pattern of mainstream expenditure, the emphasis on consultation with the black communities is seen in some cities as paving the way to a more open, less exclusionary, and more responsive pattern of decision making in local service provision.

These recent adjustments in the Urban Programme demonstrate the possibilities of introducing ethnic considerations into the policy agenda. Yet the ambiguity remains. Lord Scarman wondered 'how far it is right to go in order to meet ethnic minority needs', and posed familiar issues of the relative appropriateness of targeted schemes, schemes of a general nature under which blacks would be prime beneficiaries, and general area improvement projects under which blacks would benefit equally with, and in the same ways as, other residents.[20]

The present pattern of Urban Programme funding puts emphasis on the last of these options. In the first place this is because both the Trad UP and the IAP favour general environmental works aimed at the refurbishment of the cities. Second, it is consistent with the history of urban initiatives in Britain, which feature discrimination in favour of small areas even when the 'target population' is defined in social, rather than area, terms. Area objectives are preferred to group objectives, and this priority is often reflected in locally formulated IAP strategies. Third, there is a lingering sense of impropriety in distinguishing social groups in terms of ethnicity, a point to which I shall return later. Finally, of course, there is a powerful bureaucratic interest in using grant-aid to organisational, rather than community ends. Something similar is also apparent in the operations of grant-aid under Section 11 of the Local Government Act 1966. As Britain's other main race-related programme, Section 11 calls for some further brief elaboration.

The Section 11 scheme shares a common origin with the Urban Programme, in so far as it arose from the 1964–6 Labour Government's wish to defuse potential racial conflict and adverse electoral consequences by increased social expenditure in areas of high immigrant concentration. Like the Urban Programme, to which it is sometimes (rather optimistically) described as complementary, Section 11 provides for 75 per cent Exchequer contributions to eligible local expenditure. It differs from the Urban Programme in being a more specific scheme; indeed it is the sole exclusively race-related programme. It differs also in providing for less central discretion and in its restriction to local authority staff costs. Its relative inflexibility has led to growing problems in its administration, widespread criticism and periodic attempts at reform.[21]

In essence, Section 11 of the Local Government Act 1966 empowers the Home Secretary to pay grants in respect of the employment of staff by those local authorities who have had to make special provision in the exercise of their functions 'in consequence of the presence within their areas of substantial numbers of immigrants from the Commonwealth whose language or customs differ from those of the community'.[22] The explanatory circular which followed the Act noted that such differences of language and culture may 'throw an additional burden on local authority services'.[23] Grant-aid was originally set at 50 per cent of approved expenditure but was raised, with that payable under the Urban Porgramme, to 75 per cent in 1969. The 1967 circular also explained that, for the purposes of the scheme, a 'Commonwealth immigrant' was 'normally considered' to be someone who had been born in another country of the Commonwealth, and who had been ordinarily resident in the United Kingdom for less than ten years, and the child of such a person.[24]

Local authorities were eligible to claim grant where the proportion of immigrant pupils in the total school population was two per cent or more; 46 were listed in the first circular, but others were subsequently approved and in 1978/9 89 authorities claimed grants amounting in total to around £50m. About 85 per cent of this sum was used for educational purposes. Despite the use of a school roll eligibility test, it was never intended that Section 11 should be a specifically educational scheme. However, only in recent years has there been any significant growth of take-up within such other services as housing, social services, recreation or libraries.

Some of the problems in the operation of Section 11 reflect the changed circumstances and assumptions brought on by the passage of time. Changes in Commonwealth membership have had a direct impact on eligibility. So too has the 'two per cent rule', an arbitrary criterion whose utility was undercut by the government's decision, in 1973, to cease to collect statistics on the ethnic composition of schools. The ten year rule itself signified an assumption, common enough in 1967, that the scheme would assist in the necessarily short-term process of assimilating an immigrant community. The reality of ethnic pluralism has been one of cultural and linguistic maintenance among many black communities, and the expectation of some administrators that Section 11 would gradually become obsolete has not been fulfilled.

The passage of the Race Relations Act in 1976, with its requirement that local authorities take steps to eliminate racial discrimination and disadvantage, illuminated the weakness of Section 11 as an instrument of that purpose. The then Labour Government was concerned to tackle racial disadvantage, defined as 'a complex of problems deriving not only from newness and difference of culture but also from dispro-portionate material and environmental deprivation accentuated by racial discrimination and occurring principally in an urban context'.[25] That concern led naturally enough to proposals to replace Section 11 with a more appropriate and serviceable funding programme. The outcome was the Ethnic Groups (Grants) Bill, under which a more flexible form of grant would be available to those local authorities who sought to tackle racial disadvantage in a strategic fashion. No longer restricted to staff salaries, the new grant thus closely resembled the Urban Programme, from which it was distinguished principally by its exclusive concern with race.

In the event, the Bill fell with the Labour Government in the spring of 1979, the incoming administration declining to proceed with it. A subsequent attempt to re-introduce it in the House of Lords failed. The Home Office proposed instead a review of the administrative procedures for Section 11, a process which proceeded fitfully and with periodic prods from the House of Commons until revised proposals were announced in January 1982. Many detailed changes have been made, including the waiver of both the ten-year rule and the two-per cent rule.[26]

The use made of Section 11 to date and the discussion of its replacement illustrate the ambiguities of the scheme. Directed towards the 'additional burden' of an immigrant presence, it conferred eligibility on the basis of numbers, but left it to local authorities to assess whether or not a burden existed. Some eligible authorities do *not* claim grant, while some have evidently been unaware of their entitlement. The reference to 'language and customs' helped mould the image of Section 11 as targeted on the Asian child in school, some local officials being thereby led to believe that the presence of West Indian children did not constitute eligibility. The take-up of Section 11 grants outside the education service is still more uneven.

While the relatively few posts outside education departments are likely to be fairly explicitly geared to race-related work, there is considerable evidence that within education a substantial proportion of Section 11 funds is leaked away to general staffing support for schools. Many schools and authorities have been unwilling to identify Section 11 post-holders; accordingly, some schools simply receive additional posts while remaining unaware of the notional purpose of this supplementation. As there is a widespread resistance to designating or admitting the existence of 'immigrant teachers' the opportunity is taken to generalise the support by improving staffing ratios.[28]

Central to this absorption of national programmes to local purposes is the ambiguity which serves to 'deracialise' Section 11. To many activists and community spokesmen, and to a growing number of local politicians, Section 11 is geared to *meeting the needs* of the black population. To others, including most teachers, many local education authorities and perhaps the Department of Education and Science itself, the purpose of the scheme is to supplement resources in areas where extra burdens are generated *by the presence of* the black population. Thus, in much of the argument about Section 11, the protagonists share no common ground while there is no apparently authoritative interpretation to which they might appeal.[29]

As with the Urban Programme, the basic ambiguity about *who* is to benefit under Section 11 can be traced to the origins of these measures in the apprehensive climate of the late 1960s. In this case however, the preparation of the Ethnic Groups (Grants) Bill in 1978 is germane to the discussion. The crucial justification of the Bill as a measure distinct from the broader Urban Programme was that, while the Trad UP and the IAP were concerned with area-based disadvantage 'by whomsoever suffered', the replacement for Section 11 'would have as its specific objective the alleviation of the special features of racial disadvantage'.[30] The intention is clear and, as the Bill sought primarily to remedy the *operational inflexibilities* of Section 11, its purpose surely carries over by implication to the argument about Section 11 itself.

There remains a real uncertainty, common to many practitioners engaged in service-delivery, as to whether the remit to tackle racial disadvantage *should* be attached to identifiable staff whose special role might then relieve their colleagues of their responsibility, turning race into a 'specialist' issue and thus marginalising it. This is a real dilemma, and there has been considerable resistance to the current Home Office intention to identify Section 11 post-holders and assess their 'experience and qualifications . . . in dealing with the needs of the Commonwealth immigrants'.[31] It is of course a prerequisite of responsive service-provision under conditions of ethnic pluralism that awareness and concern should be common, and not private. But to say this is simply to elevate the argument to one about the most effective strategies for organisational change. And central to *that* discussion is the critical relationship between the sorts of specific (or potentially specific) race-related programmes that I have been discussing, and the vastly more significant patterns of mainstream provision. The intention of these supplementary programmes is to shift mainstream priorities or, in the jargon of the current inner cities debate, to 'bend main programmes'. Whether or not that can be achieved by supplementary funding, or whether such programmes *necessarily* marginalise the ethnic dimension is a complex question the answers to which are not obvious.

Moreover, a satisfactory account of the underdevelopment of British race-related policies cannot be given in terms of programme ambiguity alone, however important that ambiguity in distorting the implementation process. Behind the ambiguity lies a complex of psycho-cultural factors which bear upon the decision-making processes in central and local government, in firms, and in other public agencies. These sometimes take the form of ambivalence about the explicit identification of ethnicity, or a reluctance to shed established notions of ethnic assimilation; at worst, they take the form of covert or overt hostility towards Britain's black population. Nor are the effects of these psycho-cultural factors confined to formal government programmes. Ambivalence and equivocation are equally to be found in the application of the law relating to racial discrimination. Equally, the operations of the Commission for Racial Equality and the reservation expressed as to its promotional role reflect a low key approach to the pursuit of racial equality.

Coping with pluralism: ethnicity and the policy process

Both the Urban Programme and the Section 11 scheme have proved erratic vehicles for conferring benefits upon the black population. Indeed, in their earlier manifestations they may be read more plausibly as compensatory programmes aimed at whites living in multi-racial areas. Both schemes are recognisably products of their time. Fifteen years ago it was customary to speak of an 'immigrant problem' or (significantly) of the *burden* of the black presence in English cities. Colour itself was viewed as constituting a problem. Then, as now, language frames our perception; while immigration is today an issue of only marginal salience, such acceptable terms as 'racial disadvantage' or 'ethnic minorities' have their own conceptual overtones. The first may be misread as implying some intrinsic disadvantage in blackness, over and above the likelihood of experiencing prejudice, discrimination, or racism. The second sustains a vocabulary of majoritarianism that discounts 'minority' views and places its own limits – those of (at best) due proportionality – upon the disposition of public resources.

My choice of the term *ethnic pluralism* as an organising concept for this discussion is deliberate. It refers to a condition of multi-ethnicity which extends beyond ethnic group identity to the realm of public acts and to decisions on the allocation of public goods.[32] It is multi-ethnicity carried into the sphere of public policy-making, whether by electoral power, by campaigning activity, by pressure group politics or by unlawful and violent action in the streets. It is my contention that Britain is, by a mix of such means, close to achieving this condition of ethnic pluralism. We are now on the threshold, not of solution to those problems which the British contributors to this book have enumerated, but of redefining the policy issues and opening up the agenda of public action.

The principal obstacle to successful agenda-building is to be found in the resistance which the discussion of race-related measures has customarily encountered in Britain. While integrationist policies in an era of immigration had their own obvious appeal and apparent validity, the failure of the race relations strategy of the 1960s – increasing immigration control coupled with anti-discrimination laws and area-based social programmes – left an uncomfortable gap. A new public consensus, one congruent with the current Race Relations Act and with the analysis which underpins it, has yet to emerge.

Despite the contemporary concern for firefighting measures, resistance to a systematic response to today's multi-ethnicity still runs deep. In many local authorities, in other major public agencies, and doubtless in corners of Whitehall too, issues of multi-ethnicity are still held to be *undiscussable*.[33] Thus, the prevailing mode of discourse is one which filters out the realities of ethnic pluralism by resisting the differentiation of ethnic groups. Without differentiation there can be no understanding of indirect discrimination or 'institutional racism'. Without differentiation the consequences of public action cannot be assessed, service take-up and employment change cannot be monitored, sources of unintentional discrimination cannot be identified and the biases of organisational routines cannot be examined. Without differentiation of ethnic groups in policy discourse, the Race Relations Act's prohibition of indirect discrimination is a dead letter.

Resistance to ethnic differentiation is, however, deeply embedded in English liberal culture. While the term 'racial disadvantage' itself differentiates between different ethnic groups in terms of their likely experiences and material circumstances, it is readily deracialised by reduction to location, linguistic ability, recency of arrival, skill or social class. Ethnic identification for statistical purposes readily evokes references to Nazism; implausible scenarios of future pogroms are offered. Measures which introduce an ethnic dimension into organisational practices may be resisted as 'positive discrimination'[34]. Surveys show that the British have a high expectation of formally equal treatment at the hands of authority; the spirit of Dicey lives on in popular adherence to a version of the rule of law which views group differentiation with grave suspicion.

Hitherto, there has been a close correspondence between public *mores* and public policy on issues of race. This correspondence turned on what David Kirp, in an earlier publication, termed *racial inexplicitness*. Kirp points to the persistent unwillingness to regard race as a significant dimension of policy and he regards this as distinctively characteristic of British policy making. He argues that:[35]

> at least as a matter of official educational policy, the British minimise the relevance of colour. The same point may be made about British social policy generally. Whether with respect to health, welfare, employment or housing, Britain has self-consciously diminished the significance of race. Race plays only a small part in the policy making calculus.

True though this may have been of the 1970s (and the work of the DES Educational Disadvantage Unit and the ill-fated Centre for Information and Advice on Educational Disadvantage illustrate Kirp's thesis) it is unlikely to remain so in the next decade. The last two years have seen a remarkable shift of concern, one which may well place ethnic pluralism upon Britain's policy agenda. Whatever the shortcomings in law enforcement, the Race Relations Act is proving an important text for those who wish to challenge existing practices. Suddenly, formerly sanctioned inexplicitness is on the defensive. But before Britain can celebrate 'colour-blindness' on the American model we shall need first to achieve a greater consciousness of colour, to apply that consciousness to the distributional questions that attend public policy making and to pursue appropriate remedies. The American experience has shown us the dangers and the opportunities in that transformation.

Notes

I am grateful to my PSI colleagues Colin Brown, Naomi Connelly and David Smith for their comments on this chapter.

1 Talcott Parsons, 'Some Theoretical Considerations on the Nature and Trends of Change of Ethnicity', in Nathan Glazer and Daniel P. Moynihan (eds), *Ethnicity: Theory and Experience*, (Cambridge, Mass.: Harvard University Press, 1975), p. 56.

2 Nathan Glazer, 'The Ethnic Factor', *Encounter*, July 1981, p. 6.

3 House of Commons, *Racial Disadvantage: Fifth Report from the Home Affairs Committee, Session 1980-81*, HC424-1 (London: HMSO, 1981), paras. 67, 52.

4 There is a considerable literature on this point: see in particular John Edwards and Richard Batley, *The Politics of Positive Discrimination: An Evaluation of the Urban Programme, 1967-77*, (London: Tavistock, 1978) pp. 234, 245-6, 249-51; S. Hatch and R. Sherrott, 'Positive Discrimination and the Distribution of Deprivations', *Policy and Politics*, Vol. 1, No. 3, 1973; John Stewart, Kenneth Spencer and Barbara Webster, *Local Government: Approaches to Urban Deprivation*, (London: Home Office Urban Deprivation Unit, n.d.), pp. 33-4.

5 The speech is reproduced in *Race*, Vol. 10, No. 1, July 1968.

6 For an assessment of the immediate political impact of the speech, particularly in the Midlands, see Paul Foot, *The Rise of Enoch Powell*, (London: Cornmarket Press, 1969). A more cautious conclusion as to the longer term impact is reached by Donley T. Studlear, 'British Public Opinion, Colour Issues and Enoch Powell: A Longitudinal Analysis', *British Journal of Political Science*, Vol. 4, No. 3, 1974.

7 The Prime Minister added that 'expenditure must be on the basis of need and the immigration problem is only one factor, though a very important factor, in the assessment of social need'. Quoted in Clare Demuth, *Government Initiatives on Urban Deprivation*, (London: Runnymede Trust, 1977).

8 John Edwards and Richard Batley, *Politics of Positive Discrimination, op. cit.*, pp. 40-45.

9 *ibid*, p. 46.

10 Department of the Environment, *Review of the Traditional Urban Programme: Consultative Document*, (London: DoE, 1980) para. 2.2. See also Edwards and Batley, *op. cit.*, and D. McKay and A. Cox, 'Confusion and Reality in Public Policy: the case of the British Urban Programme', *Political Studies*, XXVI, No. 4, December 1978.

11 DoE, *Review of the Traditional Urban Programme, op. cit.* For the early period, see also Robert Holman and Lynda Hamilton, 'The British Urban Programme', *Policy and Politics*, Vol. 2, No. 2, (1973).

12 DoE, *Review of the Traditional Urban Programme, op. cit.*, para. 3.30.

13 *ibid*, para. 3.31.

14 Secretary of State for the Environment, *Policy for the Inner Cities*, (London: HMSO, Cmnd 6845, 1978).

15 Robin Hambleton, 'Implementing Inner City Policy: Reflections from Experience', *Policy and Politics*, Vol. 9, No. 1, 1981; Rupert Nabarro, 'Inner City Partnerships:

An Assessment of the First Programmes', *Town Planning Review*, Vol. 51, No. 1, 1980.

16 Department of the Environment, *Ministerial Guidelines*, (mimeo) 1981. See also Home Office, *Racial Disadvantage: The Government Reply to the Fifth Report from the Home Affairs Committee*, (London: HMSO, Cmnd 8476, 1982).

17 House of Commons, *Racial Disadvantage*, *op. cit.*, paras. 65–72; *The Brixton Disorders 10–12 April 1981: Report of an Inquiry by the Rt. Hon. The Lord Scarman, OBE*, (London: HMSO, Cmnd 8427, 1981) paras. 6.1–6.9. See also National Council for Voluntary Organisations and Runnymede Trust, *Inner Cities and Black Minorities*, (London: Runnymede Trust, 1980).

18 *House of Commons Debates*, 7 July 1982, cols. *149–50*. The information was presented in a written answer by Sir George Young, but the basis for judging projects to be of benefit to ethnic minority groups is not specified.

19 See Herman Ouseley with Usha Prashar and Danny Silverstone, *The System*, (London: Runnymede Trust, 1981) and Ken Young and Naomi Connelly, *Policy and Practice in the Multi-Racial City*, PSI Report No. 598, (London: PSI, 1981).

20 *The Brixton Disorders*, *op. cit.*, para. 6.32.

21 The Home Affairs Committee report noted that 'there is no single aspect of Section 11 payments that has escaped criticism', House of Commons, *Racial Disadvantage*, *op. cit.*, para. 49.

22 *Local Government Act, 1966*, Section 11.

23 Home Office Circular 15/1967, *Commonwealth Immigrants*.

24 *ibid*.

25 Home Office, *Proposals for Replacing Section 11 of the Local Government Act 1966: A Consultative Document*, (London: Home Office, 1978). para. 1.

26 Home Office, *Reply to the . . . Home Affairs Committee*, *op. cit.*, pp. 9–11.

27 Young and Connelly, *Policy and Practice*, *op. cit.*, chapter 7; National Union of Teachers, *Section 11: An NUT Report*, (London: The Union, 1978).

28 NUT, *Section 11*, *op. cit.* For a broad review of the defects of S. 11 see Home Office, *Proposals for Replacing Section 11*, *op. cit.*

29 Young and Connelly, *Policy and Practice*, *op. cit.*, pp. 106–113.

30 Home Office, *Proposals for Replacing Section 11*, *op. cit.*, para. 13.

31 Home Office, *Reply to the . . . Home Affairs Committee*, *op. cit.*, p. 10. During 1982 revised draft guidelines were circulated and considerable discussion within local authorities and between the local authority associations and the Home Office followed.

32 For a discussion of the significance of ethnic pluralism for government policies and programmes see Raymond Breton, 'Ethnic Pluralism and Social Equality', *Human Relations* (Ont.) December 1976.

33 Young and Connelly, *Policy and Practice*, *op. cit.*, pp. 156–64. For a fuller discussion of the processes involved in defining phenomena as 'issues' and thereby qualifying them as public policy concerns, see Ken Young and Liz Mills, *Managing the Post-industrial City*, (London: Heinemann, 1983).

34 Ken Young and Naomi Connelly, *Ethnic Record Keeping in Local Government: A Discussion Paper*, (London: Policy Studies Institute, 1981); Ken Young, 'An Agenda for Sir George: Local Authorities and the Promotion of Racial Equality', *Policy Studies*, Vol. 3, No. 1, Summer 1982.

35 David Kirp, *Doing Good by Doing Little: Race and Schooling in Britain*, (Berkeley: University of California Press, 1979), p. 2.

Notes on contributors

Colin Brown is a Research Fellow at the Policy Studies Institute. From 1974 to 1976 he worked at the SSRC Survey Unit. He then moved to the Centre for Studies in Social Policy, one of the bodies which merged to form PSI. His work at CSSP and PSI has been in the areas of housing, race and survey methodology.

Ivor Crewe is currently Professor of Government at the University of Essex. He was Director of the SSRC Data Archive from 1974 to 1982, and Co-director of the British Election Study, both at Essex University. He was from 1977 to 1982 editor of the *British Journal of Political Science*. He is co-author of *Decade of Dealignment* (CUP, 1983), a study of British electoral behaviour in the 1970s and, as editor, the *British Political Sociology Yearbook*, Vol. II, on race and politics in Britain.

Richard B. Freeman is Professor of Economics at Harvard University; he previously held positions at Yale and Chicago. He is Programme Director of Labour Studies at the US National Bureau of Economic Research. He has written widely on the labour market, especially in the fields of blacks and youth, economic discrimination, social mobility and trade unionism.

Nathan Glazer is Professor of Education and Sociology at Harvard University and co-editor of *The Public Interest*. He has served as secretary to the American Academy of Arts and Sciences. He has held a number of teaching positions, including Professor of Sociology at the University of California, Berkeley. His publications on urban and ethnic problems and policies include *Beyond the Melting Pot* (with Daniel P. Moynihan) and *Affirmative Discrimination: Ethnic and Public Policy*.

Donald L. Horowitz is Professor of Law, Public Policy Studies and Political Science at Duke University. He has served as an attorney in the Department of Justice and has done research on comparative ethnic relations at the Harvard Center for International Affairs, the Woodrow Wilson Center, and the Smithsonian Institution, as well as research on the American courts at the Brookings Institution. He is currently working on a comparative study of ethnic group conflict.

Valerie Karn is currently Senior Lecturer, Centre for Urban and Regional Studies at Birmingham University. She is closely involved in a wide range of local and national bodies, both statutory, for instance the Housing Services Advisory Committee, and voluntary. In 1979–80 she was a Consultant to HUD based at the Urban Institute, in Washington DC. She is chairman of the editorial board of the housing journal *Roof*. She has published widely on housing issues, especially on race and housing.

David Kirp is Professor at the Graduate School of Public Policy, University of California at Berkeley. He has also taught at the Harvard Graduate School of Education and from 1969–1971 was director of the Harvard Center for Law and Education. His publications include *Doing Good by Doing Little: Race and Schooling in Britain*; *Educational Policy and the Law*; and *Just Schools: The idea of Racial Equality in American Education*.

Lance Liebman is Professor of Law, Harvard Law School, specialising in property and social welfare law. In 1967–8 he was law clerk to Supreme Court Justice Byron White, and 1968–70 was assistant to Mayor John Lindsay of New York City. He has been a consultant to the Ford Foundation, the American Bar Association, and US and Massachusetts government agencies.

Laurence Lustgarten was educated in America and England and taught at Queen's University, Ontario. He is currently Lecturer in Law at Warwick University. A specialist in comparative public law, he has published numerous articles on public law and welfare law and is the author of *Legal Control of Racial Discrimination*. He is currently working on issues of police governance.

Christopher McCrudden is Fellow and Tutor in Law, Lincoln College, Oxford, and Lecturer in Law, University of Oxford. He has been editor of the 'Law in Context' series (Weidenfeld and Nicolson) since 1977.

Susan Ollerearnshaw is Principal Officer of the Commission for Racial Equality's Employment Promotion Section, and was previously employed as Principal Officer in the Reference Section of the Community Relations Commission. She has a background of advisory and research work in government and independent agencies, and has produced publications on the employment of women and ethnic minority groups.

Bhikhu Parekh is currently Vice-Chancellor of the University of Baroda, Gujarat, India, and also holds a Chair of Political Theory at the University of Hull. He has taught at the Universities of London and Glasgow and his recent publications include *Hannah Arendt and the Search for a New Political Philosophy* and *Marx's Theory of Ideology*. He was formerly a member of the Rampton Committee on the Education of Ethnic Minority Children.

Peter Sanders has been Director of the Equal Opportunities Division of the Commission for Racial Equality since 1977. Before that he was Deputy Chief Officer of the Race Relations Board. He is the author and editor of several publications on African history and literature.

Lawrence Sherman, Associate Professor of Criminology at the University of Maryland, is Director of Research, Police Foundation, Washington, DC. He was formerly at the State University of New York at Albany. His publications include *Police and Violence; The Quality of Police Education: A critical review with recommendations for improving programs in higher education*; and *The Teaching of Ethics in Criminology and Criminal Justice*.

Ken Young is a Senior Fellow at the Policy Studies Institute. He was formerly at the School for Advanced Urban Studies, Bristol, and has taught at the Universities of London, Kent, Bristol and Cambridge. He was joint editor of *Policy and Politics* from 1972–78; his publications include *Local Politics and the Rise of the Party*, *Policy and Practice in the Multi-racial City*, *Strategy and Conflict in Metropolitan Housing*, and *Metropolitan London: Politics and Urban Change, 1837–1981*.

The American Academy of Arts and Sciences

The Academy was founded during the American Revolution by individuals who contributed prominently to the philosophical foundations of the new nation and to the establishment of its government and institutions. Maintaining its initial concern with the development of knowledge as a means of promoting the public interest and social progress, the Academy has both grown and evolved since its founding. Today it is a learned society with a dual function to honour achievement in science, scholarship, the arts, and public affairs; and to conduct a varied programme of projects and studies reflecting the interests of its members and responsive to the needs and problems of society. Reflecting its national membership and identity, the Academy has added two regional centres of activity, in the midwest and on the Pacific coast, to its national headquarters in Greater Boston.

The Academy's membership represents distinction and achievement in the entire range of the intellectual disciplines and professions. Its 2,300 Fellows and 400 Foreign Honorary Members are divided into four classes – the physical sciences, the biological sciences, the social arts and sciences, and the humanities and fine arts. The Academy recognises achievement not only in election to membership but in the awarding of prizes: the Rumford Premium in the physical sciences, the Amory Prize in the bio-medical sciences, the Talcott Parsons Prize in the social sciences, the Emerson-Thoreau Medal in literature, and the American Academy Award for Humanistic Studies.

Academy members, a reservoir of intellectual talent in themselves, also enlist other scientists, scholars, and artists from the United States and abroad to participate in Academy studies. The programme of studies emphasises problems requiring the participation of representatives from several disciplines. Recent Academy projects have focused on science policy; modern technology; ethnic and racial conflict; the nature of the modern state; strategic arms limitation; defence policy; public understanding of science; the history of science and learning; intellect and imagination; and the environment and ecology. A project usually culminates in a book, article, or monograph, or an issue of the Academy's quarterly journal, *Daedalus*. Academy publications are widely read within the intellectual community; the circulation of *Daedalus* alone is 35,000.

The Academy from time to time has helped to establish new institutions to meet special needs in the scholarly and scientific communities. Examples include the International Centre for Insect Physiology and Ecology in Nairobi, Kenya; the International Foundation for Science, with headquarters in Stockholm; and the National Humanities Center in North Carolina.

Commission for Racial Equality

The Commission for Racial Equality was established by the Race Relations Act 1976 with duties to:
a) work towards the elimination of racial discrimination;
b) promote equality of opportunity and good race relations;
c) keep the working of the Act under review.

The Commission has powers to conduct formal investigations for any purpose connected with the elimination of discrimination. It can require the production of evidence and can subpoena witnesses. If the Commission finds that discrimination has occurred, the Commission may issue a non-discrimination notice which may require the organisation to undertake certain changes; compliance is monitored by the Commission and the notice is enforceable through the courts. The Commission may also assist individuals taking their own cases to industrial tribunals or county courts. In promoting equality of opportunity and good relations between people of different racial groups, the CRE has important links with statutory bodies, local government, minority groups, local communities and supports the work of local Community Relations Councils. The Commission funds a large number of groups and most community relations councils. The Commission, as a statutory body, reports annually to Parliament and its accounts are audited by the Comptroller and Auditor-General.

The Commission has a full-time Chairman (Peter Newsam) and Deputy Chairman (Clifton Robinson) and thirteen part-time Commissioners. The Commission replaces the former Community Relations Commission and Race Relations Board which were set up under earlier legislation. The Act does not apply to Northern Ireland where there is separate legislation.

Policy Studies Institute

The Policy Studies Institute was formed on 31 March 1978 by merger between Political and Economic Planning (PEP) and the Centre for Studies in Social Policy (CSSP). PSI was formally opened at its new building in Castle Lane, Westminster, by the then Prime Minister, the Rt. Hon. James Callaghan, MP, on 20 February 1979. It is an independent institute, non-party, not run for profit, and recognised as an educational charity. Its aim is to help improve public policy by obtaining relevant facts, analysing their implications and presenting the results to policy-makers and to the public.

Foundations provide the largest share of income, in particular the Joseph Rowntree Memorial Trust, which established the Centre for Studies in Social Policy. The European Cultural Foundation also provides regular support, having joined PSI in establishing the European Centre for Political Studies as an integral part of the Institute. PSI has no subsidy from public funds, but programme and project grants from a number of government departments are the second largest source of income. Subscriptions and contributions from industry comprise most of the rest.

The work of the Institute covers a wide range of subjects that are important to public policy. These include in the economic field studies of employment problems, labour relations, factors making for industrial success, energy and transport policy. PSI also has a programme of research on education policy. In social policy, it has studies of social care, voluntary organisations, health services, housing, pensions, the implications of demographic trends, the distribution and redistribution of incomes, poverty and ethnic minorities. PSI has a programme of research into political and constitutional matters, including parliaments, parties, interest groups, the European Community and relations between central and local government.

The results of research are published in PSI's own series of reports, in a European series, in PSI discussion papers and research papers, and in a series of books published by Heinemann. PSI also publishes its own quarterly journal, *Policy Studies*.

Index